Karl Marx's Theory of History

A DEFENCE

BY

G. A. Cohen

CLARENDON PRESS · OXFORD

Oxford University Press, Walton Street, Oxford OX2 6DP

Oxford New York Toronto
Delhi Bombay Calcutta Madras Karachi
Petaling Jaya Singapore Hong Kong Tokyo
Nairobi Dar es Salaam Cape Town
Melbourne Auckland
and associated companies in
Berlin Ibadan

Oxford is a trade mark of Oxford University Press

© G. A. Cohen 1978
First published 1978
Seventh impression 1991

British Library Cataloguing in Publication Data
Cohen, G. A.
Karl Marx's theory of history.
1. Historical materialism
I. Title
335.411   D16.9   78–40242
ISBN 0–19–827440–8 (Pbk)

Printed in Hong Kong

For
MY FATHER,
and in memory of
MY MOTHER

FOR

WHAT THEY

ALL SAID

WAS . . .

'It depends . . .

   It all depends . . .

      It all depends on WHERE YOU LIVE

and WHAT YOU HAVE TO BUILD WITH.'

> —*The Little Boy and His House*, by Stephen Bone
> and Mary Adshead, London, J. M. Dent and Sons,
> Ltd., 1936.

IN THE social production of their life, men enter into definite relations that are indispensable and independent of their will, relations of production which correspond to a definite stage of development of their material productive forces. The sum total of these relations of production constitutes the economic structure of society, the real basis, on which rises a legal and political superstructure, and to which correspond definite forms of social consciousness. The mode of production of material life conditions the social, political and intellectual life process in general. It is not the consciousness of men that determines their being, but, on the contrary, their social being that determines their consciousness. At a certain stage of their development, the material productive forces of society come in conflict with the existing relations of production, or—what is but a legal expression for the same thing—with the property relations within which they have been at work hitherto. From forms of development of the productive forces these relations turn into their fetters. Then begins an epoch of social revolution. With the change of the economic foundation the entire immense superstructure is more or less rapidly transformed. In considering such transformations, a distinction should always be made between the material transformation of the economic conditions of production, which can be determined with the precision of natural science, and the legal, political, religious, aesthetic or philosophic—in short, ideological forms in which men become conscious of this conflict and fight it out. Just as our opinion of an individual is not based on what he thinks of himself, so can we not judge of such a period of transformation by its own consciousness; on the contrary, this consciousness must be explained rather from the contradictions of material life, from the existing conflict between the social productive forces and the relations of production. No social formation ever perishes before all the productive forces for which there is room in it have developed; and new, higher relations of production never appear before the material conditions of their existence have matured in the womb of the old society itself. Therefore mankind always sets itself only such tasks as it can solve; since, looking at the matter more closely, it will always be found that the task itself arises only when the material conditions for its solution already exist or are at least in the process of formation. In broad outlines Asiatic, ancient, feudal, and modern bourgeois modes of production can be designated as progressive epochs in the economic formation of society. The bourgeois relations of production are the last antagonistic form of the social process of production—antagonistic not in the sense of individual antagonism, but of one arising from the social conditions of life of the individuals; at the same time the productive forces developing in the womb of bourgeois society create the material conditions for the solution of that antagonism. This social formation brings, therefore, the prehistory of human society to a close.

—KARL MARX, 1859

Foreword

1. This book defends historical materialism, by offering argument in its favour, but more by presenting the theory in what I hope is an attractive form.

The presentation respects two constraints: on the one hand, what Marx wrote, and, on the other, those standards of clarity and rigour which distinguish twentieth-century analytical philosophy. The aim is to construct a tenable theory of history which is in broad accord with what Marx said on the subject. While he would certainly have found some of what will follow unfamiliar, the hope is that he could have recognized it as a reasonably clear statement of what he thought.

That is not an arrogant hope. Marx was a restless and creative thinker, who developed many ideas in many directions. He did not have the time, or the will, or the academic peace, to straighten them all out. It is not arrogant to claim to offer a less untidy version of some of his major thoughts than he himself provided.

2. The reconstruction given here is less ambiguous than the theory in its original state. It is therefore easier to criticize, and I do not regret that. But there is one likely reaction which I wish to anticipate and deflect, namely that I have erected 'a general historico-philosophical theory, the supreme virtue of which consists in being supra-historical'.[1] I do not need to be advised that history is 'always richer in content, more varied, more many-sided, more lively and "subtle"'[2] than any theory will represent it as being. The quoted passages are warnings against a certain *misuse* of theory, but some Marxists cite them to disguise their own aversion to theory as such. They should be reminded that Marx and Lenin were not themselves against theory.

[1] Marx to the editorial board of a Russian newspaper, November 1877, in *Selected Correspondence*, p. 294.
[2] Lenin, 'Left-Wing Communism', p. 76.

3. Louis Althusser has had a strong effect on current interest in historical materialism, and I am bound to say a word about my attitude to his work, which is hardly mentioned in this book.

Althusser's *Pour Marx* persuaded me that the abidingly important Marx is to be found in *Capital* and the writings preparatory to it. That conviction helped me to write this book, and I am therefore grateful to him. But when I passed on to *Lire Le Capital*—a set of essays, by Althusser and others—I was disappointed. I obtained little from the essays by Althusser, beyond a sense of how elegantly—and evasively—the French language could be used. I liked other things better, especially the contribution of Balibar. But I did not think it profited from being cast in terms which showed Althusser's influence.

Above all, I found much of *Lire Le Capital* critically vague. It is perhaps a matter for regret that logical positivism, with its insistence on precision of intellectual commitment, never caught on in Paris. Anglophone philosophy left logical positivism behind long ago, but it is lastingly the better for having engaged with it. The Althusserian vogue could have unfortunate consequences for Marxism in Britain, where ludicity is a precious heritage, and where it is not generally supposed that a theoretical statement, to be one, must be hard to comprehend.

4. My specific doctrinal differences with the Althusserians need not be described here. They are considerable.

For it is an old-fashioned historical materialism which I defend, a traditional conception,[1] in which history is, fundamentally, the growth of human productive power, and forms of society rise and fall according as they enable or impede that growth. The focus is on the more basic concepts of the theory, those of forces and relations of production, and there will be unusually little discussion, as books on Marx and society go, of class conflict, ideology, and the state.

The main part of the book (Chapters II to X) is preceded by a sketch of 'Images of History in Hegel and Marx', so called because it deals with ideas lacking the degree of articulation suggested by the term 'theory'.

---

[1] Whose 'most pregnant' statement (see Hobsbawm, 'Introduction', p. 10) is the Preface to *The Critique of Political Economy*, quoted on pp. vii–viii above.

Chapter II opens with complex argument on behalf of the claim that what Marx called the *economic structure* consists of production relations alone, productive forces forming no part of it. The rest of the chapter, which is less intricate, says what productive forces are, and examines what can be meant by their *development*.

Chapter III is devoted to relations of production, and to the economic structures they compose. It looks at the links connecting immediate producers with their means of labour and their class superiors.

In Chapter IV the distinction between productive forces and production relations is shown to be a special case of a more general one, which runs deep in Marx, between material and social features of society. Chapter V uses the results of Chapter IV to provide an account of commodity and capital fetishism, and a partly novel interpretation of communism.

Chapter VI demonstrates that Marx attributed explanatory primacy to the productive forces, and argues, less conclusively, that he was right. Chapter VII establishes some contact between the assertions of Chapter VI and certain stretches of real history.

According to Chapter VI, economic structures are as they are because, being so, they enable human productive power to expand. According to Chapter VIII (on 'Base and Superstructure'), superstructures are as they are because, being so, they consolidate economic structures. Those statements are functional explanations, and functional explanation is widely suspected, not least within Marxism. Chapters IX and X defend it, in general terms, and with special reference to historical materialism.

Chapter XI discusses some ills of contemporary capitalist society. It argues that the relation between use-value and exchange-value under capitalism leads to a special irrationality when capitalism is advanced.[1] The first Appendix reproduces an article which relates to Chapter V, and the second defines five expressions often used in the book.

---

[1] An earlier version of Chapter XI, seriously marred by copy-editing over which I was allowed no control, appeared in Gordon Bermant and Gerald Dworkin *et al.* (eds.), *Market and Morals*, Washington, 1977.

5. This book has many weaknesses. It would have had more but for the generosity of five friends, who commented incisively on the entire first draft. To Danny Goldstick, John McMurtry, Chris Provis, Bill Shaw, and Arnold Zuboff, many, many thanks. Other helpful critics were Chris Boorse, Maggie Cohen, Irving Dworetzsky, Keith Graham, Bill Hart, Helle Kanger, Stig Kanger, Mendel Kramer, Colin McGinn, Jakob Meløe, Robin Murray, Jan Narveson, Mike O'Pray, Tim Scanlon, Chuck Taylor, Richard Wollheim, Allen Wood, and Sigurd Zienau, whose death last October deprived me, and many others, of a cherished mentor.

Katherine Backhouse and Veryan Gilliatt typed the manuscript. They were remarkably patient and kind. The Canada Council and the British Academy enabled me to spend a year free from teaching obligations. To Michael Cohen and Glanrydd Rowlands I have rather special debts. And I shall not try to describe what I owe to Maggie, and to Gideon, Miriam, and Sarah.

A new impression enables me to add two remarks.

First, I should like to thank Bertell Ollman and John Torrance, who made extremely valuable criticisms of the typescript.

Second, I regret my failure to indicate that Chapter V and Appendix I of this book are, unlike the rest of it, intended as exposition *without defence* of Marx's views. That is why the labour theory of value is prominent in Chapter V and Appendix I, despite the disclaimer in the last sentence on p. 353.

London, May, 1979

Contents

CONTENTS

A Note on References

FULL TITLES of works cited, with place and date of publication, are listed on pp. 354–61. Passages in italics are that way in the original, unless otherwise stated. With minor exceptions, editions cited of works by Hegel, Marx, and Engels are English translations, but I have often modified the translation, to produce a more literal one.

The only German works referred to which, so far as I know, have not appeared in English, are notes written by Marx in 1858, and included in the 1953 Berlin edition of the *Grundrisse*, but not in Martin Nicolaus's Pelican translation (Harmondsworth, 1973). The former is cited at *Grundrisse* (Berlin), the latter as *Grundrisse*.

Acknowledgements

EXTRACTS FROM the following works are reprinted by permission which is gratefully acknowledged:

E. P. Thompson: *The Making of the English Working Class*, reprinted by permission of Victor Gollancz Ltd.

Karl Marx and Friedrich Engels: *Selected Works, German Ideology*, and *Selected Correspondence*, reprinted by permission of Lawrence & Wishart Ltd.

Karl Marx: *Capital, Theories of Surplus Value, Poverty of Philosophy* and *A Contribution to the Critique of Political Economy*, reprinted by permission of Lawrence & Wishart Ltd.

Karl Marx: *Grundrisse*, translated by Martin Nicolaus (Pelican Books in association with *New Left Review*, 1973) pp. 78, 86, 87, 88, 90, 109, 157–8, 158, 164, 193, 208, 265, 268, 274, 320, 325, 326, 422, 462, 495, 506, 508, 510, 512, 513, 529, 612, 641, 652, 705–6, 706, 749, 754, 831, 831–2, 852–3, 872, 893, 915–16, 970. Translation copyright © Martin Nicolaus, 1973. Reprinted by permission of Penguin Books Ltd. and Random House, Inc.

Karl Marx: *Capital*, Volume I, translated by Ben Fowkes (Pelican Books in association with *New Left Review*, 1976) pp. 990, 1004, 1064. Edition copyright © *New Left Review*, 1976. Appendix translation copyright © Rodney Livingstone, 1976. Reprinted by permission of Penguin Books Ltd.

Karl Marx's
Theory of History

CHAPTER I

Images of History in Hegel and Marx

LENIN SAID that the 'three sources and component parts' of historical materialism were German philosophy, British political economy, and French socialism.[1] This chapter concerns the first source. We put forth Hegel's conception of history as the life of the world spirit, and we show how Marx took that conception, preserved its structure, and changed its content. Having acquired an altered image of history, he would then transform it into the theory subsequent chapters will expound and defend.

The world spirit is a person, but it is not a human being. Yet since human beings are the sort of persons most accessible to us, it will be useful to begin by describing one.

The picture which follows is not of an average human being, nor a typical one, and perhaps not even of a possible one. Some important ways in which all men relate to the world are featured in it, and exaggerated. The function of the picture is expository. It is a backdrop assisting the dramatization of a large vision of history.

Here, then, is a man, moving about the world. As he acts, observes, and suffers, the world reveals itself to him, and he reveals himself to it, imposing his demands on it and pursuing his purposes through it. He spiritualizes nature and it impresses a nature on his spirit. He discovers what stones and flowers and water are like, and how to look up at the stars and down canyons. He learns to change the shapes of nature, to mix and separate its elements. He learns how to live, how to make live, how to let live, and how to kill. He gains understanding of the world's glories, charms, deformities, and dangers. He intervenes in it to secure survival, power, and pleasure.

But he also experiences a substance of a different order. He is in contact and in dialogue with himself. There is a contrast between his confrontation with the world outside and his en-

[1] 'The Three Sources', p. 452.

counter with the part of the world he is. In the first exercise he
is distinct from what he examines; in the second he is not, and
his study must be part of what he studies. He may learn about his
surroundings without changing them, but his self-exploration is
always also a transformation. It leaves him no longer as he was,
investing him with a new self, one more self-aware. And if he
would keep hold of his nature he must inspect it afresh: a new
nature has supervened on the one he penetrated, because that
one was penetrated. His project of self-consciousness is a continual effort which yields continual achievement, a race whose
tape is advanced when the finish is reached. It is only possessed
by being constantly acquired and only acquired by being constantly developed.[1]

Nor is what a man knows about himself unaffected by what
he believes about himself, by the conjectures attending his
endeavour to see. If he thinks himself confident he is half way
to being so. If he thinks himself contemptible, he elicits con-
tempt. Supposing himself to be fragile, he is shaken by minor
adversity. He makes himself, guided by an image of what he
is, and what he believes he is thus contributes to what he is in
fact.

To come to know oneself has rewards but also pains, both in
the process and in the product. For in the change of self, old
manners, habits which give comfort, a residue of much living,
is worried out of existence and an undefended character is
born. Reorganization occurs, and reorganization means partial
disorganization. Each partly new structure must in time in turn
be superseded, else thought and feeling lose their spiritual status,
and the man recedes into the animal kingdom. Self-develop-
ment is the only alternative to that recession: it is not possible
to stand still.

Hegel's phrase 'the labour of the negative'[2] covers this
rending work of self-interrogation and self-alteration. Labour,
because it is hard; negative, because it is destructive. And the
model of a human being, moving painfully and in stages to
self-knowledge, helps us to understand the larger movement of
human history as Hegel conceived it.

---

[1] This sentence is drawn from Kierkegaard, who was not, however, discussing
self-consciousness. See *Edifying Discourses*, p. 10.

[2] 'Preface to *Phenomenology*', p. 390.

The story of mankind is unified by the same principle which gathered the exploits of the special individual just described. History is no miscellany of mighty deeds and catastrophes. It is the increase, now gradual, then sudden, in the self-awareness of the *world spirit*, a term whose employment in Hegel's philosophy of history we must now try to explain.

The strictly philosophical derivation of the concept of the world spirit will not be given here.[1] Instead, we consider how Hegel might have defended his use of the concept in his doctrine of society and history.

We begin by noting that the diversity of national characters, now taken for granted, was something of a novelty when it was emphasized by such writers as Montesquieu in France and Herder in Germany in the later part of the eighteenth century. We commonly expect a German to resemble in thought, feeling, and behaviour another German more than either does an Italian. The expectation is not always fulfilled, but this does not upset the fact that the phrases 'typical German' and 'typical Italian' mean something to us, and not the same thing. It may be hard to formulate the differences. We may disagree about their depth, extent, and permanence. We are very likely to disagree about their explanation, supposing we venture explanations of this difficult phenomenon. But we shall all agree that there *are* differences in national characters, however daunting the tasks of describing and explaining them may be.

Montesquieu and Herder found it necessary to insist on what for us is obvious. Their assertion of the existence of different coherent ways of being human opposed that trend within the Enlightenment which conceived men as fundamentally alike across space and time, and which looked to the construction of a science of man whose generalizations would be as free of reference to particular ages and places as were the laws of the modern science of nature. David Hume:

Would you know the sentiments, inclinations, and course of life of the Greeks and Romans? Study well the temper and actions of the French and English. . . . Mankind are so much the same, in all times and places, that history informs us of nothing new or strange

[1] For a luminous account of the matter, see Part One of Taylor's *Hegel*, especially Chapter III.

in this particular. Its chief use is only to discover the constant and universal principles of human nature.

Should a traveller report something 'new and strange' we would know that he is deceitful or mistaken 'with the same certainty as if he had stuffed his narrations with stories of centaurs and dragons, miracles and prodigies'.[1]

Hume's 'attempt to introduce the experimental method of reasoning into moral subjects'[2] envisaged a research programme contrary to that pursued by Montesquieu and the Romantics who influenced Hegel. Attention to distinct national cultures, conceived as unities organized around distinct principles, is no doubt compatible in the abstract with the claims of a generalizing sociology, but it makes for an intellectual practice opposed to what Hume sought to institute, and it was that practice, and not Hume's, which flourished in the Germany of Hegel's intellectual formation.

Hegel, then, was able to appropriate a conception of national character which he did not invent, but on which he wrought a fateful transformation. For he thought the character of a nation, though it develops only in and through the individuals of the nation and is exhibited only in them and in their works, is nevertheless something in excess of the phenomena manifesting it. The spirit or mind of the nation may not be identified with the set of individual minds nor with some aspect or abstract of them. On the contrary: it is the fact that a given nation at a certain time is animated by a spirit of a certain kind which substantively explains the thought and works we attribute to its national character.

How could Hegel have defended the idea that national character somehow transcends its terrestrial embodiment? The relative recency of the rise in appreciation of national differences might lighten his task. It was not easy to explain why nations showed the characters they did. Theory directed to that end was in a pretty raw state. Montesquieu had tried to explain what he called the 'principle' informing a nation by reference to its climate and geography. But Hegel could claim that this account, or any other which similarly relied on grossly observ-

---

[1] *Enquiry Concerning Human Understanding*, pp. 83–4.
[2] This was the subtitle of his *Treatise of Human Nature*.

able variables, was inadequate, and his reaction would not be unjust. Empirically minded persons, such as most readers of this book, will believe *a priori* that any satisfactory explanation must be an empirical one. Hegel was not an *a priori* empiricist. He would therefore be able to plead that, in the absence of a good empirical explanation of the facts of national character, a suitable non-empirical explanation should command assent.

The particular non-empirical explanation Hegel favoured came from his general philosophy, but he thought it would be supported by the study of history itself.[1] That study would show in the characters of temporally successive dominant nations or civilizations a progress in values, culture, and politics, an empirically visible line of improvement, which required explanation. Yet no empirical explanation of the fact could, in Hegel's view, be forthcoming: it was not as though the civilization which had once been the centre of progress bequeathed its achievements by an observable route to the civilization which took that progress further. Often the superior successor civilization would be spatially removed from its immediate significant predecessor, which might have flourished and decayed long before the successor arose, so that 'the transition which we have to make is only in the sphere of the idea, not in the external historical connection'.[2]

Yet something must explain the progressive sequence, and the features of its constituent nation-stages.

In the light of these supposed empirical facts which he supposed empirically inexplicable, Hegel could recommend the concept of the world spirit. The spirit of the nation explains its character, and is in turn explained as a stage in the develop-

---

[1] Although philosophy proves 'that reason is the sovereign of the world; that the history of the world, therefore, presents us with a rational process', it is also 'an inference from the history of the world, that its development has been a rational process'. *Philosophy of History*, pp. 9, 10.

Here and throughout we scale down the initial capital letter in reproducing 'spirit', 'reason', 'idea', etc. The capitals are translators' impertinences. German orthography requires that every noun be capitalized, not just names of grand entities such as those of which Hegel writes, but every noun, including names of very mundane entities, such as 'finger-nail' and 'pig'. German philosophers writing in German are unable to confer pride of place on entities by capitalizing their names. They are unable to do what translators represent them as obsessionally doing.

[2] *Philosophy of History*, p. 174.

ment of the world spirit, which controls history and directs the succession of national spirits. It is because it reflects the activity of the world spirit that the history of humanity is characterized by progress. Coherent national characters exist as phases of realization of the spirit of the world.

Someone who shared Hegel's religion, and his views about religion, would have further reason for accepting the concept of the world spirit. Hegel believed that Protestantism spoke the truth about man and the universe. But his religious faith was matched by a faith in reason which said that every truth which Christianity expresses in a wrap of myth or image may be stated without imagery by philosophy. This meant that there was a need for a philosophical formulation of the idea of Providence, of God's will manifesting itself in history. This view of the relation between Christianity and philosophic truth, fortified by the observable course of history as described a moment ago, enabled Hegel to present the empirical data as visible traces of God's engagement with the world.

Then if Hegel had been called upon to justify reference to a world spirit to someone ignorant of its derivation in his general philosophy, he might have argued as follows, if, as is false, it had been his practice to lay out arguments in this way:

1. There are distinct coherent national characters. (Empirical fact.)
2. There is cultural progress in history, and nations are its vehicles. (Empirical fact.)
3. There is no empirical explanation of 1 and 2.
4. For every image in the Christian religion there is a corresponding philosophical truth.

Therefore

5. There is a world spirit, whose activity explains 1 and 2, and which corresponds (see 4) to Providence.

The journey of the world spirit divides into chapters, or historical periods, each of which is focused in a part of the world prominent at the time, a civilization governed by a particular conception of man, of his capacities and limitations, his legitimate hopes and his inescapable fears. The conceptions match the level of self-awareness the world spirit has achieved.

Before reviewing some of them, it is advisable to describe some positions in Hegel's general philosophy.

The first of these is a doctrine of the mind which Hegel worked into his account of history and society. He thought the mind could not be understood by cataloguing its features and powers, but only by exhibiting it in process of development. Thus it would be wrong to characterize the intellect, the will, emotion, sensation, and so on, all in fairly arbitrary order (as in Gilbert Ryle's *Concept of Mind*). Instead each mode of consciousness evolves within an evolution of the whole of consciousness. We illustrate by displaying some lineaments in Hegel's construction of knowledge.

Hegel's theory of cognition postulates an epistemological ascent in three stages. The point of departure is *sensuous consciousness*, the summit is *reason*, and *understanding* lies along the route between them. These terms name not just forms of cognition but entire modes of relation between mind and the world, covering action and feeling too. The initial position is a primitive encounter which predates any form of reflection. The mind does not experience itself as separate from the world, and is incapable of distinguishing things and aspects in what lies before it. The elements of the object are merged, and the subject merges with them. Understanding is the sphere of analysis. The subject asserts a distinction between itself and the object of an absolute kind, and is able to discriminate parts and features of the object. The disposition is to hold things apart and experience them in firmly separate array. Understanding is a necessary phase in the acquisition of comprehension, but it must be surpassed by reason, which accepts understanding's distinctions, but does not maintain them intact, for reason recognizes deeper unities beyond understanding's competence. It recaptures the integration understanding suspended, without renouncing the achievements premised on that suspension.

The thesis that the mental requires evolution to manifest itself fully applies to individual human minds, but also to the mentality or culture of a community, and no less to the mind— and being—of God.

Now for Hegel the goal of the mind's—any mind's—evolution is complete self-awareness, an accomplishment impossible save in so far as it engages with something other than itself. 'An individual cannot know what he is till he has made himself real by action.'[1] Through prosecuting projects, he is able to perceive the nature and upshot of his involvement in them, and he thereby learns about himself, as he could not if he did nothing. An artist will know what sort of talent he has only after he has painted and reflected on his painting. A general will know what sort of soldier he is only after he has fought and reflected on what he has done. They must manifest themselves in the world and through understanding their manifestations they will understand themselves. There is no other way.

But the same applies to nations. The aspirations and problems of a community are also construed as instances of its self-exploration. Referring to the spirit of a people, Hegel writes that 'in its work it is employed in rendering itself an object of its own contemplation'.[2]

Mind's awareness of itself is achieved by its projection of itself into what is not itself, and subsequent recognition of itself in its expressions. That is why God creates the material world. He creates because he can come to know himself only in his creation. In order to know himself God too must make and act. He makes the world and man, and he acts through men and in and through the communities men compose.

The world spirit, then, must 'give itself an objective existence'.[3] Since God is spirit, and full spiritual reality demands self-awareness, which is impossible without self-externalization in what is not self; and since for God what is not self is the material world, it follows that in Hegel's idealism the highest form of mind requires that matter exists in order for it to be what it is.[4]

Now this idea of God is not without its blasphemous aspect, but it responds to a good question which Hegel phrased as follows: 'If God is all sufficient and lacks nothing, how does he come to release himself into something so clearly unequal to him' (i.e. nature)?[5] If we take care not to blaspheme, and assign to God the traditional plenitudes of omnipotence, om-

---

[1] 'Real' is opposed to 'potential': see pp. 13 ff. below.
[2] *Philosophy of History*, p. 76.
[3] *Lectures on the Philosophy of World History*, p. 64.
[4] A point brilliantly made by Taylor in Chapter III of his *Hegel*: see, for example, p. 109.
[5] *Philosophy of Nature*, para. 247, Vol. I, p. 205.

niscience, etc., what explains his will to create a world? Hegel answers that 'without the world God is not God'.[1] His perfections come to be only in his perfecting of himself, and that is a process demanding external instrumentalities. No mind comes to know itself except through a medium of self-expression, and in God's case that medium is the world, and history is the development of his self-knowledge in the world. The world spirit passes through stages at each of which it possesses a more adequate awareness of what it is.

The content of this growing awareness is given by the successive conceptions of themselves progressively higher cultures have. The implicit self-perception of society is revealed in the multiform phenomena of social life. 'Its religion, its polity, its ethics, its legislation, and even its science, art and mechanical skill all bear its stamp.'[2] It 'erects itself into an objective world, that exists and persists in a particular religious form of worship, customs, constitution and political laws—in the whole complex of its institutions—in the events and transactions that make up its history'.[3] Thus Hegel unites what may seem disparate expressions of the nation by discerning in each a single idea of what man is. 'The essential category is that of unity, the inner connection of all these diverse forms.'[4]

The communal mind comprises and informs the minds of the citizens, and is in turn subordinate to the world mind, which makes one history of the series of communal mentalities. There has to be a *history* of the world because God cannot know himself immediately, but only in stages, and only in the minds of men: God's 'self-knowledge is . . . his self-consciousness in man, and man's knowledge *of* God, which proceed to man's self-knowledge *in* God'.[5]

Now Hegel thinks it is his happy fate to be living fairly close to the consummation of spirit's project of coming to know itself. He therefore thinks he has a good idea of what men know when they are fully self-aware. To be specific, he thinks men know themselves when they realize that they are free, and consequently establish a relation to nature and social institutions which embodies their freedom and encourages its expression.

---

[1] *Philosophy of Religion*, i. 200.   [2] *Philosophy of History*, p. 64.
[3] Ibid., p. 74, and see also p. 53.   [4] *History of Philosophy*, i. 50.
[5] *Philosophy of Mind*, para. 564, p. 298.

But what is freedom, according to Hegel? He answers in a difficult passage we shall look at later (see pp. 15 ff.), but here we focus on one aspect of the answer: humanity's realization that it is free entails its recognition that it is separate from and sovereign over nature, where 'nature' denotes both the external environment, and the natural inclinations of man himself which, for Hegel, it is human destiny to form and control. The element external to spirit, which we saw to be indispensable to the work of achieving self-consciousness, loses its brute externality and comes under human dominion when self-consciousness is complete. The central differences between cultures in the ascent to full self-consciousness are given by the conceptions they have of the relation between mind and nature, conceptions which find fruition in the cultures' activities.

'The first step in the process presents an immersion of spirit in nature.'[1] Earliest civilization is aware of no essential difference between nature and man, who is perceived as just a part of it. Its position is analogous to the first grade of cognition (sensuous consciousness) above, as the whole of history is analogous to the whole of that progress. Hegel ascribes the primitive consciousness to the Orient, arguing that it explains the unchanging character of its economy and polity, the endless cycle of social processes, experienced as natural, he thought (in common with his European contemporaries, and Marx too) he observed in China and India. The soil is tilled and the produce harvested and the rulers served, without innovation from generation to generation, because it is not understood that these arrangements, unlike the winds and the tides, are subject to human decision and therefore alterable. Of course men know that they are different from birds and beasts, but they also know that birds are different from beasts, and they mark no distinction between these differences.

After the unfortunate Orient and before the second great stage, the Greeks, a number of intermediary peoples are reviewed, who are still more or less sunk in nature. Egypt is half-aware that men are not just creatures of nature, and therefore presents them as half-natural in its cultural works. The Egyptians are said to be labouring on the eve of spirit's full emergence. Whatever assessment Hegel's descriptions deserve

[1] *Philosophy of History*, p. 56.

from the specialist historian, their deep suggestiveness cannot be denied. Here, for example, is how Egypt's janus status is supposed to show itself in art and architecture:

> Of the representations which Egyptian antiquity presents us with, one figure must be especially noticed, viz. the Sphinx—in itself a riddle—an ambiguous form, half brute, half human. The Sphinx may be regarded as a symbol of the Egyptian spirit. The human head looking out from the brute body, exhibits spirit as it begins to emerge from the merely natural—to tear itself loose therefrom and already to look more freely around it; without, however, entirely freeing itself from the fetters nature had imposed. The innumerable edifices of the Egyptians are half below the ground, and half rise above it into the air. . . . Written language is still a hieroglyphic; and its basis is only the sensuous image, not the letter itself.
>
> Thus the memorials of Egypt themselves give us a multitude of forms and images that express its character; we recognise a spirit in them which feels itself compressed; which utters itself, but only in a sensuous mode.[1]

The spirit finally makes its exit from nature in classical Greece, as is evident in the Sophist contrast between *phusis* and *nomos*, between what grows naturally and what comes by human contrivance and agreement. The new awareness is reflected in the deliberate design of constitutions for city states, and in the sublime form assigned to the human figure in Greek sculpture.

This is not to say that the Greeks sense an opposition or hostility between spirit and nature. On the contrary, they are at home in the world, and feel it to be invested with spirituality. If the primitive mode of consciousness represented man in merely natural terms, the Greeks were able to represent nature in human terms: hence their gods who permeate nature and whose characters and deeds are plainly modelled on what is human.

This happy unity of spirit and nature, of a spirit not now sunk in nature but in repose beside it, has its limitation and price: it betokens ignorance of the full power of spirit, and the full measure of its transcendence of nature. In the balance between man and nature, mind's sovereignty is not remarked. It is characteristic that in Greek theogonies divine power does

[1] *Philosophy of History*, p. 199.

not create the world out of nothing, but shapes what exists absolutely independently of mind.

Christianity accordingly inaugurates a more advanced consciousness, initially in painful recoil from the unity that marked Greek life, in 'unhappy' alienation from the natural world and established society alike. But that is not its final posture. For in Hegel doctrines of God are also doctrines of man, and if the Christian God does indeed create *ex nihilo*, then the implicit teaching of the religion is that nature is not finally foreign to men, but subject to humanization. Man is nature's master, but this realization takes centuries to mature, and to work itself out in practice. The technological achievements of late Christian Europe inscribe and confirm the awareness man has gained that spirit is superior to nature.

Our exposition of Hegel's philosophy of history has proceeded at some distance from the sentences of his text. It is time to connect what has been said to some of his explicit formulations.

Hegel says of each of these that it is responsible for historical development: spirit, reason, freedom, and the idea.[1] Many commentators use these imposing terms almost interchangeably, as though it is so difficult to determine what each means that we may as well take them all as meaning the same vague something or other. We shall suppose that each term means something, and something different from what is meant by any of the other three, and we shall try to explain how they function in Hegel's *Philosophy of History*.

(i) *Spirit, freedom, and idea.* The relation between spirit, freedom, and idea may be given in a single sentence, which will subsequently be clarified: the idea of spirit is freedom. When Hegel attributes governance of history to the idea, it is *that* idea which he has in mind. In this use of 'idea', there is no idea *simpliciter*, but only an idea *of* something or other, just as there is in arithmetic no such thing as a square which is not a square *of* some or other number. The phrases 'the square of four' and 'sixteen' designate one and the same thing, that number; only the modes of designating it are different. So similarly 'the idea of spirit' and 'freedom' are two ways of describing one thing: the idea of spirit *is* freedom.

[1] For references, see footnotes on p. 18 below.

We can say in general what the square of x is, for arbitrary x: it is the product of x multiplied by itself. Let us say in general what the idea of an x is. We discuss the particular idea of spirit, freedom, under our next heading.

In Hegelian discourse the idea of x is the essence or nature of x,[1] and the essence of x is that which x is at least potentially: it may not be it actually. The development of x is its actualization of its potential, its becoming in reality what it once was only ideally. Not all changes x undertakes or undergoes contribute to the actualization of its potential, but we may reserve the term 'development' for just such changes. To repeat, then: for x to become what it is potentially is for x to real-ize its idea, to be no longer only idea-lly but actually what it essentially is. When Hegel says that the nature or idea of spirit is not com-pletely real,[2] he refers to the phase when spirit has not yet real-ized its potential, made manifest its essence.

The idea of a child is a mature adult, of a seed the flower which develops out of it. In Aristotelian terms, it is the form towards which the thing moves, and which explains its move-ment. It is moving so as to embody that form.

(Hegel weirdly claims that the essence of matter is gravity, and holds that any piece of matter strives towards something outside itself, indeed to a *point* outside itself, presumably the centre of gravity of the attracting object.[3] It cannot, of course, fulfil that striving, it cannot exist at or as a point, but that is supposed to show how contradictory a piece of matter is: it cannot become what it is by nature.)

Spirit fulfils its potential, manifests its deepest nature, when it achieves full freedom. That is why and because freedom is the idea of spirit. We say more about this freedom in a moment.

In explaining 'idea' we have used the unself-explanatory concept of potentiality, which deserves some account. What does

---

[1] For pertinent texts, see *Philosophy of History*, pp. 17, 23, 40. The term translated 'idea' by Sibree at p. 40 is, in fact, *Begriff*, whose more natural and more common translation is 'concept'. But there is a close connection between Hegel's use of *Begriff* in those cases where Sibree translates it as 'concept' and the uses of 'idea' (*Idee*) we seek to explicate. For the concept of a thing is given by what it would be if it realized its idea. (The German also has *Begriff* in the texts to fn. 2 below and fn. 4, p. 18.)

[2] *Philosophy of History*, p. 22.

[3] Ibid., p. 17. The claim is not necessarily peculiar in itself, but it *is* weird given Hegel's view of essence.

it mean to say of an x which is not actually y that it is potentially y? It can mean a number of things. Let us distinguish three of them, corresponding to what we can call three grades of potentiality. The third grade entails the second and the second entails the first. The idea of x will be x's potentiality of the third grade.

First grade of potentiality. X is potentially y = under some conditions (however remote), x would become y. Equivalently: the supposition that x will become y is not contradicted by any law of nature. In this sense a boulder is potentially the finest stone sculpture ever produced. This is not to say that it is *tending* to become that. It is to say no more than that it could become that, that it is possible for that very boulder to become the finest stone sculpture ever made. This is the lowest grade of potentiality, but it is not nothing. A puddle of water lacks the potentiality attributed to the stone. (It might be said that a puddle of water could, if not yet then in a scientifically more advanced future, be turned into stone by operation on its molecular structure, and that the puddle therefore qualifies as potentially a stone sculpture, on our definition. If such physico-chemical manipulation is possible, so be it. It would not be an objection to the definition if it were true that every x is potentially any y.)

Spirit is potentially free in this first meagre sense, but not only in this sense. To say that it is potentially free in this sense is just to say that it is possible for it to become free.

Second grade of potentiality. Consider a brilliant adolescent with a grave character defect of whom we feel moved to say that he might well become a fine scholar and he might well become a criminal, and nothing else rates as something *he might well become*, in the intended sense of the phrase. We mean that his personality is such that it would be quite normal for him to develop in either of those two ways. We mean more than that it is possible for him to become a criminal. It is also possible for him to become a postman, but we would not say, 'He might well become a postman', not in that tone of voice. We mean that under *some normal* conditions he would become a criminal: conditions in which he becomes one *need* not be unusual (of course they could be unusual: he could become one by a deviant route, e.g. having first become a postman; that is why we say the conditions *need* not be unusual—they would have to be unusual for him to become a postman). This concept of normality cannot be defined simply in terms of probabilities, though perhaps it can be complexly so defined. We may learn that special conditions are going to obtain, just such conditions as will ensure that he becomes a postman. Yet we would not therefore say that he is potentially a postman in this second sense. His postman potentiality remains of the lowest grade only even if it is certain that he will become one.

Third grade of potentiality. Under *some* conditions *x* would become *y*—that is first grade potentiality. Under *some normal* conditions *x* would become *y*—that is second grade potentiality. In third grade potentiality *x* would become *y* under *all normal* conditions (note that there may be more than one set of normal conditions). Illustration: we say of a sound foetus that it is potentially a child. Under all normal conditions that and no alternative to it is what it will become. It may of course fail to become one, but that would establish that conditions were abnormal.

If *y* is third-grade potentiality of *x*, then *x* becomes *y* unless its natural development is impeded. Occurrence of abnormal conditions which impede natural development may frustrate the realization of third grade potential. (It *may* do so, but it is not excluded that *x* becomes under some abnormal conditions what it becomes under all normal conditions. It would then realize its potential, but not necessarily *because* that was its potential.)

It is in this high grade sense that spirit is potentially free, that freedom is the idea of spirit. But we must add that there can be no question of obstacles blocking the attainment of its potential. 'No force can ... prevent God's purposes from being realized.'[1]

(ii) *What is freedom?* Before undertaking this review of salient Hegelian terms we said that spirit is free when it transcends and subjugates nature. Yet Hegel does not mention nature when he defines freedom in *The Philosophy of History*. He says this:

Spirit . . . may be defined as that which has its centre in itself.

---

[1] *Lectures on the Philosophy of World History*, p. 67.

It has not a unity outside itself, but has already found it; it exists *in* and *with itself*. Matter has its essence out of itself; spirit is *self-contained existence*. Now this is freedom, exactly. For if I am dependent, my being is referred to something else which I am not; I cannot exist independently of something external. I am free, on the contrary, when my existence depends on myself. This self-contained existence of spirit is none other than self-consciousness—consciousness of one's own being.[1]

Our exposition of these difficult remarks is intended to link them with the characterization of freedom given earlier.

A spirit or mind is something which is conscious, which enjoys awareness, and which may also be referred to as a consciousness. Now a fundamental premiss of the passage, and a plausible one, is that there is no objectless awareness. Awareness or consciousness is always *of* something or other. Consciousness thus depends for its existence on being related to something. That which consciousness is *of*, moreover, may be either something other than consciousness, or it may be consciousness itself. Accordingly, consciousness depends for its existence either on something other than itself, or on itself alone. But consciousness is *free* if and only if the second alternative holds, for then and only then does it depend on itself and itself alone. For it to be free, the relation without which it cannot exist must be to itself. Hence 'freedom means that the other thing with which you deal is a second self'.[2] It cannot, finally, be truly *other* if you are to be free.

That is how the identification of freedom with self-consciousness is achieved. But if freedom is the containment of consciousness by consciousness, unfreedom will be the containment of consciousness by something else. That will be its containment by what is not conscious, and what is not conscious is, precisely, nature. Then engulfment in nature will count as the bondage of spirit, and its freedom will lie, as we originally asserted, in its transcendence of nature.[3]

---

[1] *Philosophy of History*, p. 17.
[2] *Logic of Hegel*, p. 49.
[3] 'Mind is just this elevation above nature and physical modes, and above the complication with an external object . . .' *Philosophy of Mind*, paragraph 440, p. 179.

Nor does the foregoing contradict what was said earlier, that nature is an indispensable medium for the achievement of self-consciousness. There is no unmediated self-inspection on the part of spirit. The attainment of freedom requires the manifestation of spirit in nature, as in something external, but in the final consummation of freedom that nature loses its apparent autonomy: it is seen to be essentially dependent on mind.[1]

(iii) *Reason*. We have dealt with the connections binding spirit, idea, and freedom. Reason remains to be considered. Hegel states the relation between spirit and reason as follows: spirit is self-conscious reason, reason conscious of itself.[2]

What does it mean to say that spirit is *self-conscious reason*? We do no violence to the content of the thought by expressing it less floridly. The identification is of spirit and *conscious rationality*. And we do not misjudge Hegel's meaning if we trim the formulation a little further. He meant that *spirit is consciously rational*.

Why does Hegel say that spirit is consciously rational? Let us begin by asking what is rational but not consciously so, or, more floridly, what is reason not conscious of itself?

The answer is: nature.

Now it is clear that nature is not conscious, but in what sense is it rational? According to Hegel there is reason in it in so far as it is subject to law. It is easy to agree that the regularity in the movement of the planets makes their behaviour *intelligible*. For Hegel this also makes it *rational*: rules are followed, a consistency is displayed. Of course nothing here is aware of following rules. But that is because nature's rationality is not a conscious one. Nature is unconscious reason.

Spirit, by contrast, is consciously rational. When a mind follows a rule it is aware of doing so. Spirit is thus a rationality which is self-aware, or, to return to the initial formula, it is reason conscious of itself.

At a later point reason figures in a new formula: now *freedom* is the self-consciousness of reason.[3] This is substantially the same doctrine. Freedom being the essential or defining property of spirit, to say what freedom is is, indirectly, to say what spirit is.

---

[1] See *The Logic of Hegel*, p. 180; *Philosophy of Right*, p. 125.

[2] *Philosophy of History*, p. 11.

[3] Ibid., p. 70.

The new formula says that that which is by nature free is consciously rational.

(iv) *The Agency of History*. We may now assign roles to the characters said to be responsible for historical development, to wit, spirit,[1] reason,[2] freedom,[3] and the idea.[4] This plurality is not evidence of unclarity or vacillation.

History is on the one hand the work of spirit and reason, and on the other that of freedom and the idea. We pair them so because it is the work of reason and spirit in one respect, of freedom and the idea in another. And we now know that there are only two characters to consider, not four. For spirit *is* self-conscious reason, and the idea of spirit *is* freedom.

Spirit is responsible for historical development because historically significant occurrences are its acts, and the latter display an intelligible progress because spirit is rational. History is spirit's biography.

But history has not only an agent but also a purpose or goal, namely what the agent potentially is in the highest grade sense and towards the realization of which it consequently moves. Since spirit is the agent of history, and its essence is freedom, freedom, the idea of spirit, is the purpose or goal of history.

The goal of world history is described in three ways: spirit's self-consciousness, spirit's consciousness of its freedom, and spirit's actualization of its freedom (or, for short, freedom).[5] This is one purpose described from three points of view.

A proper consciousness of x is a consciousness of the essential nature of x. Since the essential nature of spirit is freedom, its self-consciousness is its consciousness of its freedom, and the first two descriptions coincide.

But why should achieving consciousness of freedom suffice for achieving freedom itself? And why is it not only sufficient but, as Hegel also implies,[6] necessary for freedom?

Here is the underlying thought: if an agent is in principle free he will act freely, that is, make his freedom actual, if and

---

[1] It is 'the director of the events of the world's history' (*Philosophy of History*, p. 8).

[2] 'reason governs the world and has consequently governed its history' (ibid., p. 25).

[3] It is 'the absolute goal of history' (ibid., p. 23).

[4] The 'general aim' of world history is 'the realisation of the idea of spirit' (ibid., p. 25).

[5] Ibid., p. 19.   [6] See ibid., p. 18.

only if he is aware that he is free. If I suppose myself enslaved to you then however much I am in truth free I shall not behave freely, I shall obey your instructions.[1] Spirit, and so men, are by nature free but they behave unfreely as long, yet only as long, as they do not know they are free. Thus it is necessary and sufficient for the realization of freedom itself that an awareness of freedom be accomplished.

The content of this developing awareness is given by the conceptions of man and nature we examined before turning to the above explication of terms. They organize the enterprises of the age and nation they control. In each epoch political life, the economic system, modes of dress, styles of painting—all social and cultural phenomena—reflect the level of self-awareness human beings, by grace of the spirit, have reached, and constitute the *medium* of their and its self-understanding.

But after serving its time the ruling motif becomes outmoded, its authority is exhausted, the old medium loses its suppleness, hardens, and cracks, and the culture which developed spirit is destroyed by that development, and must leave the historical stage.[2] In response to the decomposition of culture, social conflict erupts, and the crisis of the community is reproduced in the life of the individual: his thought and action are rent apart. He inherits images and norms whose relevance has expired and he either turns from them to nothingness or tries to live by them and finds that they cannot be realized.

Rebirth and renewal are necessary, and they are often associated with the insight and struggle of a great man, a 'world-historical' figure, an Alexander, a Caesar, a Luther, or a Napoleon. This person, in a world of roles in disarray, fashions a new role for himself and a new script for others, thereby initiating a new act in the drama. In his being the needs of the time and of the individual once more come together. He is a midwife assisting at the birth of a fresh conception of man. His insight tells him of the pregnancy of the time, but he never learns the full significance of what he delivers.

Return to the self-examining individual with whom we began. Before he undertakes his search into himself he is undivided.

---

[1] See *Philosophy of Right*, para. 21, p. 30.
[2] *Philosophy of History*, p. 71.

But once he puts himself in question he slides into shifting aspects, becomes a critic and an object of criticism. Self-interrogation rends him. He is jolted each time an image of himself on which he has lived is seen to be bounded in significance, not a final truth. In the conclusion of fruitful investigation wholeness returns. He is again a united individual, but the integration he enjoys is at a higher level, because of the self-division he has endured.

The career of mankind is in broadest overview similar. Primitive men are unthinking. They know no dualism of subject and object and they hang on to one another. History begins when men stand beside one another, when man stands beside himself and outside himself. The emergence of culture from nature brings disposition to collision in every precinct of life. History must be filled with violence and strain because spirit, like our heroic individual 'is at war with itself; it has to overcome itself as its most formidable obstacle. That development which in the sphere of nature is a peaceful growth, is in that of spirit, a severe, a mighty conflict with itself.'[1] In order to develop, spirit invests itself in forms of life it values, and it cannot subsequently break with them, except by wrenching itself away.

In history's consummation mankind will know what there is to know about itself. It will have tested itself in many dimensions and arrived at its goal. Men will recover their original unity, but it will not be mindless and brute, as it was in the beginning. Rather, they will be like mutually sustaining parts in a properly functioning organism, each occupying the place to which he is suited in the structure of roles articulated in *The Philosophy of Right*. The coexistence of primitive men rested on lack of differentiation between them. Divisive needs and contrary aims disrupted the primeval peace and supplied the impulse in history. The arrival of profound but profoundly compatible needs signifies history's end.

The epistemological dialectic given on page 7 above (from sensuous consciousness through understanding to reason) began with a phase of undifferentiated unity, followed with one in

---

[1] *Philosophy of History*, p. 55, and see p. 73. 'The history of the world is not the theatre of happiness. Periods of happiness are blank pages in it, for they are periods of harmony—periods when the antithesis is in abeyance.' Ibid., pp. 26-7.

which differentiation was achieved at the cost of disunity, and ended with a restoration of unity which did not cancel difference, a differentiated unity. The same contour is discernible in the historical dialectic just described, and the modern world bears within itself each of the three forms of relation (undifferentiated unity, differentiated disunity, differentiated unity), for 'the grades which spirit seems to have left behind it, it still possesses in the depths of its present'.[1] The replication of the stages in the emerging world appears in the main subdivisions of the last part of Hegel's *Philosophy of Right*—'Ethical Life', his essay in philosophical sociology.

Ethical life begins with the *family*, a sphere of merger, the members being immediately concerned in one another's welfare, not externally bound by calculated ties of advantage. The weal and woe of any member of the family is experienced as such by each. Counterposed to the family is *civil society*, a collection of autonomous individuals released from the family cocoon, which has prepared them to engage in economic competition and co-operation. Independence and separation predominate, and partnerships depend on unfeeling contract. But civil society is subordinate to the *state*, that is, not the political institutions merely, but the entire national community, which sustains the independence at work in economic life but complements it by providing collective identity and culture, without which an economy is impossible, for at the very least a common language is required in which contractual agreements are expressed. The family shows undifferentiated unity, civil society differentiation and disunion, and the state differentiated unity.

This rhythm of primitive whole, fragmentation, and reunification asserts itself widely in Western thought. It beats not only in Hegel and, as we shall see, in Marx, but in much religious doctrine, in the Christian triad of innocence, fall, and redemption, in Aristophanes' account of love in Plato's *Symposium*, in some psycho-analytic narrations of the genesis of the person, and—seminally for German philosophy of history—throughout Schiller's *Letters on the Aesthetic Education of Mankind*.[2]

Karl Marx was one of a generation of young German intellectuals who were captured by Hegel's philosophical and

[1] *Philosophy of History*, p. 79.   [2] See, e.g., pp. 39, 41.

historical vision. He outgrew it in the course of the 1840s, in
the middle twenties of his life. His passage into Hegelianism
and from it to Marxism will not be described here, where we
shall be content to put the gross outline of his view of history
alongside that of Hegel. But it bears mention that his own
involvement with social and political affairs, as the crusading
editor of a bourgeois radical journal, helped him to conclude
that the emphasis on thought and culture as the principal bases
of social phenomena was misguided, and served reactionary
purpose.[1] Hegelian philosophy of history transfigured exploitative class structures into realizations of concepts of human
nature, and thereby attached undeserved dignity to the images
men, and especially privileged men, had fashioned for themselves. But 'just as our opinion of an individual is not based on
what he thinks of himself, so can we not judge of [an historical]
period . . . by its own consciousness',[2] nor even by the consciousness of philosophers who decorate its demise by reading
to it the meaning of its achievements.[3]

Marx reached the conclusion that it was not spiritual attitudes, but external conditions, the wealth men enjoyed or lacked,
the ways they had to labour, which shaped society. Epochs
were controlled not by conceptions of man but by material
ends and means. The ruling interest and difficulty of men was
relating to the *world*, not to the *self*. The progress of history is
not primarily in self-consciousness: this increases, but only as a
function of man's increasing control over his environment. The
attempt to gain that control stimulates and obscures his insight
into himself. His self-image depends on it, not it on his self-
image. The battle in the soul is replaced by a battle between
man and the elements, a war of labour reproducing itself in
antagonism between and inside men. The biological and geographical conditions which for Hegel were but the instruments
of and opportunities for spirit's self-assertion have their autonomy restored to them. The character of man and society now

[1] See the Preface to *The Critique of Political Economy* for Marx's statement of the
importance to his formation of his work as a journalist, which is well described
by McLellan in Chapter IV of *Marx Before Marxism*.

[2] *Critique of Political Economy*, p. 21.

[3] See the penultimate paragraph of the Preface to *The Philosophy of Right* for
Hegel's doctrine that true understanding of a culture is possible only after its
main accomplishments are complete. See Appendix I, below, pp. 340–1.

depends on the character of the nature off which society lives, both as that nature is in the beginning, and as it becomes under the transformations wrought by the process of production.

Both Hegel and Marx faced and commented upon humanity's most serious and persistent afflictions: war, oppression, exploitation, and indignity. Hegel explained the evils by urging that humanity had not yet come to know itself fully, and justified them by maintaining that only through strife could men be introduced to themselves. For Marx the answers lay elsewhere, in the domination over human beings of the world around them, in their as yet unfulfilled attempt to prevail over what surrounded them. Men would relate in connections of mastery and servitude until they were masters of the physical world.

Unformed, unregulated, unshaped by human hand and brain, man's environment is—generally—hostile to him. Naked, he shivers. In most climes the uncooked fruits of uncultivated soil do not offer him adequate sustenance. He does not fit comfortably into the world. But, unlike other similarly unfortunate creatures, he is equipped to change his situation. He can remake the world, and in doing so he remakes himself, for he develops the powers he uses to change the world, and with those new powers come new needs. 'Needs are originally confined and only develop along with the productive forces.'[1] The growth of human power is the central process of history. The need for that growth explains why there *is* history. 'Men have history because they must *produce* their life.'[2] For Hegel men have history because consciousness needs time and action to come to know itself, for Marx because men need time and action to prevail against nature.

It will follow that there is no history when nature is unusually generous. When the earth supplies the requisites of survival with little human help nature is 'too lavish', for she

'keeps man in hand, like a child in leading-strings'. She does not impose on him any necessity to develop himself . . . It is the necessity of bringing a natural force under the control of society, of economising, of appropriating it or subduing it by the work of man's hand, that first plays the decisive part in the history of industry[3]

[1] *Grundrisse*, p. 612 n.   [2] *German Ideology*, p. 41.   [3] *Capital*, i. 513–14.

and hence, we may add by way of interpretation, in history *sans phrase*. In Arcadia the fruit falls from the tree into man's lap and men make no history because they do not have to— history is a substitute for nature.

Initially men live as equals in a classless society, in a primitive accommodation with nature, which their labour does not permanently transform. Each works, not for another, but all for the community at large, to which he is and feels united. All share depressed physical and cultural conditions.

This accommodation is upset by population growth,[1] which enjoins an expansion in production and a more aggressive technology. The original conjunction of man and nature is broken by tools which attack and alter the earth's crust. Now animals are not only hunted but raised. Vegetables are planted, not just gathered. The superior posture towards nature generates a surplus above what is required to sustain those who produce, and this enables the formation of a class which does not work on nature, which carries out society's intellectual and organizational tasks, if it does any work at all, and which exacts from the producers the maximum it can.[2] This class dominates the community as a whole, thus destroying the community *as* a whole. Unity among men is replaced by class antagonism. Men break with one another in consequence of a process which begins when they break with nature.

Capitalism brings the strife between man and nature, and man and man, to an end. It completes the conquest of nature, which is now so reshaped by industrial history that men can claim it as their own. Nature had once pressed man down to a natural level, but he has now raised it to a human level. So much technique and inanimate power are now available that arduous labour, and the resulting control by some men over the lives of others lose their function, and a new integration of man and nature in a new communism becomes possible, and will be actualized by the class oppressed under capitalism, the industrial proletariat.

This consummation is preceded by a stage of history than

----

[1] This is a somewhat controversial imputation, but see *German Ideology*, p. 32, for a little evidence. For more discussion of the dissolution of primitive communism, see p. 299 below.

[2] For elaboration, see Ch. VII, section (7).

which, in *some* respects, no other age is more hostile to human fulfilment. The oppression of the proletariat will not be traced in detail here. One summary description:

> More than any other mode of production, [capitalism] squanders human lives, or living labour, and not only blood and flesh, but also nerve and brain. Indeed it is only through the most enormous waste of the individual development that the development of mankind is at all preserved in the epoch of history immediately preceding the conscious organisation of society.[1]

It is through this very confinement of the powers of the individual that the power of the race is brought to an unprecedented height. But communism will provide for *men* the creative existence achieved under capitalism by *man*.[2]

Despite its consequences for the producers capitalism was needed for progress, since it extended man's dominion over nature and so brought forward the day when the struggle with nature could be ended, and so, too, the derivative battle of class against class. Only in capitalist organization could the enormous accumulation of productive power required for liberation be conceived and achieved. 'This antagonistic stage cannot be avoided, any more than it is possible for man to avoid the stage in which his spiritual energies are given a religious definition as powers independent of himself.'[3]

Capitalism would not last. It would, increasingly, create obstacles to its own effective functioning. Being unable to regulate the distribution and consumption of its prolific output, it would cease to be a feasible social order. The capitalist form of association would lose its pliancy as an economic medium.[4] And the class it had spawned, the propertyless proletariat, would bury its progenitor and install a classless society. In no other way would capitalism, however irrational it became, be superseded. For the class it empowers, the owners of the means of production, would resist its demolition, and would control means of destruction and oppression on a scale making determined class struggle, and not peaceful negotiation, the necessary way forward.

[1] *Capital*, iii. 88.   [2] See my 'Marx's Dialectic of Labour', p. 246.
[3] 'Results of the Immediate Process of Production', p. 990.
[4] See p. 19 above, where culture was described as a medium for consciousness. This analogy is presently extended.

In primitive communism there is community but also poverty and ignorance. History creates knowledge and a materialization of knowledge in means of production creative of wealth, but it splits the community into classes and fragments the being of the individual. Modern communism restores the original unities on the high material plane class society has provided.[1] Class struggle, and the antagonism between man and nature, come to an end.

We said that Marx's conception of history preserves the structure of Hegel's but endows it with fresh content. For Hegel, as we have seen, history shows an expansion of consciousness giving itself form in cultures, which subvert themselves through their success in advancing consciousness. The structure of his conception of history is given by the italicized words in the following summary statement of it:

> *History is the history of* the world spirit (and, derivatively, human consciousness) *which undergoes growth* in self-knowledge, *the stimulus and vehicle of which is* a culture, *which perishes when it has stimulated more growth than it can contain.*

For Marx, as we shall see in the rest of this book, the important forms are not cultures but economic structures, and the role of consciousness is assumed by expanding productive power. The following sentence, when read together with the one above, exhibits the identity of structure across diversity of content in the two doctrines:

> *History is the history of* human industry, *which undergoes growth* in productive power, *the stimulus and vehicle of which is* an economic structure, *which perishes when it has stimulated more growth than it can contain.*

Central formulations in Hegel's philosophy of history re-appear transmuted in Marx. For example:

> . . . the world spirit has had the patience to pass through these [cultural] forms in the long expanse of time, taking upon itself the tremendous labour of world history *in which it imparted as much of its content to every form as that form was capable of holding.*[2]

---

[1] For an interesting exposition of communism's many syntheses, see Goldmann, 'Socialism and Humanism', especially pp. 41, 49.

[2] 'Preface to *Phenomenology*', p. 404, my italics.

The above belongs to the provenance of:

No social order ever perishes before all the productive forces for which there is room in it have developed.[1]

Social orders (which are built around economic structures) replace cultural forms, and the development of productive power supplants that of consciousness, but the relation between the first and second members of each pair is the same.

Yet it is also not the same. For we may attribute to Marx, as we cannot to Hegel, not only a *philosophy* of history, but also what deserves to be called a *theory* of history, which is not a reflective construal, from a distance, of what happens, but a contribution to understanding its inner dynamic. Hegel's reading of history as a whole and of particular societies is just that, a *reading*, an interpretation which we may find more or less attractive. But Marx offers not only a reading but also the beginnings of something more rigorous. The concepts of productive power and economic structure (unlike those of consciousness and culture) do not serve only to express a vision. They also assert their candidacy as the leading concepts in a theory of history, a *theory* to the extent that history admits of theoretical treatment, which is neither entirely nor not at all.

The ensuing chapters attempt a reconstruction of parts of historical materialism as a theory or infant science. It will not hurt to bear in mind the vision that helps to make the theory important.

[1] *Critique of Political Eeconomy*, p. 21. The rest of the sentence reads: 'and new, higher relations of production never appear before the material conditions of their existence have matured in the womb of the old society itself'. This bears comparison with '. . . truth appears only when its time has come—and therefore never appears too early, nor ever finds that the public is not ready for it' ('Preface to *Phenomenology*', p. 456). Given the association between progress of truth and a new, more advanced culture, this is further evidence of the analogy here maintained.

CHAPTER II

The Constitution of the Productive Forces

(1) *Economic Structure and Productive Forces*

IT IS convenient to introduce the definition of productive forces in the context of a preliminary characterization of the economic structure, which will be deepened in the next chapter. We take the 1859 Preface as our guide:

> In the social production of their life, men enter into definite relations that are indispensable and independent of their will, relations of production which correspond to a definite stage of development of their material productive forces. The sum total of these relations of production constitutes the economic structure, the real basis, on which rises a legal and political super-structure. . . .[1]

The economic structure (or 'real basis') is here said to be composed of production relations. Nothing else is said to participate in its composition. We conclude *ex silentio* that production relations alone serve to constitute the economic structure. This means that the productive forces are not part of the economic structure. Given Marx's statement, they could be part of it only if they were a subset of production relations. Against this suggestion there are three considerations.

First, a force or power—for productive forces may also be called 'productive powers'[2]—is not a relation. It is not something which holds between objects, but rather a property of an object, or, in an extended use in which Marx indulges,[3] an object bearing that property, an object having productive power, and such an object is also not a relation.

Second, production relations are said to *correspond* to productive forces at a certain stage of development of the latter. Controversy rages around this word. Commentators disagree on whether its use implies that the productive forces enjoy ex-

---

[1] *Critique of Political Economy*, p. 20.
[2] See pp. 37–8 below. [3] See fn. 1, p. 38.

planatory primacy over the production relations. We hold that is precisely what it implies: we shall propound what is called a 'technological' interpretation of historical materialism.[1] But whatever 'correspond' means here, it is difficult to reconcile correspondence of production relations to productive forces with inclusion of productive forces in the set of production relations.

Third, Marx says elsewhere, in texts which will occupy us in Chapter IV, that production relations are *economic* in character, while productive forces are not. It follows that productive forces are no sort of production relations.

We take pains to insist that production relations alone, and not productive forces, constitute the economic structure, because this obvious reading of the sentences on exhibit is at variance with what other writers have found in them. It is common procedure to locate the productive forces in the economic structure, from which, we see, Marx unambiguously excludes them.[2]

Why is so manifest an error so widespread? We suggest that it reflects acceptance of a plausible but false proposition, namely:

(1) If productive forces are explanatorily fundamental, they are part of the economic basis (or foundation).

We have already asserted the antecedent of (1), but we denied its consequent, and therefore reject (1) itself. Writers who commit the error mentioned do so because they recognize that the forces are fundamental and, accepting (1), infer that they are part of the economic foundation. Others,[3] who wrongly deny the fundamental explanatory status of the forces, wrongly suppose their denial supported by the exclusion of the forces from the economic foundation, which they correctly assert. This reflects acceptance of the same false proposition, (1).

[1] See Ch. VI, and see pp. 136-8 on the meaning of 'correspond'.

[2] See Acton, 'The Materialist Conception of History', p. 312, *Illusion of the Epoch*, pp. 137-8, *What Marx Really Said*, p. 50; Calvez, *La Pensée de Karl Marx*, p. 425; Duncan, *Marx and Mill*, p. 289; Eagleton, *Marxism and Literary Criticism*, p. 5; McLellan, *Karl Marx*, p. 308; Mills, *The Marxists*, p. 82; Plamenatz, *German Marxism*, pp. 24-5; Therborn, *Science, Class, and Society*, p. 399. Keat and Urry, *Social Theory as Science*, p. 241, say that Marx 'occasionally' includes forces as well as relations in the base, but they cite no evidence, and in fact there is none.

[3] e.g. Hook, *Towards the Understanding of Karl Marx*, p. 126.

In order to expose the falsehood of (1), we must note an ambiguity in the use of the term 'basis' or 'foundation'. If x is the basis of y, then y rests on x. Now what y rests on may or may not be part of y. The foundation upon which a house rests is—arguably anyway—a part of the house, but the plinth upon which a statue stands is not part of the statue.

As commonly used, the term 'basis' does not select between the stated alternatives. Let us adopt two terms, 'basis$_1$' and 'basis$_2$', defined as follows:

x is the basis$_1$ of y = x is that part of y on which (the rest of) y rests

x is the basis$_2$ of y = x is external to y and is that on which (the whole of) y rests.

We may now say that the economic structure is the basis$_1$ of the social formation, since it is itself a social phenomenon; whereas it is the basis$_2$ of the superstructure, since it is not a superstructural phenomenon.

Now the error in (1) is to pass from the truth that the productive forces are the basis$_2$ of society—a vivid way of assigning to them primary explanatory significance—to the falsehood that they are the basis$_1$ of society. They are indeed the foundation of the economy but they do not belong to the economic foundation.

The distinction between basis$_1$ and basis$_2$ reconciles the truth of the antecedent of (1) with the falsehood of its consequent, and shows that (1) itself is false.

Marx does say, outside the Preface, that the productive forces are 'the *material* basis of all social organisation'.[1] But this is basis$_2$, as is confirmed by Marx's systematic opposition, to be demonstrated later,[2] between the *material* and the *social*.

To put the point with free use of the spatial metaphor: the productive forces occur *below* the economic foundation.[3] That the economic structure is the basis$_1$ of society and the basis$_2$ of the superstructure does not disqualify the question why a specific economic structure obtains. And the answer, on the

---

[1] *Capital*, i. 372 n.

[2] In Chapter IV.

[3] Compare Plekhanov: '. . . only in a popular speech could one talk about economy as the *prime cause* of all social phenomena. Far from being a prime cause, it is itself a consequence, a "function" of the productive forces.' *Monist View*, p. 207.

'technological' reading to be favoured in this work, is that the productive forces strongly determine the character of the economic structure, while forming no part of it.

Another misreading of the sentences quoted on page 29, less popular than the one we have just discussed, is illustrated by Acton's remark[1] that the Preface divides social *processes* into those which are basic and those which are superstructural. Yet the base/superstructure distinction does not, in the first instance, divide processes. Basic is not a set of processes but a set of relations. This is appropriate, since the base is a structure, and it is easier to construe relations as composing a structure than it is so to construe processes. The point has some importance, since the fact that certain relations obtain explains phenomena in a different fashion from the fact that certain processes occur, and the difference vitiates criticisms of Marxian explanatory theses which are insensitive to their structural cast.[2]

Also misleading in Acton's remark is its familiar suggestion that for Marx everything social is either basic or superstructural, that the distinction is exhaustive. Nothing Marx said warrants this imputation, which leads to unproductive puzzles. Not everything social has to be tagged either 'basic' or 'superstructural'.

Having made a number of rather formal points about productive forces and production relations, we now proceed to say what they are.

We say what production relations are by indicating what terms stand in production relations and (on pp. 34 ff.) how they are related by them. Let us consider dyadic relations only, for convenience. The account is easily generalized.

First, then, the terms. Persons and productive forces are the only terms bound by production relations. All production relations are either between a person (or group of persons) and another person (or group of persons), or between a person (or group of persons) and a productive force (or group of productive forces). In other words: a production relation binds at

[1] 'The Materialist Conception of History', p. 213.
[2] See also pp. 86–7 below, and the critique of Plamenatz in 'Being, Consciousness and Roles', p. 92.

least one person(s)-term and at most one productive force(s)-term, and no other type of term.

We need not state what a person is. But productive forces are less familiar. We must say what they are. The catalogue below clarifies the idea of a productive force, by listing some tradition-ally recognized kinds of productive forces (the list will be expanded in section (5)).

$$
\text{Productive forces}
\begin{cases}
\text{Means of production}
\begin{cases}
A & \text{Instruments of production} \\
B & \text{Raw materials}
\end{cases} \\
C & \text{Labour power (that is, the productive faculties of} \\
& \text{producing agents: strength, skill, knowledge,} \\
& \text{inventiveness, etc.).}
\end{cases}
$$

The catalogued items are unified by the fact that each is, in a wide sense, *used* by producing agents to make products. A denotes what they work with, B what they work on, and C what enables them to work with A on B.

To qualify as a productive force, a facility must be capable of use by a producing agent in such a way that production occurs (partly) as a result of its use, and it is someone's purpose that the facility so contribute to production. But that someone need not be the immediate producer himself. He could be a non-producer in charge of the process. Thus if a person powers a machine by running on a treadmill, the treadmill is an instrument of production even if the treader is unaware of its effect.

Our restriction of productive forces to what are used to produce things excludes from the category items other writers have placed inside it. Acton is right when he says that appro-priate laws, morals, and government can promote production, but he is wrong to infer that they can therefore be treated as means of production.[1] A means of ϕ-ing is something used in order to ϕ. Laws, morals, and government are not used by men to produce products. When they are used, as they may be, to get men to produce, they are means not of production but of motivating producers.

A similar position is espoused by Vernon Venable, who holds that x is a productive force if and only if x facilitates or stimulates

[1] *Illusion of the Epoch*, p. 167.

the process of production.[1] Venable validly infers that when production relations facilitate advances in production, they qualify as productive forces.[2] Now production relations may be congenial or adverse to production, but they are not used in production to produce products. That they stand in certain production relations may induce the capitalist to invest and the proletarian to labour hard, but nothing is materially produced out of or with such relations.

If Venable were right, a slave's religion would be a productive force if it so compensated for his misery that it made him willing to work. This result plainly contradicts the intent of Marx's theory.

Our concern to distinguish between productive forces and other requisites of and stimuli to production parallels Marx's interest in sealing off the idea of productive activity from activity which enables or assists production but which is not itself productive. He criticized Nassau Senior, who considered soldiers productive when they supplied security essential to uninterrupted agrarian labour. For Senior, the soldier participates in producing corn by protecting the farmer. But though it is true, in the case envisaged, that without the soldier no corn would be produced,

> the soldier can drop out although the *material conditions of production*, the conditions of agriculture as such, remain unchanged.[3]

It is the *social* conditions which make the soldier's presence necessary to agriculture. His indispensability does not make him productive, because his service is not *materially* necessary: it is not imposed by the nature of the soil and the technology

---

[1] This is a fair summary of pp. 105-7 of *Human Nature: The Marxian View*.

[2] This is not the mistake, mentioned on p. 28 above, of treating productive forces as production relations, but the distinct error of treating production relations as under certain conditions productive forces.

[3] *Theories of Surplus Value*, i. 289. We are here concerned with productive labour 'from the standpoint of the [material] labour process alone', not from the special point of view of capitalist production, where its characterization is different. *Capital*, i. 181 n., and cf. ibid., pp. 508-9; 'Results', pp. 1038-9. For an excellent discussion of Marx's two concepts of productive labour, see Gough on 'Productive Labour in Marx'.

We follow tradition in calling what Marx is trying to demarcate 'productive activity'. 'Producing activity' would be a better phrase. A simple way of making Marx's point is to say that not all production-promoting (and in *that* sense productive) activity is producing activity.

available for working it. That an activity is necessary to production makes it a productive activity only if its necessity is grounded in the physical facts of the situation. (This is not to say that an activity is productive only if it is essential to production: there is often more than one way of producing something. The point is that *if* an activity is essential, then its essentiality makes it a productive activity only if it is materially grounded.)

The soldier's activity *enables* production but he is not productive. Nor is activity which *stimulates* production by that token productive. If it were, the criminal would be a producer, since he

> breaks the monotony and everyday security of bourgeois life. In this way he keeps it from stagnation, and gives rise to that uneasy tension and agility without which even the spur of competition would get blunted. Thus he gives a stimulus to the productive forces. . . .
>
> The effects of the criminal on the development of productive power can be shown in detail. Would locks ever have reached their present degree of excellence had there been no thieves? Would the making of banknotes have reached its present perfection had there been no forgers?[1]

Only what contributes materially within and to productive activity as Marx demarcates it counts as a productive force. Hence, turning from the matter of who produces to the topic of the productive forces themselves, he disparages the policy of treating as '*indirect* means of production'

> everything that furthers production, everything which tends to remove an obstacle, to make production more active, speedier, easier.[2]

There is more to be said about productive forces, but first we must complete our preliminary delineation of the economic structure, 'sum total of production relations'.

Persons and productive forces are the terms of production relations. But not all relations with the right terms are production relations. Battersea Power Station is a productive force. It is larger than you are, and probably older too, but those relations between it and you are not production relations.

Production relations are EITHER relations of ownership by

---

[1] *Theories of Surplus Value*, i. 387-8.   [2] Ibid., p. 292, and cf. p. 288.

persons of productive forces or persons OR relations presupposing such relations of ownership.[1] By *ownership* is here meant not a legal relationship but one of *effective control*. We shall use legal language in our exposition, but it is to be understood as just stated. In Chapter VIII effective control will be explained at some length, the legal terms will be eliminated, and the reason for our provisional use of legal language will be given.

Representative production relations:

1 ... is the slave of ...	6 ... hires ...
2 ... is the master of ...	7 ... owns ...
3 ... is the serf of ...	8 ... does not own ...
4 ... is the lord of ...	9 ... leases his labour power to ...
5 ... is hired by ...	10 ... is obliged to work for ...

1–10 can all relate persons and persons (7 relates persons in slave societies). 1–4 and 9–10 can relate persons only. 5–8 can also relate persons and things: men can hire and own both persons and productive forces.

Further characterization of production relations is deferred to the next chapter.

Since relations of production constitute the economic structure of a society, that structure is determined by the distribution in it of (effective) ownership rights over persons and productive forces.

It will be recalled that we excluded productive forces from the economic structure, and we would exclude persons too. Yet production relations form the economic structure, and forces and persons are their terms. Is this consistent doctrine?

It is consistent if and only if the terms bound by relations do not belong to the structure those relations constitute, and this is at the very least a permissible way of speaking.

Consider some other cases: the structure of an argument and the structure of a bridge. The structure of an argument is given by the relations between its constituent statements, of a bridge

[1] In 'On Some Criticisms, I' I mistakenly included work relations in the economic structure. Work relations are *material* relations of production, and, being material, they fall outside the economic structure (see Chapter IV, section (6)). Henceforth and above whenever 'relations of production' is used without a modifying adjective, the reference, unless otherwise indicated, is always to *social* relations of production, as defined in the above paragraph.

by the relations between its constituent girders, spans, etc. (for short: parts). The statements and parts belong to the argument and bridge, but not to their respective structures. One may know what the structure of an argument is without knowing what its statements are, and one may know what the structure of a bridge is while being ignorant of the character of its parts. One may, moreover, remove the original statements and replace them with others without changing the argument's structure, and the same applies to the parts and the structure of the bridge, though the second operation requires great caution. What one changes thereby is the argument or bridge, not its structure. Hence statements and parts do not belong to the respective structures. (It is true that if the bridge changes, then there is a structure which changes, for the bridge *is* a structure. But the structure the bridge is is not the structure the bridge has.)

Of course the bridge (argument) cannot have a structure unless it has parts (statements), but we should now be satisfied that this is compatible with their exclusion from the structure.

There is no difficulty in extending these remarks to the case of the economic structure and its constituent relations. The economic structure is the structure of the economy. Suppose A owns a factory in which B works for him. Then the *economy* might be said to change—slightly—if A and B switched roles, or if B died and was replaced by C who previously lacked an economic role (perhaps he was under age). But these changes, even if changes in the economy, entail no change in its structure.

Again: there cannot be an economy without persons and productive forces, and so there cannot be an economic structure in their absence, but this has been shown to be compatible with their exclusion from it.[1]

(The structure may be seen not only as a set of relations but also as a set of roles.[2] The point to make in the context of that alternative presentation is that the role-*occupants* do not belong to the structure.)

---

[1] The point laboured in the above paragraphs may be formulated briefly as follows: a description of an economic structure employs variables in place of expressions denoting persons and productive forces. It contains no names or descriptions designating particular persons and productive forces. Hence the contemplated inconsistency does not arise.

[2] As in 'Being, Consciousness and Roles', pp. 90–6.

These conceptual rulings conform to Marx's way of thinking. He went so far as to say that

> society does not consist of individuals; it expresses the sum of connections and relationships in which these individuals stand.[1]

It would be better to put 'social structure' where Marx wrote 'society', but if society does not include individuals, then *a fortiori* its structure lacks them.

It follows from our account that it is abstractly possible—though outside the bounds of likelihood—that one and the same economic structure be present in distinct societies, just as distinct arguments and bridges may have identical structures. Identity of economic structure across societies is extremely unlikely,[2] since *all* production relations would have to be the same. But the abstract possibility is worth noting: it helps us to see that an economic structure is a *form*.

(2) *Some Terminological Points*

The Marxian phrase normally translated 'productive forces' is *Produktivkräfte*. This English translation is so entrenched that we shall usually employ it, but it is well to note that it is not a literal one. 'Productive powers' would be more exact.[3] But Marx himself used '*forces productives*' when writing in French, so the non-literal translation has an authoritative origin.[4]

Though 'productive forces' translates less literally than does 'productive powers', the latter does not apply literally to all of what Marx designated as *Produktivkräfte*, since the German itself does not apply literally to all the items he applied it to. Neither an instrument of production nor a quantity of raw material in strict speech *is* a productive power. Rather, each *has* productive power, the power to make or to be made into products. Labour power is literally a productive power, but the other two are not. This is not the only case in which Marx used power-

---

[1] *Grundrisse*, p. 265.
[2] As opposed to identity of *type* of economic structure: see Chapter III, section (6).
[3] Indeed, as Therborn points out, *Produktivkräfte* was originally Marx's translation of Smith's and Ricardo's 'productive powers': *Science, Class, and Society*, p. 355.
[4] See *Poverty of Philosophy*, pp. 149, 196. (On p. 196 '*pouvoirs productives*', the more literal translation, is also used.)

denoting terms both for powers proper and for particulars possessing them.[1]

We translate *Produktionsmittel* as 'means of production', a literal translation applying literally to what we, and Marx at least usually, designate thereby: instruments of production and raw materials. But whereas we draw a definite distinction between productive forces and means of production, Marx's usage is not similarly stable. There are passages in which he uses the terms in apposition to one another, *perhaps* intending them as interchangeable.[2] And if that is the intention, then there could be debate, with different outcomes for different texts, whether he thereby extends 'means of production' to include labour power, or contracts 'productive forces' to exclude it. But whatever the textual vagaries may be, there is a strong theoretical case, to be given in section (3), for regarding labour power as a productive force.

Marx noted the absence in some industries of raw material, and he used the phrase 'object of labour' to designate that which plays a role similar to raw material in them. He gives iron ore in mining, fish in fishing, and timber of virgin forest in lumberjacking as examples.[3] He is right that these are not raw materials in these processes. To be sure, iron ore is a raw material in the sense that there is *some* labour process in which it functions as such, but it is not a raw material in mining, and Marx is concerned to apply 'raw material' relative to a labour process in virtue of the function of the item in that process.[4]

Marx does not use 'object of labour' exclusively for non-raw materials. He uses it as a general term, to cover both raw materials and the non-raw materials just illustrated. Every raw material is an object of labour, but not every object of labour is a raw material.[5] Marx has no separate term for objects of

---

[1] The same intelligible extension is involved in his use of 'use-value', 'exchange-value' and 'value': see Appendix II, pp. 345, 348.

[2] e.g. 'Wage Labour and Capital', p. 90; *Grundrisse*, p. 109.

[3] *Capital*, i. 178, 181. 'Object of Labour' translates *Arbeitsgegenstand* (or *Gegenstand*, where it abbreviates the latter). Many English translations give 'subject of labour' instead, but that is misleading.

[4] See ibid. i. 182.

[5] See ibid. i. 178, 181, iii. 620; *Grundrisse*, pp. 715, 726, 733, 762, 768-9; *Theories of Surplus Value*, i. 131. But contrast *Theories of Surplus Value*, ii. 21, where 'raw material' is used more widely, for reasons stated by the editors.

labour which are not raw materials, and so just calls them 'objects of labour'.

While Marx is right to assert that in the industries mentioned there is no raw material, his criterion for distinguishing true raw materials from other objects of labour is incorrect: the condition he states is neither necessary nor sufficient to make object of labour raw material. He says:

> All raw material is the object of labour, but not every object of labour is raw material; it can only become so after it has undergone some alteration by means of labour.[1]

That work has been devoted to it is, according to Marx, not only necessary for it to be raw material, but also sufficient:

> If . . . the object of labour has . . . been filtered through previous labour, we call it raw material.[2]

('Alteration' and 'filtration' are synonyms in these extracts, and they should not be taken strictly: what is meant is the expenditure of previous labour.)

Expense of previous labour does not suffice to make application of 'raw material' natural. If iron ore is not raw material in mining, it is also not raw material for the labour of the truck driver who takes it to the mill, even though it is 'filtered' by the miner before it is transported. Nor is timber raw material for the lumberjack when the forest is not virgin but the product of planting.

Marx's condition is not necessary either. There are things to which nothing need be done before they function as raw materials. A tree trunk is raw material in the making of a totem pole even when it is an unfelled tree which is carved.[3]

In fact, something is raw material in a labour process if and only if it is the purpose of the process to transform it (for elaboration, see pp. 48 ff. below). Its previous history, and in particular whether labour has already been spent on it, are irrelevant.

'Raw material' translates *Rohmaterial* and *Rohstoff*. We do not accept Nicolaus's statement, *Grundrisse*, p. 521, that '*Rohstoff* is the raw material in its pristine state, before being subjected to human labour'. The *Rohstoff* translated 'raw material' in the fourth line of ibid., p. 520, cannot be pristine.

[1] *Capital*, i. 178–9.   [2] Ibid., p. 178.

[3] This example shows that there is an error in a distinction Marx draws at *Grundrisse*, pp. 768–9.

Upshot: 'raw material' does not apply to something in every labour process, but Marx's attempt to distinguish when it applies is flawed. Marx means to use 'raw material' as a functional term, but his criterion for it is inappropriate, because non-functional in character.

We shall use 'raw material' liberally, covering extracted and transported as well as transformed stuff, hence not in its ordinary meaning, but as Marx used 'object of labour', a phrase we shall drop. And, like Marx,[1] we shall take all raw materials (his objects of labour), to be means of production, even though it is unnatural to describe transported or extracted stuff as means of production in transport, mining, etc. Marx wrongly argued that such description was natural:

> It appears paradoxical to assert that uncaught fish . . . are a means of production in the fishing industry. But hitherto no one has discovered the art of catching fish in waters that contain none.[2]

Marx's quip is misjudged. Not every necessary conditiion of a productive activity qualifies as a means of producing what that activity produces. One does not use fish to catch fish, or iron ore to extract iron ore. Designating them as means of production in these processes is unnatural.

The problem arises whenever the aim of production is, as in extraction and transport, to change the *place* of something.[3] Let us rule that the thing whose place is changed is raw material and so, too, means of production. We may think of the product of extraction and transport as *x-in-place-P*. The producers transform *x-in-place-O* into *x-in-place-P*, using *x-in-place-O* to produce *x-in-place-P*. These locutions stretch their constituent terms a little, but that is harmless. What can do harm is to pretend that no stretching has occurred.

(3) *Labour Power*

In section (5) we shall consider the qualifications of various items to be accounted productive forces. We have already so classified labour power, and this section defends that decision.

---

[1] *Capital*, i. 181, p. 204.

[2] Ibid. i. 181, n. 1.

[3] For this conceptualization, see ibid. ii. 52, 150; *Theories of Surplus Value*, i. 412, and *Grundrisse*, pp. 533–4.

In determining whether or not an item is a productive force, it is of course in order to cite the definition of productive forces elaborated on pages 32 ff. above: that they are what is *used* in production. But that definition is neither so precise nor so authoritative as to leave no role for other considerations in assessing an item's claims to productive forcehood. On the contrary: when asking whether x is a productive force, we must have regard to the place of the concept in historical materialist theory. These theses of the theory are especially germane:

First, that x is a productive force only if ownership (or non-ownership) of x contributes to defining the position in the economic structure of society occupied by x's owner. (See above, pp. 34–5, and Chapter III.) (This does not entail that x is a productive force only if it is owned.)

Second, that the productive forces *develop* in history. (See section (6) below.)

Third, that the character of the economic structure of a society is explained by the nature of the productive forces available to it. (See Chapter VI.)

Fourth, that the production relations are capable of fettering, that is, restricting the use and development of the productive forces. (See Chapter VI.)

Now consider labour power. As just noted, the productive forces develop over time and condition the character of the production relations. But the development of the productive forces is very largely the growth in knowledge of how to control and transform nature, and that *is* a development of labour power. Marx writes that 'the handmill gives you society with the feudal lord, the steam mill society with the industrial capitalist',[1] but those economic structures may be inferred from the presence of those means of production only because the latter give evidence of particular and different levels of technical knowledge. Destroy all steam engines but preserve knowledge of how to make and use them and, with a bit of luck in the matter of raw materials, you can soon return to the *status quo ante*. Destroy the knowledge and preserve the engine and you have a useless ensemble of metal, a material surd, a relic of the future (unless the producers have enough skill left to rediscover the engine's *modus operandi*, but that they could, with

[1] *Poverty of Philosophy*, p. 122.

sufficient general knowledge, do so is a way of making our point).
The productive forces must include labour power because the
centre of their development is a development of labour power:

> . . . the accumulation of the skill and knowledge (scientific power)
> of the workers themselves is the chief form of accumulation, and
> infinitely more important than the accumulation—which goes
> hand in hand with it and merely represents it—of the *existing
> objective* conditions of this accumulated activity. These objective
> conditions are only nominally accumulated and must be con-
> stantly produced anew and consumed anew.[1]

The 'objective conditions' are instruments of production, and
also raw materials in so far as their productive versatility
increases with advancing knowledge. One may say that the
source of the development of the productive forces is subjective,
but that it needs an objective medium, which the stated conditions supply.[2]

We must now comment on two items related to labour power
which are sometimes considered productive forces: labouring
activity, and human beings.

Marx never provides a list of productive forces, and our
discussion of them is based partly on scattered remarks and
partly on general theoretical considerations. He does list what
he calls the 'elementary moments' of the labour process:

> 1 purposeful activity or the work itself; 2 the object of labour;
> 3 the instruments of labour.[3]

2 and 3 are said to be means of production.[4] So here we have
added to means of production not, as on p. 32 above, labour
power, but labouring activity.

'Elementary moment' is a vague enough phrase for it to be
true, in some sense, that 1, 2, and 3 are the elementary moments
of the labour process. Be that as it may, here are three reasons
for putting labour power and not labouring—the activity
itself—within the productive forces:

---

[1] *Theories of Surplus Value*, iii. 266–7, and cf. p. 295. The 'objective conditions'
are elsewhere described as 'the power of knowledge objectified' (*Grundrisse*,
p. 706).
[2] Marx speaks of 'subjective' and 'objective' productive forces at *Grundrisse*,
p. 495. See also the phrase from ibid., p. 502, quoted on p. 46 below.
[3] *Capital*, i. 178, and cf. *Grundrisse*, p. 691.   [4] *Capital*, i. 181.

(1) Labouring activity is not used in production: it *is* production.

(2) Either labouring activity is to be added to labour power, or it supplants labour power. Inclusion of both would be very strange: why not then include not only machines but also their action? So only the second alternative needs attention. But a productive force is a *Produktivkraft*, and labour power is *Arbeitskraft*. This is a strong reason for taking the latter (and not labouring activity) as a species of the former.

(3) Marx attaches high importance to the distinction between labouring and labour power, regarding it, indeed, as his crucial conceptual innovation within political economy, the basis on which he was able to surpass the theories of Smith and Ricardo. For as long as the distinction remains unmade it is, in Marx's view, impossible to explain, consistently with the laws of the market (where only commodities equal in value exchange against one another), how it is that the worker receives less than the value of what he produces: 'how does production on the basis of exchange-value solely determined by labour-time lead to the result that the exchange-value of labour is less than the exchange-value of its product?'[1] Marx answers that, contrary to the terms of the question, labour (=labouring activity), though indeed what *creates* value, itself *has* no value: 'exchange-value of labour' is a meaningless expression.[2] What has value is not labouring but labour power, that which is exercised in labouring. This, and not labour, is what the proletarian sells to the capitalist, who pays less for it than the value of what he is able to make it produce.

But if labour power is what the proletarian sells, it follows that labour power is what he owns. Neither he nor anyone else owns labouring: activities are not ownable. But then labouring cannot be a productive force, by the first thesis on page 41. It is his ownership of his labour *power* which fits the proletarian into the economic structure of society.

A human being is not a productive force except when his intentionality is suppressed and he is used as a physical object. The Nazis used human beings as raw material for lampshades,

---

[1] *Critique of Political Economy*, p. 62. Cf. 'Results', p. 1009.
[2] *Capital*, i. 537, and 'Results', p. 1073.

and if their ovens had fuelled production, they should have been using them as instrumental materials (see p. 48 below) too.

In ungrisly cases, it is a man's labour power, not he, which is a productive force. Production is an intentional activity in which men use productive forces, and they do not use themselves, but their strengths and skills.[1] (The treader of p. 32 treads intentionally, despite his unawareness of the purpose of his doing so.)

The above remarks ought to be uncontroversial, but there is a much-quoted text which is widely thought to show that, according to Marx, human beings are productive forces:

> For the oppressed class to be able to emancipate itself it is necessary that the productive powers already acquired and the existing social relations should no longer be capable of existing side by side. Of all the instruments of production, the greatest productive power is the revolutionary class itself. The organisation of revolutionary elements as a class presupposes the existence of all the productive forces which could be engendered in the bosom of the old society.[2]

We would claim that 'productive power' in the fifth line of the above excerpt is used in a special, rhetorical, way. For the class cannot itself be among the productive powers whose maturity is presupposed by its attainment of a revolutionary posture. The reference is to the power of the class to change society, rather than to turn raw material into a product. We cannot, on the basis of this text, commit the Marxian account of the material labour process to the proposition that men are productive forces in it. For by the same token they would also have to be treated as instruments of production, and no one would claim Marx thought they were that in the labour process.

The above text, then, mingles a relatively technical use of 'productive power' or 'force' with the rhetorical one noted. Less misleading as an expression of a similar thought is a slightly earlier reference to the preconditions of revolution as being '*on the one hand* the existing productive forces, *on the other* the

---

[1] Or, of course, their muscles and limbs (cf. *Capital*, i. 177). It is true that a person might use his whole body, as for example in a labour process where a heavy weight is needed, but even if persons are identical with their bodies, it is, as it were, the body *qua* used, not *qua* using, which is a productive force.

[2] *Poverty of Philosophy*, p. 196.

formation of a revolutionary mass'.[1] Here the distinction between people and their productive powers is properly respected.

Finally, we must comment on Marx's assertion that 'man himself is the chief productive force'.[2] Examination of the context shows that this is but a way of making the point, on which we have insisted, that his labour power is. (Recall—see pp. 37–8—Marx's practice of using power-denoting terms to refer not only to the power but to what has it.) It is inadmissible to treat both labour power and its possessor as productive forces, and since the first is a productive force, the second is not one.

(4) *Science*

Labour power is a productive force, and one dimension of labour power is productively applicable knowledge. It follows that scientific knowledge which is open to productive use is a productive force. (The immediate producer employing scientific knowledge need not understand what he is applying.) What is more, the development of knowledge is, as we saw, the centre of the development of the productive forces. In its higher stages the development of the productive forces therefore merges with the development of productively useful science.

Some Marxists would reject inclusion of science within the productive forces, and some critics of Marxism would find its location there suspect. We are not, of course, arguing that all of science belongs to the productive forces, but only the productively relevant parts. Nevertheless, two fairly common objections to the classification need to be considered: (i) science is superstructural or ideological, and therefore lacks the *fundamental* status assigned to productive forces; (ii) science is mental, whereas productive forces are material.[3] Marx often speaks of '*material* productive forces', and 'productive forces' is just his abbreviation of that expression.

The premiss of objection (i) is false: science is neither superstructural nor ideological.

The superstructure consists of legal, political, religious, and other non-economic *institutions*. It probably includes universities, but it does not include knowledge, for knowledge is not an institution.

---

[1] *German Ideology*, pp. 50–1, emphases added.   [2] *Grundrisse*, p. 422.
[3] See Bober, *Karl Marx's Interpretation of History*, pp. 20–1.

Ideology, on the other hand, is also not an institution but, like science, a set of ideas. Yet science is not ideology, since it is a defining property of ideology that it is unscientific. Science may contain unscientific ideological elements, but it is despite them that it is science, and despite them that it is productively useful and so a productive force. It is not in its ideological aspect that science has productive power.

Three comments on the refutation of objection (i):

1. The refutation employs a contrast between superstructure and ideology which not all will accept. But it is capable of reformulation to suit other views of their relationship.

2. The refutation depends on what some will think is a rather simple, and 'pre-Kuhnian', account of science. We would defend such an account, but cannot be obliged to do so here. Here it will suffice to point out that the view accords with nineteenth-century conceptions of science, from which Marx did not deviate. The fashionable effort to enlist him in the ranks of recent anti-positivist (Kuhn, Feyerabend, etc.) philosophy of science is entirely misguided. (For more on Marx on science, see Appendix I.)

3. Superstructural and ideological phenomena influence scientific development, and therefore influence the development of the productive forces. Hence to treat science as a productive force is to admit that secondary phenomena may affect fundamental ones. But this is a pervasive problem for historical materialism. There is no way of insulating what the theory deems fundamental against all influence of what it deems derivative. A religious proscription on the use of certain means of production, say of cattle for meat production among the Hindu, presents the same problem, but one may not therefore deny that cattle are productive forces.

Science, then, is not superstructural, since it is mental; and although ideology is mental, science is not ideology, because ideological mentation is unscientific. But this brings us to objection (ii): how can something mental be a material productive force?

At one point Marx refers to

a certain degree of development of the material (and therefore also of the mental) productive forces.[1]

[1] *Grundrisse*, p. 502.

This fragment will assist our reflections.

It is unclear whether Marx means that (a) mental productive forces are a subset of material ones, or (b) mental and material productive forces form distinct sets.

Take alternative (a). Then the question is: how can something mental be a species of something material? It cannot be if the antonym of 'material' is 'mental', but it can be if the antonym of 'material' is, in this context, something else. We submit that, *if reading* (a) *is right*, then the antonym of 'material' as used here is 'social'. This sense of 'material', which is explained in Chapter IV, makes possible the presence of mental elements in the material productive forces.

Recall the soldier (p. 33) who did not count as a producer, since his service was not materially, but socially, required. Compare a stone wall penning in plantation slaves who might otherwise escape: though material as can be, and necessary for production, it does not qualify as a productive force, since (by contrast with a wall which maintains the course of a stream of water harnessed to a productive purpose) its contribution is to social order. Whether an item is a productive force depends not on its ontology (how physical *it* is) but on whether it contributes to production in virtue of the material character of production. Productively relevant scientific knowledge does pertain to the material task to be performed, and therefore is a productive force.

If, on the other hand, reading (b) of the fragment is correct, so that there are mental productive forces *in addition to* material ones, then objection (ii) collapses, for its premiss was that all productive forces are material.

In short, and whatever Marx meant in the passage, when we oppose the material to the social, as Marx systematically did, we may classify mental productive forces as material, though they are of course not material in a more familiar sense of that term.

(5) *More Candidates for the Catalogue*

Is the list of productive forces on page 32 complete? Four items deserving of a place on it will now be considered: instrumental materials, premises, spaces, and means of subsistence.

Instrumental materials

By way of prologue to discussion of this item, a word about the difference between raw materials and instruments of production. The distinction is clear enough, but its correct statement is elusive.[1] We said on page 32 that the first is what the producer works *on*, the second what he works *with*, but these prepositions will not finally bear the weight we put on them: the potter certainly works with clay, and the maker of lamp-stands works on a lathe. In these last occurrences the preposi-tions are not used in the way the reader realized they were being used on page 32. But that shows that the prepositions do not themselves give the desired differentiation.

Raw material and instrument of production may be satis-factorily distinguished only by reference to the intentional structure of the labour process. Raw material differs from instrument in that the purpose of production is to change the first and not the second (for raw material in extraction and transport, the change is one of place). In the course of any productive process both change, partly independently of the process, and partly because of it, but it is not the purpose of the process to change the instrument of production.[2]

The producer may of course intend a change in the instru-ment of production, as when he adjusts the width of the opening of a variable spanner, but such a change will be in the service of the stated purpose: intended changes in instruments of production occur in order to effect changes in raw material.

The instrument may even, in the course of the process, be deliberately reshaped in a fashion which excludes return to its previous shape, but again this change will be dictated by what is to be done to the raw material. The act of reshaping may well be considered a separate process of production, with what is instrument in the main process being raw material and then product in this subsidiary one. It is, once again, the intentional structure which warrants the judgement that there is a separate production process here.

A given object or quantity of stuff may function as raw

material in one process and instrument in another,[1] and there can be cases in which some or all of the means of production are both instrument and material, since it is intended both to change each and to use each to change the other, as when two smooth stones are made out of two rough ones by rubbing them against one another. Such a case does not subvert the intentionality criterion, which is responsive to the reciprocity it displays.

We now turn to instrumental materials, of which fuel is a paradigm case. A fuel is by nature stuff or material, but this does not make it raw material in the relevant functional sense of the term: it is not used as raw material when it is used as fuel. Since the product is not made out of fuel but is a result, *inter alia*, of the action of fuel, fuel is an instrument of production (the same goes for grease which lubricates the machinery). It is not the purpose of production to transform fuel into ash and gas. The slower the fuel changes, the better from the productive point of view. Contrast true raw material: the faster it changes, the better. Efficient production maximizes this ratio:

$$\frac{\text{Rate of change of raw material}}{\text{Rate of change of fuel (and of instruments generally)}}[2]$$

Marx expresses himself optimally when he accepts Cherbuliez's description of 'coal, wood, oil, tallow, etc.' as 'instrumental materials'.[3] But in his most official account of the labour process his usage is less satisfactory: he speaks of 'accessory raw materials' and lists items perhaps meriting that description, such as dyestuffs (which do enter the product), along with items which do not, such as lubricating oil.[4] But despite Marx's vacillation, instrumental materials belong emphatically with instruments of production, not raw materials, in the functional description of the labour process he himself desired.

Fuel is not only used to heat raw material, as in a blast furnace or kiln. It is also used to keep the producers warm, and to protect means of production sensitive to cold or damp. Fuel

---

[1] Cf. *Capital*, i. 182.
[2] This claim is only broadly true, but broad truth will do here.
[3] *Grundrisse*, p. 680. (Wood is being thought of as a fuel in this context.)
[4] *Capital*, i. 181. Cf. ibid., p. 203; *Theories of Surplus Value*, i. 135–6.

in this last use may be likened to premises, to which we now turn.

Premises

By *premises* we understand the buildings and other containers in which production proceeds. Buildings have different utility for different productive purposes: this favours a ruling that they are used in production. We count them as productive forces, noting that ownership of a building entails occupancy of an economic-structural position, and that the productive value of buildings develops in industrial history.

In their usual role, buildings are instruments of production. They are not normally raw material, though a building could be so designed that it served as both. Perhaps cavemen chipped implements out of the walls of the caves they sat in to stay dry while chipping.

Marx did classify buildings as instruments of production. Writing in English, he speaks of 'instruments of production properly so-called, such as tools, machinery, buildings',[1] and there is a similar list in *Capital* under the rubric *Arbeitsmittel*, his German (as the similarity of the lists attests) for instruments of production.[2] He also describes 'machinery, buildings, instruments of labour, containers of all kinds' as elements of fixed capital, and Marxian fixed capital is instruments of production in capitalist ownership.[3]

Spaces

By a space we mean a particular volume of space, considered in abstraction from whatever it contains. The owner of a plot of land owns a quantity of earth, but he also and distinctly owns the space the earth fills. This is shown by the fact that he may

[1] 'Wages, Price and Profit', pp. 419-20.
[2] *Capital*, i. 203.
[3] *Theories of Surplus Value*, i. 246. In this last quotation 'instruments of labour' and 'buildings' appear separately, so that buildings are not instruments of *labour*, but neither, by the same token, are machines. 'Instruments of labour' here translates *Arbeitsinstrumente*, a narrower class than *Arbeitsmittel* (instruments of production).

In one place (*Capital*, iii. 761) Marx says a factory is a *Produktionsinstrument* at most 'to a limited extent', but that is because he is at that point impressed by the contrast between the spontaneous productive power of the land and the inertness of factories.

lose either while keeping the other. His earth may be removed, to any depth, while his rights over the space it filled are unimpaired. Or those rights may be cancelled and the material content of the space delivered to him in another place. He can sell the space with the matter missing, or sell the matter while retaining the space. The term 'land' covers both earth and space, the two things a landowner owns.

Space deserves membership in the set of productive forces. Ownership of space certainly confers a position in the economic structure. Even when a piece of space is contentless, its control may generate economic power, because it can be filled with something productive, or because it may need to be traversed by producers. He who owns a hole, even exclusive of its material envelope, is a man to reckon with if you must reach the far side of the hole, and cannot feasibly tunnel beneath it, fly above it, or make your way around it.

Thus on our account of the economic structure, space looks like being a productive force. But is it used in production? And does it develop in productivity over time, as productive forces are supposed to?

Is it used? It is certainly indispensable to putting in hand any productive process,[1] but that is perhaps not enough.[2] More pertinent is the fact that a portion of space may be more or less productively useful, because of its shape, or its location. Rectangles and circles recommend themselves to different productive uses, and the productive capacity of a space adjoining a source of energy is affected thereby, whatever, if any, its contents may be. Since space can be more or less useful, it counts as used. To be sure, unlike material facilities and labour power, it is not used up, and need not be reproduced and serviced. But its absolute reliability seems a poor reason for denying that it is used.

Does space develop? The thesis that the productive forces develop may be taken globally, so that it does not entail that every type of productive force develops. Yet something like a development of space does occur. There is, to begin with, the conquest of new spaces, which certainly expands the ability to produce, and not only because of the material content seized.

[1] *Theories of Surplus Value*, ii. 245.
[2] We must avoid sophisms, like Marx's one about the fish, quoted on p. 40 above.

There is also improved use of existing spaces, which will count, as does improved use of existing means of production in general, as development of productive power (see section (6)). Illustrations: yield-increasing repartitioning of fields, and efficiency-increasing repositioning of machines. (Field repartitioning here does not mean reallocation of ownership rights, but reorganization of agriculture's material profile, which may of course be associated with the former: for an example, see Chapter VI, p. 167.)

Spaces thus earn entry into the catalogue. But they are not raw materials and we shall not pretend that they are instruments of production. So they will receive separate mention.

Means of Subsistence

Premises were classified as means of production, in so far as they shelter the process of production, or are otherwise materially required for its smooth operation. But the producer's clothing, in certain processes at least, serves similar functions. The steelworker's facial shield must be accounted an instrument of production, and so too must specially designed overalls. Any labour process which, for *material* reasons (as opposed to reasons of social custom and convention), cannot be comfortably pursued in the nude is one in which raiment must be considered means of production, whatever else it also is.

Clothes are not the only articles serving man as producer as well as man as consumer. Other means of consumption, notably food, demand consideration. The quality of food, which influences how productive its consumers can be, has certainly improved at certain points in history. One historian opines that changes in food intake in the late medieval world were responsible for great advances in production. 'The Middle Ages', he writes, 'were full of beans.'[1] And the so-called 'adverse food-productivity cycle' in many parts of the contemporary world attests to the productive relevance of nutrition.

Marx frequently denies that food belongs to the means of production. We shall argue that it does, and then we shall explain his denial. We shall discuss food's status as means of production, first within production processes conventionally

---

[1] Lynn White, Jr., *Medieval Technology and Social Change*, p. 76.

identified as such, and then in the production of that special product, labour power itself.

Oil and grease used to maintain a machine in working order are means of production, and coffee or lunch consumed at work or in a brief respite from it fulfil a similar function: they keep the labourer in working order. Coffee is not means of production when it is laid on merely to please the workers: it is then like an appealing mural on the factory wall, or pleasant music, means of maintaining their *willingness*, as opposed to their *ability* to work. But it also contributes to ability, by helping to ensure alertness, and in that capacity it may be bracketed with materials assisting the operation of machines.[1]

We thus include food taken to sustain the action of labour power as means of production of the product that action produces. But now consider food typically consumed away from work and which creates (or reproduces) labour power itself. 'In nourishment, which is a form of consumption, man produces his own body', and, therefore, his labour power.[2]

We need to ask whether the *purpose* of the consumption of food is to produce labour power. Consider the following case. A man repeatedly strikes a log with an axe, and as a result chips of wood are produced. If he is doing so idly, just to pass the time of day, then although chips are produced, it is not his purpose to produce them, and his axe is not functioning as means of production, as it would be if the chips were supposed to be a product. Now labour power does get produced when food is consumed, but it need not be the purpose of the eater to produce labour power. To the extent that it is not, eating is not a production process with food as means of production. But in so far as men do not only work in order to eat, but also eat in order to be able to work, then, to that extent, food, wherever taken, may be classified as means of production of labour power.

[1] The important distinction between the *ability* and the *willingness* to work is understood by the promoters of Luncheon Vouchers, a British scheme for feeding employees on the cheap, who promise an increase in both:

'As an employer you obviously want to obtain the maximum output from your staff in the most cost effective way.

'Luncheon Vouchers are a sound business proposition. They are a bonus that is appreciated by employees, and an encouragement to have a midday meal, which is a sound basis for a good afternoon's work.' (Quality newspaper colour supplements, various dates.)

[2] *Grundrisse*, p. 90.

Matters become more complicated when we recall (see p. 32) that the purposes of persons other than the eater need to be considered. Food is surely means of production when ingested by a slave who would rather die and is more or less forced to eat so that he can continue working. And in so far as the capitalist intends that the worker reproduce himself by means of the goods he obtains in exchange for the wages the capitalist gives him, it becomes difficult to render judgement on the status of the workers' means of consumption.

Marx counts hay supplied to the draught-horse as means of production,[1] and there is no pertinent material difference between it and the ploughman's lunch, which might be consumed at the same time. Yet we find him saying that 'means of subsistence . . . form no part of the labour process'.[2]

The inconsistency is only apparent. Marx's remark occurs in the course of a presentation of the specifically capitalist anatomy of the labour process. He is not discussing, as we are here, the material character of production, independent of its social form.[3] Under capitalism means of production of the uncontroversial kind are purchased by capital, whereas means of subsistence exchange against wages, and it is this *social* difference which governs the quoted remark. Thus, digressing from his main subject, and speaking in material vein, Marx allows, on the same page, that sometimes

> the consumption of the means of subsistence is actually no more than an incident in the labour process, like the consumption of coal by the steam engine, of oil by the wheel, of hay by the horse, and like the entire private consumption of the labouring slave,[4]

a statement in full accord with the account given above.

Food taken to sustain labour power in action may be likened to fuel, and may therefore be considered a special sort of instrumental material. But food is not only fuel, since, in the creation of labour power itself, it enters into and helps to compose the product, and therefore functions as true raw

---

[1] *Capital*, i. 181.
[2] 'Results of the Immediate Process of Production', p. 1004.
[3] See Ch. IV, section (2) for elaboration of this distinction.
[4] 'Results', p. 1004. See also ibid., pp. 983–4, 989; *Grundrisse*, pp. 675, 693; *Capital*, i. 571–3; *Theories of Surplus Value*, i. 390.

material. If anything, apart from kitchen utensils, serves as instrument in the production of labour power, it is the hands, the teeth, etc. (but not the organs of digestion, since, if we ignore feats of Yoga, intentionality lapses once the food passes beyond the eater's mouth).

Accordingly, we suggest, in the light of the discussion of this section, the following revised catalogue of productive forces,[1] it being understood that certain means of subsistence figure among instruments of production and raw materials:

Productive forces
- Means of production
  - Instruments of production (tools, machines, premises, instrumental materials)
  - Raw materials
  - Spaces
- Labour power

(6) The Development of the Productive Forces

The productive power of a society is the power of its productive forces, working in optimal combination. The *development* of the productive forces is growth of that power. Hence the standard of the level of development of the productive forces is their degree of productivity. In other words,

the growth of the productive forces of labour means merely that less direct labour is required in order to make a larger product.[2]

Two ways of improving the productivity of means of production may be distinguished. First, there is the replacement of given means of production by superior ones. Next, and distinctly, there is the improved use of means of production already to hand.[3] The latter counts as a development of the productive

---

[1] See Shaw, 'Productive Forces and Relations of Production', pp. 32 ff., for criticism of a widely adopted alternative catalogue provided by Stalin; and see ibid., pp. 57 ff., for conceptual and textual refutation of the Althusserian view that to attempt to list the productive forces is to misconceive their nature.

[2] *Grundrisse*, p. 831, and cf. *Theories of Surplus Value*, iii. 433–4.

[3] Marx distinguishes between 'discovery of new use-values' and 'of a new use for well-known use-values': means of production are use-values, and it is means of production to which he has reference here (*Theories of Surplus Value*, iii. 440).

forces only if the principle to which the improved use answers is novel. If it has long been known, then the improved use is an application of existing productive power, to wit, that knowledge, not an extension of productive power.

What counts is not the amount of labour actually spent on what is actually made, but how much needs or would need to be spent ('is required') to make specified products. The fact that something is not produced, or that what *is* produced is produced inefficiently relative to available techniques and resources—these do not tell against the level of development of the productive forces. When relations of production 'fetter' productive forces, they inhibit not only their development but also their optimal use. But sub-optimal use does not entail a drop in the level of development of the productive forces, as it would if the power of the productive forces were measured with reference to actual rather than possible output. (Hence our concept of productivity differs from the one the economist uses when he compares the physical productivity of labour in different societies. Productivity in our sense is the maximum to which productivity in that sense could be raised, with existing means and knowledge, and in abstraction from social constraints.)[1]

Now an increase in productivity was defined as a rise in the value of this quotient:

$$\frac{\text{Size of product}}{\text{Amount of direct labour required to produce it.}}$$

Direct labour is the number of person-hours spent on the product, including the time spent producing the means of making it. It is a relatively unproblematic notion.[2] But the numerator of the fraction is less easy to handle. What can 'size' mean here?

There is no difficulty when the identity of the product is constant, for in that case 'larger product' is a simple idea. If more of product p can be produced in the same time, or as

---

[1] Nor is productivity in our sense determined by 'best practice techniques', as some economists use that phrase, for they are conditioned by factor prices, which are irrelevant here. See Salter, *Productivity and Technical Change*.

[2] Notice that there is no need here to 'reduce' skilled to simple labour: that issue is foreign to the present discussion.

much of it in less time, then productivity with respect to p has clearly risen. But historical materialism asserts that the productive forces as a totality develop in history, and therefore obliges us to compare the productive power of societies not with respect to single products separately, but globally. And this can raise problems.

Of course, if everything producible at stage $s1$ is producible at stage $s2$, and each thing at $s2$ in less time than at $s1$, then we need no common measure of the magnitude of products to claim that productivity is higher at $s2$.[1] But suppose forces at $s2$ outclass those at $s1$ with respect to some products, and are less powerful with respect to others. How can we then make a global productivity comparison between $s1$ and $s2$?

In certain instances of the type just identified comparison will still be possible without a common measure of product size. Thus suppose that at both $s1$ and $s2$ twelve hours per day is the length of time each producer is able to labour productively: marginal product is negative beyond that point. Imagine that there are just three products, p, q, and r. At $s1$ it takes 3 hours to produce a unit of p, 4 hours to produce a unit of q, and 5 hours to produce a unit of r. At $s2$ it takes 2 hours to produce a unit of p, 3 hours to produce a unit of q, and 6 hours to produce a unit of r. Then $s2$ is more productive with respect to p and q, and less productive with respect to r. Note, however, that only 11 of the 12 hours available at $s2$ are used up when it produces one unit of each of p, q, and r. Suppose the remaining hour were allocated to producing r: then as long as some r were produced in that hour, we should be able to say that $s2$ is globally more productive than $s1$, even though we have stated no ratios between units of one product and units of any other.

In the example above we assume that $s1$ is productively superior to $s2$ with respect to at least one product only if its labour hours are allocated as was stated. But the general point is the following: for all that $s1$ can produce some things (or even most things) more productively than $s2$, $s2$ remains unambiguously more productive in a global sense if, for any package of goods *per capita* producible at $s1$, there is a package producible at $s2$ in which each product is at least as large as the

---

[1] See *Critique of Political Economy*, p. 38 for an example of such a judgement, and cf. Dobb, *Welfare Economics*, p. 29.

corresponding product in the *s1* package, and at least one product is larger.

But procedures like the one just illustrated will not yield unambiguous results in all conceivable cases, and they will be inapplicable when a product produced at *s1* is absolutely unproducible at *s2*. Situations may be imagined in which, in order to settle which stage is more productive, we would appear to need a method of determining comparative sizes of quantities of distinct kinds of product. But Marx himself implies that no such method is available:

> If the productivity of two *different* spheres of production is compared, this can only be done relatively. In other words, one starts at any arbitrary point, for instance when the values of hemp and linen, i.e. the correlative quantities of labour-time embodied in them, are as 1 : 3. If this ratio alters, then it is correct to say that the productivity of these different types of labour has altered.[1]

This view allows us to say, *inter alia*, that productivity in sphere *s* has risen or dropped *x* per cent as much as it has in sphere *t*, but it forbids direct comparison of productivity across spheres.

In the above text Marx is concerned to deny the feasibility of *precise* comparisons, and they are probably unnecessary to the assessment of the relative productive strengths of societies. Here rough comparisons will do. But how can even they be made?

Two collections of different kinds of products are not *in and of themselves* relevantly comparable in size. We can of course state their volumes and weights, but ratios between those magnitudes are beside the point. If we are to find our rough comparative assessments, we must look to something causally connected with quantities of product. A natural suggestion is that we consider their capacities to satisfy human needs, to contribute to human welfare. If the forces of society *s* could be used to produce more satisfaction of need *per capita* than those of society *t*, then we may adjudge *s* more productively powerful. The reader need not be told that this gives only a rough stan-

---

[1] *Theories of Surplus Value*, ii. 85. (Marx should have said that the productivity of *at least one* of the types of labour has altered.) Marx is not here concerned with the development of the productive forces in a broad world historical sense. Cf. ibid., pp. 110 ff.

dard. Many complications threaten its viability. Here are three.

First, what people need or want is not constant in history. If it were, we could—neglecting the other complications—hazard a judgement of the comparative measures of frustration in two societies, and deem the happier one more productively powerful. But it is a Marxian insistence, and a sound one, that needs expand in history, and undergo changes of character. This does not disqualify capacity to satisfy needs as a pertinent criterion, but it makes it hard to apply in practice.

Second, recall that what counts is not actual production but what could be produced. A society's resources may be misallocated with respect to the welfare of its people. It is not easy to say, for example, how much need would be satisfied were the resources devoted to arms production diverted to other purposes, but that is something we should have to know.

Third, not all satisfaction and frustration in a society can be attributed to what it does and does not produce. Sadness due to an epidemic of disease[1] or bad weather[2] or marital instability cannot readily be blamed on insufficient productive power. It is, moreover, not always easy to say what is and what is not due to the character of the productive forces. If their efficient use requires shift work with unhappy effects on family life, does this relevantly detract from their capacity to contribute to welfare?

So reference to need makes us look in the right direction, but sometimes what we see there will not be in sharp focus.

The dimensions of the problem must not be exaggerated. Our aim is to construct a theory which may be applied to history. The course of history realizes many possibilities, but not all possibilities, so some difficult comparisons will not have to be made in practice. In addition, the claims of the theory, though large, are not unlimited. This further reduces the practical significance of the conceptual problem. We now elaborate these two points.

It should be possible to say with certainty that the productive forces of the contemporary United States are more advanced than were those of medieval England. Yet needs and tastes and

---

[1] As opposed to a generally poor level of medical provision.

[2] Though features of climate and geography are hard to disentangle from the productive forces: see Ch. IV, pp. 96–7.

opportunities have so changed that many things which were produced then are not produced now. This is not as it stands a difficulty, since what matters is not how much time it does take to produce a product, but how much time it would take: unproduced products can thus enter the reckoning. But problems arise where the skills required to make unproduced products, and/or the necessary raw materials, no longer exist. (Lack of requisite instruments of production is not an independent problem. If they are inaccessible, it is because there is not the skill or the raw material or both to make them.)

If it is known how to recover a lost skill, the problem is reduced, since we may reckon in the total time it would take to produce the thing the time required to learn the skill. But suppose the pertinent knowledge is lost, and there is no idea how to rediscover it. Then the problem remains, but it is not acute in relation to actual history. The development of knowledge is in fact so largely cumulative that difficulties presented by lost knowledge do not assume great importance. As far as constraints relating to knowledge are concerned, the United States can produce, much more abundantly per head, everything the medievals could produce, and more besides, with the exception of certain products perhaps wholly beyond its reach, such as, say, stained glass of the kind found on Notre Dame Cathedral. This being so, we may adjudge the United States as on balance possessed of more productive power than the medievals had. The concept of need is not easy to handle, but it would be hard to maintain that the unavailability of just that kind of stained glass generates an overwhelming frustration.

The supply of raw material improves when exploration (both horizontal and vertical) brings new resources within reach, and when newly created materials are introduced which are easier to work with, so that less time is needed to transform them into products.[1] But unlike knowledge, raw material does not, alas, accumulate, and we are faced with real cases in which the material for given products is sparse or no longer exists. To avoid the problem, we might rule that productivity should be a matter of knowledge alone, so that the relevant question always is: *given* what is known, how much time would it take to

---

[1] See *Theories of Surplus Value*, iii. 445, for a reference to productivity-raising changes in raw materials.

produce p, *if* the requisite raw material were to hand? But this will not do. For the level of development of the productive forces is said to determine the shape of the economic structure, and the economic structure will not be responsive to anything so counter-factual. It will be determined by what it is possible to produce, not what it would be possible to produce if something false were true. If the 'crisis of resources' is as serious as some say,[1] it is a genuine threat to the realization of forms of communism which depend upon a radically reduced working day, for those forms require astronomically high levels of productive power. It follows that the latter cannot be identified with knowledge alone.

Let us now recall the claims of the theory, for we need criteria of assessment of productive power only in relation to those claims. We have just mentioned the thesis that the level of development of the productive forces explains the nature of the economic structure co-present with them. Such explanations rely both on the quality and on the quantity of the available productive power. They depend, that is, not only on what kinds of productive forces are to hand, but also on the sheer magnitude of productive power the latter confer, the magnitude for which we seek a standard of measurement. But in so far as the character of the economic structure is explained in the second fashion, with reference to the power of the productive forces taken in abstraction from the kinds of facilities embodying that power, what chiefly matters for the explanation, it will emerge (in Chapter VII), is the amount of surplus production the forces enable. Surplus production *in this context* is production beyond what is necessary to satisfy the indispensable physical needs of the immediate producers, to reproduce the labouring class.[2] Given the explanatory role of the concept of a level of development, the development of the productive forces may be identified with the growth in the surplus they make possible, and this in turn may be identified with the amount of the day which remains after the labouring time required to maintain the producers has been subtracted. (It does not matter here how

---

[1] For brief comments on this issue, see Ch. XI, section (9).

[2] Other important but different concepts of surplus: (1) Production beyond what is necessary to satisfy the historically developed needs of the producers (see *Capital*, i. 171); (2) Production appropriated by the exploiting non-producer.

much of the available surplus time is in fact devoted to production.)

These identifications lack justification in the analysis of productivity in the abstract, but they serve the needs of the theory. It then turns out that many of the problems afflicting the concept of comparative productivity are theoretically nugatory. Thus consider two stages of development, $s1$ and $s2$. Suppose that at $s1$ it takes three man hours per consumer per day to produce indispensable means of subsistence, and in remaining time a certain package of luxury goods can be produced. By $s2$ 'necessary labour' has dropped to two hours, but in remaining time (which is one hour longer than before) only three quarters of the amount of each luxury good in the $s1$ package can now be produced, and no other kinds of luxury good are producible. Has there been growth or decline in productive power between $s1$ and $s2$? Abstractly, the question might be unanswerable, and certainly we have evolved no sure means of answering it. But in a theoretically central sense there has indeed been growth.

CHAPTER III

The Economic Structure

(1) *Ownership Rights in Productive Forces*

THE ECONOMIC structure of a society is the whole set of its production relations. Production relations are relations of effective power over persons and productive forces, not relations of legal ownership. But it is convenient to represent production relations as relations of ownership,[1] and we now deepen our understanding of the economic structure by noting some features of the concept of ownership.

To own an object is to enjoy a range of rights with respect to the use and situation of that object. (We use 'rights' widely, to cover any form of legal advantage, such as Hohfeld's claims, privileges, powers, and immunities.)[2] The rights are limited by the character of the object and the nature of the prevailing legal system. Typical ownership rights are: the right to use an object o; the right to income generated by the use of o; the right to prevent others from using o; the right to destroy o; the right to transfer o; etc.

Sometimes a person has some of these rights but lacks others, and lawyers may need to determine what sets of rights suffice to constitute *ownership*. The answer to this question, important as it may be for legal theory, is immaterial to our purposes. The law may declare that the owner of a house is the retainer of the freehold, not the long-term leaseholder who enjoys current use of it, but we need not choose between them. What matters here are the elements of ownership, not ownership itself. These elements are the rights already mentioned, and we shall designate X as (some form of) owner of o as long as he has some of the rights over o, possession of all of which marks paradigmatic cases of ownership. A diminution in the number of rights X has over o will count as a reduction in his ownership of o. Today

[1] As Marx himself did, for reasons given in Ch. VIII, where legal descriptions of production relations will be eliminated.

[2] See *Fundamental Legal Conceptions*, p. 71 *et passim*.

individual capitalists have less legal discretion over their holdings than they once did. They have fewer rights over what they own, and may be said, in our usage, to own what they do to a lesser extent.[1]

Rights over an object o may be distributed across a number of persons. X may have right r over o, while Y has right s: the freeholder has the right to transfer the freehold of an o on the income from which the leaseholder may have sole claim. Or each of X and Y may have right r over o, with the content of r reduced accordingly, as when persons jointly own a house. In such cases we may say of each person that he *partly owns* the object o.

In addition, the object o may be so divisible that X enjoys rights over one part of o while Y enjoys rights over another part, as when persons share ownership of a house but do not jointly own all of it: if, for example, one person owns the top floor and another the bottom floor. Here we may say that *each owns a part* of o.

We thus distinguish partly owning something from owning a part of it. This generates four possibilities:

1. X wholly owns all of o.
2. X partly owns all of o.
3. X wholly owns part of o.
4. X partly owns part of o.

The last three conditions are often difficult to discriminate in practice. If I have rights over the house during the day and you do at night, do we each—to that extent—own a (temporal) part of it, or do we each partly own it? If I have authority over the use of your labour power under certain conditions, do I partly own your labour power, or own (wholly or partly) a distinguishable part of it, that part capable of action in those conditions? It will often matter that ownership is partial in one of the ways 2 to 4, yet it will not matter in which one. We shall

---

[1] It does not follow that the capitalist *class* has less control over the means of production. A reduction in control by individual capitalists can result from increased control by capitalists as a class, e.g., through the state. For illustration, see Kidron, *Western Capitalism*, pp. 9-11. Cf. *German Ideology*, pp. 387-8, and see Chapter X below, pp. 294-6.

then say that X owns *some* of o, meaning this to be ambiguous across the three alternatives. We shall, moreover, use 'X owns *all* of o' as an abbreviation for 1, and we shall say of an X of whom, with respect to a given o, none of 1 to 4 are true, that he owns *none* of o.

Unlike the slaveholder, the lord of the manor has only some ownership of the labour power of the producer subordinate to him. He is entitled to tell the serf what to do with his labour power only some of the time. Unlike the proletarian, the serf has only some rights over his labour power, not all; but whereas the proletarian has no rights over the means of production he uses, the serf does have some. The lord may not expropriate his plot of land, while the proletarian has no means of production to lose, belonging as he does—and in this sense—to the expropriated class. We may tabulate the ownership positions of immediate producers as follows:[1]

TABLE I

		His Labour Power	The Means of Production He Uses[2]
SLAVE		None	None
SERF[3]		Some	Some
PROLETARIAN	OWNS	All	None
INDEPENDENT PRODUCER		All	All

The table gives three subordinate producers,[4] and one independent. Since one may own none, some, or all, of each of one's labour power and means of production, there is a total of nine cases to consider. We turn to the remaining five.

[1] For further discussion of these contrasts, and textual references, see Ch. VIII, pp. 222–3, Appendix I, pp. 333–6, and 'Marx's Dialectic of Labour', p. 244.

[2] A more complicated table would be possible, with three columns, one for labour power, one for instruments of production, and one for raw materials. For discussion and references relevant to such a table, see Therborn, *Science, Class and Society*, p. 376.

[3] This characterization applies not only to serfs traditionally so called, but to all non-slave producers burdened with duties towards exploiters which do not result from a labour contract.

[4] 'These are the three great forms of servitude': Engels, *Origin of the Family*, p. 160.

(2) *Possible and Impossible Ownership Positions of Producers*

Here are the five combinations unnoticed in Table 1:

TABLE 2

	His Labour Power	The Means of Production He Uses
(5)	None	All
(6)	Some	All
(7) OWNS	None	Some
(8)	Some	None
(9)	All	Some

Which of these positions are tenable?

Case (5) depicts an incoherent set of rights. For if *X* is the *sole* owner of *all* the means of production he uses, as (5) states, he is entitled to use them without the direction or interference of another person. Yet (5) also states that *X* has no authority whatsoever over the disposition of his own labour power. Therefore what is said regarding his labour power is incompatible with what is said regarding his means of production. (As will be seen when we consider case (7), a producer's not owning his own labour power is compatible with his retention of *some* ownership of his means of production.)

The impossibility of (5) may appear curious, since (5) is the mirror image of the proletarian, who owns all his labour power and no means of production, and the proletarian is not impossible but actual. But there is a genuine disparity between the roles of labour power and means of production in these schemata. The proletarian may do anything he wishes with his labour power, short of violating the general laws of society, and nothing may be done with it without his contractual consent. He may not, of course, work with whatever means of production he chooses, but this follows from the exclusion of illegal behaviour in general. For parity, the person described in (5) should, in virtue of his supposed ownership of means of production, be able to do whatever he wishes with them within the law, yet this is excluded by his being forbidden to work with them as he wills, which is not a general law, but a legal feature of his particular situation. Given that he owns no labour power, he cannot wholly own all of his means of production.

Case (6) is impossible for the same reason as (5) is. A man cannot have unrestricted enjoyment of means of production if his labour power is even partly owned by another.[1]

Case (7), on the other hand, is not incoherent. That a man's labour power is entirely at another's disposal is compatible with his retaining *some* rights in the means of production he uses. He may, for example, be entitled to sell or lease them. This, then, is a possible case, but it is of limited interest. It will not effectively distinguish (7) from a slave that he partly owns (some of) the means of production he uses. For consider: full ownership of another's labour power entails the right to direct its use without compensating the labourer for his exercise of it. Standardly, the alien owner will want the labourer to survive able to continue working, so he will indeed ensure that he receives indispensable means of subsistence. Now suppose the labourer is entitled to some compensation because the means of production he uses belong to him. Then the master can reduce his subsistence ration, which he gives him gratis, by whatever amount the labourer receives as 'owner' of means of production. And so the labourer's position is not effectively superior to that of a slave.[2] (To be sure, the master *need* not reduce the subsistence ration, but we are concerned with what producers obtain as of right, and producer (7) has no right against the master reducing the ration. Masters of ordinary slaves could also give their slaves more than what they need to stay alive and able-bodied.)

In case (8) the producer owns some of his labour power and none of his means of production. We may say that he is partly enslaved and partly free in the manner of a proletarian. For example: for a certain stretch of the day or year he is bound to work for some particular person, but for the rest he may sell his labour power to whomever, if anyone, he pleases. (8) is a possible transitional form between serf and proletarian, covering serfs who have lost their land (means of production) yet retained some of their traditional duties.

---

[1] Unless the physical character of the means of production is such that the respect in which he does not own his labour power constitutes no bar to his untrammelled use of them. For example, he is bound to work for another only one hour per day after nightfall, and the relevant means of production are employable in daylight only.

[2] The above reasoning fails for a case where the cost of hiring the means of production exceeds the usual subsistence ration.

Case (9) describes a proletarian who owns some of the means of production he uses, or an independent artisan or peasant who does not own all of them. We shall look at the first variant in section (4). The effective situation of such a producer is at some point (not excluding the extremes) along a continuum between independent and proletarian status.

Table 1 exhibits the central cases only, and is, even then, highly idealized. Real history exhibits important shadings and significant intermediate cases. The idea of a slave who is wholly at the disposal of his master is rarely exemplified. In ancient times slaves could own property—quite apart from the means of production they themselves used, as in case (7)—engage in trade, and contrive their own manumission.[1] Developed Roman Law defined the slave pretty well as he is presented in Table 1,[2] but the legal picture of the slave was not wholly faithful to reality.[3] Perhaps the only 'true' slaves have been galley slaves and similar imprisoned labour. For their parts, serfs lack full authority over their labour power in significantly different ways. The grip the lord has on it may take the form of labour service, dues in kind, money rent, dues for the use of monopolized facilities (such as the lord's mill), and/or a whole panoply of occasional payments (heriot, merchet, etc.). Some obligations rest on serfs individually, and others on the peasant community, which co-operatively sustains its lord. Proletarians merge into artisans, as we saw when discussing (9), and artisans enjoy many modes and degrees of independence. A craftsman who sells his entire product, year in and year out, to one merchant is unlikely to be as independent in fact as he is in law, and peasants, notoriously, can be independent in varying respects and degrees.

Table 1 purports to distinguish slaves, serfs, and proletarians *within the set of subordinate producers*. In addition, the features it ascribes to slave and serf are respectively *sufficient* for occupancy of those statuses, but a person may own his labour power and none of the means of production he uses without being a

---

[1] See Finley, *The Ancient Economy*, p. 64.

[2] See *Grundrisse*, p. 245.

[3] 'There have been individual slaves who had the bad luck to be treated by their owners as nothing but a possession, but I know of no society in which the slave population as a whole were looked upon in that simple way.' Finley, *Ancient Economy*, p. 67.

proletarian. Top-salaried architects need not own the tools of their trade, but they are not proletarians. Table 1 says that if X is a subordinate producer, then if he owns his labour power but not his means of production, he is a proletarian. The segmentation is within the set of producers who are subordinated. But what is a subordinate producer?

(3) *Subordination*

Subordinates have superiors, and in the case of slave, serf, and proletarian these are the master, lord, and capitalist, who enjoy the rights Table 1 withholds from producers by entry of 'none' and 'some' in appropriate slots. At least three facts warrant the ascription of subordinate status to our three types of immediate producer:

(i) They all produce for others who do not produce for them. The superior controls products they produce, as they do not control products of the superior, who commonly produces nothing. (Master and capitalist are the immediate recipients of the entire product, while the lord receives the surplus part of it.)

(ii) Within the production process they are commonly subject to the authority of the superior, who is not subject to their authority. (The authority may be exercised directly, or delegated to an overseer.)

(iii) In so far as their livelihoods depend on their relations with their superiors, they tend to be poorer than the latter. Each non-producer typically receives more of the fruits of production than does each producer. Some Marxists deny that differences of income and wealth play a fundamental role in the constitution of classes. But income and wealth may reflect, and may (more or less readily) be transformed into, power over productive forces. It is consequently appropriate for them to figure in a Marxian distinction between ruling and ruled classes.

Non-Marxists are wont to find reciprocity in the relations between the privileged and the subjected. It is said that the lord supplies protection in exchange for the provisions he receives, that the capitalist assumes risks in exchange for the profit he enjoys when they do not materialize.[1] These facts, if that is

---

[1] This is better than the claim that the capitalist provides wages in exchange for the workers' labour. Workers produce the means of paying those wages.

what they are, do not diminish subordination in the asserted sense, but tend rather to consolidate it. To the extent that there is reciprocity, there is some justice in the subordination, but not a lack of subordination.

How are the three features of subordination connected with the ownership relations exhibited in Table 1? In the first two cases the answer is fairly obvious. The rights over their labour power lacking to slave and serf are vested in superiors who so exercise them as to ensure that the three features obtain. Of course, there could be a kind of minimal 'enserfment', restricted to (say) one day of *corvée* per year, on the basis of which the person to whom service is due could not subordinate the person owing it. But a person so lightly burdened qualifies as a *serf* only under a pedantic reading of Table 1.

The proletarian's situation is different. No superior has rights over his labour power. His subordination ensues because, lacking means of production, he can ensure his survival only by contracting with a capitalist whose bargaining position enables him to impose terms which effect the worker's subordination. Through unionization proletarians improve their bargaining position and their consequent lot in all three dimensions of subordination. When the reduction of subordination is substantial, we may also speak of a reduction of proletarian status.[1] Increasingly self-confident workers may use enhanced bargaining power to begin to wrest control of the means of production from capital, though this is not to say that the transition to a socialist economy is possible without political action outside the immediate economic relationship.

(4) *Redefining the Proletarian*

Table 1 not only omits variants and intermediate cases, but also idealizes the central cases, as was noted above (p. 68). The table says that the proletarian owns all his labour power and no means of production, but the second part of this description is not always true. Two counter-examples:

(i) Schwartz works as a cutter in a dress factory. His job is to cut bolts of cloth into segments in accordance with patterns. Some of the cutting is done by means of a machine which Schwartz could not afford to buy. Some of it is done with

[1] For further discussion, see Ch. VIII, section (7).

scissors which belong to Schwartz. So it is false that Schwartz owns none of the means of production he uses.

(ii) Schwartz's brother-in-law Weiss works in a coat factory as an operator. He sews coats on a machine, which belongs to him. Bringing one to the factory is a condition on employment of operators.[1] He uses no other instruments of production. What is more, cloth and thread are cheap, so that Weiss is able to buy his raw material and sew coats at home.

Prima facie, Weiss constitutes not only a counter-example to, but a paradox for, the Marxian theorem that proletarians own no means of production. For an operator like Weiss is in general less well off than one whose boss supplies (maintains, etc.) the sewing-machine. Manifestly, Weiss is a proletarian, but he owns means of production, and is the worse off for it. He could wish *not* to have to own them. If he has nothing to lose but his chains, the sewing-machine he owns is one of them.

Schwartz and Weiss represent cases in which relations of legal ownership are a poor guide to relations of effective control. These counter-examples exploit the possibility of discrepancy between the *de jure* and the *de facto* situations. The connections between production relations and their legal expressions will be determined in detail in Chapter VIII. In solving the present problem, we anticipate some of that discussion.

There is a passage in which Marx describes the gradual subjection of a once independent weaver to a merchant. Initially the weaver sells cloth to the merchant, on mutually advantageous terms, and in no sense is he under the merchant's sway. But hard times supervene, and the weaver becomes dependent on the merchant's custom. Eventually the merchant supplies the weaver's raw material, and pays him what is in effect a wage, rather than buying his product:

> He purchases [his] labour and takes away, first, [his] property in the product, and soon also [his] ownership of the instrument— unless he allows [him] the *illusion of ownership* in order to diminish his costs of production.[2]

If the 'illusion of ownership' is allowed, the weaver's situation

---

[1] This rule obtained in the early North American garment industry, and it was bitterly resented.

[2] *Grundrisse*, p. 510.

is comparable to that of Schwartz and Weiss. The latter work alongside others in a factory, while the weaver works at home, but this important difference may be neglected here.

Now it is easy to see how the capitalist may gain by letting the weaver or Schwartz or Weiss own (some of) the instruments of production. But why, nevertheless, is the ownership 'illusory'? What is missing, *de facto*?

First consider Schwartz, who owns the scissors. They are not enough for him to cut the material properly. He also needs a cutting machine, which he cannot buy. Thus the scissors, though means of production he owns and uses, are not *means of production he can use productively outside subordination to a capitalist*.

Weiss meets the condition Schwartz just failed. He can do on his own what he does at the factory: sew coats. He need only take his machine home, buy properly cut material, and sew it up. But he cannot exploit his ownership of his machine to free himself from subjection to a capitalist. For he can produce domestically only on a paltry scale, and cannot enter trading connections which would enable him to compete with capitalist factories. He owns means of production, and can produce coats outside the capitalist relationship, but he cannot *live by* what he does with his means of production unless he does it under capitalist aegis. (Contrast the serf who lives by what he produces for himself on his own plot of land.)

It is broadly true that the proletariat was formed when immediate producers were deprived of their means of production. But lack of means of production is not as essential to proletarian status as is traditionally maintained. It is better to say that *a proletarian must sell his labour power in order to obtain his means of life*. He may own means of production, but he cannot use them to support himself save by contracting with a capitalist.

But now we need to consider whether the proletarian enjoys more than 'illusory' ownership of his *labour power*. His ownership of means of production is illusory because they are of little value to him unless he places them in the capitalist's service. But he must sell his labour power too. Both Weiss's machine and Weiss's labour power must be put at the disposal of some or other capitalist. Why, then, is ownership of labour power not equally illusory?

Because the worker's ownership of the machine is adventitious, whereas his ownership of labour power is not. The capitalist is able to supply the machine, and if it suited him, he would do so. If he abstains from owning it, that is because it benefits him not to. He has no such choice in the matter of labour power. He cannot own it instead of hiring it. He cannot acquire slaves or enslave proletarians. This confers on workers advantages they do not get from their occasional incidental ownership of means of production. It indicates the reality of their ownership of their labour power.

(5) *The Structural Definition of Class*

The discussion of the last section led to the suggestion that the proletarian is the subordinate producer who must sell his labour power in order to obtain his means of life. This definition retains defects, which we shall not in this work venture to repair. But we contend that it is a definition of the right type. It defines the class with reference to the position of its members in the economic structure, their effective rights and duties within it. A person's class is established by nothing but his objective place in the network of ownership relations, however difficult it may be to identify such places neatly. His consciousness, culture, and politics do not enter the *definition* of his class position.[1] Indeed, these exclusions are required to protect the substantive character of the Marxian thesis that class position strongly conditions consciousness, culture, and politics. The structural conception of class enables important distinctions between types of immediate producer. It was his perception of structure and its importance which led Marx to claim that he had discovered the *anatomy* of society.

Edward Thompson has recommended against austerely structural definitions of the proletariat. In this section we reject his advice. But the error we shall impute to him has no bearing on his historical writings proper, whose magnificence is not in question. An important truth motivates his misconceived repudiation of the structural idea, and it is the truth, not the misconception, which shapes his work as an historian.

Thompson's admonition may be found in several places. We

[1] Not even his behaviour is an essential part of it. See 'Being, Consciousness, and Roles', sections IV and V.

quote from the Preface to *The Making of the English Working Class*:

> . . . class happens when some men, as a result of common experiences (inherited or shared), feel and articulate the identity of their interests as between themselves, and as against those whose interests are different from (and usually opposed to) theirs. The class experience is largely determined by the productive relation into which men are born—or enter involuntarily. Class consciousness is the way in which these experiences are handled in cultural terms . . . If the experience appears as determined, class-consciousness does not. We can see a *logic* in the responses of similar occupational groups undergoing similar experiences, but we cannot predicate any *law*. Consciousness of class arises in the same way in different times and places, but never in just the same way.
>
> There is today an ever-present temptation to suppose that class is a thing. This was not Marx's meaning, in his own historical writing, yet the error vitiates much latter-day 'Marxist' writing. 'It', the working class, is assumed to have a real existence, which can be defined almost mathematically—so many men who stand in a certain relation to the means of production. Once this is assumed it becomes possible to deduce the class-consciousness which 'it' ought to have (but seldom does have) if 'it' was properly aware of its own position and real interests.[1]

Comments:

(i) There is an argument in this passage, which proceeds from a true premiss to an unjustified conclusion. The true premiss:

> The connection between production relations on the one hand and consciousness, politics, and culture on the other is not simple. There is logic in it but not law.

Conclusion:

> Class is not a matter of production relations alone, but involves the culture and politics growing out of them. Class embraces[2] a process of self-creation on the part of production-relations–defined groups.

A compressed statement of the argument:

---

[1] *Making of the English Working Class*, pp. 9-10. See also ibid., pp. 213, 939.

[2] A vague word, chosen to preserve the ambiguity in the extract. Some disambiguation is offered across comments (iii) and (iv) below.

Production relations do not mechanically determine class consciousness (p),

therefore:

Class may not be defined purely in terms of production relations (q).

P is true, but q does not follow from it. We are at liberty to define class, with more or less (if not, perhaps, 'mathematical') precision, by reference to production relations, without inferring, as Thompson says we are then bound to do, that the culture and consciousness of a class may be readily deduced from its objective position within production relations.

The opponent Thompson envisages commits the same fallacy as his critic. He too supposes that if p is true, then q is true. That is why he bases a denial of p on a denial of q, and erects a mechanical Marxism on a structuralist premiss. Thompson's suggestion that he reasons validly from a false premiss is unjustified. He is wrong that 'once it is assumed' that class is constituted by production relations, there is no escape from a mechanical Marxism which ignores the open drama of historical process. The difficulty is not the opponent's premiss, whose innocence Thompson fails to disprove, but the hasty reasoning with which he follows it.

Thompson's motive is to insist on p, with which we have no quarrel. But he mistakenly supposes that one who accepts a structural definition of class, and so rejects q, is thereby committed against p. There is no good reason to think that.

(ii) In the second paragraph on exhibit Thompson employs the phrase 'so many men who stand in a certain relation to the means of production'. He must accept the coherence and serviceability of the concept it expresses, for in the first paragraph he acknowledges the powerful influence of such common relationship on the cultural and political development of the men grouped by it. There is, then, nothing wrong with the concept, and 'class', in the traditional structural proposal, is just an abbreviation of the longer phrase. So at most Thompson could say that it is the wrong word for a good concept. But he has given no good reason for this view.

(iii) We have not yet argued positively for the structural

definition of class. We have only shown that Thompson's rejection of it is badly grounded. The argument becomes more positive when we proceed, as we now do, to consider the alternative definition he favours. It is in fact unclear what that is, but at least two proposals appear to be conveyed by his text. The second, which is more peculiar, is dealt with in comment (iv).

The first alternative is to regard community of production relationship as indeed necessary, but not sufficient, for class constitution. Class is formed only when the people who are thus grouped develop a consciousness of their common condition and interests.

But what is the set of men bound by similar production relations when it is not (yet) conscious of itself? Marx called it a 'class-in-itself' in just that historical writing which Thompson considers authoritative.[1] If Thompson were right, the French peasantry of the *Eighteenth Brumaire* could not be considered a class. This is a curious result, and hardly in line with the Marx Thompson invokes, who described them as 'the most numerous class of French society', the *class* base of Louis Napoleon's power.[2] It is precisely because a class need *not* be conscious of itself that the phrase 'class-in-itself' was introduced.

Thompson asks, in effect, 'Under what conditions may we identify the working class *as an active historical subject*?' He supplies a sensitive answer and a book which is a brilliant illustration of it. But there is a distinct question, namely, 'In virtue of what do the members of the working class count as members of that class?' The traditional answer is structural, and soundly so. Issues relevant to the first question have deformed Thompson's treatment of the second.

(iv) A different alternative conception of class relates to

---

[1] As opposed to a 'class-for-itself', that is, conscious of itself as a class in opposition to other classes, and acting accordingly. The distinction is taken from 'Eighteenth Brumaire', p. 334, and a similar one is made at *Poverty of Philosophy*, p. 195. Compare also these statements: '. . . the proletariat can act as a class only by constituting itself a distinct political party' and 'every movement in which the working class comes *out as a class* against the ruling classes and attempts to force them by pressure from without is a political movement' ('Hague Congress Resolutions', p. 291, and Marx to Bolte, 23 Nov. 1871, *Selected Correspondence*, p. 254, respectively). Note that what fails to *act* as a class when it does not rise to the political level is the proletariat, the working class.

[2] 'Eighteenth Brumaire', p. 333.

Thompson's denial that class is a 'thing'. This is a puzzling claim. Does 'so many men who stand in a certain relation to the means of production' denote a thing?

The denial that *x* is a thing has meaning only if there is some category with which thinghood is, in the given context, contrasted. If Thompson offers a contrast, it is the category of happening or process. He suggests it is that, not a thing, which a class may be said to be. But this way of speaking is pointlessly paradoxical. Is it not better to say that a class *undergoes* a process of cultural and political formation? How could it *be* that process?

(v) The phrase 'Making of the English Working Class' may be taken in two ways. It can refer to the making of the English working class *into* what it once was not: a self-aware group with definite political dispositions. Or it can refer to the making of the English working class *out of* what was not a class but just 'so many men who stand in a certain relation to the means of production'. Because he rejects the structural definition of class, Thompson intends his title in the second sense. But his opposition to structure is groundless, and his book loses nothing if we take its title in the first sense indicated.

(6) *The Individuation of Social Forms*

'Socialism', 'capitalism', 'serfdom', 'slavery'—these phrases denote stages in the 'economic development of society',[1] and because the economy is the centre of society for Marx, he also describes them as *social forms*. But on what principle are social forms distinguished? Are different stages of capitalism, for example, several social forms or variations within one? The answer we favour correlates social forms with types of economic structure. We must therefore state how types of economic structure are to be differentiated.

The economic structure of a society is the entire set of production relations obtaining in it. As far as the bare logic of the concept is concerned, an economic structure could consist of a quite heterogeneous collection of production relations. We have not excluded the idea of a society dividing neatly, equally, and stably into sets of slaves, serfs, proletarians, and co-operative labourers, with none of these kinds of relationship dominating

[1] *Critique of Political Economy*, p. 21.

the rest. Yet though we can imagine this, we shall never observe it. For it lacks socio-economic coherence. Because real economic structures possess coherence, the types of economic structure displayed in history are only a subset of the types it is possible to imagine. In real and stable economic structures, one kind of production relation binding immediate producers is dominant, a proposition presupposed by the following remarks:

> Whatever the social form of production, labourers and means of production always remain factors of it. But in a state of separation from each other either of these factors can be such only potentially. For production to go on at all they must unite. The specific manner in which this union is accomplished distinguishes the different economic epochs of the structure of society from one another. In the [capitalist] case, the separation of the free worker from his means of production is the starting point given. . . .[1]

'The separation of the free worker from his means of production'—the phrase encapsulates the structured characterization of the proletarian written into Table 1: his 'freedom' is his ownership of his labour power, his 'separation' is his non-ownership of his means of production. The text thus recommends individuation of social forms (and thereby 'economic epochs of the structure of society') in production relational terms, as attempted in Table 1.

Note the unstated assumption (shown by reference to '*the* specific manner') that the production relation binding immediate producers will be broadly invariant across a single social formation: there will be no unordered *mélange* of slaves, serfs, and proletarians. Equally, however, we shall not find societies which are purely slaveholding, or all of whose producers are proletarian. Hence the need to speak of the *dominant* relation binding immediate producers.[2]

We therefore say that there are as many types of economic structure as there are kinds of relation of immediate producers to productive forces. From the Marxian viewpoint, social forms are distinguished and unified by their types of economic struc-

---

[1] *Capital*, ii. 34-5.

[2] For Marx's use of 'dominant' in the intended sense, see *Theories of Surplus Value*, iii. 419-20, where he adverts to the *antebellum* American South. The concept of dominance deserves more clarification than I am able to supply here. See, further, *Grundrisse*, pp. 106-7.

ture, as individuated by the production relations dominant within them.

(7) *Modes of Production*

Up to now we have avoided the expression 'mode of production' which occurs so copiously in Marx's writings. We have preferred to discuss the economic structure instead. What are the differences and connections between the two?

A mode of production cannot be identical with an economic structure, for a mode is a way or manner,[1] not a set of relations. The economic structure is not a way of producing, but a framework of power in which producing occurs. Whatever correlations obtain between structure and mode, they are not one.

A mode of production is a way of producing. But there are many ways of differentiating ways. My way of walking may differ from yours because I take another route, or swing my legs differently, or tend, as you do not, to stop, look, and listen. 'Way of cooking' may refer to the ingredients used, to frying as opposed to boiling, to Greek rather than Italian, and so on. He who would identify social forms by their modes or ways of producing must indicate the dimension to which the relevant ways belong.

What did *Marx* mean by 'mode of production'? He used the term variously, relying on the reader to discern its import from its context of occurrence. Ambiguous use across distinct occasions is a fault only if interpretation is difficult on the individual occasion, and this is rarely true of 'mode of production' in Marx. But since he handled the phrase freely, Marxists should not employ it unexplicated in the statement of central theses.

There are, in fact, three senses of 'mode of production' in Marx, relating to what may be called (i) the material mode, (ii) the social mode,[2] and (iii) the mixed mode.

(i) *The material mode.* This is the way men work with their productive forces, the kinds of material process they set in train,

---

[1] Or, at a pinch, a process: Marx sometimes uses *Produktionsprozess* in apparent synonymy with *Produktionsweise*, e.g., at *Theories of Surplus Value*, iii. 491.

Another near-synonym of 'mode' is 'system', in the sense of a procedure or *modus operandi* (e.g. the rotation system, the seniority system), rather than a unified set of elements (like the solar system, or the system of nation-states).

[2] The propriety of the nomenclature used to distinguish (i) and (ii) will be more evident when the results of Ch. IV are to hand.

the forms of specialization and division of labour among them. There is a change in the material mode of production when enclosed fields replace strip farming, when power looms succeed hand looms, or when the quill is ousted by the typewriter. Here 'mode' means nearly the same as 'technique', and Marx used it in this sense when he wrote as follows about the beginnings of capitalist production:

> With regard to the mode of production itself, manufacture, in its strict meaning, is hardly to be distinguished, in its earliest stages, from the handicraft trades of the gilds.[1]

Capitalist relations replace gild relations, but the mode of production is unchanged because the physical character of the labour process has not (yet) been transformed. Proletarianization of labour is thus compatible with, and initially accompanied by, persistence of the pre-capitalist mode of production in this first sense of the phrase. The Soviet collective farm and the American 'agribusiness', despite their difference of social form, display the same material mode of production of grain, if they plough, sow, and reap using similar methods and instruments of production.

(ii) *The social mode.* In a second use of 'mode of production', Marx employs the phrase to denote social properties of the production process.[2] Three dimensions of production are relevant here: its purpose, the form of the producer's surplus labour, and the means of exploiting producers (or mode of exploitation).

Regarding the purpose of production, we may distinguish between production for use and production for exchange. In production for use the product, whether or not it is consumed by the producer himself, does not pass through a market on its route to consumption. A self-sufficient peasant who does not sell his produce is an obvious example, but there is also production for use when a lord or his retainers consume what a serf supplies. Another example is the production of medical services

---

[1] *Capital*, i. 322, and cf. ibid., p. 310; *Grundrisse*, p. 586. For other material uses of 'mode', see Marx to Annenkov, 28 Dec. 1846, *Selected Correspondence*, p. 31; *Capital*, i. 298, 371, 763, iii. 758; *Theories of Surplus Value*, i. 389, iii. 383; 'Results', pp. 1010, 1026-7, 1035, 1064.

[2] e.g. *Capital*, iii. 810, 857-8; *Theories of Surplus Value*, i. 390, iii. 270; 'Results', pp. 981, 1026, 1054.

in a scheme under which they are not sold to the patient but are free at the point of consumption.

In production for exchange, products are bartered or sold. Here we may distinguish further between production for exchange-*value*, and production which is for exchange but not for exchange-value. Regular barter in which each side wants a specific use-value in exchange for his product, where the idea of a substitute of equal value does not apply, illustrates production for exchange but not for exchange-value.

Within production for exchange-value, we can contrast the case where the producer or his exploiting superior seeks as high a return as he can obtain, which will be called production for *maximum* exchange-value, with the case where a limited exchange-value is sought, any more than which would be superfluous.

Finally, production for maximum exchange-value divides into that which does and that which does not subserve the accumulation of capital. A self-employed commodity producer who aims only to sustain himself as such may seek maximum exchange-value for his wares, yet devote to personal consumption whatever he receives in excess of what is needed to service and replace his means of production. He would not be engaged in accumulating capital. In a properly capitalist process, on the other hand, extra value is repeatedly used with a view to gaining still more extra value.

A tabulation of the foregoing distinctions:

TABLE 3

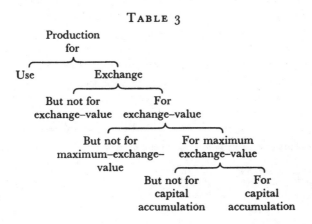

Production
for

Use   Exchange

But not for   For
exchange–value   exchange–value

But not for   For maximum
maximum–exchange– exchange–value
value

But not for   For
capital   capital
accumulation   accumulation

There are, of course, close connections between the purposes
of production and the distribution of ownership rights over
productive forces. The link between the capitalist *mode* of production, that is, production for the sake of capital accumulation,
and the capitalist *economic structure*, defined in terms of production relations, is discussed in section (2) of Chapter VII.

Two further aspects of the social mode of production are the
form taken by surplus labour, and the *mode of exploitation*. Marx
thought the first so important that he sometimes recommended
individuation of social forms by reference to it:[1]

> The essential difference between the various economic forms of
> society, between for instance, a society based on slave labour, and
> one based on wage labour, lies only in the form in which . . .
> surplus labour is in each case extracted from the actual producer,
> the labourer.[2]

The form of surplus labour is the way it manifests itself in the
society in question. Under slavery it appears in the portion of
the slave's product retained by the master after he has pro-
visioned the slave. Under capitalism it manifests itself as a
quantity of exchange-value: surplus labour is revealed only in
the disguised form of profit on investment of capital. With
serfdom, the forms vary.[3] Of central importance is the form
Marx called 'labour rent', where the producer works part of the
time 'upon the estate of the feudal lord without any compensation'.[4] This is the clearest form of manifestation of surplus
labour, with no divide between its reality and its appearance.[5]

We turn to the mode of exploitation, or means whereby the
producer is made to perform surplus labour (whatever may be
the form of the surplus). What enables the capitalist to exploit
the proletarian? The latter's lack of means of production, which
forces him to contract with a capitalist on terms which exact
surplus labour from him. Here exploitation proceeds by means
of the labour contract, and is therefore 'mediated by exchange'.[6]
In slavery and serfdom, on the other hand, there is no sale of

---

[1] The following advice differs from that quoted on p. 78 above, which is adopted
in this book.

[2] *Capital*, i. 217, and cf. ibid. iii. 772.

[3] See the varieties listed on p. 68 above.

[4] *Capital*, iii. 770.   [5] See Appendix I, p. 333.

[6] *Theories of Surplus Value*, iii. 400. Cf. 'Results', p. 1063.

labour power by producer to exploiter. Exploitation is achieved by 'other than economic pressure'.[1] Its 'basis is the forcible domination of one section of society over another',[2] assured by a combination of (threat of) violence and ideology.

There is an evident connection between modes of exploitation and production relations as described in Table 1 on page 65. Because the wage worker owns his labour power, he cannot be threatened with violent reprisal if he withholds it, but because he lacks means of production, no such threat is needed: he must, on pain of starvation, enter the labour contract. The production relations of slavery and serfdom include the authority of the superior over the producer's labour power, and he exploits it by exercising that authority.

Now either of the two basic modes of exploitation may be conceived to accompany any form of surplus labour. A producer could be coerced into working for a wage and producing surplus value.[3] A propertyless man with full bourgeois freedom could enter a contract which granted him use of means of production on condition that he regularly spend some hours producing entirely for their owner, on other means of production; or on condition that he deliver to their owner a stated portion of what he produces with them (as in share-cropping). The standard historical liaisons are: extra-economic mode of exploitation with surplus not in the form of value, and exploitation mediated by labour contract with surplus in value form.[4] But there are exceptions to these associations, and they should not be taken as obvious, as they are in even the best Marxist writing, where the distinct concepts of form of the surplus and mode of exploitation are regularly conflated.[5]

Finally, a word about the mode of exploitation of the serf. Marx's most well-known remarks on the matter[6] are not free of ambiguity. Here is how they are usually interpreted:

---

[1] *Capital*, iii. 771. Cf. 'Results', pp. 1027–8.

[2] *Theories of Surplus Value*, iii. 400.

[3] See the reference to slaves who work for wages in Ch. VII, p. 185.

[4] Section (2) of Ch. VII is, in effect, an attempt to explain the standard liaisons.

[5] For misdescription of forms of surplus labour as 'forms of extra-economic coercion', see Anderson, *Passages from Antiquity to Feudalism*, p. 147 and *Lineages of the Absolutist State*, p. 401, and contrast ibid., p. 403, where what are called 'forms of extra-economic coercion' really are such. See also Hindess and Hirst, *Pre-Capitalist Modes*, p. 221.

[6] At *Capital*, iii. 771 ff.

Given the effective possession of the subsistence-producing holding by the peasant family, the transfer of the surplus must be forced, since the peasant, as contrasted with the wage labourer, does not need to alienate his labour power in order to live.[1]

But in what sense is the said effective possession *given*? The statement suggests that the serf is in secure control of his plot *independently* of his fulfilment of his obligations to his lord. This is, however, untrue, since the direct producer is not the owner, but only a possessor' of his personal plot.[2] The rights he enjoys over it are tied to his performance of his duties: his enjoyments and obligations constitute a synthesis, neither part of which explains the other, contrary to what Hilton implies. The serf does not have burdens forcibly laid upon him *because* he controls his own little territory: they come with the territory.

The transformation of previously independent peasants into serfs is another matter.[3] It is, of course, because the peasant *was* in secure control of his means of livelihood that he had to be forced to labour for the lord: he had no need to sell his labour power. But the process of enserfment does not leave the peasant's control over his own plot intact. The Hilton formulation (which is typical among Marxists) misattributes to the structure of serfdom a feature of its historical formation.

(iii) *The mixed mode*. The material mode is the way men work with productive forces, and the social mode covers the purpose of production, the form of surplus labour, and the mode of exploitation. Lastly, we note that Marx sometimes used 'mode of production' in comprehensive fashion, to denote both material and social properties of the way production proceeds,[4] its 'entire technical and social configuration'.[5]

[1] 'Introduction' to *The Transition from Feudalism to Capitalism*, p. 14, and cf. 'Capitalism: What's in a Name?', p. 151 n., both by R. H. Hilton.

[2] *Capital*, iii. 773, and cf. ibid., p. 777.

[3] It is not clear that Marx separated these issues: see ibid., p. 771 n.

[4] See ibid. iii. 431; *Theories of Surplus Value*, iii. 491; 'Results', pp. 1019, 1021, 1034. Marx *may* be using 'mode' in mixed fashion in the 'Preface to *Critique of Political Economy*', p. 363.

For Hindess and Hirst 'a mode of production is an articulated combination of relations and forces of production structured by the dominance of the relations of production' (*Pre-Capitalist Modes of Production*, p. 9) hence a mixed mode in our usage, but one with special theoretical features. I do not find this conception clear, and in so far as I understand it, I do not f nd that the authors are faithful to it in their detailed discussions.

[5] *Capital*, ii. 385.

(8) *Varieties of Economic Change*

Every society has an *economy*, an *economic structure*, and a *social* (or economic) *form*. The differences between these will be clarified by an exhibition of varieties of economic change. We deal with (i) changes in the economy which do not change its structure, (ii) changes in the economy which are also changes of its structure but not of its social form, and (iii) changes of social form. (Recall the correlation stipulated in section (6) between social forms and types of economic structure, as individuated by dominant production relations.)

(i) *Structure-preserving changes in the economy.* These were already mentioned on page 36. A full description of an economic structure specifies how many men fill each of its various ownership positions, but it names no names: particular persons and productive forces go unrecorded. It follows that persons or productive forces may change places without there being a change in the economic structure: its full description is unaltered by economic changes of certain kinds. If Harry, who has worked for Tom, comes to work for Dick, while John, Dick's erstwhile employee, enters Tom's service, there is no change in economic structure. Such shuffling does not affect it. Nor does entry and exit of persons into and out of the economy on attainment of majority and retirement or decease; or—a rather more significant example—numerically balanced movement of firms into and out of an industry. There is no difference of economic structure, despite movement within the economy, as long as there are the same relations in the same frequency bound into the same network.

(ii) *Type-preserving changes in the economic structure.* But in fact not only the economy but also its structure is constantly changing, even in undynamic pre-capitalist society. The structure changes when the set of production relations is altered, yet the same *type* of economic structure persists as long as the same production relations remains dominant.

Two kinds of type-preserving economic structural changes may be distinguished. We shall find both kinds occurring over time periods of modest size.

First kind: the economic structure changes because the frequency of the various relations changes. We might begin with a serf-based society three per cent of whose producers are not serfs but slaves. We have a change in economic structure if the proportion of slaves rises or falls, and it is type-preserving provided that the serf relationship remains dominant.

Other examples: the petty bourgeoisie[1] swells by entry into the shopkeeper class of a number of proletarians. Or the number of owners of means of production in capitalist society declines. This means that capital is *centralized*, and if the numerical change is large, it may count as a 'transition from competitive to monopoly capitalism'. This occurs within the history of one social form because the immediate producers remain proletarian: the type of the economic structure is therefore unaffected.

The second kind of type-preserving change of structure concerns not the numbers occupying the various ownership positions but the detailed construction of those positions. The economic structure of serf society changes when money rent replaces labour rent, though serfdom remains the structure's type. Of similar import is legislation under capitalism which touches the right to strike, contracting, expanding, or otherwise modifying it. This alters the nature and scope of proletarian ownership of labour power. The schedule of workers' rights is changed. The change carries with it no alteration of social form as long as it does not render the proletariat effectively enserfed on the one hand or effectively endowed with means of production on the other.

(iii) *Changes of social form.* This is the revolutionary case in which the type of the economic structure does change, because one dominant production relation supplants another.

The economic structure is, then, variously implicated in movement and process, but to represent the structure as itself a process is to violate both the concept of structure and the intent of historical materialism. Raymond Williams is mistaken when he claims that fidelity to the movement pervasive in history

---

[1] Structural characterization of the petty bourgeois: he owns his labour power, but he does not sell it to another. If he owns means of production, then he does not do so on a scale which enables him to live without labouring. Thus he is forced to labour, though not forced to labour for another. Within the petty bourgeoisie so defined, we may distinguish between those who do and those who do not hire the labour power of others.

demands portrayal of the economic base as a process.[1] It is subject to process, but that does not make it one.

In similar vein, though more consistently, Edward Thompson rejects the very concept of the economic base or structure. 'This metaphor from constructional engineering . . . [is] inadequate to describe the flux of conflict, the dialectic of a changing social process.'[2] This is better than saying that the base *is* a process, but it is still unjustified. The metaphor is, after all, explicitly defined by Marx: the base is the sum total of production relations; and elsewhere (see p. 74 above) Thompson himself accepts the concept of a production relation. It is, moreover, obvious to a degree that the concept of structure is not intended to describe a process, but its use does not negate the existence of processes, and it is important to see that among what social processes change is the structure of society itself.

Another reason why the concept of structure must be retained is that it is sometimes appropriate to explain phenomena by reference to the economic structure itself, in abstraction from the processes enveloping it. Perhaps the emergence and strength of the ideology of liberalism are in part due not to the dynamic of capitalism but to its persistent structural requirements: this was certainly Marx's view.[3] If we do away with structure, we are liable to confuse distinct sorts of explanation.

[1] 'Base and Superstructure', p. 6.
[2] 'Peculiarities of the English', p. 351.
[3] The famous passage on 'Freedom, Equality, Property and Bentham' (*Capital*, i. 176) describes an ideology appropriate to capitalist relations of production as such.

CHAPTER IV

Material and Social Properties of Society[1]

(1) *Introducing the Distinction*

MORE THAN once we invoked without much explanation a distinction between *material* and *social* properties of society. We contrasted (p. 30) the material basis of society and its economic foundation, and denied the sociality of the former. We noted (p. 33) that it was social, not material, circumstances which would make military protection essential to agriculture. We claimed (p. 47) a sense in which scientific activity, though mental, is material, and promised a characterization of materiality which would sustain the claim. We indicated (p. 54) that the social difference between means of production and means of consumption established no material distinction between them. We contrasted (Chapter III, section (7)) the material and the social modes of production.

Marx is frequently concerned to distinguish sharply between what is and what is not an economic or social[2] characteristic:

(1) A Negro is a Negro. He only becomes a slave in certain relations. A cotton-spinning jenny is a machine for spinning cotton. It becomes *capital* only in certain relations. Torn from these relationships it is no more capital than gold in itself is *money*.[3] . . .

(2) Machinery is no more an economic category than the bullock that drags the plough. Machinery is merely a productive force. The modern workshop, which depends on the application

---

[1] It is advisable to read Appendix II before embarking on this chapter.

[2] The social characteristics of concern in this chapter are economic ones, and we shall, following Marx, use 'economic' and 'social' more or less interchangeably. For such use see, e.g., *Poverty of Philosophy*, p. 149; 'Wage Labour and Capital', p. 90; *Grundrisse*, pp. 141, 272, 872; *Capital*, ii. 225; *Theories of Surplus Value*, iii. 429.

[3] 'Wage Labour and Capital', p. 89. The text continues: '. . . or sugar the price of sugar'. Sugar is never, in fact, the price of sugar. What it may be is the value of sugar, given Marx's practice of designating as itself a value whatever has a value: see Appendix II, p. 348.

of machinery, is a social production relation, an economic category.[1]

(3) [It is a mistake to say that] from the standpoint of society there are neither slaves nor citizens: [that] both are men. Rather they are so *outside* society. To be a slave or to be a citizen are social determinations, the relationships of man A and man B. Man A is not a slave as such. He is a slave within society and because of it . . . [the] difference between capitalists and workers . . . exists in fact only from the point of view of society.[2]

(4) . . . capital is not a thing, but rather a definite social production relation, belonging to a definite historical formation of society, which is manifested in a thing and which lends this thing a specific social character. Capital is not the sum of the material and produced means of production. Capital is rather the means of production transformed into capital which in themselves are no more capital than gold or silver in itself is money. It is the means of production monopolized by a certain section of society . . .[3]

These rulings rest on a distinction between the content and the form of a society. People and productive forces comprise its *material content*, a content endowed by production relations with *social form*. On entering production relations, persons and productive forces receive the imprint of the form those relations constitute: a Negro becomes a slave, a machine becomes a portion of constant capital. Those who favour 'dialectical' language might say: a Negro is and is not a slave, a machine is and is not capital. But these are evasive declarations. The right course is to try to express Marx's distinction as clearly as possible. We shall criticize his formulations in order to clarify his idea.

1. Marx describes capital, slaves, etc., in two divergent ways. On the one hand, he insists that capital is a relation and not, like a machine, a thing; on the other hand, he allows that it may be a thing, for example a machine placed in certain relations (see (1), (4)).[4] A slave is a man in certain relations, yet he also

---

[1] *Poverty of Philosophy*, p. 149.

[2] *Grundrisse*, p. 265.

[3] *Capital*, iii. 794.

[4] Cf. 'Wage Labour and Capital', p. 90, the paragraph which begins by stating that 'capital . . . is a social relation of production' yet ends by designating 'products serving for new production' as 'capital'. See also *Grundrisse*, p. 86; *Capital*, ii. 203; *Theories of Surplus Value*, iii. 272; 'Results', pp. 996–9.

suggests that being a slave is a property not of him but of the relations themselves ((1), (3)).[1] And the modern workshop, which is instruments of production in capitalist relationship,[2] is said to *be* that relationship ((2)).

The two forms of speech are incompatible. X (a portion of constant capital, a slave) cannot be *both* (i) a relation between y (means of production, a man) and z (a capitalist, a slave-holder) *and* (ii) what y is in virtue of its relation to z. Only the second formulation is correct. A husband is a man related by marriage to a woman: he is not also a relationship of marriage. Being a husband is a property of that man, one he has in virtue of that relationship, and commonly styled a *relational property*. Being capital and being a slave are, similarly, relational properties of means of production and men. More specifically, they are social relational properties, whereas being means of production and being a man are not. The latter are possessed independently of the social form. Remove the social form in thought experiment, and those properties persist.

So, despite (4), constant[3] capital *is* a thing, namely one which has assumed a certain social character. It *is*, despite (4), a set of means of production. For if capital is, as (4) also says, the means of production transformed into capital, then once they are transformed they, the means of production, these things, are capital.

2. Let us look at the matter more closely. In the dictions we prefer, Marx acknowledges that productive forces in capitalist control are capital, and that men subject to masters are slaves. But he also wants to indicate the *in some respects* non-social character of what thus takes on social form. To this end he uses a number of phrases. Let 'S' stand for descriptions attaching in

---

[1] This might be thought a pedantic reading of text (3), which is, after all, taken from a set of often elliptically formulated notes. But Marx explicitly says that capital is a relation, and what is here said of being a slave is on a par with that. See too *Grundrisse*, p. 514, where money is said to *be* a relation. There is no money in the absence of a determinate complex of social relations, but that does not make money a relation.

[2] As used in text (2), that is. Commonly 'workshop' denotes a set of instruments of production, with no particular social character implied by use of the term. But here 'modern workshop' must mean a specifically capitalist one, or the contrast with machinery would fail.

[3] Not all capital is constant, but when means of production are capital, they are constant capital. (Labour power is, when capital, variable capital.)

virtue of the social form, and let 'M' stand for other descriptions. Then here are some of the phrases Marx uses:

M is only S in certain relations (1) (3)
M is not S torn from the S-making relationships (1)
M is not S as such (3)
M is not in itself S (4)
M is S only from the social point of view (3)[1]

The first pair of expressions are adequate, but the next two may mislead, for they suggest the consequence, which Marx tends to draw, that M is not S, that, e.g., means of production are not, ever, capital. There is also some ambiguity in the fifth expression. An object to my right may be to your left, and it cannot be said to be on the left or on the right unless some point of view is implied. It cannot be *simply* to the right. So we might think that if M is S only from a social point of view, then M is not S *simpliciter*. But in the operative sense of 'point of view' a thing is, *tout court*, whatever it is from any point of view. Suppose I chair a committee. Then I am chairman following a social process of appointment, not in virtue of my biological characteristics. One may say that 'chairman' applies to me from the social point of view. But this cannot mean that the organism I am is not a chairman, for of course it is. The fact that we need the social point of view to discern the capitalist status of means of production or the slave status of a man does not mean that the means of production are not capital or the man not a slave. Each standpoint on a thing reveals a distinct set of properties, but the thing has all of them.

If we consider a statue from the point of view of its matter we abstract from its form, and we describe it under that abstraction by stating what it is made of. Yet what it is made of does now have the form of the statue. It has both material and formal characteristics. So it is with men and productive forces. They have material and social characteristics, but *no social characteristics may be deduced from their material characteristics*, any more than the statue's shape may be deduced from its

---

[1] As opposed to the material standpoint, or—see pp. 99 ff. below—the human standpoint. Cf. *Capital*, i. 573.

matter.[1] The point Marx labours at may be expressed as follows: *M (or S) is not S in virtue of what is necessary and sufficient to make it M.* A man or slave is not a slave in virtue of what is necessary and sufficient to make him a man. A set of means of production or portion of constant capital is not constant capital in virtue of what is necessary and sufficient to make it a set of means of production. For insertion in social relations, which may not be deduced from their descriptions *as* men or means of production, is required for the further designations to apply. Yet a given man may be a slave, and means of production may be capital. Thus a machine usually has social relational, economic properties, but it is important that we can recognize it is a machine even if we ignore them.

So if we say, with Marx, that productive forces are *not by nature* or 'in themselves' ((4)) or 'as such' ((3)) social, we must not let it follow that they are *not* social, for standardly they are. Some *properties* of things are wholly social and others are wholly material, but the things which concern us have properties of both kinds.

3. In excerpt (3) Marx refers to 'social determinations, the relationships of man A and man B', suggesting that what a man is in virtue of his relations to other men is something he is from a social standpoint. But this is not always so. In the terms of the distinction we are developing, some relations between men are not social but material, and Marx recognized this. The following early statement prefigures the distinction he came to make between *material and social relations of production*:

> The production of life, both of one's own in labour and of fresh life in procreation . . . appears as a double relationship: on the

---

[1] Here and below 'deduce' is used strictly, to mean 'perform a valid deductive inference'. '*Q*' may be validly deduced from '*p*' if and only if he who asserts '*p*' and denies '*q*' contradicts himself. Thus 'There is a musical instrument in her parlour' may be deduced from 'There is an expensive grand piano in her parlour'. Put otherwise, the latter statement *entails* the former.

Not all good inferences are deductive. An example of a good non-deductive inference is from 'There is an expensive grand piano in her parlour' to 'She does not have a very low income'. Since a very low income is logically compatible with presence of an expensive piano, the inference is not deductive. It remains a good one because an expensive grand piano is unlikely to accompany very low income.

Important non-deductive inferences from material to social properties are displayed on p. 96.

one hand as a natural, on the other as a social relationship.[1]

Fresh life is conceived when a woman has sexual intercourse with a man. A description of that intercourse in natural terms will feature only those properties which belong to them as natural organisms. Now this natural relationship occurs within the frame of a social relationship, of courtship, marriage, adultery, etc., but the physical properties do not reveal its social character.

Nor is production of goods only a social process. It is also a natural or material process, man's 'interchange with nature'.[2] And some relations between men in production are material in character. If you and I carry an object, positioned on either side of it, we set up material connections by virtue of which the carrying occurs. I exert force and move my body in co-ordination with you, and our physical interaction is separable from the authority structure informing our work. The material characteristics of our labour process do not disclose the social roles we occupy *vis-à-vis* one another, or anyone else.

Section (6) provides a fuller account of the distinction between material and social relations of production, and of Marx's commitment to it. Because there are material relations between men, the appositional phrase closing this otherwise valuable sentence of Rosa Luxemburg's is misleading:

> At all stages of social development, the process of production is based on the continuation of two different, though closely connected factors, the technical and social conditions, on the precise relationship between man and nature and that between men and men.[3]

This implies that the technical or material conditions relating men with nature do not, strictly conceived, include relations between men. But while material conditions do not include social relations, they do include some relations between men, for not all relations between men are social. (Recall—see p. 35, note 1—that whenever we use 'relations of production' without a modifying adjective, the reference, unless otherwise indicated, is to *social* relations of production.)

[1] *German Ideology*, p. 41.
[2] *Capital*, iii. 794. See also ibid. i. 42-3, 183-4.
[3] *The Accumulation of Capital*, p. 32.

How may we demarcate the material from the social situation? Let us try this criterion: a description is social if and only if it entails an ascription to persons—specified or unspecified—of rights or powers[1] *vis-à-vis* other men. This proposal is rather unrefined, but it does classify descriptions of productive forces (as productive forces) and of production relations (as production relations) in the desired way, for the latter do and the former do not possess the stated entailments.

By this criterion, many facts which are fateful for society are natural or material, not social, facts. Examples: that large quantities of iron ore are available, that railways span the land, that electricity is in use, that half the labour force is engaged in agriculture. Marx calls it an 'extra-economic' fact about a developed society that

> the human being does not need his entire time for the production of necessities, that he has free time at his disposal above and beyond the labour time necessary for subsistence, and hence can also employ it for surplus labour.[2]

That he *can* so employ it belongs to the material situation, but whether he is obliged to do so, for whom, and to what extent, are facts of the social situation.

We may envisage a complete material description of a society—a 'socio-neutral' description—from which we cannot deduce its social form. It will provide extensive information, detailing the material abilities and needs of persons, the resources and facilities available to them, their scientific knowledge. But ownership patterns, distributions of rights and duties, social roles, will go unremarked.

Let us compare this delineation of the social with Max Weber's. He begins by characterizing an *action* as (roughly) a piece of behaviour informed by an intention. He then identifies a *social action* as one whose intention 'takes account of the behaviour of others and is thereby oriented in its course'.[3]

Many actions which are social on Weber's definition will be considered material here, for we may deem other-regarding

---

[1] Rights and powers are distinguished in Ch. VIII.

[2] *Grundrisse*, p. 641, and see *Capital*, i. 511, 514; *Theories of Surplus Value*, ii. 406. For misinterpretation of the first mentioned *Capital* passage, see Hindess and Hirst, *Pre-Capitalist Modes*, p. 24.

[3] *Theory of Social and Economic Organisation*, p. 88.

intentional action to be social only if some reference to social rights or powers appears in the content of the intention.[1] In so far as I carry an object with you, what I do is not social. In so far as I do it pursuant to an agreement, or under your authority, it is.

We are, however, concerned not only with actions, but with any characteristic of or fact about a society. And Weber himself extends his analysis beyond actions to 'statistical uniformities', which he deems social when they 'can be regarded as manifestations' of intentions of the other-regarding sort. He writes:

> There are statistics of processes devoid of meaning such as death rates, phenomena of fatigue, the production rates of machines, the amount of rainfall, in exactly the same sense as there are statistics of meaningful[2] phenomena. But only when the phenomena are meaningful is it convenient to speak of sociological statistics. Examples are such cases as crime rates, occupational distributions, price statistics, and statistics of crop acreages. Naturally, there are many cases where both components are involved, as in crop statistics.[3]

The Weberianly non-social phenomena listed here are material in our conception. What of his social ones? Crime rates are social, because crimes violate rights. Occupational distribution is ambiguous, as is argued in the next paragraph. Price statistics are social, for prices are rates of exchange, and exchange presupposes ownership rights in goods. How much land is sown in barley and how much in rye is not social, but the pattern of ownership of barley and rye fields is.

Though we cannot *deduce* social relationships from a material description, we can *infer* them more or less confidently, by dint of general or theoretical knowledge. To say that a man regularly makes shoes, which cover the feet of others, is to describe him only materially, but it will be extremely likely that he is a *shoemaker*, occupying a social role with established relations to

[1] A description of an intention takes, let us say, the form '. . . to do *a*' (as in '*X* intends to do *a*'). The description will be social if and only if the associated action-description, in this case '. . . does *a*', is social by the criterion given on p. 94, which this note supplements. (Intentions are social in content when they have social descriptions.)

[2] 'Meaningful' = (roughly) 'intentional'.

[3] *Theory of Social and Economic Organisation*, p. 100.

suppliers and customers, and not, for example, a shoemaking leather thief the fruits of whose toil are regularly stolen. There are, then, both material and social occupational distributions, and they are nearly isomorphic with one another.

The inference from the shoemaking man's material activity to his social role as shoemaker is an obvious one, resting on common knowledge. But Marxian theory, which is not common knowledge, is needed for more ambitious inferences, such as from the hand mill to feudal society and from the steam mill to capitalist.[1] Here the inference from material to social facts depends on the claim that feudal and capitalist relations suit the respective technologies. (If productive forces are at the hand-mill stage, they are relatively undeveloped. Most labour will be agricultural, in which case capitalist relations are unlikely.)

The material description captures a society's underlying *nature*. In this sense of 'nature', nature is of course a product of history, changing within and as a result of social forms.[2] Humanity in social organization thrusts itself against its environment, altering it and its own human nature, for it develops its own powers and needs in the course of the encounter. The development of the productive forces is expressed in the transformation of nature, and socio-economic structures are the forms in which this development proceeds, its 'forms of development'.[3]

Respecting geographical and climatic conditions, Marx and Engels wrote:

> The writing of history must always set out from these natural bases and their modification in the course of history through the action of men.[4]

The modification of the natural basis does not, of course, cancel its material character.

Facts about a society's humanly unmodified geography are facts about its productive capabilities. The distribution of rivers conditions the possibilities of irrigation and transport. Potential agricultural output depends on the nature of the soil. On hilly

---

[1] *Poverty of Philosophy*, p. 122.
[2] See *German Ideology*, pp. 87–8.
[3] *Critique of Political Economy*, p. 21.
[4] *German Ideology*, p. 31.

ground some forms of animal husbandry are unsuitable, and windmills are not possible in every climate.[1]

The external development of the productive forces—as opposed to the development of labour power—is the imposition of a *new* geography, a new material environment. If this assertion be resisted, consider the matter in stages. That there is a river here is not, on any reckoning, a social fact. Yet it may be of great social consequence, conditioning trade routes, for example. It is a material fact of social importance. Now suppose that in the course of nature the river's direction changes. That it has this (new) direction is still a physical fact. Suppose now that the change is brought about by intentional action of human beings. Does not the river's direction remain a physical matter? And if a canal is built, is this not merely a more drastic rearrangement of matter? And what is a machine, but a set of moving pieces of matter, an artificially contrived part of the environment? By easy steps we may come to see the entire productive plant of a sophisticated economy as a humanly imposed geography.

Given a certain level of development of the productive forces, or expansion of human power and its material extensions, a certain set of production relations, or social form, is appropriate as framework for use and further development of that power. But we may always abstract from the social form and display the current state of the relation between man and nature, and the material relations between men underlying their social relations. The material development ensures continuity in history:

> Because of this simple fact that every succeeding generation finds itself in possession of the productive forces acquired by the previous generation, which serve it as the raw material for new production, a coherence arises in human history, a history of humanity takes shape which is all the more a history of humanity as the productive forces of man and therefore his social relations have been developed ... Their material relations are the basis of all their relations.[2]

The relationship between man and nature is 'mediated'[3] by

---

[1] See *Capital*, i. 351.
[2] Marx to Annenkov, 28 Dec. 1846, *Selected Correspondence*, pp. 30-1.
[3] *Theories of Surplus Value*, iii. 378.

the social form: it does not occur outside it. The development of nature, described in socio-neutral terms, is therefore an abstraction. But it is a theoretically important abstraction. For central features of social institutions are explained by their contribution to the transformation of nature. Productive power is socially developed, but it is natural in character. Even scientific knowledge, though nurtured socially, is a natural power of the species man.[1]

We are arguing that the familiar distinction between forces and relations of production is, in Marx, one of a set of contrasts between nature and society. Commentators have failed to remark how often he uses 'material' as the antonym of 'social' and of 'formal', how 'natural' belongs with 'material' against 'social', and how what is described as material also counts as the 'content' of some form. (Other terms of the material vocabulary are 'human', 'simple', and 'real', while 'historical' and 'economic' consort with 'social'.) The upshot of these oppositions and identifications is that *the matter or content of society is nature, whose form is the social form.* Marx's materialism is perhaps several things, but the explanation of social history as serving material development is certainly one of them.[2]

Some critics of Marx who realize that he takes productive forces to be fundamental charge him with inconsistency when he proceeds to classify societies not materially but according to their social forms. Gellner asks why the United States is classified 'not by its tool (industrial production) but by its form of ownership (capitalism)'.[3] The question is misguided. It is often appropriate to classify entities by their form, not their content, and formal classification is correct in the present case, for individuation by productive forces would not yield *social* types.

(2) *Matter and Form in the Labour Process*

Viewed physically, production appears stripped of its social form, and that is how it is described in the chapter of *Capital* whose task is 'to consider the labour-process independently of the form it assumes under given social conditions'.[4] Production

---

[1] See *Grundrisse*, p. 700.
[2] Cf. Lange, *Political Economy*, i. 47; Goldstick, 'On the Dialectical Unity of the Concept of Matter', p. 76.
[3] *Thought and Change*, pp. 132–3 n.
[4] *Capital*, i. 177, and see iii. 803.

in its asocial aspect is '*material* production', this being the *content* of capitalist or any other form of production.[1] And that content may be described in illuminating abstraction from the form with which it is integrated. We then observe what Marx strikingly calls

> the process of production in general, occurring in all states of society, that is, without historical character, *human*, if you please.[2]

So if we look through the social form we discern something conceptually separate from it: the *human*—here opposed to *social*—interaction with nature which is material production. Having 'nothing to do with the social form' it is

> the productive activity of human beings in general, by which they promote their interchange with nature, divested not only of every social form and well-defined character, but even in its bare natural existence, independent of society, removed from all societies . . . an expression and confirmation of life which the still non-social man in general has in common with the one who is in any way social.[3]

Social man has relations with nature and with other men which are not social but, 'if you please, *human*'.

Material production does not occur in history except enveloped in a social form, for 'non-social man', if he ever existed, disappeared when history began. Hence the purely material process is an 'abstract conception which does not define any of the actual historical stages of production'.[4] The content cannot exist without form, but that does not diminish its importance.

The content of the production process is unmysterious. It is what it appears to be, and no science is required to reveal its nature. This does not make it unworthy of study, but not all study is science. Science is appropriate only when reality is belied by appearance.[5] Indeed, Marx called for a study of the content, a history of industrial technology.[6] This would not

---

[1] *Grundrisse*, p. 304. Marx emphasizes 'material' because he is referring to production in abstraction from its social features.

[2] Ibid., p. 320. ('If you please' written in English.)

[3] *Capital*, iii. 795. Cf. 'Results', pp. 1021-2.

[4] *Grundrisse*, p. 88.

[5] This thesis is explained and examined in Appendix I.

[6] 'Darwin has interested us in the history of nature's technology . . . Does not the history of the productive organs of man, of organs that are the *material* basis of all *social* organisation, deserve equal attention?' *Capital*, i. 372, emphases added.

belong to the science of economics, for 'political economy is not technology'.[1] Political economy studies the social form, which is characteristically mystified and penetrable only by theory.

So far from science being needed to understand the content, basic truths about it, which Marx calls 'natural laws', are, he says, known to every child. Children know 'that the mass of products corresponding to the different needs require different and quantitatively determined masses of the total labour of society'.[2] That is not a social law or fact of economics. It is prior to political economy, which studies the way it expresses itself in a given social form: under capitalism that way is the law of value. But '*no form* of society can . . . prevent the fact that, one way or another, the working time at the disposal of society regulates production'.[3] The fact that labour must produce means of production, and not only its own means of subsistence, is, similarly, a 'natural requisite', not 'the result of [a] specific form'.[4] These truths of the human situation lie outside the ambit of social science, for they are neither social nor scientific. Science is needed to dissolve the mystery of the form. Thus 'the mystical character of commodities'—discussed in Chapter V below—'does not originate . . . in their use-value', which is their content.[5]

The product of labour as a material process is a use-value. The character of the product of labour as a social process varies with the social form. Under capitalism it is an exchange-value:

> Tailoring, if one considers its physical aspect as a distinctive productive activity, produces a coat, not the exchange-value of the coat. The exchange-value is produced by it not as tailoring as such, but as abstract universal labour, and this belongs to a social framework not devised by the tailor.[6]

Exchange-value is a 'purely social' and hence 'non-natural' property of the product, whereas use-value is natural and sub-social.[7] 'Use-value expresses the natural relationship between things and men', while exchange-value is 'the *social existence* of

[1] *Grundrisse*, p. 86.
[2] Marx to Kugelmann, 11 July 1868, *Selected Correspondence*, p. 196.
[3] Marx to Engels, 8 Jan. 1868, ibid., p. 187. Note the emphases.
[4] *Capital*, iii. 771.
[5] Ibid. i. 71.
[6] *Critique of Political Economy*, p. 36, and cf. *Theories of Surplus Value*, i. 158.
[7] *Capital*, i. 57.

things'.[1] Materially conceived, the labour process is human rather than social (see pp. 98–9 above), and so is its product, so that whereas

> exchange-value expresses the *social form* of value . . . use-value expresses no economic form of it whatever, rather merely the being of the product etc. for mankind generally.[2]

Labour productive of use-value is concrete, or qualitatively differentiated: it is tailoring, weaving, mining, etc. Labour productive of exchange-value is abstract, just a featureless proportion of the total labour of society.[3] The sum total of use-values is the concrete or material wealth of society, whereas the ensemble of exchange-values—the same totality socially viewed—is its abstract or social wealth.[4]

It is a familiar Marxian idea that with the advent of capitalism the means of production, dead labour, come to dominate living labour, the workman himself. Less familiar is that Marx intended this in two senses, social and material, which he himself distinguished. The relevant texts describe the 'formal' and 'real' subjugations of production to capital. Capital seizes the means of production, and labour power becomes a commodity which can function productively only after it has been alienated to capital. But there are two dimensions to its inability to function independently. The first corresponds to the initial subordination of labour to capital, which Marx calls 'merely formal', a matter of the economic form alone. The means of production are transformed into capital, but the material labour process is as yet unaltered: 'the mode of working by the individual [is] for the most part unchanged'.[5] That the subjugation is formal does not mean that the labourer is not *really subjugated* to capital: it means he is not *subjugated really*, in material fashion. But his activity now serves the expansion of capital—dead labour dominates living, in a social sense. And

---

[1] *Theories of Surplus Value*, iii. 296. Cf. *Grundrisse* (Berlin), pp. 899, 909.

[2] *Grundrisse*, p. 872. At ibid., p. 680 use-value and exchange-value are distinguished as content and form.

[3] Marx criticized earlier economists (see, e.g., *Critique of Political Economy*, p. 54) for failing to note that labour may be conceived in these two ways. For a philosophical discussion of the distinction between concrete and abstract labour, see 'Marx's Dialectic of Labour', pp. 246–9.

[4] *Critique of Political Economy*, p. 59; *Capital*, i. 36; 'Results', p. 1033.

[5] *Capital*, i. 360, and cf. ibid., p. 248; 'Results', pp. 1021, 1026, 1031.

the formal subjugation leads to the real subjugation, when the form so develops the content that the worker becomes materially unable to operate except in subjection to capital. His skills are so diminished that he can produce only at a capitalist's machine, and he must follow its movements, instead of wielding tools subject to his control. He becomes '*by nature* unfitted to make anything independently'.[1] Yet

> even from the standpoint of the purely formal relation—the *general* form of capitalist production, which is common both to its less developed stage and to its more developed stage—the *means* of production . . . do not appear as subsumed to the labourer, but the labourer appears as subsumed to them[2]

since his role is to promote their expansion. Thus at all stages of capitalism

> it is not the workman that employs the instruments of labour but the instruments of labour that employ the workman; [though] it is only in the factory system that this inversion acquires for the first time *technical* and *palpable* reality.[3]

We have specified the distinction between the material and social sides of production and its product for capitalist society only, the one case to which Marx applied it in detail. The distinction might be thought inapplicable to pre-capitalist production systems, which are often, and with reason, called 'natural economies'.[4] Yet though capitalism sharpens the division between nature and society, it is not absent in earlier forms. The term 'tithe' applies to a portion of the serf's product not as a natural use-value but in virtue of its social character. In the pre-capitalist case the form of the product is determined by the social role occupancy of which generates a claim on it. There is no single form, such as exchange-value, exhibited by all goods and bringing them into systematic mutual relationship. The relation between matter and form may not be the same in pre-capitalist production, but the distinction must apply to it, and it does.

[1] *Capital*, i. 360, emphases added.
[2] *Theories of Surplus Value*, i. 390. Cf. *Capital*, i. 310, 419, 573, 645; 'Results', pp. 987–8, 1007–8, 1054.
[3] *Capital*, i. 423, emphases added. Cf. ibid., p. 386; *Grundrisse*, pp. 694–5, 699; 'Results', p. 1055.
[4] Cf. *Capital*, ii. 116, 478.

(3) *Use-value and Political Economy*

Economic science studies economic facts and laws, which manifest the social form. Accordingly, 'use-value as such, since it is independent of the determinate economic form, lies outside the sphere of investigation of political economy'.[1] The consumption of use-value is of 'purely physical interest', 'expressing no more than the relation of the individual in his natural quality to an object of his individual need'.[2]

The statement covers, among others, needs which are socially engendered.[3] It may apply, for example, to a man's need for a deodorant, which arises only in a society committed to certain norms of smell. That need is (partly) social in origin, but it is for a liquid of a certain material kind. We may prescind from the social genesis and represent the result as a relation between man and nature.[4] Society continually alters human nature, and it may become part of a man's nature to want a deodorant.

Use-value is the *substance* of the commodity,[5] and the *body* of capital.[6] Political economy examines not the content or substance or body, but exchange-value and capital, the social forms they assume. The 'material aspect' can be 'common to the most disparate epochs of production' and it 'falls outside of political economy': as far as that discipline is concerned, commonplaces serve to characterize use-value.[7]

Now while it is beyond political economy's brief to consider use-value 'as such', material facts engage its concern when they bear on properly economic ones. So although Marx says that the substance of the commodity may be ignored by the economist, since it is important only in consumption and 'it is then outside the economic relation',[8] he qualifies this in the case of the use-value of labour power, whose consumption 'enters into

---

[1] *Critique of Political Economy*, p. 28.

[2] *Grundrisse*, p. 274.

[3] Though not all such needs, for some will also be social in content. (The concept of a need which is social in content may be constructed in analogy with the concept of an intention with social content, as defined in fn. 1, p. 95.)

[4] Ian Gough questions the coherence of this abstraction, but we would defend it. See his 'Marx's Theory of Productive Labour', pp. 60–2.

[5] *Grundrisse*, p. 301. Cf. *Capital*, i. 746.

[6] *Grundrisse*, p. 646.

[7] Ibid., pp. 852–3, and cf. p. 881.

[8] Ibid., p. 208.

the economic process'.[1] The physical productivity of labour power limits the rate of surplus value, an economic magnitude, since the time available for the surplus labour which creates surplus value depends on how fast the worker can reproduce himself. Obversely, the economically grounded drive for profit promotes material productivity. And economic constraints help determine what use-values are produced: the economically inspired policy of planned obsolescence has material consequences. Marx was sensitive to the interlacing of use-value and exchange-value, and said that 'for me use-value plays a far more important part than it has in economics hitherto'.[2]

The economist's attention to use-value is consistent with its exclusion from the *domain* of political economy. He discerns the economic bearing of non-economic facts over which he lacks intellectual sovereignty. Compare the architect, who must appropriate what physicists and engineers discover about building materials, or the historian of plastic art, who must know something about the properties of paint, marble, etc.[3] The marble is the content of the statue, the stuff the sculptor forms.

Marx often criticized Ricardo for announcing a programmatic exclusion of use-value, which he could not and did not fulfil.[4] But in one case he accused Ricardo of introducing material considerations gratuitously. The accusation is unfair, and inconsistent with Marx's own views, both in detail and in principle.

Ricardo explained the declining rate of profit, which was taken as a datum in his day, by reference to the supposed diminishing marginal fertility of land, and he predicted a continued fall in the profit rate on that basis. He reckoned without the further development of fertilizers, and Marx, writing later, was able to claim that advances in organic chemistry had refuted him. Now it is clear that organic chemistry was relevant to the question. Yet Marx criticized Ricardo not only for holding to an unjustified pessimism about what was physically

---

[1] *Grundrisse* (Berlin), p. 970. See also *Theories of Surplus Value*, ii. 488–9, for 'yet another example of how important is the analysis of *use-value for the determination of economic phenomena*', and ibid. iii. 252; 'Results', pp. 979–80.

[2] 'Marginal Notes on Wagner', p. 52.

[3] This is Marx's analogy, at *Grundrisse*, p. 174.

[4] Ibid., pp. 267, 320, 646–7.

possible, but also for introducing a physical premise into a discussion of the rate of profit. He complained that Ricardo 'escaped from economics to organic chemistry'.[1]

This last criticism is tenable only if explanations of economic processes must *on principle* abstract from the physical processes underlying them. But Marx himself acknowledged the economic relevance of differential fertility, and paid great attention to it in his discussion of rent. As for Ricardo's flight to organic chemistry, Marx himself referred to 'the new agricultural chemistry in Germany, especially Liebig and Schönbein, who are more important for this thing than all the economists put together . . .'[2]

In any case, Marx's more considered general statements on use-value and economics rule out objections of principle to the introduction of material considerations in economic argument:

> Above all one must demonstrate in each analysis to what extent use-value, the presupposed substance, lies outside the economy and its categories and to what extent it enters them.[3]

(4) *Revolutionary Value of the Distinction*

The distinction between the matter and the form of society is fertile theoretically, but it also serves to sustain the revolutionary critique of capitalism. By inviting focus on the material process occurring within the capitalist economic form, it discredits capital's pretension to being an irreplaceable means of creating material wealth. Confusion of content and form supports the reactionary illusion that physical production and material growth can be achieved only by capitalist investment. When it is said, in defence of the role of the capitalist, that 'somebody has to supply the finance, somebody has to provide the jobs', then the material requisites of production are being confused with a specific social mode of satisfying them, which is thereby made proof against criticism. In the mind of the 'stupid economist . . . reproduction on an extended scale is inseparably connected . . . with *accumulation*, the capitalist form of this reproduction'.[4] Criticism requires a distinction between

---

[1] *Grundrisse*, p. 754.
[2] Marx to Engels, 13 Feb. 1866.
[3] *Grundrisse*, p. 268.
[4] *Theories of Surplus Value*, iii. 272 and see ibid., pp. 421, 424-5.

the accumulation of capital and its physical underlay, 'the simple formation of new means of production', which reveals itself once we 'leave aside the economic form'.[1]

Marx accused bourgeois political economy of mindlessly or cunningly conflating the capitalist form with its underlying matter. As useful material objects, productive forces belong to the set of use-values, so that considered just as productive forces they 'do not belong to the social framework'.[2] This truth is violated by 'The Trinity Formula', which cites 'capital, land and labour' as the three factors of production. For whereas 'land' and 'labour' designate material factors which 'have nothing to do with the social form',[3] 'capital' is a social expression, designating means of production in virtue of the capitalist form they assume at one historical stage.

In opposing the Trinity Formula, Marx contrasts the 'real [i.e. material] labour process' with the 'social process of production', which the bourgeois economist cannot separate from it.[4] The economist's mistake is not, as is sometimes said, that he assumes capitalism is the only possible economic form. Of course he knows there have been others. It is, rather, his failure to discriminate content and form in capitalism itself, which nourishes the conclusion, one he cannot openly draw, that the form is as eternal as the content, that because production always requires means of production, it therefore always requires capital.[5] Nor does he err by engaging in historically unspecific discourse about production. Marx does that himself, and it is legitimate. But the economist imports into that discourse concepts specific to a social form, as when he uses 'capital' synonymously with means of production.

In more vulgar varieties of bourgeois apologetic, the capitalist is necessary not only to provide capital but also to manage the enterprise. One objection is that the managerial function may be delegated, and if anyone is needed, it is not the delegator but the delegate.[6] A further point is that within the manager's task one may distinguish between what is due to the

---

[1] *Capital*, iii. 828.
[2] Cf. p. 100 above.
[3] *Capital*, iii. 796. Cf. *German Ideology*, p. 248; *Theories of Surplus Value*, iii. 453.
[4] *Capital*, iii. 796. Cf. ibid. ii. 388; *Theories of Surplus Value*, iii. 322, 327–8.
[5] *Grundrisse*, pp. 85–6. Cf. *Capital*, i. 608; 'Results', pp. 981–2.
[6] *Capital*, i. 193, and see ibid. iii. 379–80.

matter and what is due to the form. Organizing production belongs to the first, policing workers, seeing to it that they work, belongs to the second. Disbursements on the latter service constitute '*faux frais*' of production, costs generated not by material constraints but by antagonistic social relations.[1] One may also distinguish the true and false costs of circulation of articles, the first being costs of circulating them *qua* material goods, such as transport expenses, the second being costs of circulating them *qua* commodities, such as those of bank accounting and the remuneration received by merchants.[2]

Social arrangements cannot alter physical necessities, but social arrangements can be altered. When they are confused with the necessities they arrange, they appear to partake of the immutability of the latter. The Sophists' distinction between nature and convention is the foundation of all social criticism, and Marx's distinction is a development of it. It needs assertion because there is always an interest in hiding it, since

> from the moment that the bourgeois mode of production and the conditions of production and distribution corresponding to it are recognised as *historical*, the delusion of regarding them as natural laws of production vanishes and the prospect opens of a new society, a new economic formation, to which capitalism is only a transition.[3]

The contemporary problem of future supply of natural resources has a material side and an economic side. Partisans of capitalism reduce the difficulty to its material aspect, and leftists who cannot bear unpleasant realities attribute it entirely to the capitalist social form. Both sides of the issue need attention. That energy is in finite supply is a material fact even communism will have to confront. But the capitalist form of economy exacerbates the problem. It is prodigal with scarce resources in its monocular search for profit.

Marx's theory of revolution makes essential use of the distinction between nature and society. At any time there is 'a material outcome, a sum of productive forces, a historically

---

[1] *Capital*, i. 332, iii. 376–80; *Theories of Surplus Value*, iii. 358, 497–8; 'Results', p. 1048.

[2] *Grundrisse*, pp. 524–5, 548, 624–6, 631–3, 658–9; *Capital*, ii. Ch. VI, *passim*, e.g., p. 346; ibid. iii. 284.

[3] *Theories of Surplus Value*, iii. 429, and see ibid., p. 265; *Capital*, iii. 252.

created relationship to nature',[1] and revolution comes when this material ensemble, created by and within social forms, outgrows the society containing it. The matter pierces the form:

> To the extent that the labour process is solely a process between man and nature, its simple elements remain common to all social forms of development. But each specific historical form of this process further develops its material foundations and social forms. Whenever a certain stage of maturity has been reached, the specific historical form is discarded and makes way for a higher one. The moment of arrival of such a crisis is disclosed by the depth and breadth attained by the contradictions and antagonisms between the distribution relations, and thus the specific historical forms of their corresponding production relations, on the one hand, and the productive forces, the productive powers and the development of their agencies, on the other hand. A conflict then ensues between the material development of production and its social form.[2]

In this conflict, the material development prevails, and the social form is 'discarded'.

(5) *Against Marx on Mill*

John Stuart Mill distinguished between production, whose character, he claimed, was independent of social structure, and distribution, which he saw as socially determined. Marx criticized him, insisting that production had social as well as material properties, and he accused Mill of the conservatism that comes of conflating them. We shall argue that Mill's distinction between production and distribution resembles Marx's distinction between subsocial and social dimensions of the economy. Marx and Mill use different nomenclature, but that does not justify Marx's invective.

Marx cites Mill's contention that facts about production are 'physical', whereas distribution reflects human institutions.[3] Marx objects that production relations and distribution relations

---

[1] *German Ideology*, p. 50.
[2] *Capital*, iii. 861.
[3] *Grundrisse*, p. 832. Marx refers to pp. 239–40 of the 2nd edition (1849) of Mill's *Principles of Political Economy*. This appears on pp. 199–200 of the 1965 Toronto edition, which presents all seven of the editions Mill himself prepared. Subsequent quotations from Mill (with the exception, as indicated, of the one in fn. 3, p. 110) are from the 1849 version used by Marx, as paginated in the Toronto edition.

are sides of one coin: who owns what productive forces settles who gets what products. But Mill plainly meant by 'conditions of production' just those technical circumstances which Marx too saw as physical. And Mill's generous concept of distribution covers the pattern of ownership of productive forces, so that Marx's social relations of production are not suppressed. Marx could not have written the following sentence, but what Mill intends by it is substantially consonant with Marx's views:

> Unlike the laws of production, those of distribution are partly of human institution: since the manner in which wealth is distributed in any society, depends on the statutes or usages therein prevalent.[1]

But does Mill, perhaps, while purporting to describe production physically, insinuate socially specific terms into the description? So Marx maintains. He says that in Mill

> production . . . is to be presented as governed by eternal natural laws which are independent of history, and at the same time *bourgeois* relations are clandestinely passed off as irrefutable natural laws of society *in abstracto*.[2]

We find no basis for this indictment in the section of Mill to which Marx refers,[3] or, indeed, elsewhere. It is true that Mill uses 'capital' as Marx does not, to refer to material requisites of production *per se*. But he makes it clear that 'capital needs not necessarily be furnished by a person called a capitalist'.[4] This would be a contradiction in *Marx's* terminology, where 'capital' is invested with social meaning. He implies that Mill played fast and loose with it, employing it now socially, now materially; but this is simply untrue. (If 'capital' was widely used with the vicious ambiguity Marx deplored, Mill was as much entitled to restrict it to a physical reference as was Marx to give it a purely

---

[1] Mill, *Principles*, p. 21.

[2] *Grundrisse*, p. 87.

[3] That is, Part I of the *Principles*: see *Grundrisse*, p. 86.

[4] Mill, *Principles*, p. 59. The early champion of the working class, John Bray, made much the same point, using 'capital' as Mill did: 'It is the capital, and not the capitalist, that is essential to the operations of the producer; and there is as much difference between the two, as there is between the actual cargo and the bill of lading' (*Labour's Wrongs and Labour's Remedy*, p. 59). Marx commended this statement and did not criticize its phrasing, at *Theories of Surplus Value*, iii. 322, and 'Results', p. 999.

social meaning. And the last quoted statement shows Mill's innocence of ideological purpose in his use of the term.)

Having criticized Mill, Marx proceeds to expose the fallacy of an inference from the permanent necessity of property in the sense of physical control over objects to the permanent necessity of capitalist property, the suggestion being that Mill is among those who commit it.[1] Yet Mill himself forecasts the disappearance of capitalist private property. Referring to 'the working classes', he says that they will not

> be permanently contented with the condition of labouring for wages as their ultimate state. To work at the bidding and for the profit of another, without any interest in the work—the price of their labour being adjusted by hostile competition, one side demanding as much and the other paying as little as possible— is not, even when wages are high, a satisfactory state to human beings of educated intelligence, who have ceased to think themselves naturally inferior to those whom they serve.[2]

Here Mill foresees the demise of wage labour. (The section from which the excerpt comes is called 'Tendency of society towards the disuse of the relation of hiring and service'.)[3] True, he is not looking beyond commodity production. He envisages the persistence of a market economy, with capitalist firms replaced by co-operative enterprises, not a thorough socialization of the means of production. But this is not because he commits any such fallacy as the one Marx exposed.

So far from being a suitable target of Marx's admonition against confusing the material with the social, Mill issues similar warnings himself. One must separate the physical constraints on production from its contemporary market framework, since

> the conditions and laws of production would be the same as they are, if the arrangements of society did not depend on Exchange, or did not admit of it.

[1] *Grundrisse*, pp. 87–8.
[2] Mill, *Principles*, p. 766.
[3] *Idem.* Beginning with the 3rd edition (1852), the section ended (with minor variations) as follows: 'There can be little doubt . . . that the relation of masters and workpeople will be gradually superseded by partnership in one or two forms: in some cases, association of the labourers with the capitalist; in others, and perhaps finally in all, association of the labourers themselves.' Ibid., p. 769.

He adds that to confound what depends on those arrangements with what is independent of them leads to two mistakes, the first being the one Marx emphasized:

> on the one hand . . . political economists . . . class the merely temporary truths of their subject among its permanent and universal laws; and on the other . . . many persons . . . mistake the permanent laws of Production (such as those on which the necessity is grounded of restraining population) for temporary accidents arising from the existing constitution of society—which those who would frame a new system of social arrangements, are at liberty to disregard.[1]

Followers of Marx should not suppose that everyone he criticized was guilty as charged.

(6) *Work Relations*

We understand by 'work relations' the material relations of production distinguished from social relations on pages 92–3 above. They are relations binding producers engaged in material production, conceived in abstraction from the rights and powers they enjoy *vis-à-vis* one another, and others. It is a material fact that Sven and Lars regularly saw logs together. That they are thus related is conceptually independent of the social roles they occupy. For all that they saw together, they might be slaves, serfs, proletarians, socialist producers, or independent firewood contractors.

In addition to work relations within a producing unit, there are material relations between producing units.[2] Thus it is a material fact that shoes produced by *A* protect the feet of *B* who produces a shirt to be worn by *C* who produces wheat consumed when *A* eats a bun, whatever may be the social mechanism (market, plan, custom, etc.) mediating these material connections.

Now Marx says that

(1) The economic structure is the sum total of relations of production.

---

[1] Mill, *Principles*, pp. 455–6. Our use of this text on Mill's behalf naturally implies no endorsement of the particular claim concerning population.

[2] Cf. *Capital*, i. Ch. XIV, part 4, the distinction between 'the division of labour in the workshop' and 'the division of labour in society'.

Hence, given that

(2) Work relations are (material) relations of production,

it would follow that

(3) Work relations belong to the economic structure,

and are consequently inherently social in character. But this consequence contradicts a chief contention of the present chapter, namely that properties and relations which are material are not social. So either (1) or (2) must be abandoned.

Position (2) will be maintained. The conceptual similitude of 'work' and 'production' ensures that work relations are a species of production relations, and there is strong textual support for so designating them. It is therefore (1) which must be modified. Hence in our account of the economic structure ownership relations exhaust its constitution (see pp. 34 ff., 63 ff.).

Upshot: work relations *are* production relations, but, despite Marx's Preface of 1859, not all production relations belong to the economic structure: proposition (1) is inconsistent with his own disjunction of material and economic characteristics. We call the production relations which form the economic structure *social relations of production*, and work relations are *material relations of production*. The theoretical motivation of the adjectives should now be clear.

Here is further textual support for the identification of work relations as material relations of production:

1. Marx criticized economists who confused 'the material production relations with their historical and social determination'.[1] He therefore recognized production relations which were not social, since otherwise there could have been no such confusion. And the only plausible candidate as reference of 'material relations of production' here is the set of work relations, the connections between men as physical beings labouring in common or separately on nature and mutually providing for each other.

2. We saw that 'use-value' denotes the product from a material and not a social point of view (p. 100). In that light, the alignment between work relations—albeit not under that name—and

[1] *Capital*, iii. 809.

the production of use-value in the following sentence supports treatment of work relations as material:

> The *division of labour* as the aggregate of all the different types of productive activity constitutes the totality of the *physical* aspects of social labour as labour producing use-values.[1]

3. Marx also aligns material relations with productive forces, which suggests that material relations are, as we claim, work relations, the immediate connection in which productive forces are used. He directs attention to how

> the productive forces of man and therefore his social relations have been developed . . . Their material relations are the basis of all their relations. These material relations are only the necessary forms[2] in which their material and individual activity is realised.[3]

The first sentence implies that productive forces are the basis of social relations, and the second says that material relations are the basis of 'all their relations'. 'All their relations' must cover relations which are *not* material, namely the 'social relations' of the first sentence. Thus material work relations belong alongside the productive forces as substratum of the economic structure.

Notwithstanding the last statement, we hold that work relations are not *themselves* productive forces. Others, recognizing that work relations are not included in the economic structure, for that reason classify them as productive forces. They cite in support of this policy texts in which Marx speaks of the heightening of productive power due to efficient division of labour.[4]

We agree that *something* in this conceptual area is a productive force, but not the work relations themselves. On our account, knowledge of ways of organizing labour is a productive force, part of managerial labour power, but the relations established when that knowledge is implemented are not productive forces. It is necessary to distinguish the blueprint for the set of relations from the relations themselves, and it is the first which is a productive force. A principle for allocating tasks in a certain

---

[1] *Critique of Political Economy*, p. 51. (Emphasis on 'physical' added.)
[2] These are not *social* forms here.
[3] Marx to Annenkov, 28 Dec. 1846, *Selected Correspondence*, pp. 30–1.
[4] The following texts are cited by Wal Suchting in an unpublished paper: *German Ideology*, pp. 41, 46; *Grundrisse*, pp. 528, 585, 700, 774; 'Wages, Price and Profit', p. 421; *Capital*, i. 329, 333, 374, 386.

fashion is *used* in production, and it is *owned* by whomever owns the labour power which includes knowledge of it. Relations obtaining when tasks are divided as it prescribes are neither used nor owned.[1]

Our insistence that material relations of production are not productive forces will appear less pedantic when we put the point to theoretical use in Chapter VI, section (6).

---

[1] See the criteria of productive forcehood listed on p. 41. It could be shown, at the cost of more discussion than seems worth while, that they all tell in favour of classifying the principle as a productive force, and against so classifying the relations themselves.

CHAPTER V

Fetishism[1]

(1) Fetishism in Religion and in Economics

To MAKE a fetish of something, or fetishize it, is to invest it with powers it does not in itself have.

The term 'fetish' derives from discourse about religion. In religious fetishism an activity of thought, a cultural process, vests an object with apparent power. Since thinking does not make things so, the religious fetish does not really acquire the power mentally referred to it. But if a culture makes a fetish of an object, its members come to perceive it as endowed with the power. What is mistakenly attributed to it is experienced as inhering in it. The fetish then manifests itself as endowed with a power which in truth it lacks. It has the power not in the real world but in the religious world, a world of illusion.

Marx identified several fetishes in the sphere of the economy. The commodity fetish is most famous, but the fetishism of capital is at least as important. The economic fetish is *partly* analogous with the religious fetish. It is endowed with a power which *in a sense*[2] it lacks, whereas the religious fetish simply lacks the power.[3] And the appearance of power in the economic fetish does not result from a thought process, but from a process of production. It arises from the way production is organized in commodity society. It is 'inseparable from the production of commodities',[4] and survives even when commodity production is clearly conceived: understanding does not 'dissipate the mist'[5] through which the market economy is perceived. The false appearance is, rather like a mirage (and unlike a hallucination),

---

[1] This chapter presupposes the exposition of the idea of discrepancy between reality and appearance given in Appendix I. For a short statement of it, see p. 329.

[2] The sense is specified in section (2): it has the power, but not inherently.

[3] Except in special cases. Suppose, for example, that the worshippers believe of an idolized object that if it fell off its pedestal, they would be stricken with frenzy. It is possible that they would, therefore, suffer a frenzy if it fell.

[4] *Capital*, i. 72.

[5] Ibid. i. 74. This is the translators' phrase, but it is apt.

located in the external world. In economic fetishism there is a gulf between reality and its own appearance. The mind registers the fetish. It does not, as in the religious case, create it.

(2) *What is True and What is False in Fetishism*

Commodities possess exchange-value, and capital is productive. But these powers belong to them only by grace of the material labour process. Yet they appear to inhere in them independently of it. That appearance is fetishism.

The religious fetish does not have the power it appears to have. The economic fetish does. The illusion is that it has the power inherently, whereas it is in fact delegated by material production. The time taken to produce a commodity takes the form of the exchange-value of the commodity.[1] The productivity of men working with means of production takes the form of the productivity of capital. The forms are visible, but their foundation in labouring activity is not. *The social forms conceal the material content.*

That products have exchange-value is a result, as we shall see (section (3)), of the way labour is organized, and how much exchange-value a product has depends on how much labour is spent on it. But exchange-value appears to transcend its material basis in labour and to derive from the substance of the commodity itself. The commodity really has exchange-value, but it seems to emanate from it, not from the labour which produces it. Exchange-value is a *social* relational property of a thing, and fetishism veils its source in *material* relations between persons.

We may summarize the doctrine of commodity fetishism as follows:

1. The labour of persons takes the form of the exchange-value of things.
2. Things do have exchange-value.
3. They do not have it autonomously.
4. They appear to have it autonomously.[2]

[1] *Some* of Marx's doctrine of fetishism is expressed in terms presupposing the labour theory of value. That is not the only theory which grounds value in material conditions of production, and most of the fetishism doctrine may be stated within a competing material theory, such as Sraffa's, in which value ratios are technically determined, but not by labour alone. Our exposition will not distinguish between a generally material and a specifically labour-theoretical account of value.

[2] Statements 2, 3, and 4 explicate 'takes the form of' as it is used in statement 1.

5. Exchange-value, and the illusion accompanying it, are not permanent, but peculiar to a determinate form of society.

To characterize capital fetishism, we need the distinction between physical production and value production. Physical production is the transformation of use-values into use-values by men employing means of production. Surplus physical production is physical production whose product exceeds what is required to sustain the producers and replace used up means of production. Physical production is universal, and surplus physical production is near-universal, missing only in primitive society. Value production is specific to market economies, where the product has not only use-value but exchange-value. It is the production of the product as a value. Surplus value production is the production of more value than the value of what is used up in the productive process.

Now capital is doubly productive. First, it is value productive, because it yields a financial return: it is released, and it comes back with surplus value attached. But that surplus *value* reflects the creation of surplus *physical product*: exchange-value expands only because the productive process creates more use-value than it consumes.

Capital is also physically productive. For it is embodied in labour power (as variable capital) and means of production (as constant capital), and it is their action, hence the action of capital, which produces physical output. The physical productivity of capital depends on its being thus embodied.

Yet capital's power to produce, in both senses, appears to be a faculty inherent in it, not one it owes to the labour process.[1]

We found two phases in commodity fetishism: (1) separation of exchange-value from its material basis; (2) attachment of exchange-value to the substance of the commodity. The two phases of capital fetishism are more subtly distinguished. First, productivity is separated from its basis in material production, and attributed to exchange-value itself, to capital. Then productivity is referred back to labour power and means of production *as* physical embodiments of capital. They appear productive in virtue of being embodiments of capital, whereas in fact

---

[1] See, e.g., *Grundrisse*, pp. 745, 758, and the references in notes to section (4) below.

capital is productive in virtue of its embodiment in them.[1]
Summary of the doctrine of capital fetishism:

1. The productivity of men operating with physical facilities
   takes the form of the productivity of capital.[2]
2. Capital is productive.
3. It is not autonomously productive.
4. It appears to be autonomously productive.
5. Capital, and the illusion accompanying it, are not permanent, but peculiar to a determinate form of society.

Capital fetishism is expounded above with special reference
to *industrial* capital, capital embodied in labour power and
means of production. In fetishized perception industry produces
because capital animates it, while in reality the life of capital is
entirely due to physical production. Still, the fetishism of
industrial capital does assign a role to material production,
albeit the reverse of its true role.

Capital fetishism reaches a higher stage in the fetishism of
interest-bearing capital, which, by attracting interest, appears to
expand of its own accord, without the intervention of production. 'The relationship of capital to labour is obliterated',[3] and
surplus value, which is 'the result of the capitalist process of
production—divorced from the process—acquires an independent existence'.[4] According to Marx, 'some vulgar economists'
suppose that interest would continue to accrue even if all
capitalists only loaned their capital, and none used it productively.[5]

The interest payment is in fact derived from the surplus value
generated by production: profit and interest are parts of it,
redounding to distinct capitalists. But the route from physical
production to interest is so indirect that here 'the production of
surplus value appears purely as an occult property' of capital.[6]
It is, after all, possible for interest to accrue, for a limited time,

---

[1] *Capital*, iii. 84, 105, 728; *Theories of Surplus Value*, iii. 264, 274; 'Results', pp.
1052–6, 1058.
[2] *Capital*, i. 606–7; *Theories of Surplus Value*, i. 389.
[3] *Theories of Surplus Value*, iii. 489.
[4] *Capital*, iii. 384–5.
[5] Ibid., i. 370.
[6] Ibid. iii. 595. Cf. ibid. iii. 390, 456, 467, 479, 560–1, 794; *Grundrisse*, p. 375;
Theories of Surplus Value, iii. 453–68, 486. The fetishisms of industrial and interest-
bearing capital are compared at ibid. iii. 473–4, 476–8, 489–90, 492–5, 514–15.

without the mediation of production.[1] (An industrial capitalist whose plant is idle may still meet interest payments.)

In developed capitalism it is almost always a sum of money, or some comparably use-valueless entity, whose loan attracts more than itself in return. Gain from money lending met with hostility in pre-capitalist times, and it seems that interest-bearing capital was first tolerated when the principal was a use-value, such as a supply of seed, which could be seen to contribute materially to production.[2] Interest fetishism is limited when the principal is materially embodied.

(3) *Diagnosis of Commodity Fetishism*

Commodity fetishism is the appearance that products have value in and of themselves, apart from the labour bestowed on them. Why are commodities fetishes? Why does the labour which constitutes their value fail to appear to do so?

That commodities are fetishes does not derive from the fact that they are use-values. All products are use-values, but only when they are produced as commodities are they fetishes. No more does the fetish character result from the fact that commodities are products of a certain amount and a certain kind of labour: all products are. Nor, finally, is it grounded in the fact that commodity production is not only material production but production within a social form. All production proceeds within a social form.[3]

Mystery arises not because there *is* a social form, but because of the particular social form it is. The enigma 'comes clearly from this form itself'.[4] 'What matters is the specific manner in which the social character of labour is established.'[5] *Mystery arises because the social character of production is expressed only in exchange, not in production itself.* The product lacks social form anterior to its manifestation as a commodity. The commodity form alone connects producing units in market society. In other economies their labours are integrated from the start, by custom, directive, or plan: as producers they already have claims on one

---

[1] See *Capital*, iii. 342–3, 438.
[2] See Plekhanov, *The Monist View*, p. 87; Weber, *General Economic History*, p. 201; Mandel, *Marxist Economic Theory*, p. 100.
[3] This paragraph summarizes a long passage at *Capital*, i. 71.
[4] Ibid. i. 71–2.
[5] *Critique of Political Economy*, p. 32.

another, or on society at large. In commodity production there
is no such integration: producers connect only mediately,
through exchange, not as producers but as marketeers. Commodities are immediately social and producers' relations are
only indirectly so.

The social form is thus alienated from the productive content,
and it dominates it. Social relations between things assert
themselves against material relations between persons who lack
direct social relations.[1] It appears that men labour because their
products have value, whereas in fact they have value because
labour has been bestowed on them.[2] Men do not recognize
their own authorship of the value through which alone they
relate, and which therefore regulates their lives as producers.
They are thus in a quite specific sense alienated from their own
power, which has passed into things.

Marx contrasts market society with social forms whose production is immediately social, and therefore as transparent as
Robinson Crusoe's dealings with nature. He instances primitive
communism, production in a patriarchal tribe, feudalism, and
the future free association of producers. In patriarchal society
the product bears 'the specific social imprint of the family
relationship':[3] it is from the beginning destined, and known to
be destined, and only produced because it is destined, to be
consumed by some member of the family, or the family as a
whole. And the same holds, *mutatis mutandis*, for all other non-
commodity production: 'the social relations between individuals
in the performance of their labour, appear . . . as their own
mutual personal relations, and are not disguised under the shape
of social relations between the products of labour'.[4] The product
is socially impregnated *before* it circulates, in virtue of a nexus
of duties or agreements between people. But under commodity
production it shows a social character only in so far as it
circulates, in commodity form. Mysterious exchange-value
alone integrates dispersed producers. When production is not
ab initio social an illusiogenic market is required to link men's
labours behind their backs.

[1] *Capital*, i. 73.
[2] See *Poverty of Philosophy*, p. 86.
[3] *Critique of Political Economy*, p. 33. Cf. ibid., p. 34; *Capital*, i. 77–9; Engels,
Anti-Dühring, pp. 428–9.
[4] *Capital*, i. 77.

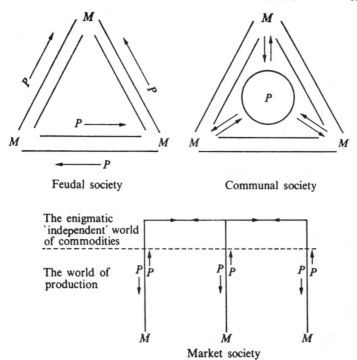

Feudal society   Communal society

Market society

The differences are depicted in the diagram. The M's are men, the P's products. Parallel lines represent bonds obtaining between men and in virtue of which products change hands. Arrows indicate the movement of products between them. First, feudal society is shown, with traditional claims of particular persons on one another. (The figure at the top is the lord, to whom products are due, but who does not, in his turn, supply any to producers.) Then we have communal production, in which each contributes to and takes from an aggregate product.[1] Finally, market society, whose 'purely atomic'[2] members are in

---

[1] 'Within the cooperative society based on common ownership of the means of production, the producers do not exchange their products; just as little does the labour employed on the products appear here *as the value* of these products, as a material quality possessed by them, since now, in contrast to capitalist society, individual labour no longer exists in an indirect fashion but directly as a component part of the total labour.' 'Critique of the Gotha Programme', pp. 22–3. Cf. *Grundrisse*, pp. 171–3.

[2] *Capital*, i. 92.

serial disconnection, linked only *via* exchange of products. The diagram portrays the duplication of worlds peculiar to commodity production. The explanation of commodity fetishism is that *if elements (here producers) which must be united are initially severed, they come to be joined indirectly on an alienated plane, in illusory forms. Division* in what needs to be unified *leads to duplication*: a second world arises to confer a surrogate coherence on the fragmented elements. (Section (6) shows the incidence of this explanatory pattern in other parts of Marx's thought.)

(4) *Diagnosis of Capital Fetishism*

We found in Marx a unitary account of the cause of commodity fetishism. In a phrase, it is lack of social connection between producers *as* producers. His explanation of the source of capital fetishism has a more complex texture. Here are some of its strands:

1. Under capitalism production is wholly dependent on capital, which advances its prerequisites, and regulates it from beginning to end. The means of production are available only as capital,[1] and it is only as (variable) capital that labour power can operate. The capitalist thus appears as the producer (or 'manufacturer'[2]), and the labourers as his instruments, 'incorporated in capital'.[3] Because capital is sovereign over the entire productive process, the power of that process appears as due to capital.

This fetishism, incipient at the stage of formal subjugation,[4] becomes

> all the more real the more . . . labour power itself becomes so modified . . . that it is powerless as an independent force . . . *outside* this capitalist relationship, and that its independent capacity to produce is destroyed.[5]

Because the extra productive power that comes of combining many labourers together

---

[1] *Grundrisse*, p. 822.

[2] In a curious transformation of meaning (evincing capital fetishism?) a *manufacturer* is now properly so called only in so far as he *makes* nothing, or at least *makes* nothing with his *hands*.

[3] *Grundrisse*, pp. 267, 297–8, 308; *Capital*, ii. 378, 385, iii. 26, 45.

[4] See Ch. IV, p. 101, on the formal and real subjugations of labour to capital.

[5] *Theories of Surplus Value*, i. 391. Cf. 'Results', p. 1024.

costs capital nothing, and because . . . the labourer himself does not develop it before his labour belongs to capital, it appears as a power with which capital is endowed by nature—a productive power that is immanent in capital.[1]

In his reduced condition, the worker cannot exert power without capital, so his power appears as the power of capital.

2. Capital's productivity is contingent on its command of the material element which is by nature productive: labour power. Yet although the amount of surplus value *created* in an enterprise depends entirely on the amount of capital it has invested in labour power (as opposed to machines, raw materials, etc.), the amount of surplus value that *redounds* to the enterprise is directly proportional to the *total* capital invested in it, in all factors of production.[2] Labour-intensive industries have a higher rate of profit-creation but the same rate of profit-appropriation as other industries. Competition induces an equalizing flow of surplus value in the direction of industries with greater investment in means of production. But this theoretically validated distinction between the locus of profit-generation and the locus of profit-accrual is not exhibited on the surface of reality, to unreflective observation. It therefore appears that what determines the amount of profit the capitalist *receives*, namely his total capital, also *creates* that profit, so that capital as such, and not particularly as invested in labour power, appears productive.[3]

3. Commercial capital (the capital of the merchant who engages in trade as opposed to production) makes no contribution to the total fund of surplus value, but competition ensures that it is remunerated on the same terms as industrial capital. This fortifies the impression that it is capital as such which is productive, and that in the industrial case actual production is only a means for the exercise of its power.[4] It is natural to suppose that it cannot be because of material production that capital is productive, when it so forcibly appears to produce

---

[1] *Capital*, i. 333. Cf. ibid., p. 360; *Capital*, iii. 627; *Grundrisse*, pp. 528–9, 585, 700–2; *Grundrisse* (Berlin), pp. 955, 960; *Theories of Surplus Value*, i. 305, 389, 391–2.

[2] *Capital*, iii. part 2; *Theories of Surplus Value*, ii. Ch. 10.

[3] *Grundrisse*, pp. 684, 759, 822; *Capital*, iii. 35, 47–8, 137, 165, 168, 172; *Theories of Surplus Value*, iii. 482–3.

[4] *Grundrisse*, pp. 632 n., 662; *Capital*, iii. 807.

without material production, in commerce, and in the hands of the recipient of interest payments.[1]

4. We noted that labour seems creative only as variable capital. It appears, moreover, that it only creates that part of the value of the product which is equal to the part of capital advanced as wages. In appearance the worker is rewarded for *all* of his labour, not merely for the part necessary to reproduce his own existence. Accordingly, 'the unpaid part seems necessarily to come not from labour but from capital, and not from the variable part of capital but from capital as a whole'.[2]

(5) *Commodity Fetishism and Money*

Capitalist society transforms quality into quantity. *Every* society embraces a set of interdependent producers, performing specific, qualitatively different material services for one another. But in a commodity economy this mutual provisioning takes place only in so far as the products achieve quantitative expression, as sums of exchange-value. Money, which is exchange-value divorced from use-value, perfects the alienated mediation of producers. 'The fact that the *exchange-value* of the commodity *assumes an independent existence* in money' reflects their disconnection as producers. In order that they may be connected,

> the definite, particular labour of the private individual must manifest itself as its opposite, as equal, necessary, general labour and, in this form, social labour.[3]

Sociality can appear only 'in this form', in the money value of labour's product, which represents just the quantity of labour bestowed upon it.

Yet 'money can possess a social property only because individuals have alienated their own social relationships by embodying them in a thing'.[4] In precommodity society men have claims on others in virtue of the roles they occupy *vis-à-vis* one another. The need for mediation through money varies inversely with the strength of direct social ties:

---

[1] See *Theories of Surplus Value*, iii. 478, 492–3, on how the fetishism of interest reinforces the fetishism of industrial capital.

[2] Marx to Engels, 30 Apr. 1868, *Selected Correspondence*, pp. 191–2. This aspect of the matter is explained more fully in Appendix I, pp. 327–8, 333–4.

[3] *Theories of Surplus Value*, iii. 130. Cf. ibid. iii. 135–7, 144–5; *Critique of Political Economy*, pp. 33–4; *Capital*, i. 77, iii. 560–1.

[4] *Grundrisse*, p. 160 and cf. ibid., pp. 223 ff.; *Critique of Political Economy*, pp. 35, 49.

The less social power the medium of exchange possesses . . . the greater must be the power of the community which binds the individuals together, the patriarchal relation, the community of antiquity, feudalism and the gild system. [In market society] each individual possesses social power in the form of a thing. Rob the thing of this social power and you must give it to persons to exercise over persons.[1]

The bourgeois revolution abolishes immediate subjection of man to man. Feudal constraints, enabling x to direct y just in virtue of who x and y are, come to an end, and no orders are valid except where the recipient has contracted to accept them. Bourgeois ideology celebrates the disappearance of the old bonds, but the new 'seeming mutual independence of the individuals is supplemented by a general and mutual dependence through or by means of the products'.[2] The rule of things is the price of bourgeois freedom.

Still, 'rob the thing of this social power and you must give it to persons to exercise over persons'. The sentence seems to favour the bourgeois claim that the suppression of the market would lead to political tyranny, and not the equality socialists preoccupied with capitalist inequality promise. Marx is sympathetic to this claim for stages of productive development short of abundance. (See Chapter VII, section (6).) But at very high levels of industry 'the power of the community' will not be exercised by some persons over others.

(6) *Commodity Fetishism, Religion, and Politics*

The explanation of commodity fetishism was: when elements which need to be united are not united directly they are joined *ab extra* through a duplicate world of illusion. In tendering this account Marx was bringing to the economic domain a form of diagnosis he applied rather earlier to religion. His Fourth Thesis on Feuerbach:

Feuerbach starts out from the fact of religious self-alienation, of the duplication of the world into a religious world and a secular one. His work consists in resolving the religious world into its secular basis. But that the secular basis detaches itself from itself and establishes itself as an independent realm in the clouds can

---

[1] *Grundrisse*, pp. 157–8 and cf. ibid., pp. 162–5.
[2] *Capital*, i. 108.

only be explained by the cleavages and self-contradictions within this secular basis.[1]

Schism in the primary world generates a second world, illusory in itself, and masking the first one.

Feuerbach does root religion in life, but he fails to see that religion will erupt as long, and only as long, as there is conflict in real life: division in the real world is necessary and sufficient for its reproduction as a religious one.

Feuerbach merits praise and blame exactly analogous to what Marx later assigned to classical political economy. The classical economists (more or less) noticed the source of exchange-value in labour time. But, in analogy with Feuerbach's error of omission, they failed to recognize that labour time takes the form of exchange-value—this blinding 'halo'[2]—only because producers are fragmented. They supposed instead that it is of the nature of labour time to take on this appearance.[3]

Feuerbach and the classical economists are commended for not taking religion and exchange-value, respectively, at 'face value'. They know the phenomenon is not autonomous, and are therefore superior to 'believers'. The believers in the economic instance are the *vulgar* economists who, like the religious, mistake illusion for independent reality.

Recall the five statements of the summary on pages 116–17. Marx knows the truth of all of them. The classical economists fail to appreciate the fifth, and are unoccupied with the question to which the fourth is an answer. The vulgar economists are unaware of the first, are therefore ignorant of the third, and taken in by the appearance mentioned in the fourth. The only truth they know is the second.

Vulgar economy alone makes value intrinsic to things:

> . . . it is characteristic of labour based on private exchange that the social character of labour 'manifests' itself in a perverted form —as the 'property' of things; that a social relation appears as a

---

[1] 'Theses on Feuerbach', p. 646.

[2] See 'Introduction to *The Critique of Hegel's Philosophy of Right*', p. 42.

[3] There is also some disanalogy, since Feuerbach hoped religion would be eliminated, while the classical economists thought of exchange-value as permanent. Feuerbach was nevertheless like them in not seeing religion as tied to a specific social reality. He therefore thought mere intellectual criticism could dispel it. (See Appendix I, pp. 339 ff. on the impotence of intellectual criticism as solvent of religious and economic illusions alike.)

relation between things (between products, values in use, commodities). This *appearance* is accepted as something real by our
fetish-worshipper, and he actually believes that the exchange-
value of things is determined by their properties as things, and is
altogether a natural property of things.[1]

The vulgar economist accepts the concepts the capitalist uses in
his business practice and systematizes them. Since the underlying reality is irrelevant to business practice—what concerns
the capitalist is not the source of value but how he may obtain
some—it goes unnoticed in vulgar economy. Classical political
economy penetrates beneath surface categories, but it thinks
that what lies beyond them is naturally and inevitably expressed
in them. Thereby it prepares the ground for the vulgarian
démarche, offering 'the vulgar economists a secure basis of operations for their shallowness, which on principle worships appearances only'.[2] A relation between men, exchange of labours,
manifests itself only as a relation between things, equivalence
of value. In not recognizing the second as but a *transient* form
of the first, the classicals encouraged the vulgarians to drop the
first altogether.

Marx holds that exchange-value necessarily dominates society
when producers are divided from one another. The economists—
classical and vulgar—do not see that exchange-value achieves
sway only because production is divided, and therefore cannot
conceive an alternative economy in which exchange-value,
money, and capital cease to regulate the social order. Compare,
finally, the petty bourgeois socialists, such as Proudhon in France
and Gray in England. They wish to preserve privatized production, but to abolish the domination of exchange-value and
capital. Hence their crackpot schemes to eliminate money and
substitute for it labour chits, which would in time acquire all the
characteristics of money, as long as producers remain fragmented.
Their futile proposals compose a programme in which 'goods
are to be produced as commodities but not exchanged as com-

---

[1] *Theories of Surplus Value*, iii. 130. Marx surely goes too far here. It is doubtful
that value has ever been conceived so purely physically by any economist, however
vulgar. The vulgar economist (e.g. Samuel Bailey, whom Marx is discussing at
this point in *Theories*) is, after all, pleased to emphasize the role of demand in
value creation, and that puts value in relation to people, however onesidedly and
inadequately.

[2] *Capital*, i. 538. Cf. ibid. ii. 372; *Theories of Surplus Value*, iii. 501.

modities'. They do not appreciate that escape from the rule of exchange-value is possible only when production itself is revolutionized, and becomes the joint enterprise of associated men.[1]

Our last illustration of the theme that division leads to duplication concerns the state.

According to *The Jewish Question*, it is because men are in conflict in their real life that they must solidarize in an ideal and false life as formally equal citizens. The state is a second and illusory society, which must be transcended:

> Human emancipation will only be complete when the real individual man has absorbed into himself the abstract citizen; when as an individual man, in his everyday life, in his work, and in his relationships, he has become a *species-being*; and when he has recognised and organised his own powers as *social* powers so that he no longer separates this social power from himself as *political* power.[2]

The Jewish Question is pre-historical materialist. A transitional text is *The German Ideology*, in which the state as illusory community and the state as organ of class rule receive equal emphasis, sometimes side by side.[3] But even the mature idea of the political superstructure has some analogy with the doctrine of commodity fetishism. The five statements on pages 116–17 are matched by these:

1. Class antagonism takes the form of political conflict.
2. There is specifically political conflict.
3. Political conflict is not autonomous but derivative.
4. It appears, however, to be autonomous.
5. Political conflict, the state, and the associated illusions are not permanent, but peculiar to class divided societies.

In a much-quoted early letter Marx credited bourgeois historians with discovery of the importance of class struggle, reserving for himself the honour of having determined that classes and their conflict are limited to a finite stretch of history.[4]

---

[1] *Critique of Political Economy*, pp. 84–6. Cf. *Grundrisse*, pp. 158–9; *Capital*, i. 94–5 n.; *Theories of Surplus Value*, iii. 296, 472, 523–7; Engels, *Anti-Dühring*, p. 434.
[2] 'On the Jewish Question', p. 31. Cf. *German Ideology*, p. 46.
[3] e.g. *German Ideology*, pp. 89, 91.
[4] Marx to Weydemeyer, 5 Mar. 1852, *Selected Correspondence*, p. 64.

This nicely parallels his conception of his advance beyond Ricardo, who did not understand how exchange-value 'is only bound up with *particular, historic phases in the development of production*'.[1]

(7) *Communism as the Liberation of the Content*

Fetishism protects capitalism. When the social form arrogates to itself the energy of the content, it makes itself appear eternal, 'simply human',[2] like the content itself. This is reflected in the discourse of the economists, which feigns a 'direct coalescence of the material relations of production with their historical and social determination'.[3] The fruits of living labour are attributed to the capital form imprisoning it.[4] The stunting quality of labour under capitalism is conceived as belonging to labouring as such.[5] There is then no prospect of liberation from capital, for labour.

The socialist revolution suppresses fetishism, and the condition of communism to which it leads may be described as the *conquest of form by matter*. For in negating exchange-value communism releases the content fetishized economy imprisoned in form. It subjects the social to the individual, thus exactly reversing fetishism. The following passage reminds us of the structure of commodity fetishism and supports the interpretation of communism advanced in this section:

> The very necessity of first transforming the products or activities of the individual into *exchange-value*, into *money*, so that they hold and display their social *power* in the form of things, proves two things: (1) that individuals now produce only for society and in society; (2) that production is not *directly* social, is not the offspring of an association which distributes labour within itself. Individuals are subsumed under social production, which operates like destiny behind their backs; but social production is not subsumed under individuals, managed by them as their common wealth.[6]

In communism individuals reclaim the power which is properly their own' but which has congealed in social structure.

[1] *Idem.*
[2] See Ch. IV, pp. 98–9.
[3] *Capital*, iii. 809.
[4] *Theories of Surplus Value*, iii. 273–4.
[5] Ibid., p. 259.
[6] *Grundrisse*, p. 158.

Use-value supplants exchange-value, and 'the material process of production is stripped of its miserable and antagonistic form'.[1] Nor is there, as in the regime before exchange-value conquered, extra-economic coercion binding men. There is just a 'free development of individualities',[2] in voluntary association. For communism makes 'it impossible that anything should exist independently of individuals'.[3] Contemplated here is a conjoint liberation of people and their productive powers. Individuals in control of historically transformed nature take over, and the reign of form ends.

Fetishism is part of the price paid for the development of production sponsored by capitalism. With fetishism the form not only dominates the content but obscures it. When communism subdues the form and enfranchises matter, obscurity retreats, and science is no longer required for human self-understanding.[4]

The form prevails because it develops the content: it is the function of society to transform nature.[5] Does it follow that, once nature is developed, society withers away? Does communism not only subject form to matter, but abolish it? Is communism formless? The answer is complicated.

Certainly communism ends the *constriction* of matter by form. It frees the material side: use-value, productive forces, individuals. But does it not *have* a social form?

A social form is a structure, an ordering of relations between persons. The total disappearance of form, so understood, is a Utopian notion. 'From the moment that men in any way work for one another, their labour assumes a social form',[6] and men work for one another under communism. But a reduction of the *scope* of form, and a change of *relation* between form and matter —these are not Utopian notions.

Since communism promises a decreasing working day, it contracts the sphere of the economy. The form of the economy, and its weight in men's lives, contract in step. As for activity

---

[1] *Grundrisse*, pp. 705–6.
[2] Ibid., p. 706.
[3] *German Ideology*, p. 87, and cf. ibid., pp. 83–4, 91.
[4] See Appendix I, pp. 336–8.
[5] See Ch. I, pp. 23–4.
[6] *Capital*, i. 71.

outside the economic zone, it is described as 'the free development of human energy',[1] which sounds like something so spontaneous as to be the opposite of anything which has a form.

But perhaps the real point is this: activity under communism, both within and outside its economy, is not unstructured, but it is also not pre-structured. No social form is *imposed* upon it, but it does have a form. One might say: *the form is now just the boundary created by matter itself.* The structure displayed by communism is no more than the outline of the activities of its members, not something into which they must fit themselves. These obscure statements will now be clarified, through attention to a neglected aspect of the idea of the abolition of the division of labour.

It is known that the state withers away under communism. But the state is not the only structure due for retirement. The social structure will also subside. The liberated association of individuals is less a new social structure than freedom from social structure:

> For the proletarians . . . the condition of their existence, labour, and with it all the conditions of existence governing modern society, have become something accidental, something over which they, as separate individuals, have no control, and over which no *social* organization can give them control.[2]

Liberation entails release of the content, and the unfettered effusion of productive power:

> . . . previous revolutions within the framework of division of labour were bound to lead to new political institutions; . . . the communist revolution, which removes the division of labour, ultimately abolishes political institutions; and finally . . . the communist revolution will be guided not by the 'social institutions of inventive socially-gifted persons', but by the productive forces.[3]

We need a reading of the division of labour which makes its abolition coincide with the suppression of social structure. This we now try to provide.

[1] *Capital*, iii. 800.
[2] *German Ideology*, p. 94.
[3] Ibid., p. 416 (quoting Max Stirner). Compare Lichtheim's perceptive description of the proletarian revolution as 'the act whereby the industrial revolution escapes from bourgeois control'. *Marxism*, p. 56.

Marx prophesied the disappearance of the division of labour in a celebrated passage of *The German Ideology*. We do not know whether this early prophecy was already accompanied by the belief he later expressed in the withering away of labour itself, as activity geared to economic ends.[1] It is unclear whether the attractively varied activity sketched below was supposed to constitute production, or take place outside it. Whatever the answer to that question may be, the passage illuminates the idea of the suppression of form:

> . . . as soon as the distribution of labour comes into being, each man has a particular, exclusive sphere of activity, which is forced upon him and from which he cannot escape. He is a hunter, a fisherman, a shepherd, or a critical critic, and must remain so if he does not want to lose his means of livelihood; while in communist society, where nobody has one exclusive sphere of activity but each can become accomplished in any branch he wishes, society regulates the general production and thus makes it possible for me to do one thing today and another tomorrow, to hunt in the morning, fish in the afternoon, rear cattle in the evening, criticize after dinner, just as I have a mind, without ever becoming hunter, fisherman, shepherd or critic.[2]

Marx here attributes three desirable features to activity—be it labour or not—in future society. First, a person does not give himself up to one activity only. Second, he does not relate to any of his several activities as to a role in a fixed social structure. And third, what he does is something he wishes to do. It is the second feature which demands examination here.

Communist man hunts, fishes, herds sheep, and criticizes, 'without ever becoming hunter, fisherman, shepherd or critic'. We submit that the quoted phrase adds to the initial assertion of variation in activity. This man is not even successively a hunter, fisherman, and critic, though he does hunt, fish, and criticize. For he is in none of these activities entering a position in a structure of roles, in such a way that he could identify himself, if only for the time being, as a hunter, etc. The thought we are trying to elicit is perhaps more apparent here:

> . . . with a communist organisation of society, there disappears

---

[1] See *Capital*, iii. 800, quoted below in Ch. XI, p. 324.
[2] *German Ideology*, pp. 44–5.

the subordination of the artist to local and national narrowness, which arises entirely from division of labour, and also the subordination of the artist to some definite art, thanks to which he is exclusively a painter, sculptor, etc., *the very name of his activity adequately expressing the narrowness of his professional development* and his dependence on division of labour. In a communist society there are no painters but at most people who engage in painting among other activities.[1]

We deny that the last sentence says: 'In a communist society there are no full-time painters but at most part-time painters.' People do paint, but the status 'painter' is not assumed even from time to time.

The abolition of roles is an exacting prescription, but Marx imposed it on future society. The reproach that he sought a complete absorption of the individual in society states the reverse of his aim. Having complained that in modern times 'a general or a banker plays a great part, but mere man . . . a very shabby part',[2] he would not be impressed by a jack-of-all-roles, who is other than mere man, whatever he took that to be. He wanted individuals to face one another and themselves 'as such', without the mediation of institutions.[3] For institutions represent 'fixation of social activity, consolidation of what we ourselves produce into an objective power above us'.[4] It is no great exaggeration to say that Marx's freely associated individuals constitute an alternative to, not a form of, society.

[1] *German Ideology*, pp. 431–2, emphases added.
[2] *Capital*, i. 44, and cf. *Grundrisse*, p. 248.
[3] *German Ideology*, p. 84, and see also, p. 49. Recall the use of 'as such' to restrict attention to the material side of things and persons: see Ch. IV above, pp. 89–91.
[4] *German Ideology*, p. 45.

CHAPTER VI

The Primacy of the Productive Forces

(1) *Introduction*

IN THIS chapter we show that Marx assigned explanatory primacy to the productive forces, and we provide some reasons for actually doing so. These tasks are prosecuted separately, in deference to an elementary distinction: the thesis that *Marx* vested primacy in the forces is distinct from the thesis that they *are* primary. This truism bears assertion, because Marxists have a habit of evaluating the first claim according to their conception of the merits of the second. That procedure is sound only if one may assume in advance that Marx's stand on the matter is correct. This may be so, as we shall ourselves argue, but it is unacceptable as an assumption. Still less acceptable is another principle sometimes implicit in Marxist thinking: that whatever Marx thought about the matter is *obviously* true. This principle is unacceptable not only as an assumption but absolutely.

The primacy maintained in this chapter is of the productive forces over the production relations, or over the economic structure the relations constitute. The primacy thesis is that *the nature of a set of production relations is explained by the level of development of the productive forces embraced by it* (to a far greater extent than vice versa).[1] The exact structure of the explanatory tie is the topic of section (5).

The primacy thesis, as we find it in Marx, is associated with a second thesis, which will be called the *development* thesis. We shall, accordingly, be concerned with the following pair of claims:

- (a) The productive forces tend to develop throughout history (the Development Thesis).
- (b) The nature of the production relations of a society is explained by the level of development of its productive forces (the Primacy Thesis proper).

---

[1] Some such qualifying phrase is always to be understood whenever the primacy thesis is asserted.

(a)   says both more and less than

(a)' The productive forces *have* developed throughout history.

(a) says more than (a)', because (a) asserts a universal *tendency* to development. The forces might have developed for a miscellany of uncoordinated reasons, and that would suffice to establish (a)', but not (a), which requires that it is of the nature of the forces to develop. On the other hand, (a) does not entail that the forces always develop, nor even that they never decline: circumstances may frustrate fulfilment of the tendency it imputes to them.

The primacy thesis ((b)) implies that changes in productive forces bring about changes in production relations. Yet some changes in productive forces are too limited in scope to have that effect. Nor is it possible to provide a *general* statement of how much productive power must increase for a consequent change in production relations to occur. Instead, we may formulate the dynamic aspect of the dependence of production relations on productive forces as follows: for any set of production relations, there is an extent of further development of the productive forces they embrace which suffices for a change in those relations, and—in virtue of (a)—that further development tends to occur. But how large the development must be will vary from case to case. The logical structure of the claim classifies it with such truths as that all liquids have boiling points, all sentient organisms have pain thresholds, etc. These do not specify the values of the critical levels whose universality they assert, and the same goes for our analogous formulation.

There are both quantitative and qualitative differences between levels of development of productive power. If level L is higher than level M, then (on the criterion adopted in Chapter II, section (6)), more surplus is producible at level L than at level M. But that quantitative difference will normally be due to incidence at the two stages of qualitatively different sorts of productive knowledge and resources. If, then, we say that production relations are explained by levels of development of productive power, it is necessary to add that it is sometimes the sheer quantity of power, sometimes its qualitative embodiment, and sometimes both, in which explanation resides.

(2) *Assertions of Primacy by Marx: The Preface*

Some arguments for the development and primacy theses will be given in section (4). In this section and the next we provide conclusive evidence of Marx's allegiance to them.

We begin with the Preface of 1859, and for ease of reference we present some Preface sentences with numbers attached:

1. . . . relations of production . . . correspond to a definite stage of development of . . . material productive forces.
2. At a certain stage of their development, the material productive forces of society come in conflict with the existing relations of production . . . within which they have been at work hitherto.
3. From forms of development of the productive forces these relations turn into their fetters.
4. Then begins an epoch of social revolution [which brings about a change of economic structure].[1]
5. No social formation ever perishes before all the productive forces for which there is room in it have developed . . .
6. . . . new, higher relations of production never appear before the material conditions of their existence have matured in the womb of the old society itself.

The sentences show commitment to the development thesis. It is not stated as such, but it is presupposed in Marx's recurrent reference to the development of the productive forces. No one could think that he is concerned with those cases in which they tend to develop *as opposed* to others in which, he would acknowledge, they do not. His subject is the trend of history as a whole, and he clearly supposes that throughout history the productive forces tend to develop and, indeed, do develop.

As to the primacy thesis proper, we contend that it is already reflected in sentence 1. When Marx says production relations *correspond* to productive forces, he means the former are appropriate to the latter, and we may impute to him the further thought that the relations are as they are *because* they are appropriate to productive development.

Yet many will say that it belongs to the meaning of the verb 'correspond' (*entsprechen*) that if x corresponds to y, then y corresponds to x, so that if relations correspond to forces, forces

---

[1] The bracketed addendum is licensed by the next sentence, which is not quoted here: see p. vii above.

must correspond to relations. If they are right, the asserted correspondence of relations to forces implies no priority either way, and our interpretation of Marx is incorrect. But they are not right. Correspondence is not always symmetrical. It is sometimes, as in 'goals in soccer correspond to runs in baseball', but sometimes it is not, as in 'nervous breakdowns correspond to increases in the pressures of life', where 'correspond' means, roughly, 'are explained by'.

Our own interpretation is not established as correct by the refutation we have just given of one bad argument for a contrary view. We still need to show that the relation signified by 'correspond' in sentence 1 is unidirectional rather than symmetrical.

The symmetrical reading is perhaps feasible when sentence 1 is taken in isolation from the rest of the Preface, but if we bring the latter to bear it fails, and our own reading is seen to be correct.

(i) The sentence following 1—it is not quoted above—states that forms of social consciousness 'correspond' to the economic structure. The proponent of the symmetry view of 'correspond' in 1 must extend his interpretation of it to this further occurrence of the word, on pain of maintaining, most implausibly, that it is used with a fundamental difference of intent in two adjacent sentences. But the extension to which he is committed is unacceptable. For later Preface sentences do assign a derivative role to social consciousness,[1] and it is reasonable to take the sentence after 1 as a summary statement of that assignment.

(ii) Sentences 2, 3, and 4 entail that productive development eventuates in incompatibility between forces and relations, whereupon the tension is resolved in favour of the forces, by transformation of the relations. But why do the relations not prevail against the forces? Because—it seems natural to reply—the relations must *correspond* to the forces: but this is a good answer only if 'correspond' is taken as we recommend.

At this point someone might say that, while the 'correspondence' of 1 is indeed unidirectional, Marx *also* held that there was as much influence in the opposite direction, by the relations on the forces, although sentence 1 does not say so. And we grant

---

[1] 'It is not the consciousness of men that determines their being, but, on the contrary, their social being that determines their consciousness' and 'Consciousness must be explained . . . from the contradictions of material life . . .'

that 1, even as we have interpreted it, is, taken alone, compatible with parallel opposite assertions to the effect that production relations develop, and, in developing, bring about changes in productive forces. Neither 1 nor passages similar to it in other works (see section (3)) state that *all* changes in production relations are responses to movement of the productive forces. Moreover, they say little about the *source* of changes in the productive forces, which might, therefore, at least in some cases, be located in the production relations. Sentence 1 and its cognates, abstractly considered, leave room for that zig-zag 'dialectic' between forces and relations, with priority on neither side, which is widely favoured.

Yet no *generalizations* asserting the putative reverse movement are to be found in the corpus. If Marx thought the influence was bidirectional, with equal weight on both sides, why did he consistently draw attention, when generalizing, to one direction only? Why does he frequently refer to correspondence of relations to forces and never to the opposite in his theoretical summations? (Marx recognizes many ways in which relations condition forces, and the bearing of this on the primacy thesis will be considered in section (5). Our present point is that his *general* statements always award priority to the forces.)

We conclude that sentence 1 of the Preface may fairly be taken as manifesting commitment to the primacy thesis (thesis (b)), in a sense which is partly elaborated by sentences 2, 3, and 4.

Further elaboration is provided by sentences 5 and 6. 2 through 6 convey a very strict form of the primacy thesis—an extremely precise governance of the production relations by the productive forces is asserted here, and when we come to defend the primacy thesis (in section (4)) a laxer version of it than what the Preface lays down will occupy us. But now we shall examine sentences 5 and 6, first in abstraction from 2 and 4, then together with them. The point of the abstraction is to distinguish distinct theses.

5 says:

No social formation ever perishes before all the productive forces for which there is room in it have developed . . .

Social formations permit ('have room for') productive development according as their production relations do. Let us therefore rewrite 5 as follows:

> No economic structure (set of production relations) ever
> perishes before all the productive forces for which there is
> room in it have developed . . .

(Note that in 5's companion, 6, 'relations of production' appears
just where, given the wording of 5, we should expect to find
'social formation'.)

Now 'all the productive forces for which there is room in an
economic structure' is, quite clearly, a reference to the maximum level of productivity compatible with that structure. (It
would be a mistake to take the quoted phrase in a literal way,
as denoting a certain *number* of productive forces.) Hence 5 says:
if an economic structure perishes, its productivity potential was
realized. At some point in its history a deceased form of economy
was as productively powerful as it was possible for an economy
of that form to be.

Two mistaken handlings of sentence 5 will now be noted. The
first is to deflate it into a truism, the second is to make its claim
out to be greater than it actually is.

When something is perishing, it is poorly placed to achieve
anything, and the weakest reading of 5 takes it as an instance
of that trivially true generalization. On this view 5 says no more
than that when it perished, the economic structure could
develop the forces no further (because it was perishing). A
somewhat stronger reading would have it that the economic
structure was already incapable of sustaining further productive
development before—perhaps just before—it began to perish:
it was sclerosed. But even this is too weak. If a man was unable
to develop further on the eve of his death, it does not follow that
all his abilities had by then unfolded; and, similarly, an economic structure might be imagined to suffer sclerosis and perish
when its productivity had not reached the maximum height
possible for it. Such a case, 5 says, is not actualized in history.

Very trivial readings being set aside, 5 remains capable of
both strong and weak construals. Thus suppose that in the
productive heyday of French feudalism a yield of grain some six

times greater than the amount of seed sown was normal.[1] (Let grain productivity alone determine a pre-industrial society's productive power.) On a strong construal of 5, 5 implies that something like that level of productivity is the highest possible for the feudal form as such, so that if some other feudalism shows an input/output ratio of, say, 1:10, then French feudalism did not reach its potential, and the French case falsifies 5. On a weaker and more plausible construal of 5,[2] French feudal society's maximum possible productivity would be set not by the feudal form as such but by the feudal form in its specific French variation. In the terms of Chapter III, section (6), not the dominant production relation alone, which is common to all feudalisms, but more specific features of its economic structure, would figure in determining a particular feudal society's potential maximum. Then the fact that other feudalisms had outclassed the French would not falsify 5.

Having rejected deflationary accounts of 5, we now indicate some respects in which it is less assertive than it might seem.

First, notice that 5 does not say that whenever an economic structure goes it is replaced by one which represents an improvement on it. 5 permits *regression*—an economic structure which has reached its productive apex being replaced by an inferior one.

Second, 5 does not entail its own converse, namely, 'if all the productive forces for which there is room in it have developed, an economic structure perishes'. A society which reaches its maximum but remains locked inside the economic form which brought it there does not falsify 5. 5 thus permits what may be called *fossilization*. Marx *perhaps* attributed fossilization to Indian civilization, and whatever difficulty the example as he describes it poses for him, it is quite consistent with sentence 5.[3]

Sentence 6 says:

---

[1] This quasi-notional figure is derived from Bloch's *French Rural History*, pp. 25–6.

[2] A construal, that is, which makes it more plausible to claim that 5 is true. It is hard to choose between the construals exegetically, for it is doubtful whether Marx considered the difference between them.

[3] See, e.g., *Capital*, i. 358. It is uncertain whether Marx discerned fossilization, as here defined, in India, as opposed to its arrested development within an economic form whose maximum productivity had not been reached. Both conceptions are consistent with sentence 5, though not with sentences 2 to 4, to which we turn in a moment.

. . . new higher relations of production never appear before the material conditions of their existence have matured in the womb of the old society itself.

We conjecture[1] that 'material' is used here in the sense explained in Chapter IV. If so, 6 says that a higher economic structure cannot be introduced without a requisitely advanced level of productivity, a level to which the forces have been developed within the old economic structure.

6 is trivialized if 'material conditions' is taken as a pleonasm, that is, as synonymous with 'conditions', for Marx would then be saying no more than that a new economic structure, like anything else, emerges only when it is possible for it to emerge. He would merely be banning miracles, not specifying substantive prerequisites of new relations of production.

On the other hand, 6, like 5, does not entail its converse, and thus also says less than might at first appear. The converse of 6 is: 'if productive forces sufficient for a new and higher economic structure have developed, the latter emerges'. For all 6 says, this need not be universally true. 6 allows historical *miscarriages*.

There are, then, a number of important theses which 5 and 6 do not entail. But the position changes when we combine them with sentences 2, 3, and 4. The amalgam 2–6 is very strong doctrine indeed.[2]

The stage referred to in 2, when production relations begin to inhibit the productive forces, is one which, 4 informs us, is followed by a revolution. But we know from 5 that if a revolution occurs, the productive forces reached the maximum level

---

[1] This *is* a conjecture, and it is *not* supported by some other uses of 'material' in the Preface, such as that quoted in fn. 1, p. 137. It is certain that the relevant material conditions include a requisitely high level of productivity, but Marx may also have in mind the germination in the old order of embryonic forms of the higher relations of production, such as merchant capital in the feudal period, and co-operative factories under capitalism. Our restricted interpretation of 'material conditions' in 6 is, on the other hand, consonant with this *Capital* passage: 'Development of the productive forces of social labour is the historical task and justification of capital. This is just the way in which it unconsciously creates the material requirements of a higher mode of production' (iii. 254).

[2] For a more precise statement of what follows, see the Addendum at the end of the chapter, which also gives a more rigorous account than that supplied above of the content of sentences 5 and 6. This material appears in an Addendum to enable the reader to bypass it.

consistent with the old economic structure. This rules out fossilization of a fully developed economic form. Since we may suppose that the revolution installs a higher economic structure, regression is forbidden as well. It now also follows—the reasoning is in section (8)—that the miscarriages formally permitted by 6 are guaranteed not to occur.

(It might be objected that we have mishandled sentence 4, which refers to an *epoch* of social revolution. It is not a briefish transformation which ensues when forces and relations are in conflict, but a protracted period of transition, possibly lasting centuries. But this enforces only minor qualifications on the above remarks. It means that *temporary* fossilization and regression are possible. The arrival of the new society may be delayed, and there may be some backward steps on the way to it, but come it must in the end.)

We sought to indicate what sentences 5 and 6 do not *per se* entail as a device for revealing a large set of theses to which, it turns out, the Preface is committed. The Preface makes many claims. When we come to defend theses (a) and (b), we shall not hope to support all the claims we distinguished. We shall not, for example, want to deny that feudal relations, had they peradventure lasted longer, might have yielded higher productivity than they ever did in fact. Their lesser productive potential partly explains their decline, but it need not follow that they must, as the Preface asserts, actualize that potential before they disappear.

(3) *Assertions of Primacy by Marx: Outside the Preface*

So at least in the Preface of 1859 Marx espouses theses (a) and (b): the development of the productive forces proceeds systematically, and production relations conform to that development. But some think this version of historical materialism is found only in the Preface. So we now exhibit passages from other works in evidence of the permanence of the Preface perspective in Marx's mature thought.

Allegiance to the primacy thesis dawns in the *German Ideology* (1846), though it is expressed in a vocabulary which is later dropped. A term notably peculiar to the *German Ideology* is *Verkehrsform*, standardly translated as 'form (or mode) of intercourse' or, misleadingly, as 'mode of (carrying on) commerce'.

Verkehrsform is a precursor of the later, better defined, 'relations of production'. We are told that 'the multitude of productive forces accessible to men determines the nature of society',[1] and this is spelled out in a diachronic dependence of the *Verkehrsform* on the forces which prefigures sentences 2 to 4 of the Preface:

> . . . in the place of an earlier form of intercourse, which has become a fetter, a new one is put, corresponding to the more developed productive forces and, hence, to the advanced mode of self-activity of individuals—a form which in its turn becomes a fetter and is then replaced by another.[2]

The propensity of the production relations to adapt themselves to the productive forces entails a corollary about the aftermath of conquests:

> . . . when there is nothing more to take, you have to set about producing. From this necessity of producing . . . it follows that the form of community adopted by the settling conquerors must correspond to the stage of development of the productive forces they find in existence; or, if this is not the case from the start, it must change according to the productive forces.[3]

The theme continues in the *Poverty of Philosophy* (1847). By now 'form of intercourse' and 'form of community' are giving way to 'production relations' and 'social relations', and the dependence of both (if, indeed, they are fully distinct) on the productive forces is crisply stated. For example:

> the relations in which productive forces are developed . . . correspond to a definite development of men and of their productive forces . . .

We know that 'correspond' is unidirectional here, for the sentence continues:

> . . . and . . . a change in men's productive forces necessarily brings about a change in their relations of production.[4]

Then there is a passage with a notorious culmination:

> Social relations are closely bound up with productive forces. In[5] acquiring new productive forces men change their mode of pro-

---

[1] *German Ideology*, p. 41, and cf. p. 87.   [2] Ibid., p. 88, and cf. p. 85.
[3] Ibid., p. 90.   [4] *Poverty of Philosophy*, p. 137.
[5] *En*—also translatable as 'by'.

duction; and in changing their mode of production, in changing their way of earning a living, they change all their social relations.[1] The hand-mill gives you society with the feudal lord; the steam-mill society with the industrial capitalist.[2]

Sidney Hook denies that the last sentence asserts the sovereignty of the productive forces:

> Marx often said that the development of technology could serve as an index of the development of society; but that is an altogether different thing from saying that we must look to the development of technology as the cause or independent variable of social change.[3]

Hook is right when he claims that '*x* gives you *y*' *may* be used to state a merely indexical connection: it does not always imply that *y* is explained by *x*. He who says 'a psychology of acquisitiveness gives you capitalist society, a psychology of loyalty and honour gives you feudal society' need not suppose that attitudes spawn economic systems. But the sentence (see above) preceding the contested remark about the mills falsifies the 'indexical' interpretation of it. So does the sentence which follows it: 'men ... establish their social relations in conformity with their material productivity'.

The same unambiguous commitment to the primacy of the forces is found in Marx's letter of 1846 to P. V. Annenkov:

> ... the social history of men is never anything but the history of their individual development, whether they are conscious of it or not. Their material relations are the basis of all their relations.[4]
>
> With the acquisition of new productive facilities, men change their mode of production, and with the mode of production all the economic relations, which are merely the relations appropriate to a particular mode of production.[5]
>
> ... as men develop their productive forces, that is, as they live, they develop certain relations with one another and ... the nature of these relations is bound to change with the change and growth of these productive forces.[6]

---

[1] Here 'mode of production' is probably the material mode (see Ch. III, p. 79). But whichever mode is meant, the sentence formulates primacy of the productive forces over the production relations.

[2] *Poverty of Philosophy*, p. 122.

[3] *Towards the Understanding of Karl Marx*, p. 126.

[4] *Selected Correspondence*, p. 31.   [5] *Idem.*   [6] Ibid., p. 34.

The Communist Manifesto (1848) offers no general statement about the relationship between productive forces and production relations, its focus being on the history of class conflict that relationship underlies. Still, the primacy doctrine is applied in the narrative:

> . . . the feudal organisation of agriculture and manuacturing industry, in one word, the feudal relations of property became no longer compatible with the already developed productive forces; they became so many fetters. They had to be burst asunder; they were burst asunder.[1]

And the pattern is repeating itself:

> The productive forces at the disposal of society no longer tend to further the development of the relations of bourgeois property; on the contrary, they have become too powerful for these relations by which they are fettered . . .[2]

It follows, as before, that the production relations can, should, and will be burst asunder: 'the proletarians . . . have a world to win'.[3]

Also from the *Manifesto*:

> The bourgeoisie cannot exist without continually revolutionising the instruments of production, and thereby the relations of production and all the social relations.[4]

What changes the productive forces *thereby* changes the production relations—this suggests the former's domination of the latter. Yet here what changes the productive forces is the bourgeoisie, and if they 'cannot exist without' doing so, that can only be because of their emplacement in the relations of production. The text thus appears to support the 'dialectical' view noticed and rejected on page 138 above. We shall come to terms with it in section (7).

Wage Labour and Capital (1849) proposes an analogy between the determination of production relations by productive forces and the determination of military relations by destructive forces:

> These social relations into which the producers enter with one another, the conditions under which they exchange their activities and participate in the whole act of production, will naturally

---

[1] 'The Communist Manifesto', p. 24.
[2] Ibid., pp. 39–40. Cf. Engels's 'Principles of Communism', Question No. 13.
[3] 'The Communist Manifesto', p. 65.   [4] Ibid., p. 37.

vary according to the character of the means of production. With the invention of a new instrument of warfare, firearms, the whole internal organisation of the army necessarily changed; the relationships within which individuals can constitute an army and act as an army were transformed and the relations of different armies to one another also changed.

Thus the social relations within which individuals produce, *the social relations of production, change, are transformed, with the change and development of the material means of production, the productive forces*.[1]

We shall take a close look at this analogy in section (5).

The passages given above come from the 1840s, but similar comment will be found in the principal later writings, as the following extracts prove:

> In the last instance the community and the property resting upon it can be reduced to a specific stage in the development of the forces of production of the labouring subjects . . .[2]

> Beyond a certain point, the development of the productive forces becomes an obstacle for capital—and the capitalist relation itself becomes an obstacle to the development of the productive forces of labour. . . . When it has reached this point, capital . . . is necessarily stripped off as a fetter.[3]

> Technology discloses man's mode of dealing with nature, the process of production by which he sustains his life, and thereby also lays bare the mode of formation of his social relations. . . .[4]

> . . . the historical development of the antagonisms, immanent in a given form of production, is the only way in which that form of production can be dissolved and a new form established.[5]

> . . . the direct relationship of the owners of the conditions of production to the direct producers . . . always naturally [corresponds] to a definite stage in the methods of labour and thereby its social productivity.[6]

> . . . the (economic) relations and consequently the social, moral and political state of nations changes with the *change* in the material powers of production. . . .[7]

---

[1] 'Wage Labour and Capital', pp. 89–90. Cf. *Grundrisse*, p. 109. On the importance Marx attached to this analogy, see his letter to Engels, 25 Sept. 1857, *Selected Correspondence*, p. 91.

[2] *Grundrisse*, p. 495, and cf. the reference to 'social conditions corresponding to a specific level of production' at ibid., p. 88.

[3] Ibid., p. 749.   [4] *Capital*, i. 372 n.   [5] Ibid. i. 488.

[6] Ibid. iii. 772, and see also 861, quoted on p. 108 above.

[7] *Theories of Surplus Value*, iii. 430.

It is not ignorance of these texts which leads commentators to deny that Marx assigned primacy to the productive forces. What then explains the widespread reluctance to acknowledge his belief in their pre-eminence?

One reason is a disposition to make assumptions like those we deplored on page 134, together with a conviction that the historical record does not support the primacy thesis.

A second reason is awareness of apparently contrary texts— we supplied one ourselves from the *Manifesto*—according to which, so it seems, the production relations control the development of the productive forces. This reason for resisting the primacy thesis will be dealt with in section (5).

A third reason is that the primacy thesis is considered demeaning to humanity, and therefore a view we cannot ascribe to Marx. Those who take this line stigmatize the thesis as 'technological determinism',[1] and complain that it presents machinery and allied subhuman powers as the agencies of history. On the technological view—so it is felt—the inhuman prevails against men.

This assessment displays a failure to appreciate the extensive coincidence in fact and in Marx's perception between the development of the productive forces and the growth of human faculties. Once we notice that the development of the forces is centrally an enrichment of human labour power[2] the emphasis on technology loses its dehumanizing appearance. A development of productive power is an advance in the 'mode of self-activity of individuals'. It proceeds in tandem with a 'development of men'.[3]

The capacity to enslave men belongs primarily to social relationships, not material powers: it is the production relations which become fetters, when they impede material development. To put the point hyperbolically: productive forces do not

[1] Technological determinism is, presumably, two things: it is technological, and it is determinist. One may envisage a non-technological determinism, and, as it were, a technological non-determinism. Our version of historical materialism may be called technological, but the issue of determinism will not be discussed in this book. One remark bearing on that issue: in so far as the course of history and, more particularly, the future socialist revolution are, for Marx, inevitable, they are inevitable not despite what men may do, but because of what men, being rational, are bound, predictably, to do.

[2] See Ch. II, pp. 41–2.

[3] These quotations are drawn from passages on p. 143 above.

enslave men because men cannot be slaves to their own capacities.

Now this *is* hyperbole, because there is a sense in which the productive forces may dominate the men whose forces they are, and Marx says so:

> . . . the multiplied productive force, which arises through the cooperation of different individuals as it is determined by the division of labour, appears to these individuals, since their cooperation is not voluntary, but has come about naturally, not as their own united power, but as an alien force existing outside them, of the origin and goal of which they are ignorant, which they thus cannot control, which on the contrary passes through a peculiar series of phases and stages independent of the will and the action of men, nay even being the prime governor of these.[1]

History is the development of human power, but the course of its development is not subject to human will. This does not put something extra-human at the centre of history. It certainly qualifies the sense in which 'men make their own history',[2] but it happens, for good or ill, to be true, until we reach the 'conscious organisation of society' that comes with communism.[3]

Some Marxists turn away from the tangled question of the respective roles of productive forces and production relations in history and assert that the 'motor' of history is the class struggle.

Now it is true that for Marx the *immediate* explanation of major social transformations is often found in the battle between classes. But that is not the fundamental explanation of social change.

Consider the partly analogous struggle between states, and how it explains what it explains. Warfare and its outcome have to a large extent determined where the borders between countries appear on the map of Europe. But no one who wants those borders explained will be content with an answer which terminates in a citation of the relative military strengths at various times of contending armies. He will want to know why the strong were strong and the weak weak.

The explanatory power of the class struggle is similarly

---

[1] *German Ideology*, p. 46, and cf. p. 82.
[2] 'Eighteenth Brumaire', p. 247.
[3] *Capital*, iii. 88.

restricted. Capitalism develops when and because the bourgeoisie prevails against pre-bourgeois ruling classes, and
socialism begins to be built when and because the proletariat
defeats the bourgeoisie. But why does the successful class
succeed? *Marx finds the answer in the character of the productive forces.*
'The conditions under which definite productive forces can be
applied are the conditions of the rule of a definite class of
society.'[1] The class which rules through a period, or emerges
triumphant after epochal conflict, is the class best suited, most
able and disposed, to preside over the development of the
productive forces at the given time. Hence Marx frequently
allows that a dominant class promotes not only its own interests
but, in so doing, those of humanity at large—until its rule
becomes outmoded, and it becomes reactionary—and he gives
no explanation of class supremacy which is not founded on the
productive needs of the relevant age. A characteristic statement:

> the interests of the species in the human kingdom, as in the animal
> and plant kingdoms, always assert themselves at the cost of the
> interest of individuals, because these interests of the species
> coincide only with the *interests of certain individuals,* and it is this
> coincidence which constitutes the strength of these privileged
> individuals.[2]

Another familiar argument against the primacy of the productive forces in Marx is stated in a clear manner by Vernon
Venable:

> . . . if any further refutation of the technological interpretation of
> historical materialism were required, it need only be pointed out
> that the Marxian revolutionary injunction calls upon the workers
> of the world to direct their energies not against the present
> instruments of production but against the *social relations* in which
> they are currently encompassed. The transition from the capitalist
> to the socialist mode of production demands the scrupulous
> preservation of capitalist technics; what goes overboard is the
> set of social relations whereby the fruits of these instruments of
> production are privately appropriated. The change is accom-
> plished not by tampering with the technics but by the substitution

---

[1] *German Ideology,* p. 85.
[2] *Theories of Surplus Value,* ii. 118. Cf. the reference to 'the common interests
and needs of society' on p. 232 below, and for further discussion and citations see
my 'Workers and the Word', pp. 381–5.

of public for the present private ownership of them—a social and not a technical matter.[1]

But Marx enjoins the workers to bring about social change, not what *explains* social change. What explains it is already present, and gives him confidence his call will be heeded—the exhaustion of the productive creativity of the old order, the availability of enough productivity to install the new.[2] The revolution does not *consist* in an alteration of the productive forces but, as Venable says, in a transformation of social relations. But it takes place because the expansion of productive power has been blocked, and the revolution will enable it to proceed afresh. The function of the revolutionary social change is to unlock the productive forces.

With focus on the development of the productive forces, history becomes a coherent story. Perhaps history is not really coherent, but Marx thought it was, and he said the development of material power made it so.[3]

(4) *The Case for Primacy*

So much for *Marx's* commitment to the development and primacy theses. We now proceed to a more venturesome and perhaps foolhardy business, namely, to assemble some reasons for thinking the theses are true. Some reasons only, and they will impress different readers differently.

We begin with thesis (a), the development thesis: the productive forces tend to develop throughout history. (a) will be defended as follows. First, we sketch an argument for it whose premises are two permanent facts of human nature, and one fact about the situation human beings face in history. The conclusion of the argument is that the productive forces have a systematic tendency to develop. But the argument has weaknesses, which are noted. We then, however, bring to bear a striking historical datum: that societies rarely replace superior productive forces by inferior ones. This datum is used, in a somewhat indirect manner, to refurbish an initially moot

---

[1] *Human Nature: The Marxian View*, p. 95.
[2] In melodramatic terms: 'History is the Judge—its executioner the proletarian.' 'Speech at the Anniversary of the *People's Paper*', p. 360.
[3] Letter to Annenkov, 28 Dec. 1846, *Selected Correspondence*, pp. 30-1.

argument. The resulting defence of the development thesis is not conclusive, but it may have some substance.

Many Marxists will be surprised by our reference to human nature, and appalled at our intention to use supposed facts of human nature as a source of argument in favour of historical materialism. Human nature, they will say, changes in the course of history: there is no single human nature on which to found reasoning about history's course.

It is a Marxist tradition to deny that there exists an historically invariant human nature.[1] The point is made against conservatives who fix on some historically virulent behaviour pattern (usually an unpleasant one), assign it to human nature, and conclude that the pattern will appear in every society, or be eliminated only by extreme tyranny. (It is against human nature: for people not to be greedy, for them to be uncompetitive, for democracy to work, for real equality to prevail, etc.) But it is not necessary to claim, in response, that there are no quite permanent facts of human nature. All that need be denied is that the particular feature the conservative emphasizes is one of them.

It must be agreed that there are enduring facts of human nature. For man is a mammal, with a definite biological constitution, which evolves hardly at all in some central respects throughout millennia of history. To be sure, one fact of this mammal's nature is that its excellent brain enables it so to transform its environment and itself that there are limits to what may be inferred about society and history from biology. But some inferences are possible, and we performed one or two in the last sentence. The proposition that human nature changes in history is importantly true in some important sense of 'human nature', but it is also true that there are permanent attributes of human nature, in some equally important, perhaps the same, sense.

Marxists who deny the existence of a general human nature declare that how people are depends on the structure of the society they live in: if society is so-and-so, personality and behaviour will be such-and-such. Must they not, however, accept that human beings have a nature in virtue of which a given form of society shapes their behaviour in a particular way?

[1] Marx was not the founder of this tradition. See, e.g., *Capital*, i. 609.

The reply might be that the 'underlying' nature is itself transient, bequeathed by previous history. But at some place in what may need to be a complex picture of layers and strata the contribution of biology will have to be acknowledged.

A distinct argument against the relevance of human nature to the explanation of historical development is that what is itself unchanging cannot explain alteration.[1] But the premiss of the argument is worthless. A well-known way of cooking meat is by constant application of a heating element at constant temperature. The same exercise, day in and day out, may turn a weakling into an athlete. And so on.

We conclude that whatever defects the argument for (a) we now begin to offer has, its reliance on claims about what people are like in all times and places is not one of them.

A measure of acceptance of the development thesis may be motivated by reflection on three facts:

(c) Men are, in a respect to be specified, somewhat rational.
(d) The historical[2] situation of men is one of scarcity.
(e) Men possess intelligence of a kind and degree which enables them to improve their situation.

Rational beings who know how to satisfy compelling wants they have will be disposed to seize and employ the means of satisfaction of those wants. Men are certainly rational to some extent in this respect, and it is the pertinent respect here.

Here is what we understand by scarcity: given men's wants and the character of external nature, they cannot satisfy their wants unless they spend the better part of their time and energy doing what they would rather not do, engaged in labour which is not experienced as an end in itself. Human need, whatever may be its historically various content, is rarely well catered for by unassisted nature. Some mammals get what they need easily, while for others life is an endless struggle for sustenance. Men would, apart from special cases, be among the unlucky ones, except that they, uniquely, can continually refashion their environments to suit themselves. This is because of (e). Mammals with less intelligence are unable to effect cumulative

---

[1] See, e.g., Plekhanov, *The Monist View*, p. 45.

[2] 'Historical', as used here, excludes situations in which nature is very 'lavish': see Ch. I, p. 23.

improvements in their habitats, with each generation building on the achievements of its predecessor.

(e) tells us that men are disposed to reflect on what they are doing and to discern superior ways of doing it. Knowledge expands, and sometimes its extensions are open to productive use, and are seen to be so. Given their rationality ((c)), and their inclement situation ((d)), when knowledge provides the opportunity of expanding productive power they will tend to take it, for not to do so would be irrational. In short, we put it as a reason for affirming the development thesis that its falsehood would offend human rationality.

Our argument sketch has two large gaps. The first is that (d) does not disclose the relative magnitude of man's material problem and consequent interest in its solution, by comparison with other human problems and interests. Perhaps certain cultural and social possessions are worth a great deal of material sacrifice, in the calculus of human welfare. Whether the falsehood of the development thesis would offend rationality demands a judgement of the comparative importance of potentially competing human interests.

Suppose the correct judgement favours our case. The argument would remain seriously unfinished. For it is not evident that societies are disposed to bring about what rationality would lead men to choose. There is some shadow between what reason suggests and what society does. Further considerations are required to show that the shadow is not unduly long.

Historical materialism fills the gulf between the demands of reason and the actual tendency of history by maintaining—see page 149—a rough correspondence of interests between ruling classes and humanity at large. But it would be question-begging to employ this claim as a means of repairing the present argument for the development thesis, thesis (a), since the claim is closely related to the primacy thesis ((b)), and it is our intention to use (a) as part of the argument for (b) (see page 158 below).

So our argument for the development thesis is incomplete. Yet it is a fact—and here we turn from general argument to the record of history—which needs to be explained, that societies rarely replace a given set of productive forces by an inferior one. And *certain* exceptions to this broad generalization are of no theoretical consequence. Natural disasters may occasion decline in productive strength, but historical theory should not be expected to handle them. It cannot legislate for or against 'chance' convulsions, even though they influence the course of history. An account of how crystals form ignores cases in which the containers of the process are violently shocked. Historical theory must, similarly, be content to grasp *normal* cases. We return to this point shortly.

Our broad generalization is that good productive forces do not yield to less good ones, in the normal run of things. Part of the explanation is inertia. There is a strong partly unreasoned attachment to the inherited productive forces, as to nearly everything in human life. People adapt themselves to what they are used to. *Yet productive forces are frequently replaced, by better ones.* So inertia is too unselective to explain, by itself, lack of regression, in face of the fact that there is often conspicuous progress.

At this point let us recall statements (c) to (e) of page 152, the premises of our original argument for the development thesis. Our faith in the explanatory reach of those statements was weakened when we noticed the two gaps in the argument we constructed around them. It was difficult to estimate the size of those gaps, and correspondingly difficult to assess the weight of premises (c) to (e). But note that if (c) to (e) are accepted as indeed weighty, they will provide us with a superior account of the marked lack of regression in productive power we have just been emphasizing. They would help to explain the mentioned discrepancy between the rarity of regression and the frequency of progress. And that is a reason for allowing that statements (c) to (e) have more weight than we came to fear. But once that is allowed, we are able to take a more sanguine view of the original argument than that to which we retreated. We are freshly entitled, once (c) to (e) are rehabilitated in the suggested manner, to say that they provide a good argument for the development thesis. In short: because the premises of the original argument would help to explain the notable lack of regression, there is reason to use them as an argument in favour of asserting the propensity to advance formulated in the development thesis.[1]

[1] The argument of the last two paragraphs has a complex structure, which it will be well to make explicit here. The relevant propositions are:

We do not claim for history as a whole that unbroken development of the productive forces which is peculiar to capitalist society. Instead, we predicate a perennial tendency to productive progress, arising out of rationality and intelligence in the context of the inclemency of nature. The tendency has more and less dramatic results at different times.

We have proceeded as though regression in productive power were in some sense always an option, yet one that is rarely selected because of the preponderance of reason against it. We may now add that reversion to more primitive productive forces is often technically unfeasible. Once agriculture is linked with town industry, which supplies machinery, fertilizers, and much of the animal feedstock to the farmer, it becomes impossible, or virtually impossible, to sustain human life under return to pre-industrial cultivation and husbandry.[1] A further point: enhanced productivity not only satisfies extant needs more easily, but also engenders new ones, which the old means could never fulfil. 'Before the discovery of the steam engine people managed without it. Now this is no longer possible.'[2] For example: once railways are in use, it is hard to go back to horse-drawn modes of transport, partly because after a time the population of horses dwindles and the crafts of coachmaking, grooming, etc., disappear, but also because it is hard to renounce the increased mobility the railways bring.

(p) The productive forces rarely move backwards (the 'broad generalization').
(q) There is inertia in human society.
(r) Statements (c) to (e) have considerable explanatory weight.
(s) The productive forces often move forwards.
(a) The productive forces tend to develop throughout history (the development thesis).

(Note that (s) is not the same as (a). (s) is an entailment of (a)', which was distinguished from (a) on p. 135.)

The argument then proceeds as follows:

   1. (p) is true.
   2. If (q) were the whole explanation of (p), we should expect (s) to be false
But 3. (s) is true
Hence 4. (q) is not the whole explanation of (p).
   5. If (r) were true, (p) would be better explained than it is by (q) alone.
Hence 6. There is good reason for thinking that (r) is true.
But 7. If (r) is true, there is good reason for accepting the original argument (pp. 152–3).
So 8. There is good reason for accepting that argument.

[1] See *Grundrisse*, pp. 527–8.
[2] Engels, 'On the Erfurt Programme', p. 58.

There are, however, exceptions to the generalization that the productive forces, though indeed capable of stagnation, do not, barring natural disaster, actually go into reverse. There is little doubt, for example, that the decline of the Roman Empire was accompanied by an appreciable deterioration in the productive forces of Europe. For one thing, the collapse of the imperial order undermined the security essential to long distance interchange of products, and this worked against the maintenance of the achieved division of labour, and hence against the transmission down the generations of the skills and techniques whose exercise could be rewarding only with that division of labour.

We noted (p. 154) that a theory of history is not answerable to abnormal occurrences, but we did not specify criteria of normality. A destructive earthquake is manifestly abnormal, but many cases, such as that of Rome, will be much harder to decide, and criteria of normality will be needed to settle them. A glance at another domain will convey some idea of what is required.

We have a concept of a healthy organism, one which functions normally. Physiology, the study of its proper functioning, contributes to but is distinct from the science of pathology, which investigates the causes of malfunctioning, and its course. Physiology says what *the* kidney does. Its statements have predictive content, but not in a straightforward way. Certainly their truth does not vary with the incidence of kidney disease in the population.

Now *if* we could devise a concept of a normal society comparable to that of a normal organism, we could then distinguish between historical theory and historical pathology, and we could enter the development thesis as an hypothesis within the former. It should not be impossible to construct a suitable concept of social normality, but the attempt will not be made here.

To be sure, we could not make it a defining property of a normal society that it tends to increase its productive power, for then a central hypothesis about our subject matter would be guaranteed true by the limitation we placed on its scope. Nor, for the same reason, could it be a defining feature of a normal society that its production relations are adjusted to its productive forces (apart from revolutionary periods, when maladjustment is normal, part of the 'birth pangs' of the new society, in Marx's metaphor). We would seek a demarcation of our subject matter under guidance of our leading theses, but they could not in and of themselves supply it, without vicious circularity. Finally, we should expect any concept of a normal society to be less clear and less easy to apply than that of a healthy organism. We must remember that the matter of history resists very refined conceptualization.

In *The German Ideology* Marx and Engels say that productive achievements are fragile when their incidence is only local, for then

> mere chances such as irruptions of barbaric peoples, even ordinary wars, are sufficient to cause a country with advanced productive forces and needs to have to start right over again from the beginning,[1]

as would not be necessary were the country surrounded by others which shared its level of productive development. This passage, by virtue of what it denominates 'chance', suggests an idea of normality, since chance events, by definition, interrupt the normal course of things. The suggestion is that a society's condition is normal when it stands in a certain relationship of equilibrium with both nature (hence earthquakes as abnormal) and other societies[2] (hence the reference to wars in the above extract). But it would be a formidable undertaking to specify with satisfying precision the form of the relevant equilibrium.

Returning to the case of Rome, we might judge that in so far as its productive decline was due to barbarian invasion the example loses force as a challenge to historical materialism. But Rome's degeneration had 'internal' causes too, and the real problem is to define the difficult notions of 'internal' and 'external' factor in a suitably rigorous way.[3]

[1] *German Ideology*, p. 69.

[2] Cf. Plekhanov's recognition that interaction between societies 'introduces an extremely powerful element of diversity into that process of social development which, from our previous abstract point of view, seemed most schematic'. *Monist View*, p. 224.

[3] According to some Marxists (see de Sainte Croix, 'Karl Marx and the History of Classical Antiquity') the internal decay of the Empire reflected intensified class struggle, but it is unclear whether this vindicates historical materialism on our interpretation of it, according to which class struggle may, indeed, temporarily inhibit the development of productivity, but not bring about so prolonged a regression as the case of Rome perhaps displays.

We turn to the primacy thesis proper, namely that

(b) The nature of the production relations of a society is explained by the level of development of its productive forces.

The first point in favour of (b) is that a given level of productive power is compatible only with a certain type, or certain types, of economic structure. Slavery, for example, could not be the general condition of producers in a society of computer technology, if only because the degree of culture needed in labourers who can work that technology would lead them to revolt, successfully, against slave status. How wide is the range of economic structures compatible with given productive forces? We shall not supply a complete answer to this question,[1] but it is clear that with given productive forces not all economic structures are possible.

Now some Marxists who accept the primacy of the forces are content to equate it with the constraint they impose on the production relations. But that is unsatisfactory. For the constraint is symmetrical. If high technology rules out slavery, then slavery rules out high technology. Something must be added to mutual constraint to establish the primacy of the forces.

The development thesis ((a)) provides the needed supplementation. We may argue for (b) on the joint basis of (a) and the facts of constraint. (a) says that the productive forces are disposed to develop. Given the constraints, with sufficient[2] development of the forces the old relations are no longer compatible with them. Either they will have changed without lag along with productive development, or—the theoretically prescribed alternative—there will now be 'contradiction' between forces and relations. But if contradiction obtains, it will be resolved by alteration of the production relations. For otherwise they would impede further productive development, which is impossible to block indefinitely, according to (a). (It is not (a) and the facts of constraint which establish that there is lag and contradiction instead of smoothly conjoint progress. This further claim depends on the interests which conspire to support the

[1] For a partial answer, see the material in Ch. VII.
[2] See p. 135 above on 'sufficient'.

existing order, interests which—(a) insists—will not be strong enough to sustain it indefinitely.)

That completes our argument for the primacy of the productive forces. We hope it is persuasive, even though, as we predicted on page xi, it is not conclusive. Perhaps the most promising line of resistance to it would be to propose a development thesis for production *relations*, a claim, that is, that production relations tend to change in some particular direction throughout history, and not because of the growth of the productive forces within them. We submit, however, that it would be extremely difficult to substantiate any such claim.

One might wonder whether the argument we have mounted for the primacy of the productive forces, based as it is on such generalities as human rationality and intelligence, and the fact of scarcity, has anything in common with how Marx would have argued for the primacy thesis, had he addressed the issue in frontal fashion. But while Marx does not explicitly set himself to account for the primacy of which, we saw, he is so convinced, he does betray an attitude on the subject, and it is consonant with the argument we sketched. That argument is really an attempt to render explicit the premisses of such passages as these:

> As the main thing is not to be deprived of the fruits of civilisation, of the acquired productive forces, the traditional forms in which they were produced must be smashed.[1]
> . . . in order that they may not be deprived of the result attained, and forfeit the fruits of civilisation, they are obliged from the moment when their mode of intercourse no longer corresponds to the productive forces acquired, to change all their traditional social forms.[2]

These are moments when, as Marx so often says, the relations have become *fetters*,[3] and because they shackle the forces, they will be broken. But why should the fact that the relations restrict the forces foretell their doom, if not because it is irrational to persist with them given the price in lost opportunity of further inroads against scarcity? It is because the capitalist

[1] *Poverty of Philosophy*, p. 137.
[2] Marx to Annenkov, 23 Dec. 1846, *Selected Correspondence*, p. 31.
[3] See passages quoted on pp. 136, 143, 145–6.

system forbids 'all rational improvement beyond a certain point'[1] that it is destined to go under.

Marx applies this doctrine to cases, not only, as is obvious, to the forthcoming transition to socialism, but also to less global phenomena, such as the English Revolution of the seventeenth century. That episode demands study at the level of class conflict. But, as we have seen, Marx holds that a class gains and possesses power because it marches in step with the productive forces. Of course he thinks the bourgeoisie made the English Revolution, but this is offered as its underlying explanation:

> . . . the privileges, the institutions of gilds and corporations, the regulatory regime of the Middle Ages, were social relations that alone corresponded to the acquired productive forces and to the social condition which had previously existed and from which these institutions had arisen. Under the protection of the regime of corporations and regulations, capital was accumulated, over-seas trade was developed, colonies were founded. But the fruits of this men would have forfeited if they had tried to retain the forms under whose shelter these fruits had ripened.[2]

(5) The Nature of the Primacy of the Forces

We shall not provide a complete taxonomy of the various ways forces and relations affect one another. Instead, we proceed to describe what we take to be the theoretically central connection between them, the connection which specifies the nature of the primacy of the forces. We begin with unqualified statement, and then take up some complications.

We hold that the character of the forces *functionally* explains the character of the relations. (Functional explanation is a contested procedure. It is defended in Chapters IX and X.) The favoured explanations take this form: *the production relations are of kind R at time t because relations of kind R are suitable to the use and development of the productive forces at t, given the level of development of the latter at t.* (In some cases, noted below, a slightly different schema is appropriate.)

When relations endure stably, they do so because they promote the development of the forces. When relations are revolutionized, the old relations cease to exist because they no

---

[1] *Capital*, i. 482, and cf. *Grundrisse*, p. 749.
[2] Marx to Annenkov, 28 Dec. 1846, op. cit.

longer favour the forces, and the new relations come into being because they are apt to do so. Dysfunctional relations persist for a time before being replaced. During that time the character of the relations is explained by their suitability to a *past* stage in the development of the forces (and a different schema from that italicized above applies: change *'are suitable'* to *'were suitable'*, and change the second and third occurrences of *'t'* to *'t − n'* to obtain the required schema).

Thus, if the relations suit the development of the forces, they obtain *because* they suit the development of the forces. And if the relations do not suit the development of the forces, they obtain because they recently did so. (In subsequent remarks the second, or dysfunctional, case will frequently be ignored, for economy of exposition.)

The proposition that the production relations condition the development of the productive forces is, it should now be clear, not only compatible with, but entailed by, what we assert as the most important way in which the forces determine the relations. The effect of the relations on the forces is emphasized in our reading of the primacy thesis. It is that effect which explains the nature of the relations, why they are as they are. The forces would not develop as they do were the relations different, but that is *why* the relations are not different—because relations of the given kind suit the development of the forces. *The property of a set of productive forces which explains the nature of the economic structure embracing them is their disposition to develop within a structure of that nature.*

A somewhat naïve story will help to illuminate the proposed explanatory pattern. Imagine a productively weak society whose members live in equality at subsistence level, and who wish they were better off. One of them suspects that the introduction of treadmills on the bank of the river on which they rely for irrigation would increase the flow of water onto the land, raise its yield, and thus enhance their welfare. He puts his idea to the community, who are impressed, and a group is forthwith commissioned to design and construct the devices. These are then installed at suitable points on the river bank, and tested, all members of the community participating in the test. They correctly perceive the benefits regular use of the treadmills would bring, and there is a request for volunteers to man them.

But none come forward: it is a task relished by no one in the society. Nor is it feasible, for reasons we allow the reader to conjecture, for everyone to contribute just some of his time to treadmilling. Many full-time treaders are needed. It is agreed to select them by lot, and this is done. So rebarbative is the job, however, that it becomes apparent it will not be efficiently performed without severe supervision. For that role there is no dearth of applicants, and a number are, by some means, selected for it. Gradually a class structure (supervisors, farmers, treaders) rises in what was an egalitarian community. One may now say that the relations have changed because otherwise the forces would not have progressed, and that the forces do progress because the relations have changed. But it is clear, despite the second part of the last sentence, that the change in the forces is more basic than the change in relations: the relations change *because* the new relations facilitate productive progress. The story illustrates the type of primacy the forces have in the Marxian theory of history.

The bare fact that economic structures develop the productive forces does not prejudice their primacy, for forces select structures according to their capacity to promote development.[1] In what sense is the development of the forces primary, if development depends on presence of the right sort of economic structure? In this sense: that the right economic structure comes to be in response to the needs of development of the forces. Suppose the forces are at level L at time t, and will develop to higher level M at time $t+n$ if and only if relations R prevail between t and $t+n$. It does not follow that whether or not the forces develop from L to M is decided independently of the forces by the character of the economic structure. For it might be a result of the forces being L at t that a structure with relations R obtains from t to $t+n$: and that is what the primacy thesis asserts. The forces develop only within suitable relations, but it is false that whether they develop is settled independently of the forces by the character of the relations, since the forces decide the character of the relations. The primacy thesis is compatible with the truth that a certain form of economy is required for productive progress. When Plekhanov claimed that '*for every given people, at every given period of its history, the further development*

---

[1] *How* do forces select structures? For pertinent discussion, see Ch. X, pp. 292–3.

of its productive forces is determined by their condition in the period under examination[1] he could not have supposed, and did not have to suppose, that that further development would be assured no matter what the production relations were like.

Now some complications.

When we say, somewhat vaguely, that the forces explain the character of the relations, we mean that they explain some features of the relations, but not, of course, all. They might explain, for example, why the economy is serf-based, without explaining the precise distribution of rights between lord and peasant. All phenomena may be described more or less specifically, and an explanation of a phenomenon succeeds or fails relative to some finitely specific description of it, not irrespective of how it is described.[2] The genetic and environmental considerations which explain why a species developed camouflage may fail to explain why its camouflage was just that mottle of red and green. What explains the fact that the boiler exploded on Tuesday—the valve was broken on Tuesday—may not explain the more specific fact that the boiler exploded at 5.30 p.m. on Tuesday. The hand mill may explain why a certain society is feudal, and be incapable of explaining why tribute is mainly in labour dues rather than in kind, which might be explained by something other than facts about productive forces.

Explanations of the relations by the forces will be more or less impressive, according to just what features of the relations the forces explain. But this variability in explanatory power does not detract from the primacy of the forces over the relations. It does not by itself show that the relations influence the forces in a way which subverts their primacy. A species with camouflage might have developed a different camouflage in the same environment, or an offensive smell instead of camouflage, but this does not show that the species influences the environment. So, similarly, the primacy of the forces is not *immediately* affected by the circumstance that the forces do not explain all the features of the relations. Yet the latter fact does, because of its further implications, modify the primacy of the forces. Let us look at the matter more closely, with the assistance of a suitable example.

[1] *The Monist View*, p. 166.   [2] Cf. Ch. IX, p. 276.

Suppose there are two types of capitalist economic structure, both of which are possible for a society at a particular level of development. Each would stimulate productive progress, but one would favour the construction of railways, while the other would promote manufacture of motor cars instead. (This could be because railway development requires larger capital outlays, and there is greater centralization of wealth in the first structure.) Call the first variety of economic structure the RF (rail-favouring) structure, and the second the CF structure. The current level of development of the productive forces does not select between RF and CF. Both would facilitate further growth in productive power, at *initially* comparable rates, *but in different directions*: different patterns of research, exploitation of resources, etc., would ensue, according as RF or CF prevails. Suppose it is RF which obtains. Then, as we saw, it is compatible with the primacy thesis that a different structure—here CF—could have obtained at the same level of productive development. But suppose the structure which did not appear would have had different effects on the nature of further productive progress, as is true in our example. It would follow that the relations do render the forces different from what they otherwise might have been. But how much does this modify their supremacy?

In so far as the difference of effect is *qualitative*—roads rather than railways, oil wells instead of coal mines, growth of petrochemical technology as against a lack of it—it does not touch those explanations of production relations by productive forces which rely on the level of the latter, in a purely quantitative sense, in abstraction from the particular ensemble in which that level is realized. Thus, for example, some aspects of the relationship between bourgeoisie and proletariat reflect the degree of development of the productive forces as such, independently of the way that degree of development is embodied. So while the production relations would here influence the productive forces, that would not as yet affect the explanation of the relations by the forces.

But many explanations of production relations by productive forces do turn on the specific character of the forces, not just their quantitative level. Thus we can suppose that, since railways are embarked upon, there will be a trend to further centralization of capital which would not have been so strong if motor car production had been dominant. But the railway option was taken because of features of the economic structure which were not in turn explained by the productive forces. Here, then, slack in the determination of the economic structure by the productive forces eventuates in a modification on the extent to which the productive forces, just by themselves, explain pertinent features of the production relations.

Finally, it must be conceded that which among the two possible structures becomes actual is likely to make a quantitative difference too: we cannot suppose that *further* productive progress would have occurred exactly as fast under CF as it did with RF. We may still say that the *course* of development of the forces, from lower to higher levels, cannot be disturbed by the economic structure, but the *rate* at which the course is traversed does depend, in part, on features of the economic structure over which the forces exercise incomplete control. It is not written into the forces how *fast* they will grow: the character of the economy contributes autonomously[1] to settling that. (But the power over the forces here conceded to the production relations is limited. The pace of productive development cannot be indefinitely accelerated or retarded.)

Summarizing, we note several respects in which the relations condition the forces. First, they promote the development of the forces, but that is entailed by the primacy thesis as we presented it: relations obtain when and because they promote development. Second, they help to determine the particular path development takes, and this restricts the independent explanatory power of the forces, to the extent that features of the path which explain features of production relations in turn reflect features of production relations not explained by the productive forces. Finally, the relations influence the rate of productivity development, and that too qualifies the primacy of the productive forces.

Despite these qualifications, it is still possible to assert, though not to prove in short compass, that the productive forces on the whole dominate the production relations, just as one may say that on the whole the character of the environment dominates

[1] Autonomously: the feature of the economy which helps explain why the pace of development is some particular rate is not itself explained by reference to the forces.

the character of an animal species, even though the species affects the environment too.

(6) *Productive Forces, Material Relations, Social Relations*

Marx's comment on weaponry and military organization in *Wage-Labour and Capital* (quoted on p. 146 above) will improve our understanding of the way productive forces explain production relations. The passage presupposes that armies tend to maximize their destructive power, and to organize themselves to that end. That is why 'with the invention of a new instrument of warfare, firearms, the whole internal organisation of the army necessarily changed'.

Now we may distinguish two dimensions of 'the internal organisation' of an army. Suppose the army moves from rifles to machine-guns, and each machine-gun needs to be manned by three soldiers. Then it will now be efficient for the artillery to be divided into groups of three, each trio manning one gun, whereas before there was one man to each rifle, and no reason to group them in threes. This is a change in *technical organization*. But it might bring about a change in *authority structure*. It might now be advisable to designate one man in each trio as a corporal, and to vest him with certain rights over the other two—with rifles there was no reason for hierarchical distinction to cut so low. If corporals are appointed, the authority relations change in response to a development in the means of destruction, whose influence on the authority structure is mediated by the new technical relations those means require. The forces of destruction determine the technical organization and thereby determine the authority structure.

There are often two comparably related stages in the determination of the social relations of production by the productive forces. New productive forces may require new material relations of production,[1] which in turn require new social relations of production, new forms of authority, and distributions of rights.

The heavy plough (or *carruca*) introduced in the early Middle Ages provides an illustration. It was impossible to use it efficiently on the small plots of land typical before its advent. 'The old square shape of fields was inappropriate to the new

[1] See *Poverty of Philosophy*, p. 149; *Capital*, i. 386.

plough: to use it effectively, all the lands of a village had to be reorganised into vast, fenceless "open fields" ploughed in long narrow strips.'[1] The altered means of production also necessitated co-operation in tilling the soil. Co-operation is a variety of material relations of production, but its institution carried social consequences: to establish open fields worked in common the previous ownership rights in small blocks or strips of land had to be abolished.[2]

Another case of two-stage determination (from productive forces through material relations to social relations) concerns rights over the disposition of labour power. The law of settlement, which restricted the mobility of the immediate producers, was undermined by

> the irresistible pressure of the new conditions brought about by the industrial revolution. For large-scale production on modern lines a free circulation of labour was absolutely necessary. The new industries had been able to develop only because the law of settlement had been constantly broken.[3]

The productive forces demanded 'large-scale production on modern lines' with larger aggregations of labour, and therefore new material relations of production. These in turn required 'free circulation of labour', the right to move, which was then denied. Since the law forbade movement, it was broken, ignored, and finally scrapped, new social production relations forming on its ruins.

Specifically social change *consists* of change in social relations of production. But its function is to promote changes in material relations and productive forces. In our examples the outmoded ownership relations inhibit the productive forces by blocking the formation of material work relations appropriate to them.

Both Acton and Plamenatz assert the impossibility of the first stage of the explanatory sequence just illustrated—the determination of material work relations by the productive forces.

---

[1] White, *Medieval Technology and Social Change*, p. 44.

[2] Ibid., p. 54. White's discussion of the *carucca* is subjected to severe and convincing criticism by Hilton in 'Technical Determinism', but the illustration is useful even if it is partly fanciful. See also Postan, *Medieval Economy and Society*, pp. 46–8.

[3] Mantoux, *The Industrial Revolution*, p. 434.

They suppose that work relations are too closely linked with productive forces to change *as a* result of changes in the latter. They fail to see how new work relations may be adopted *because* they constitute a good setting in which to use new means of production. It is false, in the sense intended by Acton, that 'technological change necessitates changes in how men work',[1] for he means it is impossible that the first should occur without the second. This is obviously—but relevantly—false for the case of newly created means of production which have not as yet been used in a productive process. But it is also false if we confine 'technological change' to cases where the new instruments are in use, simply because they might be operated with less than full efficiency.

Acton reasons as follows.[2] Suppose a society's transportation was by singly-manned row-boat, and the row-boats are now replaced by long canoes which are best operated by two men, one paddling at either end. According to Acton, since such a canoe demands two paddlers, to invent it *is* to invent something for two paddlers, and to substitute it for the row-boats *is*, therefore, to inaugurate double-manning in navigation. As soon as the productive force is employed, the required form of work relationship appears with it.

The following story refutes Acton. The canoe is invented in a row-boat society whose culture strongly supports one-man navigation. It does not matter how it does so, but for vividness suppose there is a strong ideology of nautical heroism, and co-operative sailing is regarded as sissified. The culture is tolerant of innovation in the shape and composition of boats, so it lets the canoes in: they are introduced because they are easier to build, or because the hard wood supply needed for row-boats is exhausted, or because they are very pretty. So powerful is the ideology that it successfully forbids more than one paddler per canoe. Accordingly, the canoes are used inefficiently, though we may suppose that they are superior to row-boats even when manned singly. Thus a change in technology does not *necessitate* a change in material relations in the intended sense. We should of course expect there to be a transition to double manning in the future, with graceful or awkward adjustments in the society's

---

[1] 'On Some Criticisms, II', pp. 143-4.

[2] *Illusion of the Epoch*, p. 161. In what follows, Acton's example is simplified.

ideology. The supervenience of double manning would then be functionally explained. Acton's view makes it inexplicable, for it entails that a shift to double manning must occur immediately.

Double manning is to be expected because it is the rational way to propel the canoe, and men are somewhat rational. The connection between productive forces and material work relations is quite intimate, but not as simple as Acton proposes.

Plamenatz arrives at the same conclusion as Acton, by a different route. He denies that material work relations may *fetter* the productive forces, yet that is precisely what one-man paddling does to the canoes in our example. Plamenatz's mistake begins when he writes:

> Marx says that production (or, as he often puts it, the 'forces of production') determines the relations of production.

It may seem harmless to treat 'production' and 'productive forces' as synonyms, and in some contexts it would be, but production is, after all, a process,[1] in which forces, which are not a process, are employed, and it turns out that Plamenatz's argument is founded on the confusion of the two categories. For he goes on to say that 'relations involved in production'—his phrase for material work relations—'must change as *production* changes, and therefore can hardly become fetters on it'. And however true that may be, it does not, as Plamenatz supposes, settle the question whether material work relations can fetter the *productive forces*.[2]

(7) *'All earlier modes of production were essentially conservative'*[3]

Recall the *Manifesto* sentence quoted on page 145: 'The bourgeoisie cannot exist without continually revolutionising the instruments of production.'

The bourgeoisie is a set of men defined as such by their emplacement in the economic structure. It is that emplacement which makes them revolutionize the productive forces: a policy of innovation is imposed by competition. Capitalist production relations are, consequently, a prodigious stimulus to the development of the productive forces. But this is more than

---

[1] 'Production' may also denote the result of a process, namely of the process of production, but Plamenatz must be using it to denote the process itself.

[2] *Man and Society*, ii. 279-80. Emphasis on 'production' added.

[3] *Capital*, i. 486.

compatible with the thesis of the primacy of the productive forces as we have articulated it. It is congenial to the thesis, for we assert that the function of capitalist relations is to promote growth in productive power—they arise and persist when they are apt to do so.

Now Marx holds that no previous ruling class and no previous set of production relations stimulate productivity in a similar manner. Earlier ruling classes are, as classes, wary of change, including improvements to the material mode of production, even if some members of those classes are otherwise disposed. Hence Marx calls non-capitalist ruling classes 'conservative', in contrast with the productively revolutionary bourgeoisie.[1]

It follows that such growth in productivity as occurs in pre-capitalist ages is in at least one important sense not brought about by the then prevailing production relations. It *seems*, then, that pre-capitalist societies present a problem for the primacy thesis as we have stated it. Capitalism is the society most commonly cited in rebuttal of that thesis, yet capitalism *seems* to exemplify it best, when the thesis is functionally construed.

To accommodate Marx's conception of pre-capitalist relations, we need to clarify the opening formulations of section (5). When properly understood, they are not embarrassed by what was said about non-bourgeois ruling classes.

First some analogies. If someone claims that constitutional monarchs promote democracy, it is likely he believes that, to put it in various ways:[2]

> Having a constitutional monarch in a society promotes democracy in that society.
> Democracy is promoted in a society when it has a constitutional monarch.
> The fact that there is a constitutional monarch in a society promotes democracy in that society.

He need not believe that there is an activity, namely promoting democracy, in which constitutional monarchs engage. He could hold the subtle view that though, in the sense caught by our

---

[1] *Capital*, i. 486; 'Manifesto', p. 37; *Grundrisse*, p. 605.

[2] These ways may not be equally good, but this is not the place to judge their relative merits. The reader will understand what single thought is variously expressed here.

rough rephrasals, constitutional monarchs promote democracy, a constitutional monarch is likely to be an enemy of democracy; or the still subtler view which adds that it is because constitutional monarchs tend to be enemies of democracy that constitutional monarchs promote democracy. Again: someone who believes that a 'minimal state' promotes economic development does not believe that it engages in the activity of promoting economic development. His view is that its abstention from such activity is good for economic development.

We say that the relations which obtain at a given time are the relations most suitable for the forces to develop at that time, given the level they have reached by that time. This entails that the relations, and the class they empower, promote the development of the forces, but, we may now add, in a sense which is compatible with what Marx says about pre-capitalist relations and classes. Having the relations in question, having that class in power, may be best for the development of the forces, even though the relations and the class pose many obstacles to their development.

Pre-capitalist relations are conservative not only in that they afford no direct stimulus to the productive forces, but also in that the progress which occurs within them is very slow, when compared with what happens under capitalism. Yet though capitalism encourages a faster development of the productive forces than feudalism does, it can remain true that it is best for the forces at the time when feudalism prevails that it, and not capitalism, should prevail. (Sports cars are faster than jeeps, but jeeps are faster on boggy land.)

Associated with the contrast between capitalist and pre-capitalist relations is an ambiguity in the phrase 'forms of development', as it occurs in sentences like 'the production relations are the forms of development of the productive forces'. The forms of development may be *forms by means of which* the productive forces are developed, or, differently, *forms within which* the productive forces are developed, even if not by means of those very forms. We may take it that not all relations are forms of development in the first sense. But even a set of relations which is not the means whereby the forces within it develop may be optimal for the development of the forces during the period when it obtains.

(8) *Addendum*

Here is a fuller report of what sentences 5 and 6 of the 1859 Preface (see p. 136) do and do not entail. Each is covertly hypothetical in form. Making the form explicit, we get these formulations of 5 and 6:

5a   If a social formation perishes, then all the productive forces for which there was room in it developed.
6a   If new, higher relations appear, then the material conditions of their existence matured in the womb of the old society.

For subsequent ease of handling, we rewrite again, bringing the sentences into terminological conformity with one another:

5b   If an economic structure perishes, then it actualized its maximum productive potential.
6b   If a new and higher economic structure appears, then productivity sufficient for its emergence developed within the economic structure it replaces.

If we allow ourselves a little syntactical leeway, these are the antecedents and consequents of 5b and 6b:

p An economic structure of kind R perishes.
q An economic structure of kind R actualized its maximum productive potential.
r An economic structure of kind S appears.
s Productivity sufficient for the emergence of an economic structure of kind S developed within an economic structure of kind R.

(It is to be understood that S is a kind of economic structure just higher than R: there is no kind of structure T higher than R and lower than S, whatever Marx may have meant by 'higher'.)

We may ask of each of p, q, r, and s which, if any, of the other three follow from it, *given just the truth of 5b and 6b*. That yields twelve conditional propositions. Here they are, with an indication, in each case, of whether or not the conjunction of 5b and 6b commits one to it. (In decoding the letter-formulated conditionals, it is sometimes necessary to tinker with tenses and articles to get antecedent and consequent into the right relationship.)

(1) If p, then q. YES. This is what 5b says.

(2) If r, then s. YES. This is what 6b says.

(3) If r, then p. YES. If an economic structure of kind S appears, an economic structure of kind R must have passed away: we may take it that Marx excludes 'leaps' to S from a structure lower than R.

(4) If r, then q. YES. If S appears, R achieved its maximum productivity ((4) follows from (1) and (3)).

(5) If q, then p. NO. An economic structure may persist even though it has reached its productivity maximum. We called this *fossilization* (p. 140).

(6) If s, then r. NO. Productivity sufficient for structure S does not guarantee its emergence. We called this *miscarriage* (p. 141).

(7) If p, then r. NO. An economic structure can perish without being replaced by a superior one. What we called *regression* (p. 140) illustrates this, as does the possibly more drastic outcome envisaged in the phrase 'the common ruin of the contending classes'.[1]

(8) If p, then s. NO. R can perish without having developed productivity sufficient for the emergence of S.

(9) If s, then q. NO. Productivity sufficient for S may be achieved in R although R has not attained its productive potential.

(10) If q, then r. NO. R may actualize its productivity potential without S emerging (this follows from (3) and the denial of (5)).

(11) If q, then s. NO. R can achieve its productive potential without having developed productivity sufficient for S (this follows from (1) and the denial of (8)). In such a case S would never emerge, since R cannot, of course, develop more productivity when it has already achieved its potential.

(12) If s, then p. NO. R may develop productivity sufficient for S and yet R may not perish (this follows from (1) and the denial of (9)).

As noted on page 141, the position changes radically when sentences 2, 3, and 4 are added to 5 and 6. They rule out fossilization and regression, so (5) and (7) are now affirmed.

[1] 'Manifesto', p. 34.

This entails affirmation of (8), (10), and (11). Then the only remaining denials are of (6), (9), and (12). But if any one of these is affirmed, the other two must be also, under the revisions enforced by sentences 2, 3, and 4. We may focus on (9). Though sentences 2 through 6 allow that, as the denial of (9) entails, R's maximum productivity may be greater than the minimum needed for S, they entail that once R has achieved the minimum needed for S, it will soon achieve its own productivity maximum, if it has not done so already, since 2 through 6 imply unceasing productive development. So (9), revised to permit a modest gap in time between achievement of what is needed for S and R's climax will, so revised, be true, and (6) and (12) will follow, in similarly revised form.

The 1859 Preface, then, advances a remarkably extensive set of claims.

CHAPTER VII

The Productive Forces and Capitalism

AN IMPORTANT application of the doctrine of the primacy of the productive forces is that the capitalist economic structure

(a) emerges when and because productive power reaches a level beyond which it cannot rise within existing structures

and

(b) persists because and as long as it is optimal for further development of productive power

and

(c) *is* optimal for further development of productive power.

((c) is a simple consequence of (b).)

Section (1) demonstrates that Marx affirmed (a) in his own account of the rise of capitalism. Following a discussion of the nature of capitalism in section (2), section (3) argues for the truth of (c). A case for (b) will not be made, save in so far as (c) will be defended. Nor will the historical truth of (a), as opposed to its Marxian pedigree, be demonstrated.

Sections (4) and (5) locate capitalism in the perspective of world historical growth of productive power, and sections (6) and (7) concern the preconditions of establishing a classless society.

(1) *The Emergence of Capitalism*

Part VIII[1] of Volume I of *Capital* is devoted to the 'classical case' of the genesis of capitalism, its inception in Great Britain. Marx asks how a capitalist class, owning means of production, came to face a proletariat, owning nothing but labour power. He finds the 'secret' answer in the expropriation of a more or

[1] In English editions, which classify as Part VIII what are the last two chapters of Part VII in the original German.

less independent peasantry from the soil. Expropriation was variously achieved, but notably by acts of enclosure, which were motivated in large part by new commercial opportunities, including the florescence of a wool trade which made sheep farming, with its low labour requirements, more profitable, in many cases, than agriculture.[1] Expropriation was also encouraged by improved techniques of cultivation.[2] Fewer tillers of the soil were now needed, and redundant peasants were dispossessed. The latter became paupers and vagabonds. They were hounded by 'bloody legislation', and eventually corralled into factories.

It is often said that this important stretch of Marxian historical writing contradicts the primacy thesis. One version of the claim:

> A considerable part of the first volume of *Capital* is taken up with explaining how the decay of feudal relations of production made possible the development of new productive methods. There is no question there of the methods of production peculiar to capitalism being born in the womb of feudal society and then gradually transforming it into a capitalist society as feudal relations of property, now become fetters on these methods, give way to other relations more in harmony with them. As Marx describes the transformation, capitalist methods of production could emerge only because feudal relations of property were already giving way to others. There were no limbs to break the fetters until the fetters were broken.[3]

We are expected to conclude that Marx's account of the transition to capitalism contradicts his thesis that production relations change in response to growth in productive power.

Before answering Plamenatz, let us be clear that Part VIII is not concerned with the demise of serfdom proper. The narration begins in the last part of the fourteenth century, when 'serfdom had practically disappeared', and the 'immense majority of the population [were] free peasant proprietors', from whom a

---

[1] *Capital*, i. 718.

[2] Ibid., p. 743, and see Mandel, *Marxist Economic Theory*, p. 117.

[3] Plamenatz, *Man and Society*, ii. 282–3. Plamenatz does not cite any particular segment of Volume I, but he must mean Part VIII.

Compare the following more or less Althusserian argument:

1. The formal subjugation is the installation of capitalist production relations.
2. The real subjugation is the installation of productive forces characteristic of capitalism.

surplus was nevertheless extracted, by non-contractual means.[1]
One may ask whether the transition from serfdom to widespread
smallholding was consonant with the general theses of historical
materialism. But Part VIII is occupied with the next change,
from petty proprietorship to capitalism. It recounts the transformation of post-serf pre-proletarian producers into a proletariat. If Plamenatz has a claim, it is that this description
contradicts the sovereignty of the productive forces. We shall
see that it does not.

(1) Production relations are said to go when they fetter the
use and development of the productive forces. But not all
fettering is of forces which already exist. Existent forces are
fettered when, for example, capitalist depression makes plant
and labour power idle. But fettering also occurs when relations
block the formation and/or entry into the productive sphere of
new forces. Plamenatz's last sentence extends the 'fettering'
metaphor too far, for fettering of the second kind is not a matter
of imprisoned 'limbs', of already existing forces bursting through
relational bonds. Instead, the relations are fractured because
they do not allow new forces to form, because they do not allow
productive power to grow. As we read Part VIII, pre-capitalist
relations could not harness existing forces which Plamenatz
fails to mention, but they also forbade the formation of new
forces, and both types of restraint were relevant. Trapped by
the 'fettering' metaphor, Plamenatz did not consider blockages
of the second kind.

(2) We noted that the disfranchisement of the peasantry was
expedited by the discovery of superior methods of tillage, hence
by a growth of productive power in the countryside. 'As Marx
describes the transformation'—and nothing else is in question
here—peasant smallholding did inhibit the exploitation and
further development of the new agricultural techniques. The
existing structure 'by its very nature' excluded

---

3. The formal subjugation preceded the real subjugation. So
4. Capitalist production relations did not arise in response to the development
of the productive forces, as the primacy thesis maintains.

The premises (1–3) are true, but we shall see that they do not support the conclusion. (On the distinction between the formal and real subjugations, see Ch. IV,
pp. 101–2.)

[1] *Capital*, i. 717. On the persistence of non-contractual burdens after the demise
of serfdom proper, see Anderson, *Lineages of the Absolutist State*, pp. 17–18, 348.

the development of the social productive forces of labour, social forms of labour, social concentration of capital, large-scale cattle-raising, and the progressive application of science,[1]

then in its infancy. Individual peasants could not seize and control the fresh productive powers, still less develop them further.

The pre-capitalist relations also shackled industrial productivity. Parallel to petty proprietorship on the land was the gild structure of the town, an indispensable framework in the first phases of industrial development.[2] Here the arts of the craftsman had improved and flourished. But at a certain point the gild mode impeded further progress. It had achieved the maximum productivity of which it was capable. For 'craft labour', like 'petty agriculture', does not build up a stock of material wealth. Both 'allow of only a small surplus product and *eat up* most of it'.[3] Forward movement now demanded mobility and collectivization of labour, which were antithetical to the rules of the gilds. Mobility was needed because labour must shift to new employment as techniques change; collectivization, because more advanced facilities demand producing units integrating large numbers of men. It was essential to gild organization that units be kept small, and the gilds

> tried to prevent by force the transformation of the master of a trade into a capitalist, by limiting the number of labourers that could be employed by one master within a very small maximum.[4]

Thus

> urban labour itself had created means of production for which the gilds became just as confining as were the old relations of landownership to an improved agriculture.[5]

The development of productive power was gravely inhibited in town and country alike. The result was conflict and struggle:

new forces and new passions sprang up in the bosom of society;

---

[1] *Capital*, iii. 787.
[2] Ibid. i. 761; *Grundrisse*, pp. 499, 650.
[3] *Grundrisse*, p. 506 n.
[4] *Capital*, i. 308-9, and cf. ibid., pp. 623-4; 'Results', p. 1022.
[5] *Grundrisse*, p. 508. Cf. *Capital*, i. 761-2; Engels, *Anti-Dühring*, pp. 146-7, 205, 228, 370-2.

but the old social organisation fettered them and kept them down. It had to be annihilated; it was annihilated,[1]

and a capitalist social organization supplanted it.

Marx may be forcing the facts of history. If so, the mould into which he is pressing them is, *contra* Plamenatz, supplied by the Preface to the *Critique of Political Economy*.

(3) The productive forces Plamenatz neglects were not, it is true, 'peculiar to capitalism'. They are not the technology which comes to mind when we think of an achieved capitalist society. But the primacy thesis does not say that forces *characteristic* of capitalism preceded its arrival. It rather requires that nascent forces could not be used or developed within pre-capitalist relations, and that a capitalist structure was necessary for productive progress. 'A changed form of the mode of production and a particular stage in the development of the material forces of production are the basis and precondition'[2] of the formation of capitalism, but that stage is of course not so high that capitalism is required to bring the forces up to it. The forces 'only need be developed enough so that the formal subjugation of labour to capital can occur'.[3] If the forces of what Marx called *grosse Industrie*[4] had attended the origin of capitalism, then, according to the 1859 Preface, it would have begun to sink as soon as it had been launched. There would have been no period of its rise and consolidation, no 'historical tasks'[5] for it to accomplish.

It is just when the powers 'peculiar to capitalism' are most actual that capitalism begins its decline. When the real subjugation, manifest in huge agglomerations of fixed capital, is complete, the tendency of the rate of profit to fall asserts itself most forcibly, and recovery from slump is most difficult and protracted.[6]

We observed earlier[7] that the explanatory precedence of the productive forces allows that capitalist relations of production

---

[1] *Capital*, i. 762.
[2] *Theories of Surplus Value*, i. 389.
[3] 'Results', p. 1064.
[4] 'Large-scale industry', but gratuitously translated as 'modern industry' in many translations of *Capital*.
[5] See below, p. 201.
[6] See *Grundrisse*, pp. 679, 703, 719.   [7] Ch. VI, p. 170.

promote their development: capitalism obtains *because* it stimulates growth in productive power.

We may now add that the primacy of the forces allows that capitalist relations antedated the productive forces characteristic of capitalism. That the formal subjugation of labour to capital went before the real subjugation is consistent with the primacy doctrine. Primacy requires that improved forces backed the emergence of capitalist relations, and that the latter endured because they advanced productive power. The historical record may pose challenges to that statement, but we have derived it from Part VIII of Volume I of *Capital*, which is, accordingly, consistent with the primacy thesis.

(2) *The Capitalist Economic Structure and the Capitalist Mode of Production*

A capitalist economic structure informs an economy whose immediate producers are free labourers: they constitute a proletariat. According to historical materialism, that structure arises when and because productive power attains a moderately high level, and persists because it is uniquely suited to raise that power to very high levels. Roughly speaking: productive power between the maximum possible under petty ownership on the one hand, and a level somewhere between the steam engine and generalized use of the computer on the other, is necessary and sufficient for capitalism, because capitalism alone is fit to develop productive power from moderately high to very high levels.[1] It cannot be sustained at lower levels, and it loses its utility at levels which are very high.

The thesis that

(d) The capitalist structure arises and persists *because* it is suited to develop productive power at the stated levels

entails but is not entailed by the weaker thesis that

(e) The capitalist structure *is* suited to develop productive power at the stated levels

which is in turn distinct from

(f) No other economic structure is similarly suited.

[1] Just how high the requisite 'very high' level is must be a matter for debate, which is why we do not specify it too precisely.

In section (3) we defend (e) and (f), in the interest of (d). We defend (e) because (d) entails it. (d) does not entail (f), but (f) needs defence, because (d) is implausible unless (f) is true. The disposition of capitalism to promote productive progress at the stated levels is unlikely to explain its existence at those levels if a rival economic form would promote productive progress equally well.[1]

Section (3) argues that *only production for the sake of accumulating capital* will foster the development of the productive forces from moderate to very high levels. This establishes (e) and (f) *on the assumption that* production within a capitalist structure coincides with production oriented to the accumulation of capital, a proposition which is by no means self-evident, and which we now proceed to clarify and defend.

There are two equally standard but logically distinct Marxian definitions of capitalist society. We need to show why what satisfies each definition also satisfies the other.

The first definition features the structural property of capitalism we ourselves used to identify that form of society. It defines capitalism by reference to its dominant production relation:[2] it is the society whose immediate producers own their labour power and no other productive force. It is the economy of free labour, free from serf- or slave-like burdens, free (bereft) of means of production. This is the *structural* definition.

The alternative, or *modal* definition, refers to the purpose of capitalist production, not the structure in which it occurs. It defines capitalism as the society whose production serves the accumulation of capital. The point of production under capitalism is to use exchange-value to produce more exchange-value, and then to use the additional exchange-value to produce still more, and so on.[3]

Why should societies falling under the structural definition also satisfy the modal definition, and vice versa? What is the warrant for these claims:

(g) if the producers are free labourers, production is for the sake of accumulating capital.

---

[1] Compare the point about alternative ceremonials in Ch. IX, p. 274.

[2] See Ch. III, section (6).

[3] A modal definition is implicit at *Capital*, ii. 120.

(h) If production is for the sake of accumulating capital, the producers are free labourers.

Now (g) and (h) are true, as a matter of historical fact, when, as here, they are asserted of whole economies. Wherever the great mass of producers are free labourers, production by and large is for capital accumulation; and wherever the bulk of production has that purpose, most immediate producers are free. But the factual correlation between free labour and capital accumulation could be relatively accidental. We need to argue that it is more or less necessary, something to be expected.

We begin with (g): *if the producers are free labourers, production serves the accumulation of capital.* First, we cite historical examples in which (g) is false for units smaller than an entire economy, and we depict an unhistorical but *apparently* possible case in which it is false for a whole (imagined) economy. We need to explain why the actual examples could not be typical of a whole society, and why the unhistorical case must be merely imaginary.

The mercenaries of the Roman legions constitute our first case. Any mercenaries would do, but Marx adverted to them in particular, when he said that they represent 'wage-labour [= free labour] not employed as such',[1] since they produced no exchange-value for those who hired them. The remark evidences Marx's commitment to (g): free labourers are employed *as* free labourers only when their activity augments exchange-value. We are asking why this should be their standard employment.

In capitalist society itself not all free labour is hired for the sake of capital accumulation. Marx cites the proletarian seam-stress employed to produce clothing for the capitalist's wife. She is retained so that use-value, not exchange-value, will accrue.[2]

Finally, imagine a society of free producers all of whom work for landlords who pay them a portion of the product of their labour, say rations of grain and meat, with the use of a dwelling. Part of the product is consumed by the landlord and his house-hold, part is set aside to meet the needs of reproduction, and the rest is distributed to the labourers. Nothing is marketed, so

[1] *Grundrisse*, p. 529. Cf. ibid., pp. 468, 893; 'Results', p. 1042.
[2] *Theories of Surplus Value*, i. 159, and cf. ibid., pp. 164–5; *Grundrisse*, p. 466; 'Results', p. 1041.

nothing is produced to be exchanged, nor, *a fortiori*, for the sake of increasing exchange-value. Yet the workers are free. They are able to contract with whatever landlord they wish.[1]

The cases will come under scrutiny in a moment. First, a sketch of an argument in favour of (g):

1. The labour power of a free labourer is a commodity.

2. Hence, if labour is free, there is a labour market.

3. It cannot in general be true that there is a labour market, a practice of buying and selling of labour power, unless there are also markets for goods other than labour power: if labour is free, production of commodities is well established.

4. If labour is free and commodity production is well established, there is competition between producing units.

5. Competition between producing units imposes a policy of capital accumulation: a unit not disposed to increase the exchange-value at its disposal will lack the resources to prevail in competition.[2]

6. Hence if labour is free, production serves the accumulation of capital (thesis (g)).

3 is the premiss most likely to be challenged. Yet it is surely difficult to conceive men treating their own labour power, or that of others, as a commodity, when they do not also confer such treatment on use-values in general. In historical fact a developed labour market never precedes the institution of commodity production. And the case for 3 is further strengthened by the argument we shortly give for the unreality of the recently imagined agricultural economy.

But first, the mercenary and the seamstress need to be disposed of. They are necessarily exceptional. The mercenary, because he does not produce, and a society's wage earners cannot in general be non-producers. The seamstress does produce, and she helps to increase no one's supply of capital, but the revenue disbursed on her is derived from capitalistic

---

[1] Compare 'the free day-labourer whom we encounter sporadically in all places' in pre-capitalist society. *Grundrisse*, p. 465, and cf. Engels, *Anti-Dühring*, p. 374 n. In the fantasy constructed above the phenomenon is not sporadic but universal. (g) implies that it cannot but be sporadic in reality. Thus '. . . wherever these free workers increase in number . . . there the old mode of production—commune, patriarchal, feudal, etc.—is in the process of dissolution, and the elements of real wage labour are in preparation'. *Grundrisse*, p. 469. 'Real wage labour' in this context by definition serves to expand exchange-value. See ibid., p. 465.

[2] See the argument for thesis (j) on pp. 196–7 below.

production proper, so she is an essentially parasitic case.

We come to the fantasy example. Let us ask how the society would tend to develop. The immediate producers will want good working conditions with ample rations, and the landlords will seek good workers at minimum sacrifice to the consumption of their households. A tendency to compete for workers will arise. The rations consist of meat and wheat, and, at the outset, all farms produce both, for there is, *ex hypothesi*, no trade between them. But farms with a 'comparative advantage' in wheat and meat production respectively will be disposed to swap products, if only in order to offer an enhanced basket of rations, and thus tempt good labour away from other farms. With enough development of such trade, production with a view to expanding the stock of exchange-value would become the norm. So the imaginary society, as originally described, is unstable. A propensity to accumulation of capital would soon appear within it.[1] And we contend that in general, and for similar reasons in other kinds of case, free labour without capital accumulation will fail to endure. (In an alternative scenario, the landlords might collude to restrict labour mobility, out of a preference for a traditional, settled life. So either capitalistic production will erupt, or the freedom of labour will be eroded.)

We come to (h): *if production is for capital accumulation, the producers are free labourers*, that is, owners of labour power who lack means of production. An illustration of Marx's commitment to (h):

> The concept of capital implies that the objective conditions of labour . . . acquire a personality as against labour, or, what amounts to the same thing, that they are established as the property of a personality other than the worker's. The concept of capital implies the capitalist.[2]

Capital is self-expanding exchange-value. Marx says it 'implies' capitalist production relations, which bind capitalists

---

[1] There is no parallel argument to show that feudal manors would begin to produce for exchange-value. For as long as the serf is tied to the land, a labour supply is guaranteed, and it is impossible to attract industrious serfs from other manors.

[2] *Grundrisse*, p. 512. Our discussion presupposes, what an examination of the context of the passage will confirm, that its last sentence is not the triviality it may appear to be. It is, in fact, a compressed statement of thesis (h).

and free labourers. He adds a remark which might suggest that he takes the implication, and hence thesis (h), to be true by definition: to 'speak of the existence of *capital* . . . is *merely another way of saying* that . . . labour [is] free'.[1] Yet he knows that (h) is not true by definition, for he proceeds to acknowledge that unfree labour may serve the accumulation of capital in segments of an economy whose labour is for the most part free. American slaveholders did aim at expanding exchange-value, and Marx is prepared to consider them 'capitalists', even though they did not engage proletarians. They were 'anomalies within a world market based on free labour'.[2] The *antebellum* South was possible only because it was exceptional. It could only have been what it was: a malformation in an otherwise normal capitalist economic structure.

Another affirmation of (h), this time explicitly with respect to an entire economy:

> wage-labour on a *national scale* (and consequently the capitalist mode of production as well) is only possible where the workers are personally free.[3]

'Wage-labour' is usually also 'free labour', as Marx uses the terms, but this passage is an exception.[4] Here wage-labour is labour, free or otherwise, which receives a monetary reward. If wage-labour were free by definition here, the sentence, apart from the bracketed portion, would be trivially true, and the qualifying phrase, 'on a national scale', would be inexplicably redundant. Marx is agreeing that slaves could receive wages, but denying that the great mass of producers could be wage-receiving slaves.

The sentence is syntactically complex, and what it says is easier to survey in this semantically equivalent rewrite: 'If

[1] *Grundrisse*, p. 513. Emphases added, except on 'capital'.

[2] *Idem*, and cf. ibid., pp. 224, 464; *Capital*, iii. 655, 784; *Theories of Surplus Value*, ii. 302–3.

The assignment of an anomalous status to plantation capitalism does not contradict whatever is true in the claim that 'the veiled slavery of the wage-earners in Europe needed, for its pedestal, slavery pure and simple in the new world'. *Capital*, i. 759–60, and see *Poverty of Philosophy*, pp. 124–5.

[3] *Theories of Surplus Value*, iii. 431, emphases added. 'On a national scale' is a misleading surrogate for something like 'across an entire economy', which could include more than one nation-state.

[4] The context explains the deviant use. Marx is discussing Richard Jones, who spoke of free and unfree wage-labour, the latter being slaves who receive money.

wage-labour prevails on a national scale, then so does free labour; therefore if the prevailing mode of production is capitalist (if production serves the accumulation of capital), the producers are (by and large) free labourers.' What follows the semicolon is thesis (h).

So much in evidence of Marx's espousal of (h). We proceed to consider potential challenges to (h), cases of production for expansion of exchange-value without free labour. We must show that they are necessarily imaginary, exceptional, or transitory.

The first challenge comes from what seems, initially, to be a possible variant of simple commodity production. In simple commodity production the producers are self-employed market exchangers. They are not free labourers, since they own their means of production. Yet could they not produce for the sake of accumulating capital? It is irrelevant here that simple commodity production has never in fact characterized an entire economy.[1] What does matter is that if it were general and, moreover, oriented to the expansion of exchange-value, then it would rapidly transform itself into capitalist commodity production. In the competition between producers, some would prosper and others would fail, and be reduced to labouring for the successful ones. This is just what tends to happen where simple commodity production in fact obtains. A 'process of social differentiation'[2] slices the set of simple commodity producers into a rudimentary bourgeoisie and a rudimentary proletariat.

Simple commodity production, then, supplies no refutation of (h), and we can restrict our attention to production for capital accumulation *with class subordination*. The question, is (h) true?, is the question whether the class must be proletarian. So we now reckon with cases of production for capital accumulation where the producers are unfree.

One such case has already appeared: production for exchange-value by slaves. Marx deemed it essentially subsidiary, but according to John Hicks it was purely contingent that free labour rather than slavery accompanied early Euro-

---

[1] See Catephores and Morishima, 'Is there an "Historical Transformation Problem"?', pp. 314–15.

[2] The phrase is Dobb's: *Capitalism, Development and Planning*, p. 12.

pean capitalism: there were no slaves to be had, because 'the main potential source of slaves, to the south and east, was blocked by the military power of Islam'.[1]

The 'second serfdom' in Eastern Europe of the fifteenth and sixteenth century is our next putative counter-example. Feudal burdens were imposed on the peasantry in response, so it has been claimed,[2] to mounting commercial pressures and opportunities, associated with the export of grain westwards. On this account, labour became *more* unfree as and because production became *more* oriented to exchange-value. Thus Engels, writing with special reference to Germany, says that 'the capitalistic period announced itself in the country districts as the period of agricultural industry on a large scale, based upon the *corvée* labour of serfs',[3] a formulation in apparent conflict with the correlations maintained by historical materialism, in particular thesis (h), that capitalistic production requires wage labour.

Finally, let us imagine a form of unfree labour attached to production for accumulation of capital in an industrial setting, and on a total social scale. The ironworkers of early industrial South Wales can serve as a model here. They were tied to their employers for life, so that the costs of training them would be recouped.[4] Conceive this to be general across an industrial society.

We shall now argue that, despite these examples, serfdom and slavery are in principle opposed to production for the accumulation of capital.

Take agricultural serfdom first. The landed serf sustains himself on the fruits of his own labour, consuming what he produces with means of production he controls. He largely abstains from market exchange, as buyer or as seller. Accordingly, much of what is produced is not marketed, and production for exchange, and *a fortiori* for the expansion of exchange-value, is possible only to a restricted extent. The lord may be more involved in market transactions, and hence in the pursuit of exchange-value, but the serf's self-sufficiency erects a barrier to the extension of production for exchange-value. A mass market simply is not there.

---

[1] *A Theory of Economic History*, p. 134.
[2] See Anderson, *Passages from Antiquity to Feudalism*, p. 258(19), for references.
[3] 'The Mark', p. 177.   [4] Ashton, *The Industrial Revolution*, p. 112.

What, then, of the 'second serfdom'? On Perry Anderson's account of the matter, which we shall follow, there is no case to answer: he rebuts the view that the export market was fundamental to the imposition of serfdom east of the Elbe.[1] The second serfdom embarrasses thesis (h) only if it was largely due to a heightened pursuit of exchange-value, as opposed, for example, to the relatively exposed position of the peasantry in the Eastern class struggle, which is Anderson's alternative emphasis.

According to Anderson, the enserfment of the peasantry in the East depended on the weakness of the towns in that region. Western peasants threatened with impositions could flee to the city, but their Eastern counterparts had no such recourse.[2] The urban bourgeois class in the East had lost its muscle,[3] and the grain trade with the West was conducted by the feudal landowners themselves.[4] (In so far, then, as we do find serfdom accompanying a measure of production for exchange-value, the commerce includes no local bourgeoisie and is with distant parts themselves following a more standardly capitalist path: additional reason for rejecting the second serfdom as an argument against thesis (h).)

Industrial quasi-serfdom presents a different problem, since here the labourer does not produce what he consumes: the early Welsh ironworkers did not live on iron. In some respects they were like slaves, for the whole of their output passed into the exploiter's hands, and to the extent that they resemble slaves they are indirectly dealt with in the discussion of slavery to follow. Their non-slave but serf-like quality lay in the fact that they had the right to remain for life as ironworkers in the foundries to which they were committed: this reciprocity is absent in slavery. Industrial quasi-serfdom on a social scale

[1] See *Passages*, pp. 258–9, and cf. *Lineages of the Absolutist State*, pp. 196–7.

[2] *Passages*, pp. 252–3. But see Brenner, 'Agrarian Class Structure', pp. 54–6, for scepticism about this contrast, which is also drawn by Blum in his 'Rise of Serfdom in Eastern Europe', pp. 833 ff. (Anderson's 'reservations' about Blum's excellent article—see *Passages*, p. 255(14)—are demonstrably unfounded.)

[3] See Blum, 'Rise of Serfdom in Eastern Europe', p. 834.

[4] 'In Poland', for example, 'the noble class cut out local entrepots to deal directly with foreign merchants.' *Passages*, p. 254, and see also pp. 259–60. (Anderson accepts that there was an appreciable export trade, but denies its importance for the explanation of the imposition of serfdom. He allows that it contributed to an increase in the exploitation of the already enserfed.)

would in short time prove incompatible with production for the accumulation of capital, partly for reasons listed in the treatment of slavery below, and partly because a developing capitalist economy becomes too fluid for entrepreneurs to profit by offering lifetime contracts to producers.

The considerations thus far adduced do not tell against a union of capital accumulation and slavery. The whole of the slave's product belongs to a master who could market all of it and supply the slave with a wage he would cash in for means of subsistence. So it appears compatible with slavery that all products should pass through a market and, moreover, serve the accumulation of capital. We found Marx acknowledging the capitalist character of slavery in the Southern United States, and countenancing slaves receiving wages on a local scale. Why could slavery not be general, in a context of production for expansion of exchange-value?

It might seem that a famous argument based on the labour theory of value supplies the answer. Having expounded the concept of capital as self-expanding exchange-value $(M–C–M')$, Marx asks how it is possible for exchange-value to increase in the absence of force or fraud. He replies that a commodity must be found whose use creates more exchange-value than it has. He then identifies the labour power of the proletarian as the requisite commodity. It is sold in temporal packets by the free labourer to the capitalist employer, who pays for it a sum corresponding to its costs of reproduction, hence to its value. Market justice is observed, but the value of the labour power is less than the value of what it produces, and thereby the capitalist expands his stock of exchange-value. 'The trick has at last succeeded.'[1]

But even if the labour theory of value is true, this reasoning is unacceptable as a derivation of free labour from the definition of capital as self-expanding exchange-value.[2] For two features

[1] *Capital*, i. 194, and cf. *Grundrisse*, pp. 463–4.
[2] We do not say that Marx intends the reasoning to serve this purpose. *His* concern is to find a commodity which will enable exchange-value to expand *in bourgeois society*, where by definition all men have full liberal freedom and meet as juridical equals, so that slavery is excluded. We must drop the assumption of bourgeois society, since precisely what we are trying to show is that *production for expansion of exchange-value will be the norm only in a bourgeois society*. The underlined is but a way of formulating thesis (h).

of the sale of labour power as Marx describes it are extraneous to the argument, so conceived. First, there is no reason why the labour power must be leased for a limited period only: the capitalist could obtain a freehold on it. Second, there is no reason why the vendor of the labour power must be the person in whom it inheres: instead of the producer himself, the seller could be someone who owns him. In short, the labour theory of value does not entail that the 'LP' in the circuit of industrial capital[1] cannot be the labour power of a slave. Its value would still reflect the amount of labour time required to produce what sustains him, and this could still fall short of the amount he performed, thus enabling the accumulation of capital.

No abstract proof will show that slavery and production for the expansion of exchange-value are opposed in tendency. We nevertheless agree with Marx that plantation capitalism necessarily did not arise out of slavery, but was 'grafted on to it'.[2] But Hicks thinks capitalism could have proceeded on a slave basis. Why is he wrong? Why is production for the expansion of exchange-value antithetical to slave labour?

One reason, of somewhat Marxist flavour, which Max Weber would have given in answer to the question rests on the uncertainty which afflicts production for exchange-value, the danger that what has been produced will not be sold:

> The human capital consumes more in the very moment when the market fails, and its upkeep is a very different matter from that of a fixed capital in machines.[3]

But this seems inadequate. In slavery strictly so called, the exploiter is not obliged to maintain an idle slave. It might be said that he would have an interest in feeding him, pending a revival of the market, when he could again set him to work, but the ordinary capitalist has a similar (weak) interest in preserving the life of the free labourer, yet he lets him loose, hoping to hire fresh labour when the market revives; and the capitalistic slave-owner could, analogously, buy new slaves when business improves, possibly with funds he acquires in bad times by selling surplus slaves to others whose sales are less depressed.

---

[1] See Appendix II, p. 352.
[2] *Theories of Surplus Value*, ii. 303.
[3] *General Economic History*, p. 105.

To be sure, the slave *might* be a liability, the suggested shifts might be difficult to manage: it depends on circumstances. But nothing so circumstantial can provide a reason of principle against a union of slavery and capital accumulation. Similar reservations apply to Weber's further claim that the death of a slave would be an uncompensated loss, 'in contrast with . . . conditions in which the risks of existence are shifted on to the free workers'.[1] The point has no force if a normal rate of (literally) natural wastage is assumed, and anyway someone would be quick to establish an appropriate insurance business, if the matter did present a problem.

Our own case for the contradiction between slavery and production for expansion of exchange-value does not depend on the vagaries of the market. Instead, we take as cardinal the fact that capitalistic production presupposes a considerable development of productive power, and leads to further enhancement of it.[2] Accordingly, if slavery is hard to put together with high and rising levels of productive power, it will not readily consort with capital accumulation, which is what we need to show. And there are several reasons for thinking that slavery and sophisticated, improving productive forces exclude one another.

First, it is difficult to conceive the provident habits and skilled craftsmanship which capitalism needed in the labour force it took over as faculties of slaves. The education presupposed by these abilities, and the sense of personal worth associated with them, cannot be united with slave status. In this connection, Marx avers that slavery is compatible with the use of only 'the rudest and heaviest implements and such as are difficult to damage owing to their sheer clumsiness'.[3] This is not

[1] *Idem.*

[2] These claims are expounded in section (3). Although parts of section (3) presuppose parts of the present section, the dependencies are not such as to make this particular forward reference viciously circular.

[3] *Capital,* i. 196 n.

Marx's statement may appear to be falsified by the fact that there were many skilled slaves in ancient Rome. Closer inspection suggests otherwise. The skilled slaves, despite their formal legal status, had, in practice, more autonomy than the concept of slavery allows: their labour power was not effectively controlled by others in the total way required to put them in the 'Slave' slot in Table 1 of p. 65. They were, moreover, and unlike agriculture slaves, commonly able to buy their freedom with their earnings, and it is a plausible speculation that they would not have exercised their skills quite so competently but for the prospect of manumission—and manumission could not, for obvious reasons, be the usual

the technology appropriate to the artisanship which was a necessary prelude to capitalism, nor, of course, does it permit the rapid development of the productive forces which issues from the universal pursuit of exchange-value once capitalism is established.

Secondly, slaves must not only be fed and housed, but strictly policed: they require more extensive supervision than do free workers. This prompted Adam Smith to judge that slave labour, though apparently cheap, was 'in the end the dearest of any'.[1] The point can no doubt be exaggerated, but it does mean that there is an unwelcome drain on the surplus slaves produce.

Third, rising productivity leads sooner or later to a rising standard of consumption among the producers, and that stimulates an enlarged self-awareness and a self-assertion which are difficult to reconcile with persistence of enslavement.[2]

In the last argument, the relevant aspect of rising productivity was its sheer volume, or quantitative level. But that level—and here we reach our fourth consideration—is achieved as a result of material relations of production comprising increasing interconnection of labourers both within producing units and across the labour force. The unionization of the working class, so characteristic of capitalist economies, reflects the pressures and opportunities associated with the said material relations. Those pressures and opportunities would not all be absent in a hypothetical slave capitalism, where, however, unionization would by definition be excluded. They would instead lead, in all probability, to successful rebellion against the slave condition.

Weber-like arguments turn on the supposed disutility to the capitalist of enslaved producers. Our own emphasis is on the consciousness and will of the producers themselves. There would be no incompatibility between capitalism and docile slaves at work on advanced productive forces: twentieth-century dystopian fantasies are internally consistent. But a

---

destiny of slaves in a self-sustaining slave society. See Finley, *The Ancient Economy*, pp. 64–5, 76.

We have not *proved* that skilled craftsmen cannot be wholly at the disposal of others who own them, but the claim is supported, not refuted, by the Roman examples.

[1] *The Wealth of Nations*, p. 365. Cf. *Capital*, iii. 376–7.

[2] For comparable claims, see 'Results', pp. 1030–4, which also contains Weber-like arguments of the kind we rejected.

combination of advanced productive forces and slavish docility
is difficult to accomplish.

We may now endorse Marx's judgement, which was also, in
a sense, the judgement of history, that plantation capitalism in
the South was necessarily a secondary phenomenon. It throve
on a vastly increased and growing market for textile goods,
reflecting just that burgeoning of the productive forces which
makes production for expansion of exchange-value antithetical
to generalized slavery.

(3) *Capitalism and the Development of the Productive Forces*

'The general presence of wage labour presupposes a higher
development of the productive forces than in the stages preceding wage labour'[1] for 'wage labour as such enters only where
the development of the productive forces has already advanced
so far that a significant amount of time has become free'.[2]
'Wage labour' is Marx's metonymy for the capitalist economic
structure.[3] He is therefore asserting that the capitalist economic
structure can appear only once productive power is already
fairly advanced. We saw in section (1) that he thinks it is
brought to that modestly high level by the exertions of individual
producers in urban gilds and petty agriculture.

But why should the capitalist structure require this prior
growth of productive power? With the results of section (2) in
hand, we can explain.

Until it has already reached a moderately high stage of
development, productive power can increase only slowly and
sporadically. For continuous rapid advance, productivity must
be great enough to ensure a surplus whose amplitude allows
regular formation of new means of production: 'Only when a
certain degree of productivity has already been reached . . . can
an increasingly large part [of what has been produced] be
applied to the production of new means of production.'[4]

Now to speak of 'an increasingly large part being applied to
the production of new means of production' is to use purely
material language. The phrase is a material description, but

---

[1] *Grundrisse*, p. 893.
[2] Ibid., p. 641.
[3] See *Theories of Surplus Value*, i. 200.
[4] *Grundrisse*, p. 707.

what it denotes is the material side of the social process of capital accumulation. The use of exchange-value to increase exchange-value is possible only by virtue of the denoted material process. But that material process can occur 'only when a certain degree of productivity has been reached'. Hence production for capital accumulation must await attainment of that degree of productivity.

Now we saw in section (2) that production within a capitalist economic structure will subserve the accumulation of capital: that was thesis (g). The capitalist structure cannot therefore arise until productive power is of decently large dimensions. The investment requirements of the capitalist process exclude the full appearance of capitalist relations of production before that stage is reached.

Now the fact that capitalism presupposes a technology which permits 'take-off' into sustained growth of productive power does not prove that it is the economic structure which best fosters that growth. This needs to be shown in defence of the thesis—see (d), p. 180—that the capitalist structure prevails when it does because it suits the development of the productive forces at that time. We must argue that:[1]

(i) If the productive forces progress systematically, the economic structure is capitalist.[2]

(j) If the economic structure is capitalist, the productive forces progress systematically.[3]

Section (2) established that a society has a capitalist economic structure if and only if its production aims at the expansion of exchange-value. Immediate producers are free labourers when and only when production is geared to the maximization of abstract wealth. So although (i) and (j) concern the capitalist economic *structure*, we shall be entitled, in arguing for them, to make use of the modal properties of capitalism as well as its structural ones. The modal and structural definitions (see p. 181) will be variously relevant in the ensuing arguments.

Starting with (i), we note that it is equivalent to the proposi-

---

[1] (i) and (j) are restatements of (f) and (e) respectively: see p. 180.

[2] Socialism and communism are excluded from the scope of thesis (i).

[3] (j) is, of course, false for capitalism in stagnation or crisis. An appropriate time span is implied.

tion that *non*-capitalist economic structures do *not* promote systematic productive development. Two arguments for (i) will be offered. First, non-capitalist ruling classes are not disposed to promote a prodigious development of the productive forces. Secondly, a great development of the productive forces is incompatible with unfreedom among the immediate producers.

The first argument:

1. In non-capitalist economic structures, labour is not free. Instead it is 'immediate forced labour':[1] the producers are tied to their exploiters by involuntary bonds, not as a result of contracting with them on a labour market.

2. 'In that case', if, that is, the producers are not free labourers, production will not be for the accumulation of value (this is thesis (h) of section (2)), and the only point of wealth will be 'enjoyment'.[2] The exploiter will want the producer's surplus for the sake of its use-value.

3. He will, accordingly, be content to extract a limited surplus only, since there is a ceiling to the amount of use-value he may sanely desire and feasibly dispose of:

> It is . . . clear that in any given economic formation of society, where not the exchange-value but the use-value of the product predominates, surplus labour will be limited by a given set of wants which may be greater or less, and that here no boundless thirst for surplus labour arises from the nature of the production [system] itself.[3]

4. Wanting as he does only a 'certain quantity of useful products',[4] the exploiter has no interest in promoting the means of producing greater and greater output, namely highly developed and improving productive forces.

5. Hence 'universal industry cannot unfold on the basis of immediate domination':[5] in a non-capitalist economic structure the productive forces do not progress systematically.

6. And so 'capital is an essential relation for the development of the productive forces of society',[6] which is Marx's way of asserting (i).

Step 3 appears to be the most vulnerable. Might not the exploiter want, for example, a vast number of pyramids, a

---

[1] *Grundrisse*, p. 326.   [2] *Idem.*   [3] *Capital*, i. 235.
[4] Ibid., 236.   [5] *Grundrisse*, p. 326.   [6] Ibid., p. 325.

desire which would engender a thirst for surplus labour on a massive scale? Perhaps Marx would reply: that would make the 'given set of wants' extravagant, but they would remain finite. The reply is weak, since (a) he might be so self-glorifying that he puts no limit on the number of pyramids he wants, and (b) he is mortal, and on his death the labourers subject to him will pass into the control of an heir for whom they might as yet have built nothing, and who might also want very many pyramids: an indefinite succession of large but bounded thirsts will have the same effect as a boundless thirst.

These are coherent *possibilities*, but they do not erase the main line of the argument. For, first, the thesis being propounded is that non-capitalist forms do not *in systematic fashion* promote productive growth, and that is true if, outside capitalism, 'no boundless thirst for surplus labour arises *from the nature of the production* [*system*] *itself*'. In the cases we depicted, the drive to produce more is not imposed by the economic system: it comes, instead, from the motivation of particular people. Second, pre-capitalist rulers who have the imagined extravagant desires are unlikely to combine them with a prudent disposition to set aside resources for the sake of improving productivity.[1] They want to be lavish, not sparing, with the available labour supply. It was part of the magnificence of the pyramids that great numbers of people were required to build them. They would have lost much of their point if immense effort had not been necessary for their construction.

A further basis for affirming (i) is constituted by our earlier arguments (pp. 191–3) against a union of high productive development and unfree labour. If they were sound, the productive forces can progress in non-capitalist class society only to a limited extent.

(i)'s converse, (j), is amenable to more straightforward demonstration. (j) says that capitalism *does* engender a prodigious expansion of productive power. The usual Marxist argument for (j) relies on the labour theory of value,[2] but it is

---

[1] '. . . the ancients never thought of transforming the surplus-product into capital. Or at least only to a very limited extent.' *Theories of Surplus Value*, ii. 528.

[2] The labour-theoretical version of the argument is as follows. To increase the production of exchange-value, it is necessary to increase the amount of surplus labour performed by the workers. At first this is achieved by increasing 'absolute

not essential to the conclusion. Whatever explains comparative exchange-value magnitudes, and whatever may be the source of profit on capital, exchange-value is what the capitalist firm must seek, on pain of ruin in competition. But exchange-value will not be accumulated unless use-value is produced efficiently. Opportunities to improve productivity must be found and seized, and so the productive forces move forward systematically. The imperative laid on the firm is to make money, but it can do that only by selling things, which must therefore be produced, and, because of competition, produced as competently as possible:

> . . . the goal of all capitalist production is not use-value but *exchange-value*. If one sets aside swindling, there is no way of increasing exchange-value except by increasing production. In order to increase production, it is necessary to develop the productive forces . . . To produce more goods is *never* the aim of bourgeois production. Its aim, rather, is to produce more exchange-value. It brings about the *real* expansion of the productive forces and of goods in spite of itself.[1]

So the very economy whose rulers are relatively uninterested in use-value produces more use-value, and more capacity to produce use-value, than any other class society.[2]

We conclude that the capitalist economic structure, and, among class structures, the capitalist alone, stimulates a continuous development of productive power.[3]

(4) *Four Epochs*

Disregarding sub-stages and transitional forms, we may distinguish four 'progressive epochs in the economic formation of

---

surplus value': the amount of necessary labour time remaining fixed, surplus labour time is increased, by extension of the working day, and by working labour harder ('intensification of labour'), so that the capitalist gets, as it were, more than one man-hour per worker per hour. Eventually, absolute surplus value can be increased no further, and it is necessary to increase 'relative surplus value', by raising the ratio of surplus to necessary labour in a constant working day. This requires the introduction of improved, productivity-raising, technology.

The labour-theoretical premises are not needed. It is enough that increasing exchange-value requires increasing production, and therefore demands improvement in the facilities used in production.

[1] *Grundrisse* (Berlin), p. 804, and cf. *Capital*, i. 593.

[2] This 'paradox' is explored in Ch. XI.

[3] See further *Grundrisse*, pp. 224, 334-5, 341, 770; *Grundrisse* (Berlin), p. 890; *Capital*, ii. 120; *Theories of Surplus Value*, i. 270, 282.

society', corresponding to distinct levels of development of productive power:

TABLE 4

Form of Economic Structure		Level of Productive Development
1. Pre-class society	⎫	No surplus
2. Pre-capitalist class society	⎬ Corresponding to	Some surplus, but less than
3. Capitalist society	⎪	Moderately high surplus, but less than
4. Post-class society	⎭	Massive surplus

The first correlation is obvious. A class society is by Marxian definition divided into a group which produces and a group which does not. For the latter to survive, the former must create use-value in excess of what they need themselves: there must be a surplus to sustain the non-toiling class. Accordingly, classes are excluded when productive power is so low that no surplus is available.

As long as there is some surplus, class society is possible, but if the surplus is small, it cannot yet be a *capitalist* class society (see p. 194): hence the second correlation. But why should there be classes of any kind in the second stage of productive development? The question is explored in section (7).

Next comes moderately high surplus, which is necessary for repeated introduction of new productive forces, and thus for regular capitalist investment. Like 'any other mode of production, [capitalism] presupposes a given level of the social productive forces and their forms of development as its historical precondition',[1] and this, we saw, is the level to which they are brought by small-scale industry and agriculture in dissolving feudalism and transitional post-feudal society (see pp. 178–9). Petty production generates the conditions of a further productive progress it is itself impotent to promote. Capitalism is then necessary, if development is to continue, and that, Marx says, is why it arises: see pages 175, 180–1.

If capitalism alone can promote development within productive level 3, it follows that socialism cannot do so. Its productivity precondition is massive surplus, large enough to make it no longer true that most of life and time and energy must be

[1] *Capital*, iii. 856.

spent joylessly producing means to imperative ends. The mission of capitalism is to carry humanity to that stage of abundance, whereupon it subverts itself and gives way to a classless society.

Marx would certainly have accepted the quadripartite division of social forms constructed above, and the stipulated alignment between them and distinct levels of productive power. But he did, of course, make finer structural differentiations than those given in Table 4, particularly within pre-capitalist class society, which covers a great variety of forms, of which slavery and serfdom are but the most salient. Yet did Marx suppose that *which* pre-capitalist class structure obtains may be explained in terms of the prevailing level of productive power? And if variations in productive power do not explain structural differences within pre-capitalist class society, how seriously does this embarrass historical materialism as we have presented it?

The exegetical question is not easy to answer. Marx's position on the matter is unclear, for the evidence points in opposite directions. On the one hand there is the ambitious Preface to *The Critique of Political Economy*, which certainly commits him to explanation by reference to growth of productive power of social changes beyond those canvassed in Table 4. 'Ancient' and 'feudal' society, characterized, speaking very grossly, by slavery and serfdom respectively, are among his illustrations of the theory set forth in the Preface of 1859.[1] Given that theory, and the separate billing of the ancient and feudal modes, Marx is committed to the questionable theses that serfdom requires higher productive power than slavery, that the ancient world developed productive power to a point where only serfdom could take it further, and that this explains why serfdom supervened.

Marx's numerous remarks on slavery and serfdom elsewhere, on the other hand, reveal no attempt to meet the Preface commitment. He notes the quite unPreface-like contribution to

[1] We shall not discuss the 'Asiatic Mode' of production, which is difficult to classify. See the illuminating treatment by Shaw, 'Productive Forces and Relations of Production', pp. 326–35, and the superb critique of the concept by Anderson, *Lineages of the Absolutist State*, pp. 462–96.

the genesis of serfdom of military factors,[1] and though there is also a reference to productive forces as part of its background, he does not claim that they were of a more developed character than what was known under slavery.[2] In one place he assimilates the *origins* of slavery and serfdom: both arise when producers are captured along with their means of production.[3] He also brings them together *structurally*, as societies where the immediate producer is extra-economically coerced. When he says that 'between the full development of the foundation of industrial society and the patriarchal condition, many intermediate stages, endless nuances' occur,[4] he cannot think each nuance corresponds, in the full Preface sense, to a different level of productive power. Finally, in the *Grundrisse* he essays a periodization of history more similar to Table 4 than to the divisions listed in the Preface:

> Relations of personal dependence . . . are the first social forms . . . Personal independence founded on dependence on objects is the second great form . . . Free individuality, based on the universal development of individuals and on their subordination to their communal, social productivity as their social wealth is the third stage. The second stage creates the conditions for the third.[5]

Here pre-class society is either omitted or comprehended in 'relations of personal dependence', this initially taking the unhierarchical form of unfree mutual connections.[6]

The 'endless nuances' of pre-capitalist class history resist theorization as sets of production relations whose succession reflects a series of rises in the level of productive power. But the resulting damage to historical materialism, on our strongly technological construal of it, is smaller than might at first appear:

1. Table 4, taken by itself, and unsupplemented by explanations of variants within stage 2, embodies substantial theses about the course of social development. It is, for example, no

---

[1] *German Ideology*, pp. 35, 90; *Grundrisse*, p. 165; *Capital*, i. 727 n., iii. 586.
[2] *German Ideology*, pp. 35, 90.
[3] *Grundrisse*, p. 491.
[4] Ibid., p. 193.
[5] Ibid., p. 158. The contrast between the first and second stages is related to the inverse variation between personal power and money as modes of social leverage, discussed at Ch. V, section (5).
[6] See below, pp. 211-2.

small claim to say of each pre-capitalist class society that it was one because the surplus possible at the given time was limited, and that capitalism arose when and because the surplus became moderately high.

2. In Table 4 types of economic structure are associated with quantitative levels of productive power. Quantitative levels within stage 2 do not explain the variations it shows in economic structure: the transitions do not obey the principle that a structure persists as long as it develops the productive forces, and goes when it has brought them to a level so high that it can no longer promote their progress. But explanations of economic structures in terms of the *qualitative* characteristics of productive forces are not therefore excluded. The kinds of productive facilities available might control the relations, even if their quantitative level of development does not. Distinct agricultural societies, for example, at much the same level of productive power, could have needs of different kinds for irrigation, and this might help to explain differences in economic structure they displayed.

(5) *Capitalism's Mission, and its Fate*

Capitalism arises and persists because it, uniquely, is able to take productive power from the top of level 2 to the bottom of level 4. In effecting this progress, it lays up the material requisites of a classless society. 'Development of the productive forces of social labour is the historical task and justification of capital. This is the way it unconsciously creates the requirements of a higher mode of production.'[1]

When these requirements are in store, capitalism is no longer justified, and no longer stable. It loses its rationale, and it becomes a 'barrier' to further human development. It 'enters into the same relation toward the development of social wealth and of the forces of production as the gild system, serfdom, and slavery, and is necessarily stripped off as a fetter'.[2] Having made liberty for the mass of mankind compatible with the material reproduction of the species, its 'historic destiny is fulfilled'.[3] It then reveals itself as 'merely a historical necessity,

[1] *Capital*, iii. 254, and see *Theories of Surplus Value*, ii. 405.
[2] *Grundrisse*, p. 749.
[3] Ibid., p. 325.

a necessity for the development of productive power from a definite historical starting-point or basis, but in no way an *absolute* necessity of production',[1] as bourgeois ideology would declare.

Even in its period of health capitalism does not, of course, preside over a progress which is free of friction and convulsion. The coincidence between capitalist rationality and productive rationality is imperfect: labour-saving devices are not introduced unless they are profitable,[2] the general forward movement is punctuated by periods of recession and waste. But the distortions and lurches do not nullify the fact that capitalism is, in its day, the best prescription for productive advancement.

There is some divergence between the tendency of capitalism and material progress, because the development of the productive forces is not the end of the capitalist, but just his means of accumulating value, and this means 'comes continually into conflict with the limited purpose, the self-expansion of the existing capital'. The structure of capitalism sometimes frustrates fulfilment of its 'historical task'.[3] 'It goes back on its mission whenever . . . it checks the development of productivity', and as that 'betrayal' grows in magnitude, 'it demonstrates that it is becoming senile and that it is more and more outmoded'.[4]

At 'a certain point' productivity ample enough to install a socialist society is reached, and capitalist depression tends to become more severe. There is then a

> growing incompatibility between the productive development of society and its . . . relations of production, which expresses itself in bitter contradictions, crises, spasms. The violent destruction of capital not by relations external to it, but rather as a condition of its self-preservation,[5] is the most striking form in which advice is given it to be gone and to make way for a higher state of social production.

Naturally, it does not take the advice, and needs instead to be disposed of by proletarian revolution. Then 'the last form of

---

[1] *Grundrisse*, pp. 831–2. For further discussion of this text, see 'Marx's Dialectic of Labour', p. 254.

[2] *Capital*, iii. 257.

[3] Ibid., p. 245.

[4] Ibid., p. 257.

[5] In order to endure, capitalism must undergo a crisis.

servitude assumed by human activity, that of wage labour on one side, capital on the other, is cast off like a skin'.[1]

We said that once socialism is possible, capitalism is no longer justified *and* no longer stable. It is clear why the possibility of socialism removes its justification. But why should the time when it has raised a technology which permits a transition to socialism also be a time when it suffers especially violent economic crisis? The answer is not: socialist revolution is more feasible the weaker capitalism is, and the weakness of capitalism is greatest when and because the crisis is deepest. For what a weak capitalism by itself makes possible is *potentially reversible* subversion of the capitalist system, *not* construction of socialism: the anti-capitalist revolution can be premature and can therefore fail of its socialist object.[2] What makes a *successful* revolution possible is sufficiently developed productive forces. The question is why the attainment of the latter coincides with particularly severe 'contradictions' and 'spasms' in the functioning of the capitalist system.

The interpretation of Marx's doctrine of capitalist crisis is a controversial issue, which cannot be resolved here. But let us begin by supposing, with a view to answering our question, that Marx was a 'breakdown' theorist. Breakdown theories come in different versions,[3] but we mean any one which entails that *if* capitalism lasts, then at a certain point it will come to a permanent halt, for purely economic reasons: it will be economically impossible for the cycle to continue as before, there will be a last great 'bust' followed by no regenerative 'boom'. (It is allowed that capitalism could go before it falls into the ultimate crisis it will experience if it lasts.) Such a theory does not make our question easier to answer. For now we have to ask: what ensures that enough productivity to make socialism feasible will be accumulated in advance of the final crisis? Why should the amount of time granted to capitalism by the laws which guarantee its eventual breakdown be enough to produce the required productive power?[4]

In our view, Marx was not a breakdown theorist, but he did

[1] *Grundrisse*, p. 749, and cf. *Capital*, iii. 259.

[2] See below, p. 206.

[3] For a good exposition, see Sweezy, *The Theory of Capitalist Development*, Chs. XI and XII.

[4] Cf. p. 173, implication (11).

hold that, once capitalism is fully formed, then each crisis it undergoes is worse than its predecessor.[1] But the forces improve across periods which include crises in which they stagnate. Hence they are more powerful just before a given crisis than they were before any earlier one. It follows that the more severe a crisis is, the more developed are the forces whose progress it arrests. Therefore socialism grows more and more feasible as crises get worse and worse (but not *because* they get worse and worse). There is no economically legislated final breakdown, but what is *de facto* the last depression occurs when there is a downturn in the cycle *and* the forces are ready to accept a socialist structure *and* the proletariat is sufficiently class conscious and organized.[2] Accordingly, once the concept of breakdown is dispatched, there is no puzzle in the fact that when capitalism's worst crisis occurs, productivity sufficient to establish a stable socialist society is available.

(6) *The Presuppositions of Socialism*

It is a banal but important truth that human beings on the whole prefer freedom to its opposite. That is part of the explanation why history records so much class struggle, against the bondage which has been the usual condition of the mass of mankind. They have been forced to labour, for themselves and for others, and they have enjoyed little opportunity to cultivate their talents. Unfree in their subjection to a ruling class, they have also, and consequently, been excluded from that 'development of human energy which is an end in itself'[3] and which is scheduled to flourish in the future. Some freedoms have been won in the history of class divided society, but only 'to the extent that was dictated and permitted . . . by the existing productive forces'.[4] Expansion of freedom is *dictated* by the productive forces when their further development is impossible without it, but the expansion can be no greater than what their current level *permits*.

Free time has been the special possession of privileged people, and high culture has prospered in the *milieu* of the ruling class.

[1] See Howard and King, *The Political Economy of Marx*, pp. 220-1.
[2] The third condition is not entirely independent. The maladies of capitalism and the development of the forces under it stimulate proletarian militancy.
[3] *Capital*, iii. 800.
[4] *German Ideology*, p. 475.

At productive levels 2 and 3, civilization can develop only if radical inequality is maintained:

> It is necessary that the mass of labour be a slave of its needs and not master of its time, in order that human capacities can be freely developed in the class for whom the labouring class only serves as a supporting base. The labouring class represents the absence of development in order that the other class can represent social development.[1]

The producers are 'the supporting base'. Themselves uncultivated, they create a material surplus which enables the human spirit to flower, in the environs of a leisured class. For the cultural production of class society, though restricted by its class affiliations, remains an expression of the highest human faculties.[2] Historical works of art and thought are not a set of ideological instruments whose only value is that they help to sustain class hegemony, and the proletariat does not banish traditional culture. It appropriates and extends it in a future in which each individual will have

> sufficient leisure so that what is really worth preserving in historically inherited culture—science, art, forms of intercourse— may not only be preserved but converted from a monopoly of the ruling class into the common property of the whole of society, and may be further developed.[3]

In the bourgeois epoch the guardianship of culture is assumed by the capitalist class, and Marx is accordingly prepared to accept that there is a certain liaison between capital and civilization.[4] But capitalist development lays the foundations of cultural democracy. 'In proportion as labour develops socially, and becomes thereby a source of wealth and culture, poverty and destitution develop among the workers, and wealth and culture among the non-workers', but 'in present capitalist society the material, etc., conditions have at last been created which *enable* and *compel* the workers to lift this social curse'.[5]

---

[1] *Theories of Surplus Value*, Kautsky edition, Stuttgart, 1905, iii. 111-12. Quoted by A. L. Harris in 'Utopian Elements in Marx's Thought', p. 88.

[2] See the important reference to 'free spiritual production' at *Theories of Surplus Value*, i. 285.

[3] Engels, 'The Housing Question', p. 565. Cf. *Capital*, i. 530.

[4] See *Grundrisse*, p. 634.

[5] 'Critique of the Gotha Programme', p. 20. To enable (*befähigen*) and compel (*zwingen*) is to permit (*erlauben*) and dictate (*vorschreiben*): the Gotha Critique is faithful to the formulation in *The German Ideology*. (See text to footnote 4, p. 204.)

The productive achievement of capitalism is to create a surplus which permits the producers themselves to share in civilization, nor can power now develop any further unless they *are* culturally enfranchised. The past development of the productive forces makes socialism possible, and their future development makes socialism necessary.

No socialist revolution will succeed until 'capitalist production has already developed the productive forces of labour in general to a sufficiently high level'.[1] Premature attempts at revolution, whatever their immediate outcome, will eventuate in a restoration of capitalist society. Without the 'absolutely necessary practical premise' of massive productivity 'want' would merely be 'generalized'. The ruling class might be suppressed, but in the resulting 'destitution' the working population could not establish a socialist commonwealth. A 'struggle for necessities' would ensue, 'and all the old filthy business would necessarily be reproduced'.[2]

Believing that a developed technology was an essential precondition of socialist success, Marx would be pessimistic about attempts to 'build socialism' from a baseline of comparative scarcity and industrial immaturity. But since he thought high technology was not only necessary but also sufficient for socialism, and that capitalism would certainly generate that technology, his final position was optimistic.

In this century societies have escaped the grip of capitalism when their own productive powers have fallen short of what Marx declared mandatory. But it is not clear that this refutes the pessimistic part of his position. For, in the first place, it is debatable whether they have achieved socialism, even if they have constructed economies which are in important respects superior to capitalism, both from a humane and from a 'narrowly economic' point of view. These societies, moreover, characteristically appropriate more advanced technology developed elsewhere, and might therefore not qualify as counter-

[1] *Theories of Surplus Value*, ii. 580.
[2] *German Ideology*, p. 46. Cf. Engels, 'On Social Relations in Russia', p. 387.

Marx allows for socialist revolution on a low productive base in a given country provided that it occurs in the context of a larger revolutionary transformation which engulfs advanced economies too. This complicates the question, which will not be pursued here, whether or not the Bolsheviks deviated from his prescriptions.

examples to the pessimistic thesis even were it allowed that they are genuinely socialist. What would certainly refute Marx is an unambiguously socialist society the bulk of whose production remained agricultural.

Experience accumulated since Marx's time justifies new hopes and fears. We may now be less sanguine where he was optimistic, and less gloomy where he was pessimistic. We can no longer be confident that the earth's resources will permit the astronomical productivity he appears to have thought inevitable, but it is far from evident that such productivity is a condition of human liberation.[1]

(7) *Why are Classes Necessary?*

Since Marx thinks socialist experimentation within stage 3 of productive development is bound to fail, he must hold that socialism cannot itself preside over the development of productive power to level 4: that is a task for class society to fulfil.[2] 'To obtain this development of the productive forces and this surplus labour, there had to be classes which profited and classes which decayed.'[3] A long travail of class inequality, consummated by capitalism, is needed to construct the material basis of socialism ('No antagonism, no progress'[4]).

But why should this be so? Why was it impossible to share the burden of developing the productive forces in a commonwealth of toil, without the oppression of one class by another? The rest of this chapter is a tentative discussion of this question. We want to know why

(k) class oppression is necessary to bring society to stage 4 of productive development.

Now if class oppression is necessary in productive stages 2 and 3 quite apart from its effect on the development of the productive forces; if, in particular, class oppression is, in that

---

[1] See further Ch. XI, section (9).

[2] Nothing asserted here should be taken as a denial that socialism/communism has two stages (called 'lower' and 'higher' stages of 'communism' by Marx, and later restyled 'socialism' and 'communism'), the first of which prepares the basis for the second (see 'Critique of the Gotha Programme', pp. 23–4). Productive level 4 is that which must be reached before the *lower* stage can begin.

[3] *Poverty of Philosophy*, p. 112, and see *Grundrisse*, p. 893.

[4] *Poverty of Philosophy*, p. 68.

period, necessary not merely, as (k) says, for productive *progress*, but for social *order* itself, then (k) will follow as a consequence, since productive progress is impossible without a minimum of social order. Accordingly, whatever (if anything) establishes that (m) is true, will constitute an explanation of (k):

> (m) class oppression is necessary for social order in stages 2 and 3 of productive development.

Before proceeding further, two phrases which appear in (k) and (m) need to be clarified, 'class oppression' and 'is necessary'.

Let us distinguish between class *oppression* and class *division*. For class division to obtain, it suffices that society is divided into those who produce and those who do not. Class division, so defined, is logically compatible with lack of subjection of one group to the other. Class oppression, on the other hand, will be taken to entail an antagonistic relationship in which producers are subordinated to non-producers. (These definitions are submitted solely for the purposes of the ensuing discussion.)

'Is necessary': as used here, the phrase expresses the functionality of class oppression to progress and order in (k) and (m) respectively. X may be an inevitable result of y, and in that sense necessary to it, but that is not how 'necessary' is used in (k) and (m). In the present context, if x is necessary to y, x serves to bring about y, and y is impossible without that service. A steamship will not move unless its engine is running, and it will not move without creating a wake. Only the first circumstance is necessary to the motion of the steamship in the present use of 'necessary'.

Under these clarifications of (k) and (m), it is evident that Marx was committed to the first, but there is little evidence, either way, regarding his views about the second.

In what follows, we begin by constructing a defence-cum-explanation of (m), which draws on the thought of Freud. We then present a different account of classes, which does not entail (m), and which is taken from Engels. Next we examine reasons for doubting that (m) and, accordingly, the Freudian account of it, are true. We decide to drop (m), and we offer an explanation of (k) which does not rely on it.

Some post-Freudian Marxists have been attracted to something like the following argument for (m). It begins with the fact that all productive levels below stage 4 are levels of scarcity, as that was defined on page 152. Prior to 4 society is able to reproduce itself only if enormous denial of aspiration and satisfaction is the lot of (*at least*) the great mass of its members. The labour process is, for material reasons, repellent in quality and extended in quantity. It yields few instrinsic rewards and no one engages in it except for ulterior motives: 'If capital were willing to pay [the worker] without making him labour, he would enter the bargain with pleasure',[1] and pre-proletarian labourers would happily accept similar offers. Historically, then, labour has imposed a continual painful deferral of gratification on the producers, and *men are so constituted that they do not readily accept continual painful deferral of gratification, even when it is in their overall interest to do so*:

> To put it briefly, there are two widespread human characteristics which are responsible for the fact that the regulations of civilisation can only be maintained by a degree of coercion—namely, that men are not spontaneously fond of work and that arguments are of no avail against their passions.[2]

When labour is rebarbative, men have to be driven to it. So at productive levels 2 and 3, some men have to see to it that other men work. Therefore, at those levels, a distinction between those who work and those who do not but make sure that others do is necessary.

Note that this argument for (m) meets the requirement that the relationship whose necessity (m) asserts is one of class oppression, not just class division. For the non-producing group must control and restrain, hence rule over the producers. One could say that in the Freudian account class *division* has been necessary because class *oppression* has been necessary, though it is compatible with the account that class division should have had other functions too.

A rival theory of the function of classes is provided by Engels. He distinguishes

---

[1] *Grundrisse*, p. 462.

[2] Freud, 'The Future of an Illusion', p. 7. A Marxist using this thesis would say that coercion becomes unnecessary once high stages of productivity are reached in which labour no longer need be repellent. He would also reject Freud's ignorant and otiose assumption (ibid., p. 6) that the members of the producing classes are made of especially poor psychological fibre.

between the masses discharging simple manual labour, and the few privileged persons directing labour, conducting trade and public affairs, and, at a later stage, occupying themselves with art and science.

But the foundation of this 'great division of labour' is not, as in the Freudian account, the problem of social control. Rather:

> So long as the really working population were so much occupied with their necessary labour that they had no time left for looking after the common affairs of society—the direction of labour, affairs of state, legal matters, art, science, etc.—so long was it necessary that there should constantly exist a special class, freed from actual labour, to manage these affairs.[1]

A critic of Engels could agree that scarcity ensures that *at least the majority of people* be producers, for straight material reasons. But why, he might ask, must only a majority, not everyone, produce: why is class division necessary? Why did the schedule of the 'really working population' have to be such as to leave them no time for participation in the 'common affairs of society'? Why was it impossible for everyone to work, somewhat less than each who worked actually did, with the time gained for each producer by extending labour to everyone being devoted to collective self-government? Why was no rotation system possible, obviating the need for class division?[2]

Engels does not answer these questions, but it is not hard to reply on his behalf. The critic's proposal is not really plausible. Administrative tasks require a measure of education, and an attitude of detachment from quotidian concerns, neither of which could be achieved by the masses in what would still be a very restricted amount of time free from labour. The rotation notion ignores obvious 'economies of scale' in the use of free time.

Engels has given a good account of the necessity of class division. But why could not the administrators, even if necessarily a separate group, be subject to popular control? It is

[1] *Anti-Dühring*, pp. 251–2. Engels often expressed this view: see 'Principles of Communism', questions 13 and 20; 'The Housing Question', p. 565; 'Karl Marx', p. 164.

[2] On the Freudian view rotation would conflict with the psychological constraints. The producers need to be kept in subjection, and the mentalities of subjugator and regimented cannot be combined in one person.

clear why this is excluded on the Freudian view, but how does Engels explain class oppression?

He does proceed to explain it, and his explanation does not support proposition (m). For while he represents the subordination of the producers to the others as unavoidable, he identifies no function served by it. In contrast with the Freudian account, which construes class structure as *ab initio* repressive in purpose, Engels sees it as becoming so only when and because the administrative stratum uses its position 'for its own advantage, to impose a greater and greater burden of labour on the working masses'.[1] In Engels subjugation is an outcome of class division, not its rationale: 'The law of division of labour lies at the basis of the division into classes.'[2] The oppression of one class by another would then be an inevitable cost attached to a technically necessary differentiation. It would not, as (m) says it does, itself make a contribution to society.

But now we must ask whether (m) is, after all, true. Class oppression has in fact characterized social structures at productive levels 2 and 3, but has it been required for social order?

We shall discuss two objections to (m), and hence to the Freudian argument in favour of it. The first objection relies on premisses which a Marxist defender of (m) is committed to accepting. The second objection is not attached to Marxism. The first objection can be met, but the second appears decisive.

If classes are needed at stages 2 and 3 in virtue of the limited surplus possible at those stages—and that was the beginning of the Freudian argument for their necessity—how was a classless society possible at stage 1, when there was no surplus at all? How can (m) be fitted into Marxism, which affirms the prevalence of primitive communism at the lowest level of development of the productive forces?

Marx's description of primitive communist men solves the problem:

> . . . ancient social organisms of production are . . . founded either on the immature development of man individually, who has not yet severed the umbilical cord that unites him with his fellow men

---

[1] *Anti-Dühring*, p. 252, and see ibid., p. 205; letter to Schmidt, 27 Oct. 1890, in *Selected Correspondence*, p. 398.

[2] *Anti-Dühring*, p. 390, and see his 'Introduction to *The Civil War in France*', p. 483.

in a primitive tribal community, or upon direct relations of subjection.[1]

In this portrayal primitive men lack sharp consciousness of themselves as individuals with distinct interests, and are therefore not disposed to pursue individual desires in a way that threatens social order. The need for a repressing group has not yet arisen. To put the same thought differently: the community contains and represses its members, in a crude totalitarianism without a ruling class. It is when individualization begins, notably through inter-tribal trade which stimulates internal trading,[2] that classes become not only materially possible—in virtue of the surplus associated with commerce—but mandatory for social order. The 'umbilical' psychology makes class oppression unnecessary. Once that psychology is transcended, 'direct [i.e. non-market-mediated] relations of subjection' supervene, and social stage 2 begins. Hence primitive communism, as Marx describes it, is compatible with the necessity of class oppression at stages 2 and 3, and with the Freudian explanation of that necessity.[3]

We turn to a more considerable argument against (m). It is that in large stretches of pre-capitalist history there have been self-directing peasants and artisans, who have sometimes bulked large within the set of immediate producers. They labour within class societies, but in so far as they are exploited, it is through taxation, regular or otherwise, by state or local potentate. The nature of the oppression (when there is any) to which they are subject makes it difficult to represent the ruling class as conferring on their labour a discipline which they are unable to achieve by themselves. If those whose lot it is to labour do face the problem of gratification deferral, it must be allowed that these producers solve it without ruling class assistance. Yet they are impressively individualized: we cannot say that they relate 'umbilically' to a community.

On the contrary: individualization, or lack of communal

---

[1] *Capital*, i. 79.

[2] See Ch. XI, p. 299.

[3] How would Engels cope with primitive communism, given his account of the function of classes, and his recognition (*Anti-Dühring*, p. 248) that primitive communism had 'common affairs' which needed to be regulated? He would have to say that the affairs were not so complicated and extensive as to require a special class to see to them.

connection, within the historical peasantry in some measure varies *inversely* with extent of subjection to authority. The self-dependent herdsmen on mountainous terrain have typically been under less alien control than the more communal tillers of the plain, perhaps, as has been suggested, for security reasons.[1] Lowland farming is more exposed to pillage, and the producer gets protection, in the straight and in the Chicago sense, from the ruler he feeds.

If there is a connection between class structure and problems of gratification deferral, it is not the simple one stated on pages 208–9. The Freudian defence of (m), as formulated above, must be rejected.[2] Nor shall we attempt an alternative argument for (m). A case for (k) will be constructed independently of it.

We expressed uncertainty (p. 208) as to whether Marx believed that, this side of abundance, class oppression is required for social order (thesis (m)), and we have decided to drop that claim. What other arguments can we find in Marx for (k), the proposition that class oppression is needed (if not for social order, then) to bring society to level 4 of productive development, to create the massive surplus without which, (k) entails, socialism cannot begin?

It was argued earlier (pp. 194–6) that non-capitalist class society will not create so large a surplus. (k) therefore implies that *capitalist* class society must precede socialism. Marx says that only with 'the rule of the capitalist over the worker' will

the relentless productive forces of social labour, which alone can form the material base of a free human society . . . be created by force at the expense of the majority.[3]

But why was 'private accumulation of capital' a necessary con-

---

[1] See Kosminsky, *Studies in the Agrarian History of England*, p. 144, and Anderson, *Passages from Antiquity*, p. 155. The suggestion was initially made by Eileen Power.

[2] One can imagine refurbished arguments for (m). One such would combine the considerations stressed by Engels and Freud: societies have general affairs which need to be regulated, and the producers' problem of gratification deferral can be solved only if they are not themselves in charge of them. Another idea would be that the self-directing producers sustain themselves as such partly by accepting ideologies whose availability is connected with class division. These hypotheses will not be pursued here.

[3] 'Results', p. 990.

dition of 'the development of the productive forces and of surplus labour'?[1]

Marx's answer is given in his presupposition that the development had to be 'at the expense of the majority'. It certainly was at their expense in fact. 'Large-scale industry' was undoubtedly oppressive to those who worked in it.[2] Marx believed, moreover, that only a regime of that severity could deliver the wanted surplus. Add to this the plausible contention that no group of producers will impose such a regime on themselves, by democratic process, and it will follow that socialism could not have taken humanity from scarcity to abundance. The 'severe discipline of capital'[3] was required. In short:

1. Working conditions like those which prevailed in 'large-scale industry' are necessary to reach stage 4 of productive development.
2. No group of producers will impose such conditions on themselves. So
3. Class oppression is necessary to reach stage 4 of productive development (thesis (k)).

The conclusion is supported by the premisses, and premiss 2 is hard to fault. The success of the argument therefore depends on the truth value of premiss 1. Judgement on 1 will not be passed here, but we may be confident that it figured centrally in Marx's commitment to thesis (k).

But Marx had other reasons for believing that socialism has to be preceded by capitalism. We have as yet considered only the quantitative presupposition of socialism, a massive surplus. It also has qualitative prerequisites, and they too, according to Marx, need to be created by capitalism. Capitalism collectivizes the working class, and rescues it from the parochialism of rural and craft 'idiocy'.[4] It engenders in the working class a cohesion and sophistication without which democratic self-government

---

[1] *Poverty of Philosophy*, p. 112.

[2] This is so even if the correct position in the 'standard of living controversy' is the one taken by Hartwell in Chapters 13 and 14 of *The Industrial Revolution and Economic Growth*.

[3] *Grundrisse*, p. 325.

[4] 'Rural idiocy' is mentioned in 'The Communist Manifesto', p. 38, and 'craft idiocy' in *Poverty of Philosophy*, p. 161. Idiocy is discussed in sections III and IV of 'Marx's Dialectic of Labour', which also (at pp. 251-2) gives arguments for (k) not repeated here.

of industry would be difficult. The capitalist prelude is necessary to bring into being the modern 'collective labourer'.[1] What is more, the concentration of wealth under capitalism means that the collective appropriation of the means of production by the producers is relatively easy to achieve,[2] and the struggle against capital forges a unity across the working class, which is a desideratum for the political success of socialism.

The quantitative and qualitative conditions were both important in Marx's thinking. When he says that the socialist transformation 'stems from the development of the productive forces under capitalist production, and from the ways and means by which this development occurs',[3] we may conjecture that 'the ways and means' encompass the collectivization of labour, but the development of the productive forces as such is posited first, as a separate requirement. The possibility of a reduced working day, enabling full participation in what Engels called the 'common affairs' of society, is essential, in addition to the required socialization of labour.

Our problem was why classes have been necessary, or, at any rate, why they are necessary to bring the productive forces up to level 4. The question how classes are possible is different. They are materially possible just in case any kind of surplus is available. But we may also ask how they are possible in another respect: how is the subjugation of the producing class achieved and maintained? The answer lies in the theory of consciousness and the superstructure, which will not be developed in this book. But the general location of the superstructure in the Marxian architectonic is investigated in the next chapter.

---

[1] *Capital*, i. 359–61, 508–9.
[2] Ibid. i. 764.
[3] Ibid. iii. 259.

CHAPTER VIII

Base and Superstructure, Powers and Rights

(1) *Identifying the Superstructure*

CHAPTER III examined the economic structure, the 'real foundation' upon which a superstructure rises. The economic structure was said to be the sum total of production relations, and these were provisionally construed as sets of rights of persons over productive forces. We warned that the language of rights would have to be replaced, and one aim of the present chapter is to show why it must and how it may give way to a distinct language of effective powers.

Marx gave no definite demarcation of the superstructure. Does it include ideology? We shall suppose that it does not, but little will rest on this decision, and much of what we say about the superstructure will apply to ideology too. We take the superstructure to be a set of non-economic institutions, notably the legal system and the state.[1] Our main concern will be the law, not the state as such.

Two distinct definitions of 'superstructure' are implicit in classical and subsequent Marxism:

(1) The superstructure = all non-economic institutions.
(2) The superstructure = those non-economic institutions whose character is explained by the nature of the economic structure.

No specifically Marxian terms occur in the first definition. The second is more theoretical, because of its reference to the economic structure, a concept of Marxian theory.

Whichever definition is chosen, the substantive claim is, very roughly:

---

[1] It is of interest that the superstructure is described as 'legal and political' when it is first mentioned in the 1859 Preface. See *Critique of Political Economy*, p. 20.

(3) The character of non-economic institutions is largely explained by the nature of the economic structure.

On definition (1), (3) becomes

(3)[i] The character of the superstructure is largely explained by the nature of the economic structure.

On definition (2), (3) becomes

(3)[ii] Non-economic institutions are largely superstructural.

If, as sometimes happens, *both* definitions are tacitly employed, (3) will appear true as a matter of course, since it is easy to deduce (3) from the conjunction of (1) and (2). But (3) is not in fact true as a matter of course, and so it is necessary to adopt just one of the definitions: theoretical victories cannot be scored by multiple definitions of terms.

We opt for the second, more theoretical, definition. Hence for us the substantive claim is (3)[ii], and the substantive question is: to what extent are non-economic institutions superstructural? and *not*: how much of the superstructure can be explained economically? There is no great error in the first definition, but the second does seem more apt. Thus suppose someone holds strongly anti-Marxian views, and thinks that non-economic institutions reflect the character of the economy hardly at all. Then the first definition forces him to say that the superstructure is largely independent of the economic base, which is a strange statement, since what then is the point of calling it a *superstructure*? On the second definition the opponent is able, more appropriately to his views, to deny that non-economic institutions are substantially superstructural. The second definition has gallantry in its favour: it enables critics of historical materialism to formulate their opposition more clearly.

(2) *The Problem of Legality*

In this section we venture a solution to a difficulty which arises for historical materialism, which may be called 'the problem of legality'.

The problem: if the economic structure is constituted of *property* (or *ownership*) relations, how can it be distinct from the *legal* superstructure which it is supposed to explain?[1] For

> the property relations of men belong to the sphere of their *legal*
> relations: property is first of all a legal institution. To say that
> the key to understanding historical phenomena must be sought in
> the property relations of men means saying that this key lies in
> the institutions of law.[2]

Yet, as Plekhanov recognized:

> after all, right is right, and economy is economy, and the two
> conceptions should not be mixed up.[3]

But how can they fail to be mixed up when the economic
structure is *defined* in legal terms? And is not such a definition
mandatory, since the structure of an economy is (or at least
includes) a structure of ownership?

Historical materialism is apparently committed to each of the
following four positions, but no more than (any) three of them
can consistently be maintained:

(4) The economic structure consists of production relations.

(5) The economic structure is separate from (and explanatory of) the superstructure.

(6) Law is part of the superstructure.

(7) Production relations are defined in legal terms (that is,
in terms of *property* in, or—as in Chapter III—*rights* over
productive forces).

Comment on (5): the parenthetical phrase is not required to
generate inconsistency among the positions. It is included
because we wish to show not only that production relations are
separate from legal relations, but also that explanation of the
latter by the former is coherent.

To secure consistency, one of the positions must be
abandoned. We shall abandon (7), by providing a means of
eliminating the legal terms we used when production relations
were first introduced. It was convenient to use those terms, but
they are not essential. In the course of solving the problem of
legality we indicate why they were convenient.

---

[1] For a recent reference to the problem see Nozick, *Anarchy, State and Utopia*,
p. 273, and for a longer treatment see Plamenatz, *German Marxism*, Chapter II,
section I, which is criticized in my 'On Some Criticisms, I', section (5).

[2] Plekhanov, *The Monist View*, p. 35.

[3] Ibid., p. 173.

The problem, which has two connected parts, is (i) to formulate a non-legal interpretation of the legal terms in Marx's characterization of production relations, in such a way that (ii) we can coherently represent property relations as distinct from, and explained by, production relations.

Our solution proceeds as follows. First, we display ownership as a matter of enjoying rights. Then, for each ownership right we formulate what will be called a 'matching power'. Next, we similarly describe production relations which 'match' property relations. Finally (in sections (3) and (4)), we show how production relations, thus identified, may be represented as explaining property relations.

The first step was taken in Chapter III. Though Marx uses the terms 'property', 'owns', etc., when he characterizes production relations, we thought it advisable to dispense with them, and spoke instead (p. 63) of various combinations of the sorts of rights owners typically enjoy. The offending concept in our provisional characterization of the economic structure is the concept of a right.

Now we can transform any phrase of the form 'the right to ϕ' into a phrase which denotes a power by dropping the word 'right' and replacing it by the word 'power'. Let us call the power the new phrase denotes a power which *matches* the right denoted by the original phrase. If x has power p and power p matches right r, we may say that, roughly speaking,[1] the content of the power he has is the same as the content of right r, but we cannot infer that he also has right r. Possession of powers does not entail possession of the rights they match, nor does possession of rights entail possession of the powers matching them. Only possession of a *legitimate* power entails possession of the right it matches, and only possession of an *effective* right entails possession of its matching power. One might say that the power to ϕ is what you have *in addition to* the right to ϕ when your right to ϕ is effective, and that the right to ϕ is what you have *in addition to* the power to ϕ when your power to ϕ is legitimate.

This does not mean that a man cannot have a power which

---

[1] This is rough because (a) there can be more than one power matching a single right (see p. 221), and (b) unlike rights, powers vary in degree (see section (6)).

matches an ineffective right he has. For example: a man has the right to travel, but a gang of hoodlums do not want him to. They would prevent him from travelling, and they are too strong to be restrained by the legitimate authorities, who are weak. But the man has a stronger gang at his disposal, which is able to defeat the gang that would block his movement. He has the right to travel *and* the power to travel, even though his right to travel is ineffective.

We are using 'power' as follows: a man has the power to ϕ if and only if he is able to ϕ, where 'able' is non-normative. 'Able' is used normatively when 'He is not able to ϕ' may be true even though he is ϕ-ing, a logical feature of legal and moral uses of 'able'. Where 'able' is non-normative, 'He is ϕ-ing' entails 'He is able to ϕ.'[1]

The conditions for the use of 'able' remain elastic even after normative occurrences have been excluded, and this has some implications for our programme, to be explored in section (6), where we discuss *degrees* of power. But conceptual elasticity is not obscurity. The concept of an *effective* right is clear, even though it is elastic. Our concept of power will be elastic in the same degree, and so, consequently, will be our concepts of production relation and economic structure, for the last is defined in terms of the second, and the second is defined in terms of the first.

We now list some powers pertinent to the description of economic structures, together with the rights they match:

1. right to use means of production (or labour power)
   power to use means of production (or labour power)
2. right to withhold means of production (or labour power)
   power to withhold means of production (or labour power)
3. right to prevent others using means of production (or labour power)
   power to prevent others using means of production (or labour power)
4. right to alienate means of production (or labour power)
   power to alienate means of production (or labour power)

---

[1] We ignore cases of ϕ-ing *by fluke*, not because the entailment fails there, but because ϕ-ing by fluke is not evidence of a power to ϕ in the appropriate sense.

Match 4 introduces a complication: the description of the power contains the legal term 'alienate'. The right-hand phrase designates a power rather than a right,[1] but it is a power described in essentially legal terms. Since we aim to eliminate legality from production relations, we cannot be content with powers specified in a legal way. The remedy is to locate the rights contained in the concept of alienation, and to continue the translation, as follows:

To alienate is to arrange for another to have over an object the rights I now have over it.[2] The right to alienate is therefore the right to arrange . . . over it. The power matching the right to arrange . . . over it is the power to arrange for another to have over an object the *powers* I now have over it.

Now the power to alienate is not the same as the power to arrange for another to have over an object the powers I now have over it,[3] even though the first matches the right to alienate, the second matches the right to arrange . . . over it, and they are one and the same right. It is a consequence of the purely syntactical character of the definition of 'matching power' (p. 219) that a single right may have more than one power matching it. Under the definition of 'matching power', the following argument is invalid:

> Power p matches right r
> Power q matches right s
> Right r = right s
> therefore, Power p = power q[4]

Powers with legal terms in their descriptions are perfectly

---

[1] A person will have the right to alienate without the power, if, for example, someone threatens to kill him if he sells his property. The right to alienate real property is not accompanied by all of the matching power when racist groups force a white man not to sell his house to a non-white person.

Whether one can have the power to alienate without the right is a tricky question, which is left as an exercise to the reader.

[2] For the sake of readability, 'arrange for another to have over an object the rights I now have over it' will be abbreviated as 'arrange . . . over it' in the next three sentences.

[3] Where transfer of property is legally forbidden, one could have the second power without the first. (Note: the power to alienate *is* identical with the power to arrange for another to have over an object the *rights* I now have over it.)

[4] It does follow from the premises that power p matches right s and that power q matches right r. Powers match rights, not descriptions of rights, even though they match rights in virtue of descriptions of rights.

proper and indeed quite interesting powers,[1] but no such power is ever the same as a power whose description is free of legal terms. But powers of the first sort are inadmissible as constituents of the economic structure, and henceforth, when we speak of powers, we shall mean ones whose definitions lack legal terms.

We now have a way of excising legal terms from the description of production relations. We can construct *rechtsfrei* production relations which match property relations in just the way powers match rights. We proceed to illustrate the use of the method. The method works only if the *rechtsfrei* characterizations of production relations it supplies do not alter the intent of the claims Marx made about production relations using a legal vocabulary.

Consider the contrasting relations of production, described in legal terms, as in Table 1 of Chapter III, which distinguish the ideal-typical slave from the ideal-typical proletarian. (Here we reflect on ideal types only. We come closer to reality in section (7).) Neither owns any means of production. Marx differentiates them by pointing out that whereas the proletarian owns his labour power, the slave does not. Unlike the latter, the former has the right to withhold it.

Our programme enjoins us to translate as follows: the proletarian has the power to withhold his labour power, while the slave does not.

Objection: The reason the slave is said to lack this power is that if he does not work he is likely to be killed, and he will certainly die. But a similar fate awaits the withholding proletarian, since he loses his means of subsistence. Therefore the proletarian is also unable to withhold his labour power. Therefore the descriptions of the production relations of slaves and proletarians no longer contrast when they are purged of legal terms in accordance with our programme.

Reply: It is relevant that the withholding slave is liable to be killed and the proletarian is not, but we shall not rely on this difference. We concede that the withholding proletarian dies.

---

[1] Such powers match those rights which Hohfeld calls powers (which are legal enjoyments and hence not powers in our sense), for I have a Hohfeldian power when I (legally) may so act as to change the distribution of legal enjoyments.

But note that he may be able to withhold his labour power from a given capitalist, including his current employer, without fear of death. The slave cannot withhold his labour power from his particular master and still live.

The proletarian is constrained to offer his labour power not to any particular capitalist, but to some capitalist or other. If he wishes to survive, he must present himself on the labour market to the capitalist class, and he is forced to serve that class. This accords well with Marx's frequent statement that the proletarian is owned not by any given capitalist, but by the capitalist class as a whole.[1] The matching non-legal statement of his position is true.

That is how to carry out the programme in one important case. It is impossible to demonstrate the viability of the programme except on a case-by-case basis, but we submit that it will generate the appropriate results quite generally.

Two objections will now be dealt with.

(1) A critic familiar with the thought of Engels might complain that we have replaced the legal conception of production relations by the 'force theory', which Engels, presumably with Marx's approval, condemned in *Anti-Dühring*.[2] The complaint would be misdirected, since our definition of production relations does not stipulate how the powers they enfold are obtained or sustained. The answer to that question does involve force, but also ideology and the law. The programme says what production relations are, not what maintains them. The distinction will be clarified in section (4), but the following comparison conveys the essence of our reply to the objection.

An illegal squatter on a tract of land might secure his dominion by dint of retainers who use force illegally on his behalf, and/or by propagating a myth that anyone who disturbs his tenure of the land thereby damns himself to eternal hellfire. The squatter has something in common with a legal owner of similar land whose tenure is protected by the legitimate authorities. Both have the power to use their land. That one

---

[1] See 'Wage-Labour and Capital', p. 83; *Grundrisse*, p. 464; *Capital*, i. 168, 574, 613–14; 'Results', p. 1032; *Theories of Surplus Value*, i. 229, 349; Engels, 'Principles of Communism', Question 7.

[2] Part II, Chs. II to IV. Cf. *German Ideology*, p. 357.

employs force (or myth) and the other relies on the law to sustain his position in that production relation is in neither case part of the content of the relation. This comparison shows that we are not advocating a variant of the 'force theory'.

(2) Even if our programme is internally sound, it might seem misguided as an explication of *Marx's* idea of production relations, for the question remains, why did he describe them in legal terms? The answer is that there was no attractive alternative. Ordinary language lacks a developed apparatus for describing production relations in a *rechtsfrei* manner. It does have a rich conceptual system for describing property relations, strictly so called. Given the poverty of the vocabulary of power, and the structural analogies between powers and rights, it is convenient to use rights-denoting terms with a special sense, for the sake of describing powers. It is certainly more convenient, though less conceptually strict, than instituting something like our rather complicated programme.

Marx regularly used legal terms in non-legal senses. Obvious examples: he refers to means of production which 'were, in fact or legally, the property of the tiller himself',[1] and of instruments of production being 'transformed into the property of the direct producer ... first in fact, and then also legally'.[2] Since 'property' is a legal term, it might be argued that there could not be property which is the tiller's in fact but not legally. That argument would be entirely scholastic. 'Non-legal property' is perhaps a *contradictio in adjecto*, but there is not a trace of conceptual confusion in Marx's use of such expressions. His phrasing achieves concision, and our programme shows that what he means can be stated in a wholly unobjectionable way, at the cost of a certain prolixity. (We are not, of course, advising anyone to adopt our programme, or to desist from using legal terms in non-legal senses. The point is that one could dispense with them, not that one should.)

Sometimes production relations are established without legal sanction, which they acquire at a later time. A conquering army might subject a defeated peasantry to new production relations, by enforcing a set of decisions which have no legislative or other legal backing. Once the relations have endured

---

[1] *Capital*, iii. 660, and see ibid., p. 770.
[2] Ibid., p. 777. Cf. *Capital*, i. 237.

for a certain period, they will probably acquire the support of legal authority. The two stages in the aftermath of the conquest illustrate the distinction between production relations and the property relations which typically—but not necessarily—accompany them.

But a passage in the *Grundrisse* might be taken as a rejection of our distinction:

> The bourgeois economists have a vague notion that it is better to carry on production under the modern police than it was, e.g., under club-law. They forget that club-law is also law, and that the right of the stronger continues to exist in other forms even under their 'government of law'.[1]

If club-law is also law, there appears to be something wrong with our description of the aftermath of the conquest. The appearance is deceptive.

Marx says 'the right of the stronger continues to exist in other forms' in capitalist society. He plainly means that even in his civilized age there are, underlying the property relations describable in terms of *legal* rights, what we have called *powers*, and what Marx, perhaps infelicitously, calls 'the right of the stronger'. The latter is the real content filling the bourgeois legal form, and so 'club-law' is not different in content from bourgeois law. Marx is certainly bringing together the sophisticated legal situation and the legally underdeveloped one, but his assimilation proceeds backwards in time. 'Club-law' society, where powers are openly visible, illuminates the society where rights screen powers: not vice versa. Marx's point, far from contradicting our analysis is, we should claim, explicated by it.

(3) *Explanations of Property Relations and Law by Production Relations*

Having acquired *rechtsfrei* descriptions of production relations, we must now show how production relations, so described, may be said to explain property relations. In this section we illustrate the explanatory connection, which is discussed in more general terms in section (4).

Examples of the connection appeared in earlier chapters,

---

[1] *Grundrisse*, p. 88.

though not explicitly, since up to now we have not been concerned to distinguish finely between production relations and property relations. Recall, for instance, the collapse of the law of settlement, as described by Mantoux (see Chapter VI, p. 167). There were evidently two stages in that process. First, the law was violated, as production relations allowing mobility of labour were formed illegally. Later, the law was scrapped, so that conformity was re-established between rights and powers, the *de jure* situation and the *de facto*, property relations and production relations.

The general explanatory thesis is that given property relations have the character they do because of the production relations property relations with that character support. Thus property relations change in order to facilitate, or, as in the Mantoux case, to ratify, changes in production relations. The production relations change so that the productive forces can be properly used and/or developed, and the property relations change to allow for or to stabilize the required changes in production relations. Sometimes, as in the Mantoux case, the economic change precedes the legal; sometimes the reverse is true; and sometimes the changes proceed simultaneously. But in all cases, so historical materialism contends, the property relations change in the service of changes in production relations (which in turn reflect development of the productive forces).

Four types of case will be illustrated below:

I. At time t circumstances favour the formation of production relations forbidden by existing law. Because the law, if obeyed, would fetter the productive forces, it is broken between t and $t+n$. At $t+n$ the law is changed, so that consonance between property relations and production relations is restored. (The Mantoux case belongs here.)

II. As in I, conditions favour the organization of currently forbidden production relations. But in this case the legal system is too strong to allow formation of production relations in defiance of it. Accordingly, the law is sooner or later changed, so that new production relations can be established.

III. In types I and II the new production relations are illegal unless the law is changed. In type III new production relations form which violate no law, since no law forbids them.

Fresh laws are nevertheless desirable, to make the economic change more secure, and they are consequently passed.

IV. In types I to III the law is changed at some point or other. In IV property relations change although no change in the law occurs.

History is full of examples of these patterns, and commonly there is multiple patterning: in a complex transition we find that some new powers are exercised illegally, while others await a change in the law. The same legal change typically both ratifies achieved powers and permits the formation of new ones, if only because ability and willingness to break the law are unevenly distributed in society. Thus in the course of the decline of the gild system, regulations limiting the numbers that could be employed by one master were violated here, and grudgingly accepted there, until the legal impediments were removed and what had happened locally could be generalized.[1]

So our types of case mingle in historical reality, but we can still cite examples which are dominantly of one type or another.

Three fairly clear instances of I:

The early European bourgeoisie was in part formed out of serfs who ran away from the lords to whom they belonged and settled in fortified cities. Legally speaking, they carried their serf obligations with them. But in fact, though not without frequent bloody battle, they were able to resist lords who would recall them to their established duties. 'City air makes a man free' even when the law says otherwise. 'But the fact had to be transformed into a right',[2] and what had to be, came to be. Here then, 'legitimation only confirmed an illegitimate act'.[3]

The English Statute of Artificers of 1563 declared, *inter alia*, against entry into the clothing industry of men whose parentage was below a certain economic rank. It was not conducive to the development of early manufacture, and was widely abused, sometimes with the legal authorities turning a blind eye. Finally, in 1694, the offending clause was repealed, and 'this allowed a proletariat of textile workers to exist *de jure* as well as *de facto*'.[4]

[1] See *The German Ideology*, p. 70.
[2] Pirenne, *Economic and Social History of Medieval Europe*, p. 51.
[3] Weber, *The City*, p. 108.
[4] Hill, *Reformation to Industrial Revolution*, p. 139.

A century or so later, that proletariat began to form trade unions, and there were strikes, in defiance of Combination Acts designed to prevent development and exercise of working-class power. Workers combined and struck illegally until their ability to do so was transformed into a right. They established effective control over their own labour power, and this led to changes in property relations:

> In England combination is authorised by an Act of Parliament, and it is the economic system which has forced Parliament to grant this legal authorisation ... The more modern industry and competition develop, the more elements there are which call forth and strengthen combination, and as soon as combination becomes an economic fact, daily gaining in solidity, it is bound before long to become a legal fact.[1]

A pure type II case is hard to find, for the same pressure which leads to the legal change is likely to produce an illegal anticipation of it. Still, the following passage perhaps supplies an example:

> After the restoration of the Stuarts, the landed proprietors carried out, by legal means, an act of usurpation, effected everywhere on the continent without any legal formality. They abolished the feudal tenure of the land, i.e. they got rid of all its obligations to the State ... [and] ... vindicated for themselves the rights of modern private property in estates to which they had only a feudal title.[2]

British landed proprietors used the law to achieve a result their continental cousins attained without it. In long historical perspective the difference of means loses its importance. Compare Marx's reference to the 'more or less plausible legalistic subterfuges' big landlords used to justify enclosures which expropriated the peasantry.[3] The degree of legality in the subterfuge is of secondary interest.

Early British factory capitalists tried to exact intolerably intensive labour from their employees, but the workers resisted,

---

[1] *Poverty of Philosophy*, p. 192.

[2] *Capital*, i. 723. Cf. Weber's discussion of the different degrees of legality in the emancipation of the peasantry from feudal burdens in France and Germany (*General Economic History*, p. 87).

[3] *Capital*, iii. 751.

and conflicts about the pace of work were endemic, in which neither side could cite law definitely in its favour, since no legislation was addressed to the matter in contention. The struggle led to fairly well recognized practices, and then the law broke its silence and gave the facts legal form:

> . . . these minutiae, which, with military unifirmity, regulate by stroke of the clock the times, limits, pauses of the work, were not at all the products of Parliamentary fancy. They developed gradually out of circumstances as natural laws of the modern mode of production. Their formulation, official recognition, and proclamation by the State were the result of a long struggle of classes.[1]

This example illustrates our type III.[2]

Type IV is of great historical significance. Here certain forms of production relation are legally allowed for, but property and production relations to which the relevant laws apply are, at a certain stage, marginal in extent. If the productive forces subsequently encourage more widespread production relations of the given kind, they can develop unimpeded by the law, and even facilitated by it, so that property relations change in perfect coincidence with changes in the economic structure. In this way a once secondary production relation can become dominant[3] without much change in the law, even though what happens entails an alteration of the entire social form. A major illustration of this is the use of Roman law in capitalist society. Marx thought Roman law raised a problem for his theory of base and superstructure. His solution to it is given in section (8) below.

If certain critics of historical materialism were right,[4] property relations could not be explained by production relations, by the very meaning of the terms denoting them. In section (2) we clarified the terms, and now we have seen that what the

---

[1] *Capital*, i. 283.

[2] Cf. *The German Ideology*, p. 80: 'Whenever through the development of industry and commerce, new forms of intercourse have been evolved . . . the law has always been compelled to admit them among the modes of acquiring property.' This statement covers changes of types I and III.

[3] On 'dominant production relation', see Ch. III, section (6).

[4] Notably J. P. Plamenatz and H. B. Acton. See fn. 1, p. 218, and section (5) below.

critics declare impossible is a phenomenon familiar to historians. But even historians sometimes fail to distinguish properly between economic and legal facts. Mantoux's criticism of Arnold Toynbee Sr.'s pioneering work on the industrial revolution is most instructive:

> In the whole economic history of the seventeenth and eighteenth centuries, the protection of industry by central or local governments was, for a long time, the subject that attracted most attention. This is not surprising, since it is much easier to study legislation, when all the texts are available, than scattered elusive facts of which it is hard to find even a trace. It may be for this very reason that the importance of this branch of research has long been overestimated. Toynbee even went so far as to assert that the change from protective regulations to freedom and competition was the main feature of the industrial revolution. This was to mistake effect for cause, and *the legal aspect of the economic facts for the facts themselves* . . . on the contrary, it was the new organisation and the new industrial processes which burst the cramping bonds of obsolete laws by which they were still fettered.[1]

Mantoux's diagnosis of the tendency of historians to identify production relations ('the economic facts') and property relations ('the legal aspect' of those facts): it is difficult to discern production relations except by studying property law and assuming the conformity of the former to the latter. This *methodological* problem is related to the *semantic* problem mentioned on page 224, the absence of a ready-made non-legal language for compendious description of production relations.

Mantoux's remarks nicely complement Marx's thesis that, although economic changes have usually to be registered juridically, the law does not explain the economic changes. 'Revolutions are not made by laws.'[2] But it is essential that they *make* laws, since, as we now explain, bases need superstructures.

---

[1] *The Industrial Revolution*, p. 83, emphases added.

Another historian who stressed the importance of distinguishing rights and powers was Marc Bloch. He noted that '*de jure* status' could be 'in stark contrast with . . . *de facto* status', and he presented many cases in which 'legal tradition . . . finally yielded to the facts'. *Feudal Society*, pp. 341, 344. See his *French Rural History*, pp. 42–4, 69, 179–80, for his skilful employment of distinctions some philosophers think cannot be drawn.

[2] *Capital*, i. 751.

(4) *Bases Need Superstructures*

We said (Chapter VI, p. 160) that production relations are
functionally explained by the development of the productive
forces. Here we add that property relations are, in turn,
functionally explained by production relations: legal structures
rise and fall according as they promote or frustrate forms of
economy favoured by the productive forces. Property relations
have the character they do because production relations require
that they have it.

In human society might frequently requires right in order
to operate or even to be constituted. Might without right may
be impossible, inefficient, or unstable. Powers over productive
forces are a case in point. Their exercise is less secure when it
is not legal. So, for efficiency and good order, production
relations require the sanction of property relations. Hence men
fight, successfully, to change the law so that it will legitimate
powers they either have or perceive to be within their grasp,
and lawmakers alter the law to relieve actual or potential strain
between it and the economy. (This is not to say that the
adjustment of the legal order to the economy is always carried
out consciously.)[1]

If production relations require legal expression for stability,
it follows that the foundation requires a superstructure. This
seems to violate the architectural metaphor, since foundations
do not normally need superstructures to be stable. We must be
careful if we are looking for a visual image to go with the
metaphor. One slab resting on another would be inappropriate.
One correct picture is the following.

Four struts are driven into the ground, each protruding the
same distance above it. They are unstable. They sway and
wobble in winds of force 2. Then a roof is attached to the four
struts, and now they stay firmly erect in all winds under force 6.
Of this roof one can say: (i) it is supported by the struts, and
(ii) it renders them more stable. There we have a building whose
base and superstructure relate in the right way.

The picture does not display the claim that the base explains
the character of the superstructure. One has to add a caption
which says that when and because struts would otherwise be

---

[1] For other possibilities, see Ch. X, sections (4) and (5).

unstable a roof which secures them tends to be imposed. Non-metaphorically: the property relations are as they are because their being so is conducive to the initiation or maintenance of the production relations (demanded by the productive forces).

In law-abiding society, men's economic powers match the rights they have with respect to productive forces. Do they have the rights because they have the powers, or do they have the powers because they have the rights? The question is ambiguous.

Consider a man who has a right r. Since society is law-abiding, his right is effective. So he will also have power p, which matches r. Moreover, he has p because he has r. Society being law-abiding, he can only have p as a result of having r. The same is true with respect to all economic powers and all economic agents. So we can say: in law-abiding society men have the powers they do because they have the rights they do.

That seems to refute the doctrine of base and superstructure. But the above analysis, though correct, is incomplete. Historical materialism takes the analysis further, and it is in fact compatible with the truths of the last paragraph. For it says that right r is enjoyed because it belongs to a structure of rights, which obtains *because* it secures a matching structure of powers. The content of the legal system is dictated by its function, which is to help sustain an economy of a particular kind. Men do get their powers from their rights, but in a sense which is not only allowed but demanded by the way historical materialism explains rights by reference to powers.[1]

Now some texts which show that Marx and Engels affirmed a functional account of the relation between base and superstructure. Here is what Marx told the jury at the trial of the Rhenish Democrats in 1849:

> Society is not founded upon the law; this is a legal fiction. On the contrary, the law must be founded upon society, it must express the common interests and needs of society—as distinct from the caprice of individuals—which arise from the material mode of production prevailing at the given time. This Code

[1] Compare the parallel points about forces and relations of production at Ch. VI, p. 161.

Napoléon, which I am holding in my hand, has not created modern bourgeois society. On the contrary, bourgeois society, which emerged in the eighteenth century and developed further in the nineteenth, merely finds its legal expression in this Code. As soon as it ceases to fit the social conditions, it becomes simply a bundle of paper.[1]

Capital articulates the idea that the base needs a superstructure:

> . . . regulation and order are themselves indispensable elements of any mode of production, if it is to assume social stability and independence from mere chance and arbitrariness . . .[2]

Since the base needs a superstructure, it 'creates' one:

> . . . every form of production creates its own legal relations, forms of government, etc. The crudity and the shortcomings of the bourgeois conception lie in the tendency to see but an accidental reflective connection in what constitutes an organic union.[3]

Bases need superstructures, and they get the superstructures they need because they need them: this is what is meant by saying that the two are *organically* connected.

The fact that production relations require the order law supplies may lead to misperceptions of the historical process, as Mantoux claimed it did in the case of Toynbee (see p. 230). Engels makes a similar point:

> Since in each particular case the economic facts must assume the form of juristic motives in order to receive legal sanction; and since, in so doing, consideration has of course to be given to the whole legal system already in operation, the juristic form is, in consequence, made everything and the economic content nothing.[4]

We saw that law can look more fundamental than the economy, when the underlying functional explanation of law is ignored (p. 232). The role of force in history is open to similar misconstrual. Engels's main criticism of the 'force

---

[1] 'Speech at the Trial of the Rhenish District Committee of Democrats', p. 232.
[2] *Capital*, iii. 774.
[3] *Grundrisse*, p. 88.
[4] 'Ludwig Feuerbach and the End of Classical German Philosophy', p. 397. Engels is allowing that the *way* the economic content expresses itself legally depends in part on the already existing legal system. This is an aspect of the 'relative autonomy' of the superstructure, which will not be discussed in detail here.

theory' is that it mistakes the fact that force functions to sustain economic structures as a proof that force is more basic than the economy.[1] When he protests 'that force is only the means, and that the aim is economic advantage'[2] he is asserting, in crude terms, a functional connection between base and super-structure. Another primitive formulation:

> Every socialist worker, no matter of what nationality, knows quite well that force only protects exploitation, but does not cause it; that the relation between capital and wage-labour is the basis of his exploitation, and that this was brought about by purely economic causes and not at all by means of force.[3]

The statement is primitive because it does not accommodate the fact, known to Engels, that force figures considerably among the *immediate* causes of economic power, just as rights do (see p. 232). Indeed, effective rights are effective partly because of the force behind them.

An important Preface sentence says:

> At a certain stage of their development, the material productive forces of society come into conflict with the existing relations of production, or—what is but a legal expression for the same thing—with the property relations within which they have been at work hitherto.[4]

We can now say that when productive forces 'come into con-flict' with property relations it is because the forces conflict with the production relations those property relations formulate and protect. The solution is either a change in production relations in violation of the law, with the law later falling into line, or a change in law which facilitates a change in production relations. History is full of both solutions.

(5) *Is the Economic Structure Independently Observable?*

In the *Illusion of the Epoch*[5] H. B. Acton provides an argument which purports to prove that factors Marx placed outside the

---

[1] 'Force' here is not the 'might' of p. 231, the latter being power as that was defined on p. 220. In our usage your power is what you are able to do, regardless of what makes you able to do it. Force is one source of power.

[2] *Anti-Dühring*, p. 221. [3] Ibid., pp. 211–12.

[4] *Critique of Political Economy*, p. 21. [5] pp. 164–5.

economic structure cannot be appropriately separated from it. We shall not review the argument. It shows only that non-basic institutions are functionally necessary to basic arrangements. So far from disturbing historical materialism, this thesis about the superstructure is, we have argued, one of its principal claims.

Elaborating his conclusion, Acton writes:

> The 'material or economic basis' of society is not, therefore, something that can be clearly *conceived*, still less *observed*, apart from the legal, moral and political relationships of men.[1]

We have submitted a method of *conceiving* the economic structure which excludes from it the legal, moral, and political relationships of men. The powers we defined are sustained by law, morality, and the state, but they are not legal or moral or political in content.

We have not, however, tried to show that the economic structure can be '*observed* apart from' superstructural relationships. It is not immediately clear what we are to understand by *observing* an economic structure. Consider, for comparison, a divorce rate. A divorce rate in a given country during a given period is identical with the number which is the ratio of divorces to marriages in that country in that period. Can a divorce rate be observed? No, since it is a number, and numbers are unobservable. But *what the divorce rate is* can, of course, be determined by observation.

Is it possible to determine by observation what the divorce rate is without at the same time observing all kinds of circumstances which are closely connected with divorces? Presumably not, but it does not follow that the fact that a certain divorce rate obtains cannot explain other facts about the society or its individuals, including facts 'inseparable' from the fact that divorces are occurring. A high rate of divorce might explain a high rate of juvenile delinquency, or a low marriage rate (if, e.g., the high divorce rate promotes disillusionment with matrimony). A high divorce rate might also explain the fact that a large proportion of divorces are effected by unusual

---

[1] *Illusion of the Epoch*, p. 167, emphases added. (Readers convinced by Chapter IV of this book will recognize 'material or economic basis' as a solecism. For the difference between the material basis and the economic one, see Ch. II, p. 30.)

means, recourse to which is necessary because so many are seeking divorces.

Similar comments apply to the economic structure. It is determined by observation, but it is not felicitous to say that it can be observed, since, like a number, it is an abstract entity.[1] And even if its character cannot be observationally determined without concomitant observation of the relationships Acton mentions, that in no way rules out an explanation of those relationships by reference to features of the economic structure. How could the fact that economic and non-economic variables occur together in experience invalidate an attempt to explain the second in terms of the first?

These are banal contentions. They are evidenced by the practice of theorists in any developed science. Is molecular biology debarred from explaining biological phenomena in physico-chemical terms when the relevant physical processes are unobservable apart from the biological processes they explain? Acton-like strictures on the capacity of a *rechtsfrei*, (*moralitätasfrei*, etc.) economic structure to explain law (morals, etc.) rest on a conception of explanation which is alien to science. Historical materialism may therefore ignore them.

(6) *More on Rights and Powers*

The account of rights and powers in section (2) was deliberately simplified, since it seemed wise to postpone complications until after the main points had been made. One major simplification lay in the treatment of every right of ownership as a *right to do* something. A landowner has the right to use his land, which is, indeed, a right to do something. But he also has a right that no one else use it, and that is not a right to do something. There is no right to do something which x has and which is identical with his right that y not use his land. (Standardly, if x has the right that y not use his land, he will *also* have the right *to* prevent y from using his land. But that is an additional right, arising out of the first, and not identical with it.) Instead, x's right that y not use his land, this right he has *against y*, is identical with y's duty (to x) not to use x's land.

---

[1] We suppose here that relations are not observable, a debatable philosophical claim. If it is false, so be it. We have no *need* to deny that the economic structure is observable.

Now what power matches x's right that y not use his land? The answer is not x's *power that y not use his land*, for that is a meaningless phrase. A power is always a power to do something. But given the identity of x's right that y not use his land and y's duty not to use x's land, we may say that what matches x's right is y's lack of power to use x's land. Y's lack of power is the *de facto* analogue of x's right. In section (2) one man's right was matched by that same man's ability. Sometimes, we now see, one man's right is matched by another man's inability.

Generalizing, we have to recognize duties to ϕ as no less basic than rights to ϕ within the legal framework. And in the matching economic framework we must put not only powers or abilities but also inabilities or constraints. But just as a power is distinct from the effective right ensuring it, so a constraint is distinct from the enforced duty imposing it. It is not trivial to say that the serf is constrained to work because he is legally obliged to.[1]

. Section (2) also made things sound simpler than they are by its failure to observe that powers vary in degree.

Consider a person A and a right r: either A has r or he does not have it. It is false that he has it to some *degree* or another. And if both A and B have right r, neither has it *more* than the other. Rights possession does not vary in degree.

A right may be divisible into parts, and a person might have some parts of it and not others. To take an easily managed example, a man's right to play the trumpet in his home at any time for as long as he likes divides into his right to play it between 9 a.m. and 10 a.m., his right to play it between

---

[1] The most effective—because entirely general—way of handling difficulties like that dealt with above would be to begin with a general analysis of rights, which reduced them to their basic elements, and then to construct *de facto* matches for the basic elements. Thereby *de facto* matches could be generated for rights of every type. A good place to start would be the excellent analysis of rights furnished by Kanger and Kanger in 'Rights and Parliamentarism'. The basic notions in their analysis are those appearing in the following schema, together with negation:

'It shall be that Y sees to it that S(X,Y)',
where 'S(X,Y)' = 'the party X stands in the relation S to the party Y'.

We should want *de facto* analogues for the above sentence schema and three others like it (with variously placed negation signs) out of which twenty-six atomic types of rights are constructed. A good match for the schema above might be:

'Y is constrained to see to it that S(X,Y).'

10 a.m. and 11 a.m., etc., and subdivides further, as finely as time itself does. Another trumpeter, restricted by bye-laws, will have some of these rights but not others. The first man has more trumpet-playing rights, but no greater degree of any right.

Powers, however, do vary in degree. Or if someone insists, against what was said, that rights vary in degree, then powers vary in degree in ways rights do not.

Nigel and Fred are both able to go to Brighton, but Nigel is better able than Fred is. His ability to get there is greater, because, unlike Fred, he owns a car, and Fred can barely afford the train fare.

Wage-workers have the right to withhold their labour power. Apart from extreme cases, they are also to some extent able to do so. But how far they are able to do so varies from worker to worker. It also varies for representative or average workers at different stages in the history of capitalism.

This contrast between rights and powers does not upset our solution to the problem of legality. The procedure for generating descriptions of powers which match rights still has the virtues we claimed for it. But when, in pursuing our programme, we eliminate a *rechtsvoll* description in favour of a matching *rechtsfrei* one, we can go on to ask what degrees of the denoted powers people enjoy, a question which, we have seen, has no legal analogue, and the answer to which is of prime importance for an accurate understanding of economic structures.

Power varies in degree in a number of dimensions, two of which will concern us, because of their relevance to the topic of section (7). What matters to us is that the power to ϕ of a person (who is able to ϕ) depends for its degree on how *difficult* it would be for him to ϕ, and on how *costly* it would be for him to ϕ. These are distinct ways in which it can be *hard* for him to ϕ.[1]

The difference between the cost and the difficulty of doing something will be seen in an example. A friend desperately needs to get to the airport, and I can secure his presence there

---

[1] 'Difficult' is distinguished from 'costly' in the next paragraph, and by 'hard' we mean 'difficult and/or costly'. We are making simple distinctions which are not marked by the chosen words in their ordinary senses, for any pair of the three adjectives, and sometimes all three, can be used interchangeably in many contexts. We need to stipulate quasi-technical senses because no single words or short phrases natively have the senses we wish to distinguish.

on time either by giving him ten pounds for a taxi fare, or by driving him there on my bicycle, with him sitting on the bar. I am poor, but I have ten pounds in my pocket at my fingertips, so it is not *difficult* but it is *costly* for me to give him the money for the taxi fare. It is costly because giving ten pounds involves a large sacrifice for me, but it is not difficult for me to supply him with it, as it would be if I had to go to a bank the other side of London to get the money. Contrariwise, I enjoy driving my bicycle, especially with a passenger aboard over long distances, so it would cost me nothing (and maybe gain me something) to drive him by bike to the airport, even though it is a difficult thing to do. I spend almost no energy but sustain a large sacrifice in the first way of ensuring that he gets there, and I spend much energy but sustain no sacrifice in the second way. The first way is *costly*, the second is *difficult*.

I have less power to get him there than I would if I were a richer man, and less than I would if I had a helicopter on the roof instead of a bicycle in the yard.

Very often what is difficult is also costly, because it is difficult, but this is not always so, and the two considerations are sufficiently distinct in practice to require separate billing as factors which reduce power.

The dimension of cost is explored by Alvin Goldman, who maintains that the amount of power to ϕ a person has is inversely proportional to the cost to him of ϕ-ing.[1] It is in virtue of this, says Goldman, that to threaten someone with an undesired consequence if he acts in a certain way is to reduce his power to act in that way. He is still able so to act, but less able than before.

Goldman's discussion is valuable, but imperfect. He mistakenly ranges what we have called the difficulty a person may have in ϕ-ing under the concept of cost, for he regards expenditure of energy as a form of cost,[2] and it is not in fact a cost, even

[1] 'Towards a Theory of Social Power', p. 249. (On p. 257 Goldman acknowledges that power and cost are perhaps not so simply related as the unqualified inverse proportionality thesis says, but for our purposes the latter may stand as a rough truth.)

[2] Ibid., p. 251. The conception that expenditure of energy is, *ipso facto*, a sacrifice runs deep in bourgeois consciousness. It appears, for example, in Adam Smith's idea of labour as essentially 'toil and trouble', against which Marx protested. (See *Capital*, i. 46–7.) Much of Scitovsky's *Joyless Economy* is an exhibition

if it often imposes one. Thus—to adapt an example of Goldman's[1]—suppose there are two senators, each of whom can get his favourite bill passed, but the first can do it just by making three telephone calls, while the second has to lobby extensively. Intuitively we would say that the first senator has, *ceteris paribus*, more power to get his bill passed, and this is so even if each Senator hugely enjoys what he respectively has to do to get his bill passed, and neither need forgo greater pleasures for the sake of getting it passed. So the second senator, though less powerful, is not less powerful because it costs him more to get the bill passed. Difficulty is a consideration germane to power distinct from cost.

It is a staple of bourgeois propaganda that in a capitalist society every worker can become a boss. That is probably false, but certainly some workers can, though usually at considerable cost and/or with great difficulty. Note that it is compatible with the fact that x can become a boss that it would be extremely hard for x to become a boss. That logical consistency receives little emphasis in pro-capitalist ideology.

(7) *Rights and Powers of the Proletariat*

The proletarian described in section (2) has the legal right to refuse to work for any given capitalist, and also the legal right to refuse to work for all capitalists whatsoever. But he has no power matching the second right, for he is forced, on pain of death by starvation, to work for some or other member of the capitalist class.[2] We saw that this was the *rechtsfrei* meaning of Marx's frequent claim that he is owned not by any particular capitalist, but by the capitalist class as a whole. *Vis-à-vis* the class, he is *de facto*, though not *de jure*, in the position of a slave.

If this was ever true it is certainly now false, when stated, as Marx does, without qualification. The proletarian does not currently face the capitalist class as a slave does his particular master. The self-assertion of the working class has strained that

---

of the consequences of this conception in the economic culture of the United States: see pp. 160–1 for a telling illustration.

[1] 'Towards a Theory of Social Power', pp. 249–50.

[2] In the view of Robert Nozick, it need not be true of even the most abject proletarian that he is forced to work for some capitalist or other. See *Anarchy, State and Utopia*, pp. 262–4, which is criticized in my 'Robert Nozick and Wilt Chamberlain', pp. 19–20.

analogy to breaking point. We now attempt, necessarily in merest outline, a more realistic statement of the rights and powers of contemporary workers, in countries where bourgeois legality prevails.

We may distinguish the power of the proletarian acting alone, and his power as a member of a group (or the whole class) of workers acting collectively. Also, we must distinguish the power of the worker *within* capitalism from his power to *escape* capitalism. We begin with individual and collective power within capitalism.

'The boss won't listen when one guy squawks, but he's got to listen when the union talks.'[1] The 'feeble strength of one'[2] worker in confrontation with capital is widely understood. His strength in unity with others is another matter. It varies with innumerable concrete circumstances, but is always great enough to make this now false:

> The Roman slave was held by fetters: the wage-labourer is bound to his owner by invisible threads. The appearance of independence is kept up by means of a constant change of employers, and by the *fictio juris* of a contract.[3]

Contemporary employers might wish that the labour contract were merely *fictio juris*. Once workers bargain collectively, the abstract possibility of withholding labour power turns into a real threat, which is constantly made and frequently carried out. The workers' position within capitalism is thereby considerably improved.[4]

To strike is to withdraw labour power from some capitalist(s) without offering it to any other. Workers who can strike are not *de facto* 'owned' by the capitalist class. The power to strike is legally recognized in liberal capitalist countries, with greater or lesser restrictions upon it, which the workers are able to violate, to different extents, at different places and times.

Does the right to strike accord with basic bourgeois ideology, or does it, on the contrary, contradict it?

[1] From 'Talking Union', by the Almanac Singers.
[2] The phrase comes from the union song 'Solidarity Forever', by Ralph Chaplin.
[3] *Capital*, i. 574, and see also the references in fn. 1, p. 223.
[4] To be sure, not all workers belong to trade unions, but union members are not the only workers who benefit from the existence of unions.

Basic bourgeois ideology[1] prescribes and protects the right of the individual to contract with others, howsoever he may wish, provided he exercises no force and perpetrates no fraud. The ideology also imposes a reciprocal duty to abstain from interference in the prospective contractings of others. But if circumstances, for example earlier contracts between others, disable someone from contracting as he would wish, the basic ideology affords him no grounds for complaint.

A strike may be regarded as a fulfilment of a contract among workers who have agreed with one another to cease contracting with a third party—the employer—until his offer meets certain conditions. The basic ideology allows each worker so to contract, despite the resulting limitations on the employer's market power. The closed shop too appears to be in accord with the fundamental bourgeois norm, for it is merely mutually contracting workers writing into their contract with the capitalist that he may employ no one who does not also contract with them. (The use of force to prevent the entry of scab labour into a struck establishment is clearly not bourgeois-licit, for he who decides not to contract with someone may not forcibly prevent others from doing so, though he may inform them of his views, for example by non-obstructive picketing.) Early prohibitions of combination and strikes were not applications of basic bourgeois principles but class-interested backsliding from them.

Basic bourgeois ideology is potentially self-defeating. For unless certain types of free contract are forbidden, freedom of contract will fail to be maximized. The basic principle of *allowing* all free contracts to take place therefore often gives way to a derivative principle of *promoting* the freedom of contract in general, for example by *forbidding* free contracting which would restrict future contracting. That is the rationale given for outlawing certain kinds of closed shop.

The dictate of the basic principle is fairly clear, but the implications of the derivative principle are less evident. How far is market freedom to be protected against the consequences of its own use? What transactions constitute action 'in restraint of trade'?

The right to strike is guaranteed by the basic ideology but

[1] As identified by Marx at *Capital*, i. 176. What we call *basic* bourgeois ideology is articulated and defended by Nozick in *Anarchy, State and Utopia*.

threatened by its derivative replacement. Blood was spilled to get capitalism to conform to its basic ideology in this respect, and what was won then is not likely to be lost through application of the derivative surrogate:[1] the workers have too much power.

For all that was said above, each worker must still, in the end, work for some capitalist. But because of the union he has considerable say in the terms of the contract he enters, and is not powerless before the capitalist class as a whole. He is therefore not *de facto* 'owned' by that class.

We turn to another restriction on that 'ownership'. It is of massive ideological importance, and it has some real significance apart from ideology too.[2] It is the fact that at least some workers can rise into the petty bourgeoisie, and some can go further and become fully fledged capitalists, even though, as was noted (p. 240) the fact that they can does not make it an easy thing to do.

But if individual escape is to some extent, though in very different degrees, open to many proletarians, *sensu diviso*, it is evidently closed to the proletariat as a whole, *sensu composito*. After the advent of modern technology it is too late for everyone to become a self employing Jeffersonian petty bourgeois or farmer. And the idea that all workers can become capitalists so that no proletarians are left is ruled out by the very definition of capitalism:

> . . . it is impossible for the individuals of a class . . . to overcome [the production relations in which they stand] *en masse* without destroying them. A particular individual may by chance get on top of these relations, but the mass of those under their rule cannot, since their [i.e. the relations'] mere existence expresses subordination, the necessary subordination of the mass of individuals.[3]

Collective emancipation cannot come through a series of individual exits, but only collectively, through the exercise of class power.

[1] We have in mind recent attempts in Western countries to limit the right to strike, such as the now repealed Industrial Relations Act introduced by the Heath government in Britain.

[2] As Marx recognized: see *Capital*, iii. 587; 'Results', pp. 1032, 1079.

[3] *Grundrisse*, p. 164, and cf. 'Results', p. 1079.

Do the proletariat now have the required power, in, for example, Britain? And if they do, why have they not overthrown capitalism?

Recall (see section (6)) that power varies in degree. We should therefore not imagine that the answer to the first question is an unqualified 'yes' or 'no', as is sometimes presupposed in left-wing factional debate. If the price of socialist revolution in Britain today would be a substantial immediate reduction in the standard of living, that bears on how much power to overthrow capitalism the working class disposes of. Turning from the costs of revolution to the difficulties in the way of it, the magnitude of such tasks as detaching parts of the broad middle classes from their currently strong commitment to capitalism needs to be reckoned. This is hardly the place to do more than insist that no uncomplicated answer to the first question is correct.

The right answer to the first question is probably a properly qualified 'yes'. But this brings us to the second question. Why have they not overthrown capitalism? Partly because of the qualifications which attach to the answer to the first question. But other considerations also bear mention.

A man is in a windowless room whose door he mistakenly thinks is locked. Unlike a man in a locked room, he can leave it. Yet since he does not know he can, he is not likely to try the door. One reason why people sometimes do not exercise their power is their lack of awareness that they have it.[1] Capitalist society propagates and reinforces ignorance of power, whenever it projects an image of workers as incapable of collective self-organization.

Knowledge and belief are particularly important for the enjoyment and exercise of *collective* power:

> If all the slaves acted in unison, they would overwhelm their masters. But it does not follow that they have much (or any) collective power over their masters

since even if each knows that, acting together, they could prevail,

[1] See Goldman, 'Towards a Theory of Social Power', pp. 229–30, though he would prefer to say that the man in the unlocked room lacks the power to leave it. See, however, ibid., n. 7, which proposes a distinction between 'epistemic' and 'non-epistemic' senses of 'power'. Ours is the latter sense.

each is insufficiently confident that rebellious action on his part would be supported by others.[1]

This is one reason why solidarity is a major virtue in revolutionary struggle.

It might be said that the problem of mutual confidence does not arise in a parliamentary democracy. The worker can vote for a revolutionary candidate, an initiative which is 'costless' even if unaccompanied by similar 'rebellious action' on the part of others. Let us suppose, naïvely,[2] that the ballot box is, just by itself, an excellent instrument for the achievement of socialism. Why, then, do workers not elect revolutionary candidates?

From a non-socialist point of view the answer might be: capitalism is in the objective interest of the working class, so they vote to preserve it.

A revolutionary point of view needs different answers. A 'Marcusean' reply was popular in the 1960s. Bourgeois ideology, it went, has so captured the minds of the workers that they are hooked on capitalism and virtually unaware of a socialist alternative. This answer no doubt gives a part of the truth, in exaggerated form. But it is important to realize that it is not the whole truth. For it neglects the costs and difficulties of carrying through a socialist transformation. Workers are not so benighted as to be helpless dupes of bourgeois ideology, nor all so uninformed as to be unaware of the size of the socialist project. Marxist tradition expects revolution only in crisis, not because then alone will workers realize what burden capitalism puts upon them, but because when the crisis is bad enough the dangers of embarking on a socialist alternative become comparatively tolerable.

(8) Addenda

(i) Roman law and capitalism. In the Grundrisse 'Introduc-

---

[1] Goldman, 'Towards a Theory of Social Power', p. 238. In 1594 an Essex labourer asked, 'What can rich men do against poor men if poor men rise and hold together?' Hill, Reformation to Industrial Revolution, p. 93. The rub is that it is hard for poor men to rise and hold together. For similar exultant remarks from the grass roots, see Hill, Puritanism and Revolution, p. 112, and Prothero, 'William Benbow', p. 164.

[2] It would take us too far from our theme to explain why the supposition is naïve. For excellent recent comments on the character of bourgeois parliamentarism, see Anderson 'The Antinomies of Antonio Gramsci', pp. 27 ff.

tion' Marx adverts to examples of 'disproportionality' between material and spiritual development. He views with comparative equanimity the possibility that art is out of step with the economy.[1] Autonomy in the educational system is more worrying But 'the really difficult point'

> is how the relations of production as legal relations take part in this uneven development. For example the relation of Roman civil law (this applies in smaller measure to criminal and constitutional law) and modern production.[2]

How is it that modern capitalist production relations find legal expression in property relations governed by laws whose content owes so much to the laws of ancient Rome, a society whose economy was based on slavery?

The problem is solved in the main body of the *Grundrisse*. The essence of the solution: the *elements* of capitalist property and exchange long predated the formation of the capitalist economic structure proper, and the ancient laws which governed them are applicable to transactions within the special organization of them which is capitalism.

Thus although 'exchange-value did not serve as the basis of production' in antiquity, there was an exchange sector, and in that sector, 'in the realm of free men', 'the moments of simple circulation, at least, were developed'. Hence

> it is explicable that in Rome . . . the determinations of the legal person, the subject of the exchange-process, were developed. The essential determinations of the law of bourgeois society were [thereby] elaborated.[3]

If laws devised to regulate undeveloped commodity production in a non-capitalist economy are framed with sufficient generality, they will also suit fully formed capitalist commodity production:

> The same right remains in force, whether it be at a time when the product belonged to the producer, and when this producer,

---

[1] Some evidence that he regarded art as not, on the whole, properly superstructural: see section (1) above, and Ch. VII, p. 205.

[2] *Grundrisse*, p. 109.

[3] Ibid., pp. 915–16. See also ibid., p. 157, and three clear statements by Engels: 'Ludwig Feuerbach', p. 396; 'Introduction to *Socialism, Utopian and Scientific*', p. 107; 'Decay of Feudalism', p. 217.

exchanging equivalent for equivalent, could enrich himself only by his own labour, or whether it be under capitalism, where the social wealth becomes in an ever increasing degree the property of those who are in a position to appropriate to themselves again and again the unpaid labour of others.[1]

The principal powers exercised by capitalists are complexes whose elements are powers which Roman law recognized. The transition to capitalism is the accession to centrality of powers which were legitimate but only peripherally exercised in pre-capitalist societies. Here, then, property relations may change utterly, without a commensurate change in the law being required:[2] a type IV (see p. 229) example of the determination of the legal superstructure by the economic foundation.

(ii) *Anderson on base and superstructure.* We saw (p. 224) that Marx's legal descriptions of production relations cannot be taken literally. Perry Anderson is therefore wrong to construe Marx's investigation of the 'forms of agrarian property' as a study of property strictly so called.[3] It is a study of 'what is . . . *designated* property',[4] whether or not that which is so designated is legally valid.

Anderson's misinterpretation[5] disqualifies his attempt to use Marx in support of an unfortunate proposal ventured at this point in *Lineages*. Rightly disparaging the latitude with which some Marxist historians apply the term 'feudalism', he argues that when 'Ming China, Seljuk Turkey, Genghisid Mongolia' (etc.) are all called 'feudal', it becomes impossible to explain, from the character of the economic structure alone, why

[1] *Capital*, i. 587. See Ch. II of Renner's *Institutions of Private Law* for an extended discussion of this point. 'The kind of subject-matter which is the object of the property norm is irrelevant to the legal definition of property. One object is as good as another. The norms which make up the institution of property are neutral like an algebraic formula, for instance the formula of acceleration. But if one factor in this formula of acceleration is the avalanche, everybody is crushed, and if one factor in the property-norm which makes a person the owner of a thing, is the machine, generations are devoured.' Ibid., p. 112.

[2] Though in fact Roman Law had fallen into disuse in the Middle Ages, and it needed to be revived and refined.

[3] *Lineages of the Absolutist State*, p. 405.

[4] Marx to Annenkov, 28 Dec. 1846, *Selected Correspondence*, pp. 33-4, emphasis added; quoted by Anderson, *idem.*

[5] Which is the more curious given his recognition of the characteristic 'lag in the juridical codification of economic and social relationships' (*Passages from Antiquity to Feudalism*, p. 147). Anderson cannot think that Marx was concerned only with *juridically codified* forms of agrarian 'property'.

capitalism arose in Europe and not in these other societies. If it was feudalism which gave rise to capitalism in Europe, why did it not do so elsewhere? On the view Anderson opposes, the answer is sought in the contrasting superstructural features of European and non-European societies, a procedure he calls 'idealist', for obvious reasons.[1]

Anderson's own solution, in support of which he misuses Marx, is to say that in pre-capitalist societies 'the "super-structures" of kinship, religion, law or the state necessarily enter into the constitutive structure of the mode of production'.[2] Here the 'superstructure' does not rise on the economic base. It is part of it. Hence, presumably, the quotation marks.

But this solution is no less idealist than its competitor. When critics of historical materialism claim that dimensions other than the mode of production are fundamental, it is no reply to insert those dimensions into the mode of production.

The fact that capitalism did not arise spontaneously outside of Europe is a serious problem for historical materialism. It will be solved, if at all, by finer distinctions among production relations proper, together with attention to different strictly material conditions in different regions. If the problem cannot be solved in that way, then so much the worse for historical materialism, not for the claim that historical materialism distinguishes between base and superstructure.

[1] *Lineages*, pp. 402–3.
[2] Ibid., p. 403.

CHAPTER IX

Functional Explanation: In General

(1) *Introduction*

THE PRESENT chapter is more philosophical than any of the rest, and non-philosophical readers are likely to find it particularly difficult. Most of them will wish to proceed immediately to Chapter X, where functional explanation is discussed with greater reference to historical materialism. Chapter X is not philosophically technical, and it does not presuppose this one. The present chapter is justified because, beyond the disquiet about functional explanation felt by social scientists and historians, which Chapter X seeks to allay, there exists a deep strictly philosophical scepticism, felt no doubt by very many, but articulated by philosophers, and it is appropriate to confront that scepticism in a book which has made free use of the functional-explanatory mode.

For historical materialism has been presented as a functionalist theory of history and society, most obviously in Chapters VI and VIII. The former said that production relations have the character they do because, in virtue of that character, they promote the development of the productive forces; the latter, that the superstructure has the character it does because, in virtue of that character, it confers stability on the production relations. These are large functional-explanatory claims.

Here are some explanatory sentences of apparently similar structure, from various fields:

Birds have hollow bones because hollow bones facilitate flight.

That robin on the fence has hollow bones because hollow bones facilitate flight.

Shoe factories operate on a large scale because of the economies large scale brings.

This rain dance is performed because it sustains social cohesion.

A rain dance was performed yesterday because social cohesion was threatened yesterday, and the rain dance reinforced it.

Protestantism achieved strength in early modern Europe because it promoted the development of capitalism.

The intelligibility of these statements creates a *prima facie* case for the existence of a distinctive explanatory procedure, in which reference to the effects of a phenomenon contributes to explaining it. It is generally thought that the case collapses on further scrutiny, that each such remark is either misguided, or, if sound, then only by virtue of compressing or pointing to one or other *familiar* kind of causal story. We judge that the general opinion is ill-considered. The alternative view, that a single properly distinctive form of explanation is advanced in these sentences, deserves more examination. We shall hypothesize that there is a *special* type of causal explanation advanced in these and like instances, deriving its peculiarity from generalizations of distinctive logical form.

Explanations which possess the distinction we seek have been called 'functional explanations', and there is a large literature on the meaning of the statement-form 'The function of x is to ϕ'. It is widely assumed that such statements are, by virtue of their meaning, functional explanations,[1] but we shall not make that assumption: we shall not identify attributing a function with providing a functional explanation. We shall, moreover, maintain that it is possible to characterize the nature of functional explanation while offering no analysis of the statement-form 'The function of x is to ϕ'.

Following a terminological prelude, which stipulates a preferred sense of 'explanation', we show (section (3)) that there is functional explanation in that sense, and we separate the task of characterizing it from that of analysing function-attributing statements, which we forsake. In section (4) the concept of a *consequence law*, here claimed as the basis of functional explanation, is introduced. Section (5) concerns the confirmability of functional explanations, and section (6) defends them against a likely scepticism. Section (7) vindicates functional explana-

---

[1] Though, as we shall see (p. 252), those who hold this view do not all mean the same thing by 'explanation'.

tion in social science against criticism due to C. G. Hempel.

(2) *Explanation*

Consider a request or question of, or transformable into,[1] the form 'Why is it the case that p?', 'p' being an empirical sentence, to the effect, e.g., that copper conducts electricity, that $S = \frac{1}{2}gt^2$, that Napoleon was defeated at Waterloo, that birds have hollow bones, that the Hopi have a rain dance in their cultural repertoire, that this Hopi group performed a rain dance last Tuesday. Call such a request or question a *why-question*, and an answer to it a *why-explanation*. (A why-explanation need not be correct to qualify as such.)

Not all demands for explanation admit rephrasal in the form of a why-question. 'Explain the rules of chess', uttered by one who wants to know what they are, not why they are what they are, is a case in point. So is 'Explain what is happening in Northern Ireland', from one who knows only that something remarkable is going on, and is not inquiring into its causes. So too is 'Explain the structure of DNA', if the speaker will be content with an answer not disclosing why it is structured as it is. So indeed is 'Explain the function of the liver', if no more than a list of the useful services it performs is sought. These requests for explanation may be called *what-questions*.

An answer satisfying a request of the second kind may also be a correct reply to a why-question. 'He was in the trough of a manic-depressive cycle', which might be offered in response to 'Explain what mental state Napoleon was in at Waterloo', might also be used to explain why Napoleon was defeated at Waterloo. But uttering it with why-explanatory intent carries commitments and liabilities of a kind which are absent when it is used to answer a what-question only.

Hempel holds that all genuine explanations answer why-questions. We do not follow suit in hereby legislating confinement of the term 'explanation' to what answers a why-question.[2] 'Explain', 'explanatory', etc., will be similarly restricted. We do not, like Hempel, deny that non-why-explanations are explanations, or assert that they are explanations in a different sense,

---

[1] A request or question is so transformable if and only if casting it in that form preserves its intent.

[2] This legislation comes into force in section (3).

but we just elect not to call them such, since our interest is in why-explanations.[1]

Authors who call statements of the form 'The function of x is to ϕ' 'functional explanations' disagree about which of our two kinds of explanation they provide. Most of those who have tried to analyse such statements equate them with statements ascribing useful effects to x. For them 'the function of x is to ϕ' is equivalent to a subform of 'the beneficial effect of x is to ϕ', a subform, since no one says that *all* beneficial effects are functions.[2] A functional explanation of x is, on their account, an explanation of the function of x, a clear, systematic description of a restricted class of its useful effects. It is not an explanation of x by reference to those effects. It does not purport to say, for example, why x is to be found where it is. In this view 'the function of the liver is to promote digestion' carries no implication that the liver is in the body *because* it promotes

---

[1] For Hempel's view, see *Aspects of Scientific Explanation*, pp. 334, 414, and 'Explanation and Prediction by Covering Laws', pp. 125 ff.

Hempel is wrong when he contends that 'explanation' (etc.) is ambiguous across why-explanatory and other occurrences. He presents himself as analysing the concept of explanation, or at least the or a central concept of explanation. But in fact he is investigating the conditions of adequacy of one *kind* of explanation, the why-explanatory kind. The distinction would be tedious were it not that, misdescribing what he is doing, Hempel replies ineffectively to those who criticize him on the assumption that what he offers to analyse is the concept of explanation as such. A general analysis of the concept is less interesting than Hempel's enterprise. Probably to explain is, quite simply, to make clear, so that to explain why is to make clear why, to explain what is to make clear what, etc. Hempel is really concerned with the conditions under which we may be said to make clear why something is so.

Nor may Hempel correctly say that his concern is with *scientific explanation*. Not all scientific explanations are explanations-why, and not all explanations-why are scientific explanations. A good explanation of the structure of DNA is a scientific explanation, but it need not explain why anything is so. On the other hand, why-questions occur and are answered pre-scientifically, and science, Hempel would agree, is but a more rigorous and more theoretical body of doctrine available for answering them. An account of scientific explanation-why is incorrect if it represents it as different in principle from ordinary explanation-why. Hempel respects that condition, and in so far as his account is right and wrong, it is similarly right and wrong for both contexts.

[2] A typical benefit theorist is John Canfield, who writes: 'A function of I (in S) is to do C means I does C and that C is done is useful to S.' For example, '(In vertebrates), a function of the liver is to secrete bile' means 'the liver secretes bile, and that bile is secreted in vertebrates is useful to them'. 'Teleological Explanation in Biology', p. 290. (Canfield's analysis does not make all beneficial effects functions because of special restrictions—see ibid., p. 292—on the meaning of 'useful' in the *analysans*.)

digestion: it just explains *what* the function of the liver is.[1]

Dissenting from these accounts is Wright, who thinks that it belongs to the meaning of statements of the form, 'the function of x is to ϕ' that they are answers to why-questions, and are therefore functional explanations in our preferred sense of 'explanation'. He accordingly rejects all analyses which identify ascriptions of function with ascriptions of (special sorts of) beneficial effect.

In section (3) we dissociate the question of the analysis of functional ascriptions from the question of the nature of functional explanation, and we adopt a posture of neutrality on matters of analysis. A preview of the standpoints to be distinguished: for the 'benefit theorists' and for Wright, but not for us, a functional ascription *is*, as such, a functional explanation. For Wright and for us, by contrast with them, a functional explanation answers a why-question. Unlike Wright, we do not contend that function attributing statements answer why-questions by virtue of their meaning; but unlike the benefit theorists, we hold that they do answer why-questions under certain conditions.

(3) *Function-statements and Functional Explanations*

Abbreviations: A *function-statement* ascribes one or more functions to something. A *benefit-statement* ascribes one or more beneficial effects to something. A *precedence-statement* says of one event that it preceded another event.

Larry Wright opposes analyses of function-statements which reduce them to benefit-statements of one or other kind. He claims that these analyses fail to note that function-statements always serve to answer why-questions:

(1) . . . functional ascriptions [i.e. function-statements] are—intrinsically if you will—explanatory. Merely saying of something x, that it has a certain function, is to offer an important kind of explanation of x.[2]

---

[1] It is unfortunate that some philosophers use 'functional explanation of x' to mean 'explanation of the function of x'. As Christopher Boorse has remarked, one might as well call an explanation of a person's marital status a *marital explanation* of that person. (For explication of the usage, see Scheffler, *Anatomy of Inquiry*, pp. 52–3, and for protest against it, see ibid., p. 123.)

[2] 'Functions', p. 154.

Accordingly, Wright holds that it is part of the meaning of 'The function of x is to ϕ' that 'X is there because it ϕ's'.[1] Every function-statement is suited to answer a question of the form 'Why is x there?'

Wright gives two arguments for (1), only the second of which will be examined here.[2] We shall show that it supports not (1) but this weaker thesis:

(2) At least some function-statements are intended as explanatory.

The premiss of Wright's argument is the 'contextual equivalence' of such questions as 'What is the function of the heart?' and 'Why do human beings have hearts?' He does not elucidate 'contextual equivalence', but we may agree that, 'in the appropriate context', 'The function of the heart is to pump blood' answers both questions mentioned. But what is the appropriate context? Wright does not say, but clearly it is one governed by a belief that an answer to the function-question will explain why human beings have hearts, will, that is, answer the stated why-question.

Now this argument supports (2) and not (1), as a parallel demonstrates. Similar 'contextual equivalence' may obtain between the questions 'What preceded event e?' and 'Why did event e occur?'. The answer to both might be 'Event e was preceded by event f'. This shows—what needs no showing—that an event may be explained by a precedence-statement. It does not show—what is false—that precedence-statements are inherently explanatory.

This does not *disprove* (1), for the belief on which the 'contextual equivalence' between the function-question and the why-question rests might be conceptually grounded. But it does prove that Wright's argument supports the weaker thesis (2) only. It no more substantiates (1) than does the 'contextual equivalence' of function-questions and benefit-questions establish that benefit-statements entail function-statements, a conclusion Wright would reject. 'Why do human beings have hearts?' is contextually equivalent to 'What is the function of

---

[1] 'Functions', p. 161, with slightly different symbolism.

[2] See ibid., pp. 154–5. Wright's first argument turns on a supposed analogy between functional ascriptions and statements assigning goals to conscious agents. It cannot be assessed without more discussion of the explanation of animate agency than would be justified here.

the heart?' but the latter is contextually equivalent to 'What good does the heart do?' Thus an argument precisely similar to Wright's would prove exactly what he wishes to deny.

Wright's argument nevertheless provides some support for the weaker thesis, (2) ('At least some function-statements are intended as explanatory'), which we wish to affirm. And here is a further argument for (2), which does not involve the vicissitudes of interrogation. Sometimes a speaker who asserts a function-statement also cites comparable and contrasting cases in a manner reminiscent of explanation at large, and finds himself faced with counter-examples as one does when one is purporting to explain something. In uninvited commentary on a cow's long tail, a man points out that its hairy back attracts flies, and that one function of the tail is to keep them off. For contrast he cites the pig, whose sleek back is less enticing to insects, and whose curly little tail simply protects its anus. Finally, he exhibits the wild boar, rather pig-like, but sporting a substantial tail at the end of its unpiggishly hairy back. His friend may then point to the stubby tail of the hairy moose, thereby challenging what he said about the cow.[1] If, in saying it, the original speaker had intended only to indicate a benefit accruing to the cow from the tail, the case of the moose would be irrelevant: the cow is not worse off than he claimed because it is better off than the moose. The dialogue, being quite natural, shows that function-statements are, at least sometimes, intended and received as explanatory claims.

Two differences from Wright's position will now be remarked. First, though we maintain that there is functional explanation, we do not assert that every true function-statement correctly answers a why-question, still less that function-statements are explanatory as a matter of their meaning. Secondly, we do not restrict functional explanation to a select range of *explananda*. Wright does so restrict it, since for him a function-statement pre-eminently explains why the functional item 'is there'. On the view to be developed here, a functional explanation is *logically* in order in answer to any why-question. It could explain why a certain event occurred, why a particular thing has a certain property, why something regularly behaves in a certain

---

[1] For help in constructing this dialogue, I thank Gideon Cohen, who thinks the roe deer is an even better example than the moose.

manner, and so on, without restriction: note the heterogeneity of the examples with which we began on pages 249–50. Only the facts decide whether a why-question has a functional answer, not the structure of the question itself.

The account of functional explanation to be given in section (4) supplies no analysis of the meaning of function-statements. We ask, 'What renders an explanatory function-statement explanatory, whether or not every function-statement is explanatory?' An analogy will clarify the nature of the question. Consider the following:

(4) Event f brought about event e.

(5) Event f preceded event e.

To assert (4) is to venture a causal explanation of e. To assert (5) is to do so in certain circumstances, to wit, when an explanation of e is sought or promised. Now what makes (4) explanatory is the same as what makes (5) explanatory when it is explanatory, namely some relevant true generalization: that there is one is *entailed* by (4), and *implied* when (5) is uttered as providing an explanation of e. (4) entails

(6) There is a true generalization in virtue of which, because f occurred, e occurred.[1]

(5) does not entail (6), but proferring (5) as an explanation of e commits one to (6). (6) makes both (4) and (5) explanatory, even though (4) is explanatory as a matter of meaning and (5) is not.

Now consider

(7) Event f led to event e.

The meaning of (7) may be difficult to decide. Specifically, it is unclear whether it entails (6).[2] But it should now be evident that we can say what makes (7) explanatory (to wit, (6)) if or when it is, without deciding whether it entails (6). The question of the analysis of statements (4), (5) and (7) is distinct from the question what makes them explanatory, when they are.

We return to our object of inquiry:

[1] Less briefly: there are types of event T and T' such that f was of type T and e was of type T', and whenever an event of type T occurs, an event of type T' occurs.

[2] Readers who think otherwise will concede nothing substantial if they agree to pretend it is unclear.

(8) The function of x is to ϕ.

(9) The beneficial effect of x is to ϕ.

According to those Wright criticizes, (8) entails a refined version of (9), and nothing else, and is, like (5), not inherently explanatory.[1] According to Wright (8), like (4), by nature explains, and so cannot be equivalent to anything like (9). If we ask, as proposed, 'What makes explanatory instances of (8) explanatory?', we are not obliged to decide between these rival views. And to emphasize our escape from the issue of meaning, we may change the question to: 'What makes explanatory instances of (9) explanatory?'

The change may be justified by recourse to the analogy. Though (5) is not by nature explanatory, in asking what is needed to make it so one is investigating the nature of causal explanation. So, similarly, an appropriately refined (9) does not by nature explain, but in asking what makes it explain when it does, one is investigating the nature of functional explanation, whether or not some refined form of (9) gives the *meaning* of (8).

To summarize. Wright criticizes those who analyse functions as benefits for failing to acknowledge the existence of functional explanation. We concur, but the analysis of functions as benefits might nevertheless be correct. We adopt a neutral posture towards benefit-statement analyses of function-statements. We agree with Wright that such analyses are not accounts of functional explanation, but we withhold from him agreement that function-statements inherently explain and that therefore no such analysis is correct.[2]

---

[1] Though, as we saw (p. 252), many of them nevertheless *call* (8) a 'functional explanation', but the terminological policy laid down on p. 251 is now in force. (They call (8) a functional explanation because it *explains what* the function of x is.)

[2] I am, in fact, disposed to reject Wright's claim that function-statements are explanatory by virtue of their meaning. It appears to me that, often enough, when the life and human sciences attribute a function to an organ or a physiological process or a social custom, no more is intended by 'function' than '(possibly hidden) beneficial effect'. What is indicated is a service the item performs as though it were intended to do so—from which it does not follow that it is there *because* it performs that service.

It is certain that sociologists apply 'function' to hidden beneficial effects they do not think explanatory. In the course of the 'Hawthorne Experiment' (a study of a factory) there occurred a significant and at first unexplained rise in the morale and productivity of the factory's workers, the cause of which was in time identified

When is a function- or benefit-statement a correct answer to a why-question? A precedence-statement correctly answers one when an appropriate generalization of familiar form is true. We shall propose that function- and benefit-statements do by virtue of generalizations of a somewhat special form.

(4) *The Structure of Functional Explanation*

What makes a benefit-statement explanatory? More precisely: what makes a benefit-statement explanatory in whatever way a generalization linking the successive events makes a precedence-statement explanatory? We claim only *that* a generalization makes a precedence-statement explanatory, *how* it does being (even more) debatable.[1] But some remarks on the character of the generalization are appropriate.

---

as the experiment itself: the workers liked being studied. In his seminal paper on 'Manifest and Latent Functions' Robert Merton describes this beneficial effect as a 'latent function' of the experiment. Yet he cannot think it was conducted because of its probable effect on factory morale. (Also symptomatic of lack of explanatory intent is the common use—in biology and sociology—of 'dysfunction' as an antonym of 'function', uncomplemented by a suggestion that the fact that *x* is dysfunctional calls for a special explanation of its presence.)

Non-explanatory occurrences of 'function' appear to abound in uses of the term which Wright regards as peripheral. According to him (ibid., p. 141), one should first analyse 'the function of *x* is to ϕ' and then treat 'a function of *x* is to ϕ' as true when more than one thing meets the discovered criteria. This strategy he thinks superior to its opposite (analyse 'a function' and apply 'the function' when only one thing meets the criteria) since, he says, there are many peripheral uses of 'a function'. He does not examine why this is so. If the term has a copious peripheral use, why does it resist the definite article in that use?

No doubt Wright prefers 'the function' because he is interested in functional *explanation*, and 'the function' has a more explanatory ring. But the latter may derive as much from the article as from the noun. If, absent during the previous interchange, one hears it said that 'the event preceding *e* was *f*' the incidence of 'the' makes it a safer bet than otherwise that the speaker thinks *f* brought *e* about. But it would be improper to analyse 'the preceding event' as explanatory and then segment 'a preceding event' into central (because explanatory) and peripheral (because not) cases.

Now *the* preceding event need not be explanatory. The focus licensing 'the' may be different: thus the event might be the clown's act preceding but not explaining the sea lion's on a certain evening at the circus. But is 'the function' different? Perhaps it means, roughly, 'the chief beneficial effect', and it is only pervasively—not conceptually—true that what makes a beneficial effect chief and so the function is that it is explanatory.

For good criticism of Wright's analysis, some of which parallels the above, and for an alternative account of functions (as contributions to goals) on which we have not tried to comment, see Boorse on 'Wright on Functions'.

[1] The most familiar thesis in the latter debate is Hempel's: see p. 272.

It is usually supposed that the generalization must be a matter of law, and that tenet is adopted here. It is widely recognized that it need not be known for the precedence-statement explanation to be true and justified; that it may admit of exceptions; that it may relate event-types individuated by descriptions other than those used in the precedence-statement to identify the particular events: the generalization conferring an explanatory role on 'f preceded e' is rarely 'Whenever F occurs, E occurs'.[1] (George's having drunk four cups of coffee may explain his subsequent sleeplessness even though not everyone who drinks four cups of coffee is sleepless afterwards.)

The truth about what makes precedence-statements explain is complex. This could impede our inquiry, for we seek to answer 'What makes benefit-statements explain?' in an analogous way, and it would be awkward to have to construct an analogue which reflects all the complexity of the model. We therefore sacrifice accuracy to simplicity and seek an analogue in the case of benefit-statements to the simplest justification of a precedence-statement's explanatory role: where 'f preceded e' is explanatory because whenever F occurs, E occurs.[2]

A benefit-statement assigns beneficial consequences to some item. Let us generalize the question 'What makes benefit-statements explanatory?' by asking instead: what makes citation of consequences, be they beneficial or not, explanatory? What are the truth conditions of what we may call a *consequence explanation*? We return to functional explanation proper on page 263.

Our proposal is that a consequence-statement explains when it relates to a *consequence law* in whatever way an explanatory precedence-statement relates to a pertinent law. A consequence law is a universal conditional statement whose antecedent is a hypothetical causal statement. A consequence law relevant to the explanation of an event (as opposed, e.g., to the explanation of an object's having a certain property) takes this form:

---

[1] We use small letters to represent phrases denoting particular events, and capital letters to represent phrases denoting types of event. Where the small letter and the capital letter are the same, the denoted particular event belongs to the denoted type in virtue of the meanings of the phrases denoting them. Thus anything of the form 'e is of type E' (e.g. 'the collapse of the bank was a collapse of a bank') will be true *ex vi terminorum*.

[2] Some of the complexity ignored below will be catered for in section (7).

IF it is the case that if an event of type E were to occur at t_1,
then it would bring about an event of type F at t_2,
THEN an event of type E occurs at t_3.[1]

The antecedent of the conditional is itself a conditional, to
wit the *minor* conditional, the *major* conditional being the whole
statement.

The temporal ordering of t_1, t_2, and t_3 will differ in different
consequence laws. In no case will t_2 precede t_1, and in no case
will t_3 precede t_1. If causes can be contemporaneous with their
effects, then t_1 may or may not precede each of t_2 and t_3, and
t_2 may precede t_3, succeed it, or be identical with it. If causes
necessarily precede their effects, t_1 always precedes each of t_2
and t_3, but all three relations between t_2 and t_3 (precedence,
succession, identity) remain possible.[2]

By deleting 'IF' and replacing 'THEN' by 'IF' we obtain the
form of a consequence law stating a necessary condition of the
occurrence of an event of a certain type. (This corresponds to
reversing the direction of the unboxed arrow in the formal
version given in note 1 below.)

A consequence law supporting the explanation of an object's
having a certain property (e.g. a species' having a certain organ)
would be relevantly analogous in form to the one given above,
with mention of types of events being replaced by mention of
properties:

---

[1] More formally:

$$(\exists x)(Ex \text{ at } t_1 \; \Box\!\!\rightarrow (\exists y)(Fy \text{ at } t_2)) \longrightarrow (\exists z)(Ez \text{ at } t_3),$$

where 'x', 'y', and 'z' range over events, '$\Box\!\!\rightarrow$' is a connective expressing hypothetical causation, and the unboxed arrow is to be interpreted in whatever is the
right way of interpreting the arrow between the antecedent and the consequent
of a statement of natural law. 't_1' and so on are temporal variables, related as
stated in the next footnote.

Not all of my more logical colleagues agree that the above is the correct formal
version of what appears in the text, and the wrangle, in which I am an innocent
observer, continues as this book goes to press.

[2] Causes cannot succeed their effects, but whether a cause must precede its
effect is a philosophical question on which we need not form a judgement here.
If causes can be contemporaneous with their effects, the temporal possibilities in
the above schema are: $t_1 = t_2 = t_3$; $t_1 = t_2 < t_3$; $t_1 < t_2 = t_3$; $t_1 < t_2 < t_3$;
$t_1 < t_3 < t_2$ ('$<$' is short for 'is earlier than'). If causes must precede their effects,
only the last three orderings are possible, and references to contemporaneous
causes in the rest of this chapter should be construed as references to causes which
are immediately succeeded by their effects.

IF it is true of an object *o* that if it were *F* at *t1*,
then it would, as a result, be *E* at *t2*,
THEN *o* is *F* at *t3*.[1]

(The same temporal possibilities as were listed for the event law form hold here too.)

To convey the role of consequence laws in explanation of events, we propose an analogy between '*e* occurred because *f* occurred, since whenever *F* occurs, *E* occurs' and '*e* occurred because of its propensity to cause *F*, since whenever *E* would cause *F*, *E* occurs'.

Consider the examples with which we began on page 249. In light of our proposal we contend that, contrary to what is sometimes said, those remarks do not purport to explain causes by effects. They are not mirror-images of ordinary causal explanations. Rather, and very differently, it is the fact that *were an event of a certain type to occur, it would have a certain effect*, which explains the occurrence of an event of the stated type.

To get a particular law-statement of the first form explicated, let *E* = a performance of a rain dance of kind *R*, let *F* = a rise in social cohesion, and suppose *t1* = *t3*, which precedes *t2* by a short period. Then the law-statement says:

Whenever performance of rain dance *R* would bring about, shortly thereafter, a rise in social cohesion, rain dance *R* is performed.

It is false that, in an explanation relying on such a generalization, the resulting social cohesion is put forth as explaining the performance of the rain dance. Instead, the performance is explained by this dispositional fact about the society: that if it were to engage in a rain dance, its social cohesion would be increased.

In informal explanatory remarks, such as those on page 249, an event subsequent to the one to be explained may be cited, but only, we claim, in evidence of a disposition which holds before (or at least not after) the event to be explained occurs, the purport of the remark being that the prior or concurrent disposition explains the occurrence of the event. *It can be explanatory to cite the effect of the rain dance, not because its effect*

---

[1] $(x) [(Fx \text{ at } t1 \ \Box\!\!\rightarrow Gx \text{ at } t2) \longrightarrow (Fx \text{ at } t3)]$ is the formal version.

explains it, but because the fact that it had that effect allows us to infer that the condition of the society was such that a rain dance would have increased its social cohesion, and it is implied that that inferrable condition occasioned the performance of the dance. (Subsequent events are commonly cited in informal explanatory remarks. An example from non-functional explanation: the question 'Why was he looking so terrible yesterday?' may be satisfactorily answered by 'He died of cancer today'. That answer can be appropriate, not, of course, because today's death by cancer explains yesterday's sickly appearance, but because today's death by cancer allows inference of a cancerous condition yesterday which, the respondent implies, accounted for yesterday's sickly look.)

To get a particular law-statement of the second form explicated, let o be the species cow, let F = long-tailed, let E = possessed of the power to swish flies away, and let $t1 = t2 = t3$. We then obtain a consequence law-statement relevant to the explanatory claim—see page 255—that the function of a cow's long tail is to swish away flies. Of course that explanation is not in fact supported by a law so neatly generalizing it,[1] but recall our decision (p. 259) to go for simplicity of presentation. 'George was sleepless because he drank four cups of coffee' is not supported by 'Whenever a man drinks four cups of coffee he is sleepless', since that is false. Those who find probabilistic weakening of the latter plausible may adopt that course here too, though a more reasonable policy would be a retreat to a law sketch.[2] It is a question about explanation in general how to back up a particular explanatory claim when it is not supported by an easily recovered generalization. We need claim only that, whatever the right course is, it can be pursued in the case of consequence explanation.[3]

---

[1] Nor is the rain dance explanation supported by so simple a law as that given on p. 261. For other possibilities, see section (7).

[2] A 'law-sketch' is a law-like generalization in which some (but not all) of the antecedent properties are specified only by reference to an object which has them. For example: anyone who drinks four cups of coffee and is relevantly like George suffers sleeplessness thereafter. For the cow case: any species which is relevantly like a cow and which is such that if it has a long tail it has, as a result, the power to swish away flies, has a long tail.

[3] Some would reject explanations of features of organisms (or societies) in terms of their adaptive value on the ground that organisms (and societies) frequently fail to acquire adaptive features. Adaptive failure certainly is frequent, but an

This being the form of the laws presupposed in consequence and so[1] in functional explanation, we readily see that not every causal connection enables formulation of a functional explanation of the occurrence of the cause, quite apart from whether or not the cause benefits anything. It is virtually always true that if lightning occurred it would bring about thunder, but lightning occurs only infrequently. So lightning is not consequence explained and hence not functionally explained by its propensity to cause thunder. There is decisive reason for denying that lightning is functionally explained, independently of the fact that it has no function.

To summarize afresh: in a consequence explanation a dispositional fact explains the incidence of the property (or event-type) mentioned in the antecedent of the hypothetical specifying the disposition. A consequence explanation of the *striking* of a brittle tumbler (that is, one which, struck sufficiently hard, would break) would be in order if it were true as a matter of law that its being brittle raised the probability of its being struck. It would be wrong to think so, but not, we claim, because of the form of the thought.

What distinguishes functional from consequence explanation? In our view, a functional explanation is a consequence explanation in which the occurrence of the *explanandum* event (possession of the *explanandum* property, etc.) is functional for something or other, whatever 'functional' turns out to mean. Thus consequence explanations which are functional explanations may be conveyed by statements like 'The function of x is to ϕ', whatever may be the correct analysis of the latter.

An evident corollary of the present account: the fact that the consequence it cites is functional is not a fact about the structure of functional explanation, which is just that of consequence explanation in general.

But it might be claimed that no consequence explanation is ever offered which is not also a functional explanation. If

objection to functional explanation on that basis conflicts with our standard explanatory practices. For what one might call 'causal failure' is also common. Jones couldn't sleep because he overate, even though plenty of people sleep after overeating. Similarly, then, the cow may have a long tail because a long tail is functional for it, even though it would also be functional for a moose, and moose lack them.

[1] This slide is defended presently.

functionality is, as claimed, not germane to explanatory structure, why are all tendered consequence explanations functional explanations?

All explanation operates against a background of theoretical presupposition to which candidate explanations which satisfy structural and confirmational criteria must conform. The presuppositions of early modern physics, for example, included a principle forbidding action at a distance, and Newton's laws of motion, despite their theoretical economy and predictive success, were not regarded as explanatory, not even by Newton, because they were thought to violate the constraint on explanation the principle imposed. The restrictive presupposition was in time abandoned, so that Helmholtz could write in the mid-nineteenth century: 'To understand a phenomenon means nothing else than to reduce it to the Newtonian laws. Then the necessity for explanation has been satisfied in a palpable way.'[1] In earlier days Newton's laws were structurally sound but were considered materially inadequate for explanation.

We may similarly distinguish structural and material aspects of functional explanation, and our account of the former is not impugned by its neglect of the latter. The background against which consequence explanation is offered in biology or anthropology or economics is a conception of species or societies or economic units as self-maintaining and self-advancing, and consequence explanations are accordingly accepted only when they are also functional explanations. If we had background belief representing entities as self-destructive, we might accept consequence explanations which deserved to be called 'dysfunctional explanations'. It is not, indeed, evident that all of us lack such belief. If one way of taking psycho-analytic explanations which go beyond the pleasure principle to posit unconscious self-destructiveness is correct, some already have it. To elaborate would mean discussing the relation between consequence explanation and explanation of human action, which would take us too far afield.

Thus the fact, if it is a fact, that all plausible consequence explanations are functional explanations, does not tell against an account of the structure of functional explanation which abstracts from its functional character.

[1] Quoted by Hanson, *Patterns of Discovery*, p. 91.

(5) *Confirmation*

The confirmation of consequence explanations and laws raises no unusual problems. To stick to simplifying statement, the law-statement (and hence the explanation it would support), is confirmed by instances satisfying its major antecedent and consequent, and disconfirmed by instances satisfying its major antecedent only. A complication arises in assessing whether the major antecedent is satisfied, since it attributes a dispositional property. We therefore confront the problem of counterfactuals, but not in any novel way.

Thus suppose we wish to test the claim that the average scale of production in the *shoe* industry expanded because of the economies attending large scale in that industry. We may know of the *garment* industry that if it were to expand the scale of its production, economies would result. So the major antecedent of this consequence law-statement, which would support the claim about the shoe industry, is satisfied in the case of the garment industry:

> Whenever an expansion of scale would lead to economies, an expansion of scale occurs.

We then predict satisfaction of the major consequent in the case of the garment industry, the fate of the prediction being a test of the hypothesized law. If the prediction that scale will expand is falsified, there may be a suitable way of modifying the law-statement. The counter-example may motivate adding a conjunct to the major antecedent which says, e.g., that adequate funds to finance scale expansion are available.

So much for simple forms of confirmation. There are, of course, more complex ones, which cannot be surveyed here. It is sufficient to observe that unsimple ways of testing causal explanations will have their counterparts for the special kinds of causal explanation consequence explanations are.

A causal explanation of familiar form may be assessed without explicit examination of possible causal laws, and the same is true here. Professional intuition may respond to a particular functional-explanatory hypothesis: 'Such an item would have a similar effect in this other case too, yet we do not find it there'; or: 'and having searched for it, we have found it'.

It is of the utmost importance to note, particularly with regard to some Marxian functional explanatory claims, that a consequence explanation may be well confirmed in the absence of a theory as to *how* the dispositional property figures in the explanation of what it explains. In other terms, we may have good reason for thinking that a functional explanation is true even when we are at a loss to conjecture by what means or mechanism the functional fact achieves an explanatory role. We return to this point at the end of section (6), after we have faced and answered a sceptical challenge.

(6) *Are any Functional Explanations True?*

If we are right, there exist functional explanatory claims (see section (3)), their structure is as stated in section (4), and they may be tested as outlined in section (5). *But we have not yet shown that any such claims are true.* Our account of what a functional explanation is might be correct, yet there might be no true functional explanations. Indeed, some—if there are any—who accept our account might take it as a proof that there are no true functional explanations. They might say that dispositional properties never contribute to explanation in the asserted manner. Those who allow that, abstractly speaking, they could, might deny that they ever do in the world as we know it.

But we hold not only that the structure of functional explanation is as was claimed, but also that some explanations having that structure are correct. We must now defend this thesis against a likely scepticism.

The sceptic to be answered here would treat all supposed examples of functional explanation as really and only involving natural selection, or negative feedback mechanisms, or the results of conscious choice, and so on. He would say that what is truly explanatory is a phenomenon or process the relevant description of which involves no citation of the dispositional characteristics we favour. Confronted by what we called 'consequence laws' and 'consequence explanations', he would say that the first are at best non-explanatory generalizations and the second are not explanations at all.

The sceptic can accept the concept of a consequence generalization. He must even admit that there are true consequence generalizations: an abundance of them hold in natural history.

By a consequence generalization we understand a (possibly mere) correlation between a dispositional property and a concurrent or subsequent incidence of the property mentioned in the antecedent of the hypothetical specifying the disposition. That is a coherent concept and it is exemplified. The controversial question is whether such a generalization, even one which is a law, ever has any explanatory power.

Not all lawful generalizations are explanatory. Suppose it is a law that whenever F occurs, E occurs. An occurrence of F will nevertheless not explain an occurrence of E, if, for example, there is a third type of event, G, which causes each of F and E, and causes E other than by virtue of causing F. Pictorially, we would then have:

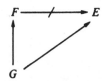

the arrow here representing a causal relationship. For example, let F be a barometer reading at t_1, let E be the weather at t_2, and let G be the atmospheric pressure at t_0 $(t_0 < t_1 < t_2)$. Whenever the barometer reads thus and so, the weather will be such and such, but it is false that barometer readings explain weather conditions. The barometer reading is only a *concomitant*, not an explanation, of the subsequent weather.

The sceptic claims that the dispositional property (the fact that were E to occur, it would cause F) is never more than a concomitant of the occurrence of E. The dispositional property is only a concomitant when what causes it to obtain is what causes E itself, and not by virtue of causing the disposition to obtain, as in this picture:

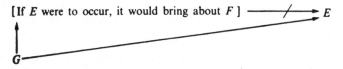

The sceptic says that what is pictured above is true of all consequence generalizations. His thesis may be formulated as follows:

Whenever a correlation holds *between* the fact that were E to occur, it would bring about F, *and E*, there is a G which causes the disposition (were E to occur, it would bring about F) to hold, which also causes E, and which does not cause E by virtue of causing the disposition to hold. Hence such a disposition is never more than a concomitant of E.

Here is an example of an apparently correct functional explanation which, on closer inspection, confirms the sceptical thesis.

Some flowers close their petals just when doing so will prevent wastage of their fragrance, thus enhancing their reproductive chances. Their reproduction depends on visitations by insects attracted by the fragrance. They close their petals at the onset of night, when the insects have retired. It looks as though the petals close because the closure is preservative, and that is a functional explanation.

Let E = petal closure, and let F = fragrance preservation. Then it is true that whenever E would cause F, E occurs.

The sceptic predicts that there is a G which (1) causes the petal closure to be fragrance-preserving, (2) causes the petal closure, and (3) does not cause the latter through causing the former.

Now the 'immediate' cause of the fragrance-preserving value of the petal closure (of the fact that E would cause F) is the departure of the insects, but the departure of the insects does not cause the petals to close. The plants are quite insensitive to presence or absence of insects. Hence the departure of the insects (call it D) is not the required G.

But further examination does reveal a relevant G. For what stimulates the closure of the petals is the reduction of light associated with the onset of night, and that reduction also causes the insects to leave, and therefore, by the transitivity of causation, causes the petal closure to be fragrance-preserving. The reduction of light is the G predicted by the sceptical thesis. Pictorially:

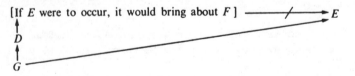

A functional explanation of the closure of the petals on a particular occasion would, accordingly, be a pseudo-explanation. But the result cannot be generalized. It is false that dispositional facts are never more than concomitants of what functional explanations claim they explain.

Two sorts of consequence generalization are supported by the fossil record, current observation, and inferences therefrom. In the first, or *diachronic* case, it is true at a time t that were a species to have a certain feature it would fare better, and true at a later time $t+n$ that the species has the feature. (More precisely, the disposition obtaining at t raises the probability of the truth at $t+n$ of the antecedent of the hypothetical specifying it.) In the second, or synchronic case, the time when the feature would be valuable and the time when it obtains are the same. We shall argue that in the diachronic case the generalization provides a genuine explanation, though in the synchronic case it does not.

An illustration of the diachronic case. A population of giraffes with a mean neck length of six feet lives in an environment of acacia trees, on whose leaves they feed. The height of the trees makes it true that if they now had longer necks, their survival prospects would be better. They subsequently come to have longer necks. So far all we have is evidence of a consequence generalization. But if Darwin's theory of evolution is true,[1] then the fact that were they to have had longer necks, they would have fared better, contributes to explaining the elongation. The environment selects in favour of variants with longer necks precisely because it is an environment in which longer necks improve life chances. On no construal can that dispositional fact be reduced to an unexplanatory precursor of the acquisition of the feature. Its explanatory relevance to the elongation of the neck is entailed by the Darwinian theory.

Or consider the plants discussed a moment ago, but change the question from 'Why do those plants now close their petals?' to 'Why did that species of plant acquire its sensitivity to light and darkness?' The answer will include the fact that were it to have had it in the past, it would have prospered better. Specimens having it were favoured, by virtue of that dispositional fact, over those lacking it.

[1] Though not *only if* it is true. Alternative theories give different accounts of why the dispositional feature is explanatory: see p. 271.

The sceptic says that the dispositional property is only correlated with what *really* explains the change in the species' equipment. In the giraffe example, what causes the longer-necked variants to be favoured, and thereby causes the species neck length to increase, is, he says, the presence of the trees, a quite undispositional circumstance.

We can agree that it is the trees which, aided by the chance genetic variation, cause the neck of the species to grow. But what is it about the trees which makes them have that effect? Answer: where trees are of the given height giraffes with longer necks would prosper better. The dispositional fact is an essential element in the explanatory story.

Turn now to *synchronic* natural-historical consequence generalizations. They do lack a genuine explanatory use. The species has the desirable feature because it was desirable earlier, not because it is desirable now. The current adaptive value of the feature, unlike the fact that it would have had adaptive value in the past, is causally irrelevant to its presence. If the environment were now different, so that the feature lacked value, the species would still have it. The flowers would continue to close their petals even if the insects suddenly changed their habits. Synchronic functional explanation in natural history is pseudo-explanation. The dispositional fact is merely correlated with the feature to be explained.[1] By contrast, had the disposition not obtained in the past, the species would not now have the feature. The diachronic explanation is genuine. Hence the sceptical thesis is false. There are true functional explanations. (And some of them, we contend, are provided by historical materialism.)

If someone says, 'That cow has a long tail because a long tail is good at swishing away flies', his remark is ambiguous across true and false interpretations. If he is assigning explanatory significance to the particular service provided by the tail to that particular cow, what he says is false. If, instead, he means that the cow has a long tail because such tails provide such service,

---

[1] The correlation holds because environments change slowly. If a feature would be adaptive now, it would probably have been adaptive in the past. If the species now has the feature, that is because it was adaptive in the past. The past adaptive value of the feature explains its current incidence and, because of environmental stability, probabilifies its current adaptive value. So the current adaptive value of the feature is an unexplanatory concomitant of its presence.

then what he says is sketchy but true, and the sketch is filled in when we add that, from an explanatory point of view, it is *past* occasions when tails would give such service which are relevant.

The sceptic holds that whenever a functional explanation appears to be apt, appearances are deceptive, and in fact some one of a short list of non-functional explanations applies (see p. 266). In the case of the characteristics of biological species, the correct alternative to functional explanation is supposed to be Darwin's theory, or, rather, a modern development of Darwin which draws upon genetics unavailable in his day.

In our view, Darwin's theory is not a rival of functional explanation, but, among other things, a compelling account of why functional explanations apply in the biosphere. It is possible to know *that x* explains *y*, and yet find it very puzzling that *x should* explain *y*, through failure to see *how x* explains *y*. Among Darwin's achievements was an attractive theory of how the fact that a facility would benefit a species helps to explain its acquisition.

Darwin discovered the way in which functional facts about the equipment of species contribute to explaining why they possess the equipment they do. In a different account, for example that of Lamarck, the functional facts would get their explanatory power from quite different considerations.[1] Both doctrines acknowledge the explanatory relevance of the dispositional features we have emphasized. What we have are rival theories of why a consequence explanation holds, not rival alternatives to consequence explanation.

We may say that these theories provide contrasting *elaborations* of natural-historical consequence explanations. Our experience of the world assures us that wherever a consequence explanation holds, it has some or other further elaboration, and we contend that the sceptic misconstrues as various alternatives to functional explanation what are in fact various more complete forms functional explanations may take. One object of Chapter X will be to propose directions of elaboration of Marxian functional-explanatory claims. But such claims may be rationally tenable before suitable elaborations are available. If a Marxist says that the bourgeois media report industrial conflicts in a style which

---

[1] For more on Lamarck, see Ch. X, pp. 288–9.

favours the capitalist class *because* that style of reportage has the asserted tendency, he may be able to justify his explanatory claim even when he cannot yet display *how* the fact that reportage in the given style favours the capitalist class explains the fact that industrial conflicts are reported in that way.

(7) *Consequence Explanation and the Deductive-nomological Model*

A consequence explanation relates to a consequence law in whatever way explanations relate to laws. It is not our task to say what that relation is. But it may be clarifying to exhibit how consequence laws figure in explanations on the supposition that the correct answer to the question here suspended is Hempel's. For Hempel every satisfactory and fully explicit explanation is an argument, either deductively valid or inductively sound, and containing among its premises at least one statement of law. Only one of the arguments thus licensed, the deductive-nomological (D-$\mathcal{N}$) will be considered here.

The simplest D-$\mathcal{N}$ argument contains two premises, one a law of conditional form, and the second a statement instantiating the antecedent of the law and thus together with it enabling deducibility of an instantiation of its consequent, which is the *explanandum*. An elementary consequence explanation, D-$\mathcal{N}$ construed, would contain as first premise a consequence law and as second a statement asserting an instantiation of its major antecedent. The schema, where what is to be explained is the occurrence of an event of a certain type, would be as follows:

L   IF it is the case that if an event of type E were to occur at t_1 then it would bring about an event of type F at t_2, THEN an event of type E occurs at t_3.

C   Were an event of type E to occur at t', it would bring about an event of type F at t''.

E   An event of type E occurs at t'''.[1]

[1] Or:

L $(\exists x)(Ex \text{ at } t_1 \ \Box\!\rightarrow (\exists y)(Fy \text{ at } t_2)) \longrightarrow (\exists z)(Ez \text{ at } t_3)$
C $(\exists x)(Ex \text{ at } t' \ \Box\!\rightarrow (\exists y)(Fy \text{ at } t''))$

E $(\exists z)(Ez \text{ at } t''')$

The symbols are to be read as in fn. 1, p. 260 except that 't''' and so on denote particular times, the relations between which are just those required to make E follow logically from L and C.

In his 'Logic of Functional Analysis' Hempel himself explores $D\text{-}N$ presentations of functional explanations. He first construes function-statements as benefit-statements in which the functional item is said to ensure 'the satisfaction of certain conditions . . . which are necessary for the proper working of' some system.[1] He then seeks a $D\text{-}N$ derivation of the presence of the item, whose operative premiss is that it fulfils one or more of the system's needs.[2]

In our view—and here we trespass into assessment of the $D\text{-}N$ model itself—the derivation Hempel seeks would not be an explanation even if it were successful, no more than *deriving* a flagpole's height from the length of its shadow, the position of the sun, and the laws of optics, would *explain* its height. For Hempel, the conjunction of a law about a system to the effect that it survives only if some condition C is satisfied and a statement saying that the system *is* surviving *explains*—what it doubtless *entails*—the fact that condition C is satisfied. If Hempel were right, the law that mammals exist only if there is oxygen in the atmosphere, in conjunction with the fact that mammals exist, would explain the fact that there is oxygen in the atmosphere; and that consequence of his theory is quite unacceptable. It is equally unacceptable to represent the fact that mammals exist, in conjunction with a law that hearts are necessary to their existence, as explaining their possession of hearts. Their possession of hearts may not be explained, and hence may not be functionally explained, in that manner.[3]

So much by way of critical aside. For Hempel, if the derivation of the presence of an item is, as a derivation, sound, then it also qualifies as an explanation. But he argues that in typical cases where functional explanations are offered, an effective derivation is unavailable. The deduction is either invalid,[4] or valid but with a disappointingly unspecific con-

---

[1] *Aspects of Scientific Explanation*, p. 305.

[2] The schema he suggests reads as follows:

(a) At time t, system s functions adequately in a setting of kind c

(b) s functions adequately in a setting of kind c only if a certain necessary condition, n, is satisfied

(c) If trait i were present in s then, as an effect, condition n would be satisfied

(d) (Hence), at t, trait i is present in s. Ibid., p. 310.

[3] Compare the point about societies and religions made at pp. 281–2 below.

[4] The schema of fn. 2 is clearly invalid: see *Aspects*, p. 310.

clusion, what is deduced being not that the functional item exists, but that some one or other of a (possibly unspecified) set of need-satisfiers exists.[1] The trouble arises because in typical cases something other than the functional item whose presence is to be explained might have satisfied the need. The item is a sufficient condition of its satisfaction, but a valid derivation of it would require that it be a necessary condition. Applied to the claim, taken as explanatory, that the rain-making ceremonials of the Hopi fulfil the function of reinforcing group identity, Hempel's basic point is that 'the function of the rain dance might be subserved by some other group ceremonial'.[2]

The point does not penetrate arguments instancing the schema on page 272 above, for they do not essentially contain benefit-statements, nor, a fortiori, statements to the effect that something satisfies a need. But it is reasonable to expect that, though aimed at something else, the point can be redirected against our different form of D-N argument. Let us accordingly examine how it might affect the latter.

Suppose, then, we have not Hempel's D-N candidates for the rain dance case, but a D-N argument whose law premiss is: if a rain dance would reinforce group identity, a rain dance is performed.[3] Hempel's point would not fault the derivability of the desired conclusion. But it might create doubt that the law premiss is true.

This is not because the law states—it does not—that only a rain dance would reinforce group identity. Hempel's point does not contradict the law. But it makes it dubious: why should the rain dance's potential suffice for its actualization when other ceremonials with similar potential are not actualized?

We are not, of course, obliged to vindicate this particular explanation. But since it is typical enough of functional

---

[1] In the alternative schema, (a) and (b) are as in fn. 2, p. 273 and (c) and (d) are replaced by:

(c′) I is the class of empirically sufficient conditions for n, in the context determined by s and c; and I is not empty

(d′) (Hence), some one of the items included in I is present in s and t.

Ibid., p. 313.

[2] Ibid., p. 311.

[3] Note that our explanandum is the performance of a rain dance on a particular occasion, not the presence of the rain dance in the society's cultural repertoire. Treatment of the latter would be exactly analogous to what follows, but the first is easier to handle.

explanations, it is worth outlining how it might be defended against what Hempel says.

Hempel's point may be correct, but it is far from obviously correct: it only seems so. It is not obvious that performance of a ritual other than a rain dance would reinforce group identity among the Hopi. It may be that such rituals reinforce only under certain conditions, which are met by rain dances alone in the cases where rain dances and not other rituals occur. One plausible condition is that the ritual be part of the traditional repertoire of the tribe. If rain dances have this property only when other rituals do not, then other rituals, contrary to Hempel's claim, will lack comparable reinforcing potential among the Hopi. If this is so, the original explanation retains whatever plausibility it had. Nothing Hempel says would tend to fault it.

But suppose Hempel is right that alternative ceremonials would reinforce Hopi group identity. We may then retreat to a second line of defence, as follows.

Hempel's point now being granted, the law as originally stated becomes suspect, but a modified version of it which retains the consequence-legal element may nevertheless hold. The original major antecedent, which describes the rain dance's potential, is now insufficient to imply that a rain dance is performed. But perhaps we obtain a sufficient condition by adding a conjunct to the major antecedent, one stating, e.g., that a rain dance is part of the traditional repertoire of the society in question. Neither this nor the rain dance's potential, we are supposing, by itself suffices for the performance of a rain dance, but together they do. The revised law-statement says: if a rain dance would reinforce group identity *and* rain dancing belongs to the society's tradition, then a rain dance is performed. If the *C*-statement is also revised, by addition of a corresponding conjunct, we are again able to derive the original *explanandum*.

Note that tradition (or whatever condition—it might be a less obvious one—we appeal to) plays a different role in the second defence from what it did in the first. There it was a condition of a ritual's integrating effect that it be a traditional one. Tradition generated an argument for retaining the original law-statement. In the second defence it is allowed that tradition is not required for a ritual to have an integrating effect: rather if a ritual would have that effect, *and* it is traditional, then it is performed.

The evidence may be unfavourable to both lines of argument. Then a third defence becomes appropriate. It is to admit that the law does not hold, even in qualified form, and regress to one which says that if a (here unspecified) ceremonial would reinforce group identity, then some or other such ceremonial is performed. We may then deduce not the original *explanandum* but merely that some or other appropriate ceremonial is performed. The price of this loss of specificity is not as great as Hempel might contend.[1]

Hempel has himself frequently stressed that every explanation fails to account for innumerable properties of the *explanandum* phenomenon. Whether the respect in which it is explained represents an achievement depends on our interests. When glass breaks, we care little about the pattern its bits make, and are therefore satisfied with an explanation of why it broke at all, which is usually as far as we can get anyway. So similarly an anthropologist may find it interesting that some or other ceremonial is performed at all, and, having functionally explained that, he may proceed to investigate its specific character without pretence that it too is functionally explained. Given that they perform a ritual, there may be no *functional* explanation why it is this ritual rather than that, and yet that they perform a ritual may be functionally explained.

It is, then, no more a condition of sound functional explanation than of sound explanation generally that phenomena be explained in some ordained measure of specificity. Hempel emphasizes the point for the general case, but he wrongly fails to apply it to the functional instance.[2]

Hempel's basic claim is that the reinforcing power of the rain dance does not explain why the Hopi perform it, since other

---

[1] He would presumably call the result 'rather trivial'. See *Aspects*, p. 314.

[2] The same considerations show that Charles Taylor makes the position of what he calls 'teleological explanation' more difficult than he need by requiring that the fine structure of the *explanandum* (how fine he fails to say) be captured teleologically. See *The Explanation of Behavior*, p. 9 n., and 'The Explanation of Purposive Behaviour', p. 55 n.

Readers of Taylor will have realized that the concept of a consequence law is in some respects a development of his concept of a teleological law.

ceremonials would have the same effect. Because the example is typical of functional explanations, the claim becomes a critique of functional explanation as such. Here is a résumé of our response to that critique, in language which does not presuppose our particular theory of functional explanation.

(i) It is easy to overestimate the availability of substitutes for a given functional device. The fact that ceremonials which are not rain dances reinforce social cohesion in other tribes does not show that they would do so among the Hopi. In general: if device d fulfils function f in system s, and device d' fulfils the same function f in a distinct system s', it does not follow that d' would fulfil f if it occurred in s.

(ii) Suppose, though, as will sometimes be true, that d' would fulfil f in s. Then the fact that d fulfils f in s is unlikely to explain its presence there. But d's presence might still have a *partly* functional explanation. For example: the facts of genetic variation are part of the explanation why a species developed a certain adaptive feature, the other part being its adaptiveness. (Other features would have been just as adaptive, but the genetic variation excluded them.)

(iii) Where responses (i) and (ii) both fail, we might still be able to sustain a functional explanation, not of the presence of d, but of why some or other item which fulfils function f is present, that is, of why there is an x in s such that x fulfils f in s. It is not trivial to say: the cow has a device which dispatches flies because such a device dispatches flies—even though that is not why what it has is a *tail*.

CHAPTER X

Functional Explanation: In Marxism

(1) *Introduction*

CHAPTER IX defended functional explanation, an intellectual device indispensable to historical materialism as expounded in this book. The defence continues here. We deal with objections to a functionally construed historical materialism likely to be raised by Marxists, and by non-Marxist social scientists. Following that, various elaborations (see p. 271) of Marxian explanatory claims are conjectured.

The Preface to *The Critique of Political Economy* uses a number of explanatory expressions: relations of production *correspond* to productive forces; the legal and political superstructure *rises on* the real foundation; the social, political, and intellectual life process *is conditioned by* the mode of production of material life; consciousness *is determined by* social being. In each case Marx distinguishes two items, the second of which he asserts to be in some way explanatory of the first. He fails to say, here and everywhere else, what kind of explanation he is hypothesizing, and semantic analysis of the italicized phrases would not be a good way of discovering what he meant. We have said that central Marxian explanations are functional, which means, *very roughly*, that the character of what is explained is determined by its effect on what explains it. One reason for so interpreting Marx: if the *direction* of the explanatory tie is as he laid down, then the best account of the *nature* of the tie is that it is a functional one. For production relations profoundly affect productive forces, and superstructures strongly condition foundations. What Marx claims to explain has momentous impact on what he says explains it. Construing his explanations as functional makes for compatibility between the causal power of the explained phenomena and their secondary status in the order of explanation.

Thus to say that an economic structure *corresponds* to the achieved level of the productive forces means: the structure provides maximum scope for the fruitful use and development of the forces, and obtains *because* it provides such scope. To say that being *determines* consciousness means, at least in large part: the character of the leading ideas of a society is explained by their propensity, in virtue of that character, to sustain the structure of economic roles called for by the productive forces.[1]

Putting the two theses together, we get such hypotheses as that Protestantism arose when it did because it was a religion suited to stimulating capitalist enterprise and enforcing labour discipline at a time when the capital/labour relation was pre-eminently apt to develop new productive potentials of society. When Marx says that 'Protestantism, by changing almost all the traditional holidays into workdays, plays an important role in the genesis of capital'[2] he is not just assigning a certain effect to the new religion, but proposing a (partial) explanation of its rise in terms of that effect.

While Marx was inexplicit about the structure of the central explanations he hypothesized, there are some hints:

> The first 'Statute of Labourers' (23 Edward III, 1349) found its immediate pretext (not its cause, for legislation of this kind lasts centuries after the pretext for it has disappeared) in the great plague that decimated the people.[3]

The Statute cannot be explained by the circumstances of its origin, but only by reference to the persisting effect of legislation of that kind on the developing social structure. We must avoid the error of the 'English, who have a tendency to look upon the earliest form of appearance of a thing as the cause of its existence . . .'[4]

There is no well-stated alternative to the view that major Marxian explanatory claims are functional in character. The functional construal is nevertheless not popular, for a number of bad reasons, which will shortly be exposed. In practice Marxists advance functional explanations, but they do not theorize their practice accurately. They recoil from the

---

[1] For extended commentary on 'Social being determines consciousness', see my 'Being, Consciousness, and Roles'.

[2] *Capital*, i. 276. Protestant reformers themselves stressed that the abolition of Saints' days would have a salutary effect on industry. See Hill, *Puritanism and Revolution*, p. 51 and *Change and Continuity*, p. 81.

[3] *Capital*, i. 272.

[4] Ibid., p. 403. See also the passages quoted on pp. 232–3 above.

functional construal when it is made explicit, for reasons to be reviewed. They then have recourse to opaque ideas of 'structural causality',[1] to invocation of Engels's unexplained 'determination in the last resort',[2] to the facile suggestion that the priority of the base lies in the fact that it limits the superstructure, as though the converse were not also true;[3] or they effectively abandon the master theses of explanatory priority by interpreting them as merely heuristic.

Marxists regard functional explanation as suspect for a variety of reasons, the most important of which are dealt with in the next two sections.

(2) *Conceptual Criticisms of Functional Explanation*

This section is an informal restatement of some of the principal contentions of the last chapter, in confrontation with a typical critique of functional explanation.

Let us begin with a simple functional explanation. In some industries there is, over a period of time, a marked increase in the median size of the producing units: small workshops grow into, or are replaced by, large factories. The increased scale reduces the costs of producing a given volume of output. It generates economies of scale. If we find that scale grows just when growth in scale would have that effect, and not otherwise, then it is a plausible explanatory hypothesis that scale grows *because* the growth brings economies. Note that we may be justified in proposing this explanation before we know *how* the fact that enlarged scale induces economies explains large scale. We can know that something operated in favour of large scale, because of its cost effectiveness, without knowing what so operated. We may not know whether the increase was deliberately sought by wise managers, or came about through an economic analogue of chance variation and natural selection. We might be able to claim *that* the change is explained by its consequences without being able to say *how* it is so explained.

Let us now delineate the form of the explanation more carefully. We have a cause, increase of scale, and an effect,

---

[1] Althusser, whom we may associate with this phrase, himself employs functional explanations when dealing with actual social phenomena. See, for example, 'Ideology and the Ideological State Apparatuses', in *Lenin and Philosophy*.

[2] Engels to Bloch, 21–22 Sept. 1890, *Selected Correspondence*, p. 394.

[3] Cf. p. 158 above.

economies of scale. It is not proposed that the cause occurred because the effect occurred. Nor even—though this formulation is closer to the truth—that the cause occurred because it caused that effect. Instead, the cause occurred because of its propensity to have that effect: *the increase in scale occurred because the industry was of a sort in which increases in scale yield economies.*

This being the form of functional explanation, a common objection to it is misplaced. We take the objection as it is stated by Percy Cohen. His examples of functional explanation are

> that religion exists in order to sustain the moral foundations of society . . . [and] . . . that the State exists in order to coordinate the various activities which occur in complex societies. In both these cases a consequence is used to explain a cause; the end conditions of moral order and coordination are used to explain the existence of religion and the State . . . Critics rightly argue that this type of explanation defies the laws of logic, for one thing cannot be the cause of another if it succeeds it in time.[1]

Now it is true (if not, perhaps, a law of logic) that what comes later does not explain what comes earlier. But it is false that the theses mentioned by Cohen violate that truth. It is a plausible generalization that a society develops and/or sustains a religion when a religion is necessary for (or would contribute to) its stability. The religion of a society might, then, be explained in terms of this feature of the society: it requires a religion to be viable. That feature is not a consequence of having a religion, and there would be no contortion of time order in the explanation.

Now suppose a society requires a religion for stability, and has a religion fulfilling that need. It does not follow that its need for a religion *explains* its having one.[2] The society may indeed require a religion, but it is a further question whether it has one *because* it requires one. It may have one not at all because it needs one, but for other reasons. Imagine ten godless communities, each, because it lacks a religion, teetering on the brink of disintegration. A prophet visits all ten, but only one of them accepts his teaching. The other nine subsequently perish, and the single believing society survives. But they took up

---

[1] *Modern Social Theory*, pp. 47-8. Cohen's other criticisms are implicitly answered in the last chapter.

[2] This would follow on Hempel's theory of explanation: see p. 273.

religion because they liked the prophet's looks, and not because they needed a religion (though they did need a religion). So the fact that there is a religion, and it is needed, does not show that there is a religion because it is needed. That demands further argument. Perhaps some sociologists mistake the need for further argument as a defect in functional explanation itself.

To say that

(1) f occurred

is not to advance an explanation of why e occurred.[1] Yet it might be true that

(2) e occurred because f occurred.

(2) may or may not be true, and if it is true, it is not true simply because (1) is true.

Analogous remarks apply to functional explanation. One does not propose an explanation of the existence of religion by saying that

(3) Religion is required to sustain social order.[2]

Yet it might be true that

(4) Religion exists because it is required to sustain social order.

(4) may or may not be true, and if it is true, it is not true simply because (3) is true.

The mere fact that f preceded e does not guarantee that f caused e, though it may be true that f caused e. Similarly, the mere fact that g's propensities are beneficial does not guarantee that g is explained by those propensities, but it may be true that it is so explained. The existence of the fallacy *post hoc ergo propter hoc* does not disqualify all causal explanations. Neither does the comparable fallacy of supposing that, if something is functional, it is *explained* by its function(s), rule out all functional explanations.

So Percy Cohen is misled when he rejects a theory of religion solely because it explains religion functionally, and when he impugns Durkheim's account of the division of labour on the ground that it is functional in form.[3] There is nothing in

---

[1] Unless (1) is offered in response to 'Why did e occur?', in which case uttering (1) is tantamount to uttering (2).

[2] Again, unless (3) is a response to 'Why is there religion?'

[3] *Modern Social Theory*, pp. 35–6.

principle wrong with functional explanations, though to identify a function something serves is not necessarily to provide one. Failure to recognize both truths generates confused debate in sociology, for many catch one truth only.

Thus while Cohen mistakenly argues that assigning a function to a phenomenon cannot be explanatory, others suppose that to show that a usage or institution is required or eufunctional is *ipso facto* to explain its existence. Merton's classic paper tends towards the supposition that to establish that an item has functions is automatically to contribute to explaining it. He never satisfactorily distinguishes between explaining something by reference to its function(s) (functional explanation proper), and explaining the function(s) of something (see p. 252). He identifies a function the Hawthorne experiment had (see p. 257), but fails to note it is not a function which explains why the experiment took place.[1]

Sociologists often identify interesting functions, but it is always a further question, whose answer needs further evidence and argument, whether what they identify explains why something is so. Sometimes good evidence and argument is forthcoming, but not always.

(3) *Functionalism, Functional Explanation, and Marxism*

Other objections to the functional explanation of social phenomena spring from the historical association between *functional explanation* and the theory of *functionalism*. Defects in the latter have affected the reputation of the former. This is regrettable since, as we shall see, there is not a necessary connection between them.

By functionalism we understand the trend in anthropology whose chief proponents were Malinowski and Radcliffe-Brown. It affirmed three theses,[2] here listed in ascending order of strength ((3) entails (2) and (2) entails (1)):

(1) All elements of social life are interconnected. They strongly

---

[1] It might be claimed in Merton's defence that he was concerned only with *identifying* functions of social patterns and institutions, not with functionally *explaining* them. This is a highly implausible reading, and if it is correct, then we may object that in an article recommending the study of functions Merton neglected their explanatory significance.

[2] Not often clearly distinguished from one another.

influence one another and in aggregate 'form one inseparable whole'[1] (*Interconnection Thesis*).

(2) All elements of social life support or reinforce one another, and hence too the whole society which in aggregate they constitute (*Functional Interconnection Thesis*).

(3) Each element is as it is *because* of its contribution to the whole, as described in (2) (*Explanatory Functional Interconnection Thesis*).

Thesis (3) embodies a commitment to functional explanation, and it has therefore been criticized on grounds like those discussed and rejected in the last section. But there has also been separate criticism of thesis (2), which proposes no functional *explanations*, but asserts the universal eufunctionality of social elements. It is objected that (2) is falsified by the conflict, strain, and crisis so common in so many societies. How could Malinowski think that 'in every type of civilisation, every custom, material object, idea and belief fulfils some vital function, has some task to accomplish, represents an indispensable part within a working whole'?[2]

(2) is widely thought to be not only false but also viciously conservative in its implications. Marxists have, accordingly, been strong opponents of functionalism, a fact which helps to explain their failure to acknowledge the functional nature of their own explanatory theses.

Whether functionalism is in truth inescapably conservative is a question we need not discuss, though we may note how natural it is to conclude that if everything serves a useful purpose or is, indeed, indispensable, then there is no scope for desirable social change. Radcliffe-Brown's principle of the 'functional consistency of social systems'[3] seems hard to reconcile with the reality of class struggle, and whatever serves to deny the latter is a comfort to conservative convictions.

It should be obvious that a Marxist can assert functional explanations without endorsing any of theses (1) to (3). Functional explanation is compatible with rejection of the doctrine of functionalism, and functional explanation is not necessarily conservative. Functional explanation in historical

[1] Malinowski, *Argonauts of the Western Pacific*, p. 515.

[2] Malinowski, *A Scientific Theory of Culture*.

[3] See *A Natural Science of Society*, pp. 124–8, and *Structure and Function in Primitive Society*, p. 43.

materialism is, moreover, revolutionary, in two respects: it predicts large-scale social transformations, and it claims that their course is violent.

To say that forms of society rise and fall according as they advance and retard the development of the productive forces is to predict massive transformations of social structure as the productive forces progress. The master thesis of historical materialism (thesis (b) of p. 134) puts the growth of human powers at the centre of the historical process, and it is to this extra-social[1] development that society itself is contrained to adjust. The conservative tendency of functionalism lies in its functionally explaining institutions as sustaining (existing) society. There is no conservatism when institutions, and society itself, are explained as serving a development of power which prevails against forms of society resisting it.

The theory is also revolutionary in that the means whereby society is transformed is class conflict. Transitions do not occur quietly and easily. Society adjusts itself to nature through access to power of a new class. Class struggle is a large part of the answer to the question: *how* does the fact that a new economic structure would benefit the productive forces explain its actualization? We must now consider such 'how-questions' more generally.

(4) *Elaborations*

We argued in Chapter IX (pp. 269 ff.) that sound functional explanations apply to the development of biological species. The theory of chance variation and natural selection does not displace functional explanation in that domain. Instead, it shows, *inter alia*, why functional explanation is appropriate there. The theory entails that plants and animals have the useful equipment they do because of its usefulness, and specifies in what manner the utility of a feature accounts for its existence.

Now in the absence of such a theory we shall still observe provocative correlations between the requirements of living existence and the actual endowments of living things, correlations fine enough to suggest the thesis that they have those endowments because they minister to those requirements. We can rationally hypothesize functional explanations even when

[1] In the sense of Ch. IV.

we lack an account which, like Darwin's, shows how the explanations work, or, as we put it in Chapter IX (see p. 271), even when we lack *elaborations* of the explanations. A satisfying elaboration provides a fuller explanation and locates the functional fact within a longer story which specifies its explanatory role more precisely.

Now the fact that functional explanations may reasonably be proposed, in the light of suitable evidence, but in advance of an elaborating theory, is very important for social science and history. For functional explanations in those spheres often carry conviction in the absence of elaborative context. And it would be a mistake to refrain from taking those explanatory steps which are open to us, just because we should prefer to go farther than our current knowledge permits.[1] *If*, for example, the pattern of educational provision in a society evolves in a manner suitable to its changing economy, then it is reasonable to assert that education changes as it does because the changes sustain economic evolution, even when little is known about *how* the fact that an educational change would be economically propitious figures in explaining its occurrence. To be sure, there are grounds for caution pending acquisition of a plausible fuller story, but that is not especially true of functional explanations.

For it is not only explanations of functional cast which, though accepted as explanations, are yet felt to require further elaboration. We are frequently *certain* that p explains q yet unclear *how* it explains it. Someone ignorant of the contribution of oxygen to combustion may yet have overwhelming evidence that when a match, having been struck, bursts into flame, it bursts into flame *because* it has been struck, for all that his ignorance prevents him from saying how it is that the friction leads to ignition. So similarly, to return to functional explanation, one ignorant of genetics and evolutionary theory, will, when he finds species of insects regularly developing means of resisting pesticides introduced into their environments, naturally conclude that they develop those means because they are protective, although he can say nothing more. Perhaps historians and social scientists never record cases of adaptation as unarguable as the biological ones. But the rest of their explanatory hypothesizing is also based on less impressive

[1] Cf. Plekhanov, *The Monist View*, p. 330.

evidence than what natural scientists are in a position to demand.

Functional explanations, then, have intellectual validity and value, even if it is said that 'they raise more questions than they answer'. For they answer some questions, and the further ones to which they give rise point research in the right direction.

But now let us examine some ways in which functional explanations may be elaborated.

Consider once again an industry in which average scale of production expands because of the economies large scale brings. We imagined (p. 280) this explanatory judgement being passed without detailed knowledge of a connection between the fact that scale yields economies and the (consequent) fact that scale expanded. Two elaborations readily suggest themselves.

First, we can suppose that the industry's decision-makers knew that increased scale would yield economies, and that they enlarged their producing units out of awareness of that functional fact. The functional fact would then play its explanatory role by accounting for formation of the (correct) belief that an increase in scale would be beneficial; that belief, together with a desire for the relevant benefits, being a more proximate cause of the expansion in size. For obvious reasons, we call this a *purposive* elaboration of a functional explanation.

In the above elaboration we neither assert nor deny that the industrial units operate in a competitive environment. The decision makers might be Gosplanners, setting the course of an industry wholly subject to their will. But purposive elaboration can also apply in a competitive setting, in which case among the known benefits to be had from expanding scale might be the very survival of each of the firms in question.

In a competitive economy a purposive elaboration is, as noted, possible, but so is a second important form of elaboration. Imagine a competitive economy in which a certain industry would function more efficiently under increased scale, but suppose the managers of the industry's firms are ignorant of the fact. Then if mean scale expands, it is not because anyone seeks the economies increased scale promises. Still, some firms increase the scale of their producing units, perhaps because prestige is attached to size, or because the move is seen as a way of reducing tension between managers; or suppose that there is no intention to increase scale, but, in certain firms, an ungoverned drift in that direction. Then we could not say of any particular firm that its scale grew because of the associated economies. But the functional fact might still explain a change over time in the industry's scale profile, if only those firms which expanded (for whatever reason) would have succeeded, in virtue of having expanded, against the competition. Competition is bound to select in favour of firms whose practice is efficient, regardless of the inspiration of that practice. In the case described, we have what may be called a *Darwinian* elaboration of a functional explanation, for these are its salient elements: chance[1] variation (in scales of production), scarcity (in virtue of finite effective demand), and selection (on the market of those variants which, by chance, had a superior structure).

A third kind of elaboration may be called *Lamarckian*. In Lamarckian biological theory, by contrast with that of Darwin, the species evolves in virtue of evolution within the life history of its specimens, which acquire more adaptive characteristics, and transmit them to offspring.[2] An organ not fully suited to the creature's environment becomes more suited as a result of the struggle to use it in that environment. (An example would be teeth becoming sharper as a result of regular chewing on food best chewed by sharp teeth.) The suggested elaboration is not purposive, because it is not the intention of the organism so to alter its equipment: it is altered as a result of a use which is not intended to alter it, but which reflects the environment's demands. Nor is the elaboration Darwinian. The initial varia-

---

[1] This designation does not imply that the variation is uncaused or inexplicable. What is meant by 'chance' is that the explanation of the variation is unconnected with the functional value of greater scale. Darwin calls genetic variation *chance* only because it is not controlled by the requirements of the environment.

[2] Following Ritterbush (*Overtures to Biology*, p. 175), we may distinguish between the *acquisition* of inheritable characteristics and the *inheritance* of acquired characteristics, and it is the former which interests us here: we are not concerned with the transmission of features from one social entity to another. Lamarck is relevant for his concept of an adaptation to the environment which is not mediated by a prior chance variation. The movement towards the adaptation is from the beginning controlled by the environment's demands.

Lamarck's specification of the mechanism of adaptation, in terms of 'the influx of subtle fluids', is also irrelevant here. What has social application is the concept of plasticity, of organs being able to develop new uses under new constraints.

tions, which are then preserved, do not occur by chance relative to the environmental requirements, and there *need* not be any competitive pressure on the organism, expressing itself in differential survival rates as between well- and ill-equipped specimens.

A fourth form of elaboration—really a special case of the first—is appropriate in cases of *self-deception*. By contrast with the second and third forms, the functional fact operates through the minds of agents, but unlike paradigm purposive examples, it does so without the agents' full acknowledgement. An elaboration of this form for the economies of scale case would be quite fanciful, but it is relevant to Marxian theory, as will be seen.

The above classification is not exhaustive, and the types of elaboration reviewed admit of combination with one another: there are often several interlaced routes from the functional fact to the fact it explains. C. Wright Mills contrasted 'drift' and 'thrust' in social development,[1] and it is easy to envisage agglomerations of the two. Thus, returning once again to economies of scale, there could initially be an unplanned drift to greater average size, controlled by competition, and later a perception of the functional relationship, with increasing thrust as a result.

(5) *Marxian Illustrations*

Our discussion will be confined to two central topics: the generation and propagation of ideology, and the adaptation of the economic structure to the productive forces.

When Marxists venture functional explanations of ideological and superstructural phenomena, they are often accused of espousing a 'conspiracy theory of history'. A Marxist says 'it is no accident that' left-wing commentators receive little space in major American newspapers, or that British trade union leaders end their careers in the House of Lords. He is then criticized for imagining that an omnicompetent élite exercises fine control over these matters. He sometimes tries to forestall the response by disclaiming an assertion of conspiracy, but too commonly he fails to say in what other fashion phenomena like those mentioned are explained by the functions they serve.

[1] See *The Causes of World War Three*.

Our discussion of non-purposive elaborations of functional claims suggests ways of filling that lacuna, but it is also necessary to point out that Marxists can be too sensitive to the charge that they perceive conspiracies. There is more collective design in history than an inflexible rejection of 'conspiracy theories' would allow, and richer scope for purposive elaboration of Marxian functional theses than that posture recognizes. Thus, while ideologies are not normally invented to fit the purposes they serve, a fairly deliberate and quite concerted effort to maintain and protect an *existing* ideology is not unusual. According to Christopher Hill, nobility and gentry in seventeenth-century England doubted they 'would still be able to control the state without the help of the church', and, there-fore, 'rallied to the defence of episcopacy in 1641 . . . for explicitly social reasons'.[1] Ruling class persons of no special devotion to an Anglican God frankly professed that the established church was required to ensure political obedience, and acted on that inspiration. Or, to take another example, when a high state functionary, reflecting on the unequal distribution of information in society, concludes that 'this inequality of knowledge has become necessary for the main-tenance of all the social inequalities *which gave rise to it*',[2] he may be expected to see to the persistence of an educational structure which reproduces ignorance in the right places.

Conspiracy is a natural effect when men of like insight into the requirements of continued class domination get together, and such men do get together. But sentences beginning 'The ruling class have decided . . .' do not entail the convocation of an assembly. Ruling class persons meet and instruct one another in overlapping *milieux* of government, recreation, and practical affairs, and a collective policy emerges even when they were never all in one place at one time.

There are, of course, many shades between the cynical[3] handling of ideology just emphasized and an unhypocritical commitment to it, and a division of labour between lucid and *engagé* defenders of dominant ideas can be quite functional. If

---

[1] *Reformation to Industrial Revolution*, pp. 153, 92. Cf. *Change and Continuity*, p. 191.

[2] Jacques Necker, as quoted at *Theories of Surplus Value*, i. 307.

[3] What was cynical was not the belief that the existing order ought to be defended, but the use of religion in its defence.

awareness of the true name of the game penetrates too far down the élite, it could leak into the strata beneath them. There is always a mix of manipulation, self-deception, and blind conviction in adherence to an ideology, the optimal proportions varying with circumstance.

All classes are receptive to whatever ideas are likely to benefit them, and ruling classes are well placed to propagate ideologies particularly congenial to themselves. But before an ideology is received or broadcast it has to be formed. And on that point there are traces in Marx of a Darwinian mechanism, a notion that thought-systems are produced in comparative independence from social constraint, but persist and gain social life following a filtration process which selects those well adapted for ideological service. Thus it is true but in one respect unimportant that the idea of communism has been projected time and again in history,[1] for only when the idea can assist a viable social purpose, as it can now, by figuring in the liberation of the proletariat, will it achieve social significance. There is a kind of 'ideological pool' which yields elements in different configurations as social requirements change.

Yet it is unlikely that ideas fashioned in disconnection from their possible social use will endorse and reject *exactly* what suits classes receptive to them. Here a Lamarckian element may enter, to make the picture more plausible.[2] In Lamarck's theory the equipment of the individual organism is somewhat plastic, for it changes under environmental challenge when it is put to a novel use. Because of the delicacy of intellectual constructions, sets of ideas enjoy a partly similar plasticity: one change of emphasis, one slurred inference, etc., can alter the import of the whole. Such 'Lamarckian' possibilities are intimated in Marx's review of the numerous uses to which a self-same Christianity is liable,[3] and it is not because 'liberalism' is an ambiguous term that its presumed teaching varies across space and time. And if it is true of revolutionaries that

[1] *German Ideology*, p. 51.
[2] Plekhanov invoked Lamarck in the service of historical materialism: 'In the same way must also be understood the influence of economic requirements, and of others following from them, on the psychology of a people. Here there takes place a slow adaptation by exercise or non-exercise . . .' *The Monist View*, pp. 217–18.
[3] See 'The Communism of the Paper *Rheinischer Beobachter*', p. 82.

just when they seem engaged in revolutionising themselves and things, in creating something that has never yet existed, precisely in such periods of revolutionary crisis they anxiously conjure up the spirits of the past to their service and borrow from them names, battle cries and costumes in order to present the new scene of world history in this time-honoured disguise and this borrowed language,[1]

then it is perhaps not only for the reason Marx states that they so behave, but also because the only symbols and thought-forms available are those which come from the past, and which they must now adopt and adapt.

Chapter VI upheld the thesis that transformations of economic structure are responses to developments within the productive forces. Production relations reflect the character of the productive forces, a character which makes a certain type of structure propitious for their further development. We denied that this formulation removed class struggle from the centre of history, saying instead that it was a chief means whereby the forces assert themselves over the relations, and challenging those who assign a more basic role to class struggle to explain what else determines the rise and fall of classes (pp. 148–9). Those remarks constitute a preliminary elaboration of the functional explanation of forms of economy, which must now be extended.

Classes are permanently poised against one another, and that class tends to prevail whose rule would best meet the demands of production. But how does the fact that production would prosper under a certain class ensure its dominion? Part of the answer is that there is a general stake in stable and thriving production, so that the class best placed to deliver it attracts allies from other strata in society. Prospective ruling classes are often able to raise support among the classes subjected to the ruling class they would displace. Contrariwise, classes unsuited to the task of governing society tend to lack the confidence political hegemony requires, and if they do seize power, they tend not to hold it for long.

Sometimes, too, as in the gradual formation of capitalism, the capacity of a new class to administer production expresses

---

[1] 'The Eighteenth Brumaire', p. 247.

itself in nascent forms of the society it will build, which, being more effective than the old forms, tend to supplant them. Purposive and competitive elements mingle as early growths of capitalism encroach upon and defeat feudal institutions that would restrict them. There is also adaptive metamorphosis. For example: a pre-capitalist landed ruling class in an epoch of commercialization requires finance from a not yet industrial bourgeoisie. When landlords cannot meet the commitments engendered by their new connections, they lose their holdings, so others, in fear of a similar fate, place their operations on a capitalist basis. Some see what is required for survival, and undergo an alteration of class character; others fail to understand the times, or, too attached to an outmoded ideology and way of life, fight against the new order, and disappear.

The ideological and superstructural supports of the old order lose their authority. The sense of oppression and injustice always latent in the underclass becomes more manifest, encouraged by the class whose hour of glory is at hand, and the dominating illusions become pallid. Marx supposed that the ideological defences of existing conditions begin to collapse when those conditions no longer accord with productive growth. Thus

> when the illusion about competition as the so-called absolute form of free individuality vanishes, this is evidence that the conditions of competition, i.e. of production founded on capital, are already felt and thought of as *barriers*, and hence already *are* such, and more and more become such.[1]

In similar spirit, Engels opined[2] that ideas of equality and rectification of injustice are perennial, but that they achieve historical power only when and because there is contradiction between the productive forces and the production relations. The class able to take hold of the forces rides up on the resentment of the exploited producers.

Recall the distinction (Chapter III, section (8)) between a change in economic structure which institutes a new dominant relation of production, thus altering the economic structure's type, and a lesser change, which leaves the latter intact. We

[1] *Grundrisse*, p. 652.   [2] *Anti-Dühring*, p. 369.

have been looking at the more dramatic case, the replacement of one type of economic structure by another. But adaptations of the economic structure falling short of total transformation also occur. One such change was the legislated reduction of the working day in Britain, which modified the dominant relation of production, by altering the space in which the wage bargain between bourgeois and proletarians was to be struck.[1]

Marx states two reasons for the contraction of the working day effected by the Factory Acts, and he establishes no bond uniting them. Having presented his reasons, we shall sketch a possible connection between them, which will suggest a generalization about the way functional requirements sometimes assert themselves.

The reasons: 'apart from the working-class movement that daily grew more threatening, the limiting of factory labour was dictated by' the need to 'curb the passion of capital for a limitless draining of labour power'.[2] These are cited as separate forces, whose confluence produced the Factory Acts. (Marx does not say whether either would have been enough without the other.)

Marx conceived that the health of the system required a brake on capitalist exploitation, which was reaching a pitch inimical to the reproduction of the labour force:

> ... capital is reckless of the health or length of life of the labourer, unless under compulsion from society. To the outcry as to the physical and mental degradation, the premature death, the torture of overwork, it answers: Ought these to trouble us since they increase our profits?[3]

Here 'capital' is capital embodied in the individual capitalist, and the behaviour ascribed to him is imposed by the regime of competition, a set of 'external coercive laws having power over every individual capitalist'.[4] The coercion of competition can be countered only by the coercion of society, in the shape of its political guardian, the relatively responsive capitalist

---

[1] In the classification of p. 86, this illustrates the second kind of type-preserving change of economic structure.

[2] *Capital*, i. 239.

[3] Ibid. i. 270. In comparable fashion, overintensive capitalist farming threatens the productivity of the soil: see ibid. i. 239, 265, 507, iii. 603, 792.

[4] Ibid. i. 270.

state. The state must intervene because, despite the behaviour forced upon the capitalist, 'the interest of capital itself points in the direction of a normal working day'.[1] 'Capital' in this last excerpt refers to the system as opposed to its members, or to the capitalist as stake-holder in, not puppet of, the system. Large capitalists, whose positions are relatively secure, and whose enterprises would survive—or improve—under additional state constraint, often rise to the stake-holding attitude, and press upon the state the need for reform.

The capitalist state, legislator of the Factory Acts, is, then, the eye of the otherwise blind capitalist, the stabilizer of a system capitalist activity itself endangers. The needs of the system cannot be attended to by dispersed entrepreneurs severally driven to maximize individual profit. Collected in the state, they may see, and see to, those needs, and may respond to working class demands which suit those needs but which they necessarily repel in civil society.

Let us now take stock. The workers demand remission of exploitation because they want to live; the state grants it because capital needs living labour. The suggested generalization (not a universal law) is that substantial changes in economic structure which favour the immediate welfare of the subordinate class occur when the class fights for them *and* they increase—or at least preserve—the stability of the system (for reasons independent of allaying a felt grievance of the exploited[2]). The elements are connected because ruling class perception of the need for change is quickened by the pressure of underclass demand, and the latter gets bigger in consequence.

Class insurgency is more likely to achieve its object when the object has functional value, a fact which bears on the undialectical question whether it was systemic need, or, on the supposed contrary, militant struggle, which accounted for the coming of welfare capitalism. A reform essential to capital's survival can also qualify as a 'victory of the political economy of labour over the political economy of property'.[3] There is

[1] *Capital*, i. 266.
[2] That is, the change is functional for the system other than because it reduces the anger of the proletariat. Recall the distinction (p. 53) between being willing and being able to work, which is relevant here.
[3] 'Inaugural Address of the W.M.I.A.', p. 383. That is how Marx described the Ten Hours Bill.

victory when capitalism is able to sustain itself only under the modification the reform imposes on it.[1]

[1] Merton ('Manifest and Latent Functions', p. 104) requires of items to which functions may be assigned that they be 'standardized, i.e. patterned and repetitive', for example: 'social roles, institutional patterns, social processes, cultural patterns, culturally patterned emotions, social norms, group organization, social structure, devices for social control, etc.' There is no good reason for this restriction, as the case of the Factory Acts shows. It is possible to offer functional explanation of a particular event, such as the passage of a bill, or, for that matter, an enactment of a social role on a particular occasion, or a change in a cultural pattern, which is not itself a cultural pattern, and which may occur because of its salutary consequences for the culture.

In our view, no special type of phenomenon or fact is by nature an object of functional explanation (see Ch. IX, pp. 255-6).

CHAPTER XI

Use-value, Exchange-value, and Contemporary Capitalism[1]

(1) *Introduction*

THIS CHAPTER begins by describing the displacement of use-value by exchange-value as the fulcrum of economic life, and proceeds to argue that the dominance of exchange-value under capitalism generates a peculiar contradiction when capitalism is advanced. We present contemporary 'affluent' capitalist society as the climax of the history of use-value and exchange-value, and as the prelude to the suppression of exchange-value as regulator of the social organism.

A *contradiction* obtains when a society's economic organization frustrates the optimal use and development of its accumulated productive power, when prospects opened by its productive forces are closed by its production relations. The term is taken from the 1859 Preface,[2] and no connection is intended between our use of it and the meaning it has in logic.

The concept of advanced capitalism will be clarified by the exposition of its contradiction, on pages 306–7 below. It will prove plausible to assert that at least American capitalism is advanced in the appropriate sense. The chapter offers an indictment of that society based on considerations wholly independent of its severe domestic inequality and imperialist

---

[1] The reader may wish to review the definitions in Appendix II before embarking on this chapter.

[2] 'At a certain stage of their development, the material productive forces of society come into contradiction with the existing relations of production. . . . From forms of development of the productive forces these relations turn into their fetters.' *Critique of Political Economy*, p. 21.

The contradiction to be attributed to advanced capitalism involves, in the first instance, restriction on the *use* of productive power, as opposed to on its *development*. Compare the 'antagonism between modern industry and science on the one hand . . . and the social relations of our epoch' ('Speech at the Anniversary of the *People's Paper*', p. 360), which does not, in the main, concern impediments to scientific progress, but misuse of its fruits.

world posture.[1] They would condemn it even if the United States were a society of substantial equality, isolated from the rest of the world.

The capitalist essence is at issue here, not the accidents of geography and history. Advanced capitalism as here defined relates to contemporary American capitalism as the capitalism of *Capital* does to Victorian British capitalism. In each case the consequences of principles animating the society are explored *in abstracto*, but the results bear on reality, since the animating principles are really there.[2]

Declarations in Appendix II[3] entail that the labour theory of value plays no role in this chapter. We venture a critique of capitalism which is Marxian in its use of the fact that capitalist production serves to expand exchange-value, but the critique is committed to no account of the source of variations in exchange-value.

(2) *The Subjugation of Use-value by Exchange-value*

In this section we examine how exchange-value supplants use-value as the determinant of productive activity and, to a lesser extent, as the object of human desire. Using Marxian materials, we construct a sequence in the course of which there arises the pursuit of exchange-value as an independent aim and, later, the subordination of society to that pursuit. The steps in the sequence have occurred in history, though not in the regimented manner in which they will appear here. But the degree of historical verisimilitude of what follows does not affect the subsequent exposition of a distinctive contradiction of advanced capitalism. All that matters is that the last member of the sequence is real.

Market exchange does not occur without production, but production may proceed and products circulate without market exchange. Use-values go from producer to consumer without passing through a sphere of exchange when they move in accordance with customary rules (e.g. of ritual gift), or in

---

[1] These phenomena condition the mode of incidence and the degree of importance of the contradiction, as well as its relevance to political practice.

[2] See *Capital*, iii. 141. It need hardly be said that there is no intention here to produce anything as penetrating as *Capital*.

[3] See pp. 348, 353.

accordance with a distributive plan, whether democratically adopted or imposed by a dictatorial authority.

Marx thought use-values circulated without market exchange in earliest history. The first instance of market exchange is trade between independent tribes. Trade first appears between (not within) tribes because it presupposes separate ownership on each side of the trading transaction. Separate ownership in turn presupposes a certain independence of the owners from one another. But the members of the tribe experience themselves as united with one another in the tribe. They lack the requisite independence. They have it only collectively, *vis-à-vis* other tribes, so that if two tribes, or members of two tribes meet, trade is possible. Those conducting it will be agents of their respective tribes, not independent merchants.

Once trade between tribes develops, the principle of market exchange begins to penetrate the interior of the community, and intra-tribal trade is inaugurated. Commerce dissolves primitive solidarity.[1]

At first trade takes the form of barter, $C–C^1$.[2] But the barter form restricts the volume and pace of commodity circulation. The scope of exchange is extended by the emergence of money, as medium of exchange and measure and store of value. Now trade takes the form $C–M–C^1$. The producer exchanges his product for money in order to purchase and then consume the product of another producer, who does likewise: each sells in order to buy in order to consume. C and C^1 issue from production and end in consumption, and M only facilitates their passage between these termini. Production and exchange are oriented to consumption and therefore to use-value.[3]

[1] See *Grundrisse*, pp. 170, 496, 740, 873; *Grundrisse* (Berlin), pp. 904, 921; *Critique of Political Economy*, p. 50; *Capital*, i. 87–8, 351–2, iii. 174; Engels, *Anti-Dühring*, p. 223, and *Origin of the Family*, p. 100.

This and other steps in the sequence assign to commerce a transforming power not anticipated in the 1859 Preface, which never mentions *exchange* of products, and our presentation of historical materialism in earlier chapters also concentrates on the domain or production. I had planned to include a chapter reconciling the 'dissolving influence' of commerce on existing structures with the primacy of the productive forces, but that exercise will now be left for another occasion. (Clues are available at *Capital*, iii. 326–7 and *Grundrisse*, pp. 256–7.)

[2] See Appendix II, p. 351, for explanation of these symbols, and the ones to follow.

[3] Compare the discussion of craft labour at *Grundrisse*, p. 512, and see 'Results', p. 1030.

Nevertheless, in this consumption-grounded form of trade, exchange-value has achieved an independent manifestation, in an object useless for consumption, which has no use-value apart from its exchange-value: M. The precondition of the merchant's entry is fulfilled.[1] His activity rationalizes and accelerates commodity circulation. It suits producers to sell C to him and buy C^1 from him. For them M remains a medium of exchange, but for him it is capital. The circuit of his activity is $M–C–M^1$: he buys in order to sell. He uses exchange-value to increase exchange-value, though he recurrently transforms M into what has use-value for consumption (C) in order to increase it. *Qua* merchant, he neither produces nor consumes the C he handles, and its qualities are of no interest to him: he cares only about its exchange-value.

Initially the merchant who uses M as capital lacks what we shall call a *capitalist mentality*. He does not 'personify'[2] capital, for his final object is to cash M^1 in for consumables, thus benefiting in use-value from the difference between M and M^1. But there is a natural progression from him to the merchant who is a living embodiment of $M–C–M^1$, who aims to increase his stock of exchange-value without limit, or at least beyond the limits set by his consumption demands. The merchant who thus personifies the capitalist principle is likely to grow larger and stronger than the modest merchant who does not.

Thus barter leads by easy steps to the *capitalist principle*, the *use* of exchange-value to increase exchange-value; and the capitalist principle engenders the *capitalist mentality*, the *quest* for exchange-value which is not controlled by a desire for use-value, or not, at any rate, by a desire to exchange it for use-value. The reality of the principle and the mentality is undeniable,[3] though the story just given of their genesis is highly stylized.

To personify capital is to practise the principle *and* possess the mentality. Such a person is not necessarily crazed. Exchange-value is purchasing power, but it can be agreeable and rewarding to have a great deal of purchasing power even when there is nothing one wants to purchase (except as a means to

---

[1] Not in a logical sense, but effectively. It is difficult to operate as a merchant in the absence of a monetary medium of exchange. See Appendix II, p. 352.

[2] See *Capital*, i. 152–3.

[3] But the extent to which the mentality informs an individual or a society is a highly complex question.

increasing one's purchasing power). The accumulation of the capitalist who personifies capital is not motiveless. Among other things, 'to accumulate is to conquer the world of social wealth, to increase the mass of human beings exploited by him, and thus to extend . . . [his] . . . direct and . . . indirect sway'.[1]

The mentality and the principle need not go together. A man who handles the funds of an orphanage, in an attempt to increase them for the sake of the children's welfare, employs the principle but lacks the mentality. He may well drive harder bargains than a mentally capitalist trader, who may be restrained by the fact that his trading—unlike that of, say, the Commissioners of the Church of England—lacks underlying moral justification.

Conversely, a man who does not use exchange-value to increase exchange-value may have a capitalist mentality. A miserly craftsman who transforms his earnings into a hoard of gold operates non-capitalistically but possesses a capitalist mentality. A modern worker has something of a capitalist mentality if his furniture pleases him because it costs a lot, and not just because he enjoys its comforts.

In general, however, the principle and the mentality promote one another.

Both the principle and the mentality antedate capitalist society. In capitalist society *all* the elements of the productive process have become objects of purchase and sale, and the principal capitalist is no longer the merchant but the industrialist, who travels in circuit V (see p. 352), and whose enterprise, unlike the merchant's, essentially involves the employment of labour power. (This differentiation does not depend on the labour theory of value, for it does not imply that labour is the sole source of the industrialist's profit.)

As society develops towards capitalism, larger and larger portions of the productive process fall subject to the capitalist principle. Capitalism is preceded by a succession of mercantile conquests. At first the merchant disposes only of the surplus product of producers. As the division of labour deepens (partly as a result of new market opportunities created by mercantile enterprise) he comes to handle the entire product. Next, he controls the producer's raw materials, and then the tools, which

[1] *Capital*, i. 592.

the producer must rent from him. Finally the producer's labour power becomes a commodity, and the capitalist becomes an industrialist.[1] The formation of the labour market completes the subordination of production to exchange. Now consumable use-values are produced only because they have exchange-value, and only if the industrialist expects to expand exchange-value through their production and sale. Concrete wealth, an ensemble of qualitatively different use-values, cedes precedence to abstract wealth, a quantum of featureless exchange-value. For 'the immediate purpose of capitalist production is not "the possession of . . . goods", but the appropriation of value, of money, of abstract wealth'.[2]

(3) *A Distinctive Contradiction of Advanced Capitalism*

The pursuit of abstract wealth proceeds apace in the capitalism of our own day. Whatever other goals a corporation has, it must, on pain of bankruptcy, obey the imperative: seek to expand the exchange-value at your disposal. This holds whether firms aim at profit or at growth, for they are different modes of increasing exchange-value, and no firm can aim at neither. It also holds whether or not managerialist theses are true: whoever wields ultimate corporate power is constrained to favour decisions which enlarge the difference between M and M^1.

It is a paradox (in a loose sense of that term) that in just this society, consumption, whose requirements are by nature finite according to a tradition descending from antiquity,[3] eventually

[1] This sequence occurred in the textile industry, as Marx tells the story. It illustrates the 'non-revolutionary' mode of formation of the industrial capitalist. In the contrasting 'really revolutionary way' it is the immediate producer himself who grows into a capitalist. (See *Capital*, iii. 329–30.) This fertile distinction is tangential to the present discussion.

[2] *Theories of Surplus Value*, ii. 503. Cf. ibid., p. 495.

[3] Aristotle, developing an idea of Plato's, contrasted trade servicing the consumption needs of a household, whose circuit is $C–M–C^1$, and 'retail trade' ($M–C–M^1$), whose aim is the accumulation of money. He endorsed the first and condemned the second as a perversion of it. There is a natural term to the accumulation of C's, but the virtues of order and limit are violated by the search for M, which is by nature endless. This criticism of the Sisyphean character of mercantile enterprise is often heard in Western intellectual history. Hume derided the merchant who knew 'no such pleasure as that of seeing the daily increase of his fortune', and similar disdain informed much of the nineteenth-century socialist and conservative (e.g. Carlyle) response to capitalism. The recommended alternative was not asceticism—at root the merchant exhibits that—but enjoyment of

knows no bounds. We shall argue that consumer demand becomes bloated when and because production does not have consumption as its controlling goal, when 'the product is from the outset subsumed under capital, and comes into being only for the purpose of increasing that capital'.[1] If the aim of production were use-value, much less use-value would be sought, produced, and consumed than is in fact produced and consumed.

This paradox is not what is meant by 'a distinctive contradiction of advanced capitalism', for that is a matter of productive forces and production relations. We first explain how advanced capitalism produces the paradoxical situation, and then reveal the contradiction associated with it.

Capitalist society is responsible for technological power on an unprecedented scale, progressing at an unprecedented rate. This is because the competitive position of its industrial decision-makers compels them to increase the productivity of production processes. The compulsion does not lapse when capitalism reaches its misnamed 'monopoly stage', for competition persists in pertinent respects. Since total consumer spending power is finite, heterogeneous products of monopolized industries compete against one another for buyers. There is also competition for shareholders, for skilled labour, etc.

Improvement in productivity is a condition of persistence and success in the multidimensional competition which characterizes capitalism in *all* of its stages. 'It is therefore the economic tendency of capital which teaches humanity to husband its strength and to achieve its productive aim with the least possible expenditure of means.'[2]

Now improvements in productivity, whether labour-saving or capital-saving,[3] are open to two uses. One way of exploiting

---

use-value, the desire for which was supposed to be satiable. Better 'the accumulation of pleasures' than 'the pleasure of accumulation'. *Theories of Surplus Value*, i. 282-3. For more in this vein, see ibid., pp. 174, 302, 367, 374; *Grundrisse* (Berlin), pp. 928-9; and *Capital*, i. 588.

[1] *Theories of Surplus Value*, i. 401.

[2] Ibid., ii. 548.

[3] 'Capital' is here used in a non-Marxian sense. In Marx's language, capital-saving is 'cheapening of the elements of constant capital' (*Capital*, iii. 230). Capital-saving poses problems for the thesis of the falling rate of profit, but it does not threaten the present argument, since it clearly enables labour-reduction with constant output.

enhanced productivity is to reduce toil and extend leisure, while maintaining output constant. Alternatively, output may be increased, while labour stays the same. It is also possible to achieve a measure of both *desiderata*.

'Leisure' is used broadly here, in rough synonymy with 'freedom from unappealing activity', and 'toil' refers to activity in so far as it is unappealing. One is lesiured to the extent that his time and energy is *not* spent in the service of goals he would prefer fulfilled without such expenditure. One toils to the extent that the motivation of his activity is remuneration or other external reward. It follows that leisure time can be filled strenuously. It also follows that amelioration of working conditions counts as expanding leisure.

The economic distinction between job time and time off coincides imperfectly with the distinction here envisaged between toil and freedom from it. Some 'gainful employment' is enjoyable, and some time off is spent toilsomely. But the distinctions are sufficiently coextensive for the purposes of our argument. What particularly matters is that, as things are, for most people most of the time earning a living is not a joy. Most people are so situated that they would benefit not only from more goods and services[1] but also from reduced working hours and/or enhanced working conditions. It is clear that advances in productivity enable gains in either direction, typically at the expense of gains in the other direction.

Now capitalism inherently tends to promote just one of the options, output expansion, since the other, toil reduction, threatens a sacrifice of the profit associated with increased output and sales, and hence a loss of competitive strength.[2] When the efficiency of a firm's production improves, it does not simply reduce the working day of its employees and produce the same amount as before. It produces more of the goods in question, or, if that course is, because of

---

[1] This could be challenged, but to the extent that it is false, our argument gains in strength. Here we can afford to concede its truth, but for a closer assessment see section (7) below.

[2] See *Grundrisse*, pp. 701, 707–12; *Theories of Surplus Value*, i. 223, 226–8, ii. 468.

An interesting early example of the bias of capitalism was the introduction of safety lamps in mining after 1813, which initially brought 'not greater security of life to the miner, but a larger output of coal—from seams that had previously been considered too dangerous to be worked at all'. Because explosions would have damaged the mine too much? Ashton, *The Industrial Revolution*, p. 65.

the structure of the market, not optimal, it adopts another non-labour-reducing strategy, to be described shortly.

But first let us note that there has indeed been a titanic growth of output and a comparatively small reduction of labour expenditure since the inception of capitalism (date that where you will). That the reduction in the working day has been small by comparison with the volume of output expansion is beyond controversy. But it is arguable that it has also been fairly small in absolute terms, if sophisticated but defensible criteria of the amount of time people spend supporting themselves are used. Meriting consideration here are such activities as travelling to work, shopping in so far as it is felt to be a nuisance, and any activity in itself unattractive but performed as a means to fulfilling consumption purposes.[1] In sheer hours of work per year (admittedly, not the only relevant index), the modern American worker is not obviously better off than the European peasant of the Middle Ages, many of whose days were made idle by the weather and by observance of the Christian calendar.[2] Nor has there been stunning progress since, say, 1920, if everything pertinent, notably overtime, is taken into account. There has of course been an impressive decline in labour time since the earlier part of the nineteenth century, but the capitalist system need not be thanked for effecting it, since it was capitalism which stretched the working day in the first place. In any case, even that decline loses force in comparison with the accompanying increase in output, and the bias here attributed to capitalism is sufficiently evidenced by the relative position.

Output expansion takes different forms. If the market for the good whose production has improved is expansible, output

[1] Also needing attention, in more than just a footnote, is the complicated effect of capitalism on the amount of labour performed by women. In *some* respects their leisure can increase since the output bias leads to a proliferation of devices which reduce domestic labour. But the same devices enable women to join the remunerated labour force, so their total effect is not easy to judge.

According to Galbraith, the net result of the increasing flow of goods into the home is to make housewives hard-pressed managers of consumption, so that 'the menial role of the woman becomes more arduous the higher the family income'. Galbraith is evidently no connoisseur of low-income family life, but there may be a grain of truth in what he says. See *Economics and the Public Purpose*, p. 32.

[2] For further discussion, see Parker, *The Sociology of Leisure*, p. 24, the references he cites, and those cited by Howard and King, *The Political Economy of Marx*, p. 124, n. 7.

expansion may take the immediate form of more products of the same kind. Otherwise, and especially if the market in question is more or less saturated, output expands elsewhere, as newly available funds (generated by reductions in the wages bill) flow into another line of production. This does not always occur promptly or smoothly, but eventually it occurs. Jobs are generally destroyed and created in the process.

As long as production remains subject to the capitalist principle, the output-increasing option will tend to be selected, and implemented in one way or another. Whether or not they have capitalist mentalities, it is imperative for capitalists to continue accumulating exchange-value, and thus to expand output. But it is unlikely that the principle should prevail while the mentality is wholly absent, and the mentality fortifies and augments the output-favouring effect of the purely objective constraint of competition.

Now the consequence of the increasing output which capitalism necessarily favours is increasing consumption. Hence the boundless pursuit of consumption goods is a result of a productive process oriented to exchange-values rather than consumption-values. It is the Rockefellers who ensure that the Smiths need to keep up with the Jones's.[1]

The productive technology of advanced capitalism begets an unparalleled opportunity of lifting the curse of Adam and liberating men from toil, but the production relations of capitalist economic organization prevent the opportunity from being seized. The economic form most able to relieve toil is least disposed to do so.[2] In earlier periods of capitalist history the bias towards output conferred on the system a progressive historical role: capitalism was an indispensable engine for producing material wealth from a starting point of scarcity, and there lay its 'historical justification'.[3] But as scarcity recedes the same bias renders the system reactionary. It cannot realize the possibilities of liberation it creates. It excludes liberation by

---

[1] For a case in which the 'conspiracy' to achieve this result may be described without inverted commas, see Sklar, 'On the Proletarian Revolution', which reports the concerted plan to stimulate consumption conceived under the aegis of the Hoover administration.

[2] See *Capital*, i. 235–6.

[3] *Theories of Surplus Value*, ii. 405. Cf. *Grundrisse*, p. 701.

febrile product innovation, huge investments in sales and advertising, contrived obsolescence. It brings society to the threshold of abundance and locks the door. For the promise of abundance is not an endless flow of goods but a sufficiency produced with a minimum of unpleasant exertion.

The dynamic of advanced capitalism is, arguably, hostile to the prospect of a balanced human existence. It certainly upsets the equilibrium of physical nature. The disaffection with its forms of work and consumption shown by part of the young middle class may anticipate in miniature a wider response to advanced capitalism. The pollution/resources impasse, present or future, is the unequivocal answer it gets from the elements.

The permanent contradictions of capitalism discussed in Marxist economic literature, or the difficulties known to Keynesians, or forces of some other kind—it does not matter here that economists are disagreed what they are—incline the system to an underemployment of resources. The contradiction distinctive of advanced capitalism generates their overemployment. But there is no wizard who or mechanism which nicely balances these effects against one another, and the result is grotesque overemployment in some directions and injurious underemployment in others.

(4) *Mishan and Galbraith*

The consequences of the distinctive contradiction are familiar. They figure in the critique of 'economic growth',[1] as illustrated by the writings of E. J. Mishan and J. K. Galbraith. This chapter is an attempt along Marxist lines to explain what they deplore.

Mishan sees what he calls 'growthmania' as a property of advanced industrial society as such, or of the 'growthmen' whose ideology governs it. He largely ignores the capitalist structuring of industry. A small section of his *Costs of Economic Growth* is entitled 'Profit-propelled growth'. Yet the evils he identifies in the rest of the book are also attributable to profit-propulsion, to the enclosure of production within circuit V. Mishan grounds them in the mania for growth, a syndrome he

---

[1] Scare-quotes, because the critique is of economic growth very narrowly defined. In calling what they oppose 'economic growth' the critics make a gratuitous concession.

does not attempt to explain. We say it is the natural reflection in consciousness of practical adherence to the capitalist principle.

Galbraith's purview is larger than Mishan's. He does not refer the bias in favour of output to growthmania. He believes it is not 'the images of ideology' but 'the imperatives of technology and organization' which 'determine the shape of economic society'.[1] High technology generates new power relationships, which in turn establish the primacy of production. In particular, technology shifts power to the highly trained persons who operate it. The 'technostructure' of salaried engineers, economists, market analysts, personnel experts, etc., wrest control from entrepreneurs, shareholders, and bankers. Let us accept that there is this transfer of power. The rest of the argument is the following. Since 'the technostructure is principally concerned with the manufacture of goods and with the companion management and development of demand for these goods',[2] a strong bias in favour of more goods is assured.

But once we recall that advanced technology may also be used to reduce toil, this account is seen to be question-begging. Grant that sophisticated technology confers power on technical experts. It does not follow, unless the need to make profit—of secondary import for Galbraith—is introduced, that they will favour output, not leisure. One elaboration of this point follows.

Members of the technostructure have skills of two kinds. Some (e.g. those of the sales force) are especially suited to promoting consumption, but others (e.g. those of production engineers) could also be used to extend leisure.[3] The proposition that technology gives authority to possessors of technical knowledge does not explain the demand for the first set of skills, nor the use to which the second set is put. It does not explain why the skilled obtain advancement and kudos by delivering goods rather than free time and a better work environment, conceived as an end in itself. What explains these phenomena is the extra-technological fact that this technology appears within a capitalist economic structure. The supposed

---

[1] *The New Industrial State*, p. 18.

[2] Ibid., p. 169.

[3] Skill individuation is a hazardous business, and the illustrations could be challenged, but rigorous demarcation is not required for the argument offered here.

circumstance that industry is in the grip of unchallengeable experts leaves the choice between output and leisure open. It is closed by the imperative of capital accumulation alone.

The great fault in Galbraith's position is that he relates the output emphasis to the modern firm's (supposed) *transcendence* of market constraints, whereas it derives from the *persistence* of those constraints. The huge corporation is well placed to meet them, but it does not follow that it has escaped them. While the 'market-controlling' enterprise has less need to fear insolvency than the old-style 'competitive' firm, it has no less need to avoid it, and to pursue the output-expanding policies which help to insure against it.

The humble truth that even the megacorporation must earn money receives more attention in the last book of the Galbraith trilogy,[1] in the course of his discussion of the 'protective purposes' of the technostructure.[2] There is also a momentary acknowledgement that public enterprise need not so protect itself,[3] and at one point a recognition that the ideology of output preceded the technostructure's advent.[4] A proper development of these submerged truths sustains the conclusion that output fanaticism belongs to capitalism as such, whatever variation the technostructure may play on the theme.

(5) *The Argument Reviewed*

Key positions in the argument:

1. Capitalist competition promotes increases in productivity.

2. Increases in productivity enable both expansion of output and reduction of toil.

3. Capitalist competition engenders a bias in favour of expanding output as against reducing toil.

---

[1] *Economics and the Public Purpose.* (The first two are *The Affluent Society* and *The New Industrial State.*)

[2] *Economics and the Public Purpose*, Chapter X. We are nevertheless told that 'the power of the technostructure, so long as the firm is making money, is plenary' (ibid., p. 40). Even if this is true, the qualification is of momentous import. The need to make money by itself induces an output bias, and explains why we have the kind of technostructure we do.

[3] Ibid., p. 219.

[4] 'It has always been a prime tenet of the neoclassical model that wants do not diminish in urgency and hence goods do not diminish in importance with increased output' (ibid., p. 158). Galbraith aligns the neoclassical model with *pre*-technocratic capitalism.

4. Both more output and less toil benefit people. The current endowment of goods and leisure will determine which use of productivity improvement is currently preferable. Sometimes, the leisure-increasing use will be preferable.

5. Because capitalism always favours expanding output, it will, for that reason and to that extent, be a detrimental economic system under certain conditions.

6. For some value of 'very high' and some value of 'substantial', capitalism is detrimental when consumption is very high and the working day is substantial.

7. Consumption is relevantly high and the working day is relevantly substantial in the United States now. Hence (at least) American capitalism now functions detrimentally to human welfare in the stated respect.

Different kinds of claim are lodged here. Statements 1 and 3 depend on elementary economic reasoning. To prevail in competition capitalist firms must be favourably disposed to technical innovation and to an output-expanding use of that innovation. 1 and 3 require no special premisses about human nature. They follow from what is true of the mere structure of capitalist economies.

Productivity is here understood as the ratio of volume of output to extent of labour input. Hence statement 2.

Statement 4 ventures claims about the sources of human welfare, but not controversial ones.

Statement 5 follows from statements 3 and 4.

Statement 6 identifies a type of case illustrating the truth of statement 5.

Statement 7 maintains that American capitalism is an example of what 6 describes. 7 is a judgement, and it has not been defended. But it is not a judgement which may be dismissed as merely eccentric.

To recapitulate. The argument is that even if and when it becomes possible and desirable to reduce or transform unwanted activity, capitalism continues to promote consumption instead, and therefore functions irrationally, in the sense that the structure of the economy militates against optimal use of its productive capacity. It is undeniable that capitalist relations of production possess an output-expanding bias. So the only way of denying that they are potentially irrational in the stated respect is to assert that labour is so enjoyable (or not so unenjoyable) and resources are so plentiful and the satisfaction to be had from goods and services is so limitless that no matter how much is being consumed it remains desirable to consume more, instead of expanding freedom from labour: a rather large assertion.

The heart of the matter is that capitalist firms are so placed that they will assess productive activity only in terms of its extrinsic value. Its meaning for the producer is irrelevant, except where that has extrinsic effects (improved working conditions sometimes raise output, but the point has limited significance[1]). The same considerations commonly used to argue that capitalism promotes an optimal allocation of factors of production serve to show that it promotes the use of human energy and time *as* a factor of production.[2] But human energy is not only a potential factor of production. Even if labour power tends to be used efficiently, that it tends to be used *as* labour power will only *per accidens* and under restricted conditions promote the total welfare of society.[3]

For a long time the benefits of this tilted decision-making perhaps outweigh the sacrifice exacted in labour. But when output is of a very high order and it remains true that most people devote most of their substance to doing what they would rather not do, then to persist in favour of further output at the expense of relief from undesired work is irrational.

---

[1] The bias we attribute to capitalism is in the first place *towards* more output, and it is only in virtue of broad empirical generalizations that it is *therefore against* more leisure. These generalizations are not exceptionless, and sometimes better working conditions or even shorter hours will increase profits. But as a rule the antagonism described by Schumacher prevails:

> We produce in order to be able to afford certain amenities and comforts as 'consumers'. If, however, somebody demanded these same amenities and comforts while he was engaged in 'production', he would be told that this would be uneconomic, that it would be inefficient, and that society could not afford such inefficiency. *Small is Beautiful*, p. 87.

While *society* can certainly afford to give to the producer whatever it would otherwise give to the consumer, the options of the capitalist firm are more confined.

[2] For it is 'a mode of production in which the labourer exists to satisfy the needs of self-expansion of existing values, instead of, on the contrary, material wealth existing to satisfy the needs of development . . . of the labourer' (*Capital*, i. 621). See also 'Results', p. 1037.

[3] Something else which capitalism tends to use as a factor of production, when it is actually other things too, is the planet Earth.

The basis of the argument is the incontrovertible proposition that, *in Marxian terms*, capitalist production is production for exchange-value. Acceptance of that proposition involves no commitment to the controversial labour theory of value. Once its meaning is explained, its truth is obvious, and it can be expressed in a quite unMarxist way. Alfred P. Sloan (one-time head of General Motors) recognized the truth when he said that it was the business of the automobile industry to make money, not cars. That, indeed, is why it makes so many cars. It might make fewer if its goal were not making money but, say, providing people with an efficient and inoffensive form of transport.

The result we derive from Sloan's insight, that capitalism will favour output at the expense of freedom from toil, follows pretty immediately. Yet the textbooks which present the arguments in favour of capitalism do not devote attention to it. It is not, after all, an uninteresting result. Its neglect by established economics needs to be explained, because, though fairly trivial intellectually, it bears on the assessment of capitalism. And that is the explanation. It is neglected *because of* its relevance to the assessment of capitalism.

One argument favouring capitalism has as its conclusion statement 1 on page 309 above: capitalist competition promotes increases in productivity. It needs little rehearsal here, so familiar is it from economic discourse, both high and low. Its premiss is that capitalist firms which produce incompetently are defeated in competition. They are therefore constrained to produce as efficiently as possible, and to seize on opportunities to improve their productive facilities and techniques.

Some socialists have complaints against that argument. They say that it may run well in theory, but that practice does not follow suit, since in practice market economies are not as vigorously competitive as the premisses of the argument assert. But that is a mistaken response. Of course capitalism has never been *as* competitive as its ideology pretends, but the argument, properly understood, does not require that competition be wholly unrestrained. There has, after all, been uncommonly rapid technological improvement in the history of capitalism, and the best explanation of that fact is that capitalism has been at least as competitive as the argument requires it should be.

Now the argument for statement 3, which calls capitalism into question, proceeds analogously. Again a bias is derived from the constraints of competition, this time not in favour of productivity improvement, but in favour of a one-sided and potentially damaging use of that improvement. And this argument too is subject to qualification, which, once again, does not destroy its importance. In both cases qualifications are needed to meet objections. Thus it might be said, against the main contention of this chapter, which rests on the competition model, that if people do not *want* to consume more, but prefer more leisure, they will offer less labour power, and capitalist firms, on the competition model,[1] need not care, so long as the attitude is quite general. A given firm will survive even if it produces no more than it did before productivity increased, as long as other firms behave similarly, as broadly speaking all will have to if the aversion to increased consumption is general.

Section (7) deals with what is true in this objection. But here we point out that quite the same order of comment may be directed against the more familiar argument for statement 1. Capitalists need have no interest in increasing their efficiency apart from the danger that other capitalists will do so, and the danger disappears to the extent that workers are successful in resisting technological change, something they are not unknown to do.

Statement 3 needs to be defended against objections, but so does statement 1, and nothing justifies the enormous disparity between the consideration given the latter and the utter neglect of the former in bourgeois economic theory and publicity.

(6) *Is Capitalism a Necessary Condition of the Distinctive Contradiction*

Now the argument shows only that capitalism is a *sufficient* condition of the distinctive contradiction. Is it also a necessary condition? Do other economic forms generate the same irrationality? Would the overthrow of capitalism ensure escape from it?

Capitalism is a society whose production is governed by the capitalist principle *and* which exhibits a division between a

---

[1] That model, as understood here, abstracts from the fact that capitalists may actually *want* more exchange-value, other than because they *need* it for survival in competition.

capitalist and a labouring class.[1] But capitalism's preference for output depends largely on the first feature. We may envisage class undivided societies whose production follows the capitalist principle. Three such will be depicted, and then a society whose production is not subject to the principle will be considered.

The three may be called 'egalitarian market societies'. In each competition induces a tendency to output expansion, but to only two of them may we also ascribe movement towards the distinctive contradiction. None has occurred in history, and none represents a viable alternative for the future.

The first is a variant of what Marx called 'simple commodity production', a market economy of self-employed producers who hire no labour. Given sufficient competition, each producer will be motivated to raise his productivity, lest competitors who do so drive him out of the market by outselling him. (Productivity is improved by, for example, use of superior producer goods sold by innovating blacksmiths.) What is more, he will be inclined to exploit increased productivity for output expansion, since only by the extra sales thereby gained will he be able to finance further needed productivity improvements. But simple commodity production is incompatible with really advanced technology—which socializes labour—and so also with really high output. Its tendency to promote 'economic growth' would lead to its self-destruction and replacement by capitalism, before it came in sight of the distinctive contradiction.

The second type is a set of firms each of which is wholly owned by its employees, who share fairly equally the firm's income. Here 'the associated labourers' are 'their own capitalist'.[2] If this structure could be sustained, there would be movement towards the contradiction; though the bias in favour of output might receive less ideological and political support than in capitalism proper, since no powerful class would benefit differentially from it. Transcendence of the capitalist principle would not discriminate against the interests of a dominant minority.

The third case—call it 'people's capitalism'—differs from the second in that share ownership is not restricted to the employee's firm. In addition—to keep the thing egalitarian—there is a duty

[1] See Appendix II, p. 352.   [2] *Capital*, iii. 431.

of all to work and an income ceiling aimed at preventing the formation of distinct classes. If these stringent conditions were realized, there would be movement towards the contradiction. Once again, however, no particular section of society would benefit especially from it.

The last two models are instructive. They show that it is not in virtue of its inequality that capitalism slides towards the contradiction.[1] But they have never occurred, and they are not reasonable options now.[2] In the course of an inevitably 'uneven development', some firms would outpace others,[3] and this would foster (what would in effect be) a division between employers and employees. If the competition is real, some firms would be threatened with bankruptcy, and it would suit the more successful ones to offer them subcontracting work, but only on terms which made them in effect wage-earners. Such tendencies might be arrested by insurance schemes, but they would probably have to be so comprehensive that the economy would lose its market character. The envisaged forms are counter-examples to the proposition that capitalism is *in principle* a necessary condition of the contradiction, but their likely unviability confirms that it is a necessary condition *in practice*.

Turn now to a non-market society, with production integrated by a plan, democratically formed (as in genuine socialism) or otherwise. This will not generate the contradiction. For the decision-makers are free, *as far as systematic economic constraints are concerned*, to choose between expanding output and reducing labour, when there is progress in productivity. A dictatorship might for some reason seek to maintain labour constant, even in conditions of affluence, for example out of fear that people with free time would be more difficult to rule. But this would be political choice, not, as with capitalism, a dictate of the impersonal logic of the economic system. But the latter is required to impute contradiction, which by definition holds between productive forces and production relations, not between productive forces and the will and interests of particular

---

[1] The inequality does, however, exacerbate the tendency to excessive output. See p. 322.

[2] Hugh Stretton presents a powerful case to the contrary in *Capitalism, Socialism, and the Environment*, which reached me too late for proper consideration here.

[3] The post-war economic history of Yugoslavia is of some relevance here.

men. We are looking for irrationality in the nature of the economic system itself.

We therefore conclude that the capitalist principle alone induces an economic-systemic bias towards output expansion, and that, if we consider feasible economies only, then capitalism is not just a sufficient but also a necessary condition of the emergence of the distinctive contradiction.

Now the foregoing, even if correct within its own terms, may seem disappointing. For it is conceded that a non-capitalist regime may in fact sustain a drive for more and more output, the insistence being merely that the economy over which it presides does not dictate that choice. And indeed there is good reason to think that the Soviet leadership, bent on 'overtaking capitalism', would continue to stress production before all else even when that emphasis ceased to be defensible.[1] The author once remarked, in conversation with Soviet academics, that whereas an American manager is motivated to conceal pollution caused by his plant, a Soviet manager can publicize it and request subventions to counteract it. One sociologist replied: 'You are naïve. If he publicizes it, he will be replaced by someone who is more discreet.'[2]

For all that, the distinction between a policy choice and the natural result of the normal functioning of an economic system retains intellectual and practical importance. There are surface resemblances between the maladies of the Soviet Union and the United States, but different diagnoses apply, and different remedies are required. Political change in the Soviet Union could lead to altered priorities with no dramatic reshaping of its economic system. In America the problem is different. It is hard to conceive governmental measures which would arrest the impulsion towards output expansion without striking hard at the capitalist system itself, not to mention its powerful ideological encasement. It is even questionable whether American capitalism will be able to deal effectively with

[1] Though to the extent that the Soviet Union attempts to overtake capitalism by taking over capitalist structures, the link between capitalism and output expansion is further confirmed.

[2] The Soviet Union is a poor model of what socialism need be like, for it was threatened by capitalism from its inception, and was compelled to 'catch up', on pain of extinction. A socialist revolution in an advanced capitalist country would not have to catch up with capitalism.

pollution, which is just one side of the problem. Capitalist enterprise does not thrive hedged round by regulations and directives, even supposing that their passage and enforcement are politically feasible in the face of corporate power.

(7) *An Objection*

Here is one way of developing the objection mentioned on page 313: 'You have proved at most that capitalism *tends* to select output expansion. It does not follow that if it actually expands output, then this is adequately explained by the bias you identified. There are other tendencies attributable to capitalism on similar grounds—the need to accumulate capital —which are completely unfulfilled. One is the tendency of firms not to raise their workers' wages. The tendency is there, but its effect is neutralized by countervailing trade union power. Why does that same power not check the propensity towards output? Why do unions generally press for more income rather than less labour? If the system's bias harms their members' interests, why do they co-operate with it? When the contradiction looms, why does union policy not change? If the United States has crossed the border into contradiction, why is union policy what it is?'

Note the nature of the objection. It is *not*: output expansion is favoured not by the system but only by the aims the population wants the system to accomplish. That claim cannot stand, since the system demonstrably possesses an output-expanding bias. But the presence of that tendency does not show that it explains the realization of what it is a tendency to. That lesser claim is the basis of the objection.

We shall meet the objection by exploiting quite uncontroversial premises. It is easily met on the radical premiss that much of what is consumed gives no real satisfaction, but people cherish it because they are dupes of advertising and ideology. Later, a reduced version of that thesis will be defended, but first let us magnanimously assume that by and large the given consumer goods are desirable, that desire for them is in some relevant sense awakened, not contrived, by advertising and affiliated processes, and that the satisfaction they afford is genuine.

On the other side, the opponent must concede that plenty

of labour is not desired. If God gave workers *gratis* the pay they now get, and granted them freedom to choose whether or not to work at their jobs, for as long as they pleased, without remuneration, then there would result a very substantial decline in labouring activity. Superficial observation suggests that people enjoy what they consume, but it also reveals that they do not enjoy much of what they must do to be able to consume it.

Then what advertising (etc.) may be said to do, on the most generous account, is to draw attention to and emphasize (what we have supposed are) the independently desirable qualities of the products it displays. This is balanced by no similar campaign stressing the goods of leisure. No ads say: WHEN *YOUR* UNION NEGOTIATES, MAKE IT GO FOR SHORTER HOURS, NOT MORE PAY. ELECTRIC CARVING KNIVES ARE FINE, BUT NOTHING BEATS FREEDOM. There are no 'leisure ads' because firms have no interest in financing them, nor in paying for public reminders of the unpleasant side of the labour which buys the goods.

There is, of course, promotion of so-called 'leisure products', but rising income is required to procure them, and the advertisements do not mention the sacrifice of leisure needed to sustain that income. One can imagine someone saying, in an extreme case: 'I am taking a week-end job to maintain the payments on the snowmobile I use at week-ends.'[1]

Thus labour acquiescence in the bias is itself traceable to the bias: workers are influenced by its operation in the emphases promoted by the media.[2]

The foregoing scepticism about the process of desire formation in capitalist society does not rest on a theory disclosing the optimal desire structure for human beings: that would be difficult to supply. It would, more particularly, be hazardous to attempt a realistic general statement of the relative merits of increments of consumption and leisure at varying levels of each. Such doctrine being foresworn, what are the principles behind the critique that was given?

[1] Cf. Roberts, 'On Time', p. 650.

[2] We have dealt only with the most manifest messages in favour of goods projected by capitalist society. To show how much else in its culture has the same end is more than can be done here. Advertising is no doubt a relatively secondary influence, reinforcing much deeper sources of commitment to consumption.

A distinction obtains between what a man is disposed to seek, and what would in fact afford him satisfaction. We can, on that basis, distinguish, more elaborately, between two schedules pertinently descriptive of a person's make-up and circumstances: his *pursuit* schedule and his *satisfaction* schedule. Each orders objects of his desire, but from different points of view. The pursuit schedule orders them by reference to the relative strengths of his dispositions to seek them. The satisfaction schedule orders them according to the amounts of satisfaction he would obtain from possessing them. (We ignore (a) satisfactions he would obtain from objects he does not pursue, and (b) probabilities of attaining pursued objects: suppose that whatever is pursued is attained.) These schedules are, of course, constantly changing with changes in information, taste, and external conditions, but we can say that a person's situation at a given time is likely to be unfortunate to the extent that objects are differently ordered in his two schedules. If the ordering in his satisfaction schedule differs from the ordering in his pursuit schedule, he is unlikely to be making optimal use of the resources available to him.

Now if an agency increases a man's pursuit of an object, without commensurately increasing the satisfaction he would get from possessing it, then it probably produces the unwanted misalignment of schedules, and therefore has a negative effect on his welfare, *unless* his pursuit of the object increases because the agency supplies a more accurate account than he had before of the satisfaction it would give him (in which case, an— in that respect—improved alignment results). But the agencies in capitalist society which promote a preference for output over leisure cannot be credited with a comparable tendency to increase the satisfaction to be had from output as opposed to leisure, nor may they be said to provide a more accurate account than might otherwise be available of the relative values of the two. There is therefore a case for saying that they corrupt the individual's preference structure, a claim we can make without describing the content of an uncorrupted preference structure.

We criticize capitalism not because it causes desires which might otherwise not have arisen, but because it causes desires the fulfilment of which does not afford an appropriate degree of satisfaction. The system requires the pursuit of consumption goods: it is indifferent to the quality of satisfaction which lies at the end of it, except in so far as high satisfaction might reinforce the pursuit. But it is naïve to think that a particularly effective way of sustaining the commitment to consumption is to make consumption rewarding. On the contrary, there is reason to suppose—and here we approach the 'radical premiss' (p. 317) not used in our reply to the objection—that the pursuit of goods will, in important ranges, be stronger to the extent that their power to satisfy the pursuer is limited. The system cannot abide consumers who are content with what they already have. As Baker says:

> . . . while trying to increase sales and profits, a business enterprise will want to create tastes that are (1) cheapest to develop or stimulate and (2) for which palliatives can be produced but (3) which are never completely satisfied and do not cause other desires to be satiated.[1]

Business wants contented customers, but they must not be too contented. Otherwise they will buy less and work less, and business will dwindle.

Finally, a reply to those who use their leisure time arguing that if people had lots of it they would not know how to use it. No well-confirmed propositions about human beings support this arrogant pessimism. It is, moreover, predictable that a society rigged up to maximize output will fail to develop the theory and practice of leisure.[2] And this further manifestation of the output bias adds to the explanation of general acquiescence in it. Free time looks empty when the salient available ways of filling it are inane.

(8) *The Bias of Capitalism and Max Weber*

We have seen that in capitalist *practice* it is a mistake to reduce labour time when output can be raised instead. The same emphasis is unthinkingly taken for granted in much

---

[1] 'The Ideology of the Economic Analysis of Law', p. 38.
[2] '. . . we are now at a point at which sociologists are discussing the "problem" of leisure. And a part of the problem is: how did it come to be a problem?' Thompson, 'Time, Work-Discipline, and Industrial Capitalism', p. 67.

bourgeois *ideology*, and it operates as an unstated premiss quite widely in academic analysis.[1] We limit ourselves to one instructive example.

Max Weber did not welcome every aspect of capitalist civilization. But he did turn its pathetic preference for output into a canon of rationality:

> At the beginning of all ethics and the economic relations which result, is traditionalism, the sanctity of tradition, the exclusive reliance upon such trade and industry as have come down from the fathers. This traditionalism survives far down into the present; only a human lifetime in the past it was futile to double the wages of an agricultural laborer in Silesia who mowed a certain tract of land on a contract, in the hope of inducing him to increase his exertions. He would simply have reduced by half the work expended because with this half he would have been able to earn [as much as before]. This general incapacity and indisposition to depart from the beaten path is the motive for the maintenance of tradition.[2]

Weber regarded the labourer's response as other than rational, for he tendentiously contrasted 'traditional' and 'rational' behaviour. Suppose we allow that contrast. Then Weber still fails to show that the peasant reacted traditionally and hence, on his view, non-rationally. For he did *not* continue to do what he had always done. He began to work a lot less than before. To cease to work from sunrise to sunset is to forsake tradition at least as much as to work no less hard, or harder, at twice the old wage rate. Only a fixation on material goods as against freedom from toil could incline one to think otherwise. Indeed, the labourer's choice was probably rational. He could not be certain what increase in consumption welfare would attend the rise in money income—clearly it would not have doubled as a result. Reasonable conjectures regarding the marginal utility of goods and the marginal disutility of labour—in his particular situation—suggest that in opting for labour-reduction he won a more substantial benefit.[3]

---

[1] 'By some accident in the development of economic thought, the choices made by persons *qua* consumers became pivotal in the economic theory of resource allocation' in contrast to 'their choices *qua* workers'. Mishan, 'Ills, Bads and Disamenities', p. 73. It is surely no accident, comrade.

[2] *General Economic History*, pp. 260-1.

[3] Compare the 'utterly delightful' example reported at *Grundrisse*, pp. 325-6.

(9) *Obiter Dicta*

(1) We promised (p. 297) to ignore the inequality character-istic of capitalism, but two inequalities of real capitalist society will now be remarked.

First, there is now among the higher echelons of the employed a considerable amount of what can be called 'job-time leisure'. This must modify our judgement (p. 305) of the degree to which the anti-leisure tendency has manifested itself in practice. Note, though, that the uneven distribution of agreeable working conditions receives less attention than it might, because the output bias makes off-work consumption levels the preponderant criterion of individual welfare.

Turning to consumption, we confess our awareness that output under capitalism is shared very unequally. And that uneven distribution, reflecting differential class power, helps to sustain the output emphasis. Having overtaken the Jones's, the Smiths now set themselves to catch up with the Jacksons. The skewed distribution of the overvalued fruits of production reinforces the overvaluation.

The structure of consumption under capitalism fosters a desire for goods which necessarily outruns the capacity of the average person to satisfy it. More reason to be sceptical about the contribution of consumption to personal well-being in capitalist society.

(2) This chapter has made little reference to the grave problem of future provision of natural resources and energy. No one knows how big the problem is, but we may perhaps be guided by the mature judgement of the authors of *Only One Earth*,[1] for whom it is great but soluble, *if* major changes are instituted in inherited patterns of production and consumption. An attempt will now be made to relate this important issue to the preceding discussion.

Whatever the size of the problem would otherwise be, it is certain that capitalism aggravates it. The pressure to sustain and expand output makes for a more rapid exploitation of existing resources than could otherwise be expected to occur, and the finite time horizon of the capitalist firm discourages

[1] Barbara Ward and René Dubos.

investigation of alternative paths of development. What is more, the consequent conditioning of society to forms of consumption which draw upon prodigious quantities of irreplaceable material makes new paths harder to embark upon. The longer capitalism and its bias prevail, the more difficult will be the transformation which appears to be necessary.

The 'resources crisis', then, scarcely gives reason for tempering this chapter's critique of capitalism. But it could be thought that it makes the implied account of the post-capitalist prospect look naïve. For if natural resources are to be used more sparingly, recourse to them must to some extent be replaced by continued reliance on human labour power, and it then might seem that the promise of increased leisure cannot be fulfilled.

But those reflections depend upon a crude concept of leisure, quite different from the one defined on page 304 above. By 'leisure' we have meant freedom from unwanted activity, not freedom from productive activity. That the two have gone together under capitalism does not mean that they are fated to coincide in the future. The rhythm of development of the productive forces in capitalist history has been heedless of the quality of the work experience, and the growing knowledge at the centre of productive power has been objectified[1] in highly limited ways. Productive knowledge might now be objectified in civilized forms, even if repellent objectifications were unavoidable in the past.[2] It is possible to envisage creative labour processes which are less appetitive of scarce resources and which meet the concept of leisure as understood here.

An enriched working day is not a 'second best' to be embraced only if a contracted working day is impossible. That should be obvious, yet it runs against a deep current of thought in Marx, which finds its most articulate expression in the following passage, one which Marxists like to quote in evidence of Marx's lack of Utopianism, but which may be too pessimistic:

[1] See pp. 41–2 on growth of knowledge as the main line of development of the productive forces, and on physical productive facilities as 'mere' objectifications of that knowledge.

[2] 'It is too often assumed that the achievement of western science, pure and applied, lies mainly in the apparatus and machinery that have been developed from it . . . The real achievement lies in the accumulation of precise knowledge, and this knowledge can be applied in a great variety of ways, of which the current application in modern industry is only one.' Schumacher, *Small is Beautiful*, p. 156.

... the realm of freedom actually begins only where labour which is determined by necessity and mundane considerations ceases; thus *in the very nature of things* it lies beyond the sphere of actual material production. Just as the savage must wrestle with nature to satisfy his wants, to maintain and reproduce life, so must civilised man, and he must do so in all social formations and under all possible modes of production. With his development this realm of physical necessity expands as a result of his wants; but, at the same time, the forces of production which satisfy these wants also increase. Freedom in this field can only consist in socialized man, the associated producers, rationally regulating their interchange with nature, bringing it under their common control, instead of being ruled by it as by a blind power; and achieving this with the least expenditure of energy and under conditions most favourable to, and worthy of, their human nature. But it nonetheless still remains a realm of necessity. Beyond it begins that development of human energy which is an end in itself, the true realm of freedom, which, however, can blossom forth only with this realm of necessity as its basis. The shortening of the working-day is its basic prerequisite.[1]

On this account, freedom inside socialist industry is regrettably limited, and Marx looks for what he calls *true* freedom beyond the economic zone. His idea is not that 'labour is no longer a means of life but life's prime want',[2] but that, being a means of life, it cannot be wanted, and will be replaced by desired activity as the working day contracts.

This negative appraisal of future working conditions, however warranted it may be on other grounds (and we must hope that there are none), here rests on a fallacious conflation of distinct ideas. Granted, there will always be a set of operations on whose completion the provisioning of the race depends. But it does not follow, and it is not equally undeniable, that there will always be tasks which men perform against their inclinations because they have to. That a task must be and is fulfilled does not imply that the motive for its performance is that its performance is necessary. (Some eating is enjoyable.) But Marx asserts this implication when he says that the 'realm of freedom', first glossed as activity not *determined* by mundane requirements, must 'in the very nature of things' lie beyond the sphere servicing

---

[1] *Capital*, iii. 799–800, emphasis added.
[2] 'Critique of the Gotha Programme', p. 24.

those requirements. Up to now the character of the productive forces has imposed on work the property of not being performed for its own sake. Whether it must retain that property in future is a complex question of technology and psychology, not a matter of the manifest 'very nature of things'.

The possibility Marx swiftly excludes is that material necessities might be met, at least partly, by 'that development of human energy which is an end in itself'. One cannot settle *a priori* the extent of compatibility between labour and creative fulfilment. Marx thought he knew the compatibility would always be small. Hence his need to forecast diminishing quantities of labour. It is not a prediction believers in human liberation are forced to accept.

APPENDIX I

Karl Marx and the Withering Away of Social Science[1]

> If there were no difference between reality and appearance, there would be no need for science.

THE FOLLOWING pages explore the ramifications of the above dictum. In section 1 I try to explain what Marx intended by it. I then (section 2) display discrepancies between reality and appearance in feudal and bourgeois society, by stating some differences between exploitation on the medieval manor and exploitation in the capitalist factory. Next (section 3) I demonstrate that the dictum entails that, for Marx, socialism and social science are incompatible— as socialism develops, social science must wither away. In section 4 I relate the antagonism between socialism and social science to the doctrine of the unity of theory and practice. Finally (section 5), I criticize Marx's idea of science, but I defend his belief in the desirability of a society whose intelligibility does not depend upon it.

1. Marx frequently pronounced his teaching on essence and appearance when he was at work on *Capital*, which he conceived as an attempt to lay bare the reality underlying and controlling the appearance of capitalist relations of production. In Volume II[2] of the work he identifies the 'really scientific' explanation of a phenomenon with the 'esoteric' view of it. In Volume III he declares that 'all science would be superfluous if the manifest form [*Erscheinungsform*] and the essence of things directly coincided';[3] and in a lecture to workers in 1865 he warns that 'scientific truth is always paradox, if judged by everyday experience, which catches only the delusive appearance of things'.[4] He often crowns his demonstrations in *Capital* by glorying in the fact that common observation contradicts his analysis;[5] and in the course of a letter to

---

[1] Revised version of an article which originally appeared in *Philosophy and Public Affairs*, Winter 1972. Reprinted by kind permission of Princeton University Press.
[2] p. 212.   [3] p. 797.
[4] 'Wages, Price and Profit', p. 424.
[5] See, e.g., *Capital*, i. 307: 'This law clearly contradicts all experience based on appearance [*Augenschein*].' See also ibid. iii. 42–3, 205, 846–7.

Dr Kugelmann he complains that recent bourgeois economists (unlike their classical predecessors[1]) use only the ordinary concepts of price and profit with which every merchant is familiar. He finds no science in economic studies which fail to penetrate beneath the phenomena a businessman can see.[2]

Marx mentions achievements of natural science which help us to gauge what he means when he distinguishes appearance from reality and maintains that science discovers the latter. The air we breathe appears to be elementary, but chemistry discloses that it is composed of distinct substances, which are not detected by the nose. The sun appears to move across the heavens, but science replaces this proposition, which ordinary experience supports, by the thesis that it is the earth which is the moving body.[3]

These cases are intended as analogues of the relation between capitalism as Marx analyses it and capitalism as it appears to those who live inside it.

It is a cardinal tenet of Marx's theory that only the expenditure of labour creates economic value, and in proportion to the amount of labour that is expended. It follows that because workers do not receive the whole value of what they produce they are not paid for all the labour they have performed. It also follows that capital investment enables the creation of profit only to the extent that it is investment in labour power.

Notwithstanding these theorems, the wage worker appears to receive payment, whether high or low, for every unit of labour time he completes. If his wage is eight shillings for each hour and he works ten hours, he will receive four pounds, which is the exact product of ten times eight shillings. But in the reality divulged by the theory of surplus value, the four pounds compensate the worker for only part of his time, and the unremunerated remainder creates what is appropriated as profit. Yet since the worker appears to be

[1] Notably Smith and Ricardo. For a fascinating comparison of them, see *Theories of Surplus Value*, ii. 164-9.

Though he formulated important truths about capitalism, Smith did not keep the 'esoteric' and 'exoteric' parts of his work properly separate. Reality and appearance mingle in his presentation. Marx excused him on the grounds that the surface—the observational data—had first to be charted, and as a pioneer Smith could not always distinguish it from the depths. Ricardo was more consistently scientific in aspiration, but even he did not always succeed (see ibid. ii. 106, 191). It was Marx himself who, according to Marx, rendered economics fully scientific, and put appearances in their place.

See further ibid. ii. 347, 351, 437, iii. 500-1, 515.

[2] Marx to Kugelmann, 11 July 1868, *Selected Correspondence*, p. 197. See also Marx to Engels, 27 June 1867, ibid., p. 179, and *Capital*, iii. 760, which credits Hegel with the insight that genuine science thrives on paradox.

[3] *Capital*, i. 316, 74.

rewarded for all the effort he expends, the profit appears to have a source other than his labour. Economists in the thrall of appearance therefore attribute it to the capitalist's decision to invest instead of consume his wealth, or to his entrepreneurial ingenuity, or to the power of the machines he owns. They tend to impute to capital itself the faculty of profit-creation.[1]

This imputation is encouraged by the unavailability to those who inspect appearances alone of a critical distinction between the locus of profit-creation and the locus of profit-allocation. Although the amount of profit[2] *created* in an enterprise depends entirely on the amount of capital it has invested in labour power (as opposed to machines, raw materials, etc.), the amount of profit that *redounds* to the enterprise is directly proportional to the *total* capital invested in it, in all factors of production.[3] Labour-intensive industries have a higher rate of profit-creation but the same rate of profit-appropriation as other industries. Competition induces an equalizing flow of profit through the economy from labour-intensive to other industries. It is therefore irrelevant to the capitalist's practice that labour alone creates value and profit. He will not be especially tempted by the opportunity of investing in a labour-intensive industry. He cares about the volume of his return, not the dynamics of its creation. He therefore regards what determines the share of profit he receives as tantamount to what creates it, and the economist who does not penetrate below the surface, on which the distinction between profit-creation and profit-allocation is not exhibited, follows him.[4]

Let us return to the rudimentary illustrations from natural science. For Marx the senses mislead us with respect to the constitution of the air and the movements of heavenly bodies. Yet a person who managed through breathing to detect different components in the air would have a nose that did not function as healthy human noses do. And a person who sincerely claimed to perceive a stationary sun and a rotating earth would be suffering from some disorder of vision, or motor control. Perceiving the air as elementary and the sun as in motion are experiences more akin to seeing mirages than to having hallucinations. For if a man does not see a mirage under the appropriate conditions, there is something wrong with his vision.

[1] See also Ch. V above, pp. 117–19, 122–4.
[2] Strictly: surplus value.
[3] See *Capital*, iii. part 2; *Theories of Surplus Value*, ii. Ch. 10; ibid. iii. 455, 459, 482–3.
[4] 'To the unscientific observer' things appear just as they do 'to him who is actually involved and interested in the process of bourgeois production'. *Theories of Surplus Value*, ii. 165, and see pp. 218–19, 266–7, 318, 333, 427, iii. 187, 265, 272, 453, 485, 503, 514–15.

His eyes have failed to register the play of light in the distance.

The ideas of the air as a uniform substance and of the sun rising and setting do not come from faulty perception. That is how the air and the sun present themselves. Neither are the notions that the worker's labour is fully rewarded and that every unit of capital participates in the creation of profit results of misperceiving the shape of capitalist arrangements. Those notions record surface features of capitalist society. But anyone who thinks the real lineaments of that society are exposed on its surface and open to immediate observations misunderstands its nature.

The appearances just reviewed are, like mirages, part of the world around us. They comprise the outer form of things, which enjoys an objective status, and which science alone can strip away. To express the thought with less imagery, let us say that *there is a gulf between appearance and reality when and only when the explanation of a state of affairs falsifies the description it is natural to give of it if one lacks the explanation.* Gulfs are due to the way reality itself appears, and only when they exist is science required for a state of affairs to be intelligible.

(The italicized formulation could be taken as allowing that a *theory* describes appearance and not reality if it is replaceable by a 'deeper' theory which falsifies it. But Marx, like the age he lived in, believed in a two-dimensional contrast between observation and theory, and in expounding him I follow him. Hence the description mentioned in the italicized formulation is to be understood as based on pre-theoretical observation. I shall ignore challenges to the absolute distinction here presupposed between the world of experience and the world of theory.)[1]

Now if the nose channelled nitrogen through one nostril and oxygen through the other, and if the respirer sensed a difference

---

[1] Criticism of Marx's way with the contrast between observation and theory may be based on the (now unfashionable) view that theoretical concepts serve to connect observation statements without denoting constituents of a reality underlying experience; or on the (highly fashionable) contention that experience is always shaped by a theoretical perspective; or on the distinct claim that the contrast in question is relative to a context of inquiry.

According to Howard and King (*The Political Economy of Marx*, p. 163), 'when Marx says that reality is unobservable he does not mean it in an epistemological sense, but in a *sociological* sense'. Why, then, did he use natural scientific examples to explain his meaning?

According to Keat and Urry (*Social Theory as Science*, p. 179), 'when Marx says that the essence of air is different from its appearance, what he must mean is that the original observation is incorrect, because it assumes the truth of a false theory'. The only basis for this interpretation is a desire to bring Marx up to date with contemporary philosophy of science. His own views were more Victorian than the authors appreciate.

between the gases, he would not need science to inform him that the air is heterogeneous. (Science might still outdo the nose by revealing the proportions of nitrogen and oxygen in the air, and the chemical structure of each; but not by asserting the fact of atmospheric diversity.) If enormous fleshy telescopes were attached to our eyes, and we could control them as snails do their horns, then the Copernican revolution might never have had to occur.

But it is fortunate that we do not always perceive the essential natural phenomena: it expedites our survival. Nasal siftings of nitrogen and oxygen could be taxing and distracting, and the telescopes would make us less efficient perceivers of what is nearer to hand. The gulf between reality and appearance in nature benefits the human organism. And we shall see that, for Marx, the survival of a class society, in particular of capitalism, also depends on a disparity between what it really is and the appearance it displays to its members, rulers and ruled alike.

Vico said that society is more intelligible to man than nature, because it is his creation. But according to Marx this creation is riddled with mystery: curious theoretical constructions are required to understand the setting in which men act, and, consequently, what they are doing. The schism between reality and appearance in society could well provoke disquiet. It is not hard to appreciate the desire to establish a social order in which things are as they appear to be. We shall see that socialism is expected to satisfy that desire. But first we must ask why class societies present themselves in a guise which differs from the shape correct social theory attributes to them.

2. Part of the answer is that they rest on the exploitation of man by man. If the exploited were to see that they are exploited, they would resent their subjection and threaten social stability. And if the exploiters were to see that they exploit, the composure they need to rule confidently would be disturbed. Being social animals, exploiters have to feel that their social behaviour is justifiable.[1] When the feeling is difficult to reconcile with the truth, the truth must be hidden from them as well as from those they oppress. Illusion is therefore constitutive of class societies.

I say 'constitutive' because more is claimed than that the members of a class society acquire false beliefs about it. The falsehood maintains its grip by permeating the world they experience: their

---

[1] Marx never states this explicitly psychological thesis, but it must be attributed to him if we are to make sense of a great deal of his theory of ideology. See my 'Workers and the Word', pp. 382-3.

perceptions are false because what they perceive is a distortion of reality. According to Plato (on some interpretations), men observing the material world are under illusions not because their thoughts fail to correspond to it, but because they faithfully reflect what is an illusory world. Marx was not untouched by the philosophical tradition Plato began, and when he writes that workers take seriously the appearance *(Schein)* that their labour is fully rewarded, the phrasing[1] shows that he thinks of the appearance as an attribute of the reality. It is only derivatively a reflection of reality in men's minds.

Hence the discovery of the labour theory of value does not 'dissipate the mist'[2] through which commodity relations are observed. Those who know the theory continue to 'move about in forms of illusion *[Gestaltungen des Scheins]*'.[3] Things do not *seem* different to a worker who knows Marxism. He knows they *are* different from what they continue to seem to be. A man who can explain mirages does not cease to see them.

The table on page 333 purports to display what is obvious and what is hidden under two regimes of exploitation, feudalism, and capitalism. Before turning to the table, a brief exposition of two analytical constructs which enable us to identify some general differences between the societies.

Nineteenth-century German sociology, drawing on Marx and Hegel and Sir Henry Maine, established a distinction between two ideal types of human society, the *Gemeinschaft* and the *Gesellschaft*. No pair of English nouns adequately conveys the intended contrast, but we may translate *Gemeinschaft* as 'community' and *Gesellschaft* as 'association'.[4] They are distinguished by the different relations between people characteristic of each. In an association men connect

---

[1] *Capital*, i. 558. Other passages demand a similar construal, e.g., 'everything appears reversed in competition, and *thus* in the consciousness of the agents of competition' (ibid. iii. 220, italics added); 'The mystification . . . lies in the nature of capital' *(Grundrisse*, p. 640). See also *Critique of Political Economy*, p. 213; *Capital*, i. 550; iii. 165–6, 802, 810, 845; 'Results', p. 998; *Theories of Surplus Value*, ii. 69, 165, 217; *Theories of Surplus Value*, iii. 137.

These citations are from Marx's later writings. No list of passages is required to show that he conceived of reality and apearance in this manner in his earlier work. In his response to Feuerbach he formed the view that the 'inversions' the latter had identified in consciousness occurred because consciousness was of an inverted world. See, for example, the opening page of 'Introduction to *A Contribution to the Critique of Hegel's Philosophy of Right*', and for further discussion, see section 4 below.

[2] *Capital*, i. 74. The translation is free here.

[3] Ibid. iii. 810.

[4] As in the English title *(Community and Society)* of Tönnies's *Gemeinschaft und Gesellschaft*.

with one another only when each expects private advantage from the connection. Links between people are impersonal and contractual. The perfect capitalist market embodies this idea. But the feudal manor *looks*[1] more like the opposite social type, a community, with personalized relations. The bond between lord and serf does not derive from contract: it is conceived in the imagery of kinship. The lord fights for the sake of his manorial dependents. He is their paternal protector. The serf labours in a spirit of filial homage to provision the lord's household. Ties between master and servant, it seems, are not utilitarian, not rooted in prudential calculation. Each appears concerned for the welfare of the other, not interested in the other merely as protector or as provider of consumables.[2] The incursion of commerce dissolves these bonds and reduces human contact to patently cash-determined transactions. A man is merely a means to another man under capitalism, but in the *Gemeinschaft* (and, to all appearances, under feudalism) his position is respected by his fellows. It restricts the uses they are prepared to make of him, and the uses he is prepared to make of them.

Now neither a *Gemeinschaft* nor a *Gesellschaft* is of necessity exploitative. To be sure, in a market society, or pure association, men make use of one another, but mutual use is not exploitation unless it yields unequal rewards.[3] What Marx called 'simple commodity production' could constitute a *Gesellschaft* which is not exploitative. In simple commodity production men meet at a market to exchange their wares, but the marketeers themselves produce the commodities they bring. No one is subordinated to them in the productive process. The simple commodity market may not be an enthralling ideal of social organization,[4] but where it prevails there need be no systematic injustice.

Again, the idealized manor sketched a moment ago, though it involves exploitation in the technical Marxian sense (a surplus product is extracted), contains no serious unfairness. My neighbour does not exploit me if in friendship I dig his garden for him, particularly if he stands ready to defend mine against marauders. If capitalism were simple commodity production, and if feudalism had measured up to its *gemeinschaftliche* ideology, then neither could be

---

[1] See *Grundrisse*, p. 165.

[2] See *Grundrisse* (Berlin), pp. 873–4, 913.

[3] See ibid., pp. 911–12.

[4] It was a component in the ideals of Sismondi, Proudhon, and some anarchists, but Marx spurned it, because it was incompatible with modern technology, and because even if it were possible to return to it, it would inevitably lead to capitalist commodity production again. Marx associated yearning for simple commodity production with the petty bourgeoisie. See *Grundrisse* (Berlin), p. 916, and discussion above, pp. 127–8, 186, 314.

deemed exploitative, if exploitation entails oppression. But both societies are in fact oppressively exploitative, because the stipulated conditions are not fulfilled. Capitalism is not simple commodity production. Its propertied marketeers exert power over propertyless producers. And feudalism, according to Marx, is not the intimate community it presents itself as being. The relation between lord and serf is utilitarian in basis, however much the parties to it are unaware of the fact.

The following table captures some differences between the two societies.

	Under Feudalism	*Under Capitalism*
That surplus product is extracted	is evident	is concealed
That human relations are utilitarian	is concealed	is evident

Both societies really have the two features noticed in the table, but in each society only one of them is readily observable.

Consider the first feature. It is obvious to all concerned that the serf spends a part of his time working for the benefit of his lord. If labour rent is exacted, that part is spent tilling the lord's demesne, instead of his own plot; alternatively, or in addition, some of the effort the serf expends on his own and on the common land is directed to raising produce he will deliver to the lord's table, or sell to provide money for the lord's coffers. Nothing is more obvious than that a definite quantity of the fruits of his labour goes to his master.[1] But under capitalism the manner in which a portion of the product of the worker's toil is retained by the capitalist obscures the fact that he keeps it. The working day and the working year are not manifestly divided into stretches of time for which the worker is compensated and stretches for which he is not. It is false that at any given moment the worker is either producing the product-equivalent of wages or producing the product-equivalent of profit, yet theory enforces a division of his total time into those two segments.[2] Nor is the palpable physical product divided between capitalist and worker. They share only the money it fetches on the market, and this mystifies the transaction between them. So what feudal rent reveals, the wage system conceals.[3] 'A child could tell the sources of wealth of an ancient slave-holder or medieval feudal

[1] *Capital*, i. 77; *Theories of Surplus Value*, iii. 484.

[2] 'The product is always divisible in its value form, if not always in its physical form.' *Grundrisse*, p. 427, and see also *Grundrisse* (Berlin), p. 888.

[3] See *Grundrisse*, pp. 283, 593, 772; *Capital*, i. 236–7, 539–40, 568–9, ii. 385–6, iii. Ch. 47, Part 2; *Theories of Surplus Value*, i. 46.

baron. Not so with our non-producing classes. The sources of the wealth of our merchant-princes are shrouded in mystery.'[1]

Now consider the second feature. Under capitalism, production relations are obviously utilitarian. Capitalists pretend no affection for their workers, and the indifference is reciprocated.[2] But, Marx believed, manorial relations only appear to be otherwise. Though men seem bound by non-economic ties of tradition and loyalty, historical materialism entails that it is really economic necessity that glues them together. The level of productivity characteristic of the medieval period made the manorial scheme an appropriate device for provisioning the species. A patina of *Gemeinschaftlichkeit* is required to reconcile men to the scheme, whose ground is utilitarian. If the members of the manor knew that its ideological ratification was a sham, the peasants would not serve their lord, and the lord could not maintain his patriarchal posture. In his early *Manuscripts* Marx goes so far as to treat the fact that feudalism is a *Gesellschaft* masquerading as a *Gemeinschaft* as the reason for its demise. The economic reality underpinning the superstructure of quasifamilial relations must reveal itself. Capitalism supersedes feudalism because the truth must come into view.[3] Marx later abandoned this Hegelianizing explanation of the transition to capitalism, but he retained the contrast on which the explanation relies.[4]

To conclude. Feudalism and capitalism have two features. One is veiled under feudalism, the other under capitalism. It is a plausible suggestion that in any society qualified by those features, social stability requires that one of them be concealed.[5] If serfs knew that the communality of the manor was a sham, they would not do what they in fact do, for they knowingly surrender a part of their produce to the lord. If factory workers knew that they were not recompensed for all of their labour, they would resist working for capitalists,[6] since their sole motive for doing so is self-interest. No traditional bonds inhibit them from revolting against the system, so when they become apprised of the truths of Marxist science they do revolt.

---

[1] Boudin, *The Theoretical System of Karl Marx*, p. 59.

[2] See *The German Ideology*, p. 448.

[3] 'In general, movement must triumph over immobility, overt self-conscious baseness over concealed, unconscious baseness . . . and money over the other forms of private property.' 'Economic and Philosophical Manuscripts', p. 143, and see p. 115.

[4] For its retention, see *The German Ideology*, p. 239; *Poverty of Philosophy*, pp. 178–81; 'Communist Manifesto', pp. 36–8; *Critique of Political Economy*, p. 189; *Capital*, iii. 603–4.

[5] The stated condition is not *sufficient* for stability, if only because the concealed features may become known while continuing to appear to be absent. See p. 331.

[6] See Marx to Kugelmann, 11 July 1868, *Selected Correspondence*, p. 197.

But they must learn those truths to become revolutionaries. They must penetrate through the mirage of the wage form.

It might be objected that even if historical materialism committed Marx to the thesis that economic necessity generated the manorial structure, there is no evidence that he accepted it. I therefore offer some documentation. According to *The Communist Manifesto*, only capitalism compels man 'to face with sober senses his real conditions of life, and his relations with his kind'.[1] The relations obtained under feudalism, but men were blind to them because they did not 'surface'. Under capitalism men are 'no longer bound to other men even by the *semblance* of common ties'.[2] Marx did believe that the second feature, concealed though it was, characterized feudalism.

But did he believe, as I have claimed, that under feudalism the first feature was a matter of observation? A statement in the *Manifesto* may seem to refute my interpretation: 'In one word, for exploitation, veiled by religious and political illusions, [the bourgeoisie] has substituted naked, shameless, direct, brutal exploitation.'[3] If this is inconsistent with my presentation, it is equally inconsistent with the texts[4] on which I based it. But there is in fact no inconsistency, or even tension. Exploitation in the technical sense (the first feature of the table) is not at issue here: it is not asserted that the extraction of surplus product was made more evident by the bourgeoisie. The passage patently means that capitalism made the utilitarian treatment of men by their masters more obvious, and that is something I affirmed.[5]

Marx also contrasted the illusions of capitalism and slavery. Whereas the wage worker seems to perform no unpaid labour, the slave seems to perform unpaid labour only. But the latter is as much a false appearance as the former, since the slave is allowed to consume part of his product. Worker and slave are both paid in that they both receive necessities of life in return for labour. Yet 'since no bargain is struck between [the slave] and his master, and no acts of selling and buying go on between the two parties, all his labour seems to be given away for nothing'.[6] 'The ownership-relation conceals the

---

[1] p. 37.
[2] *The Holy Family*, p. 156.
[3] p. 36.
[4] Listed in note 3, p. 333.
[5] Cf. Balibar: '. . . the capitalist mode of production is at once that in which the economy is most easily recognised as the "motor" of history and that in which the essence of this "economy" is in principle misunderstood.' *Lire Le Capital*, ii. 212.
[6] 'Wages, Price and Profit', p. 429. Cf. *Capital*, i. 574, iii. 30.

labour of the slave for himself; . . . the money-relation conceals the unrequited labour of the wage-labourer.'[1]

3. One corollary of the dictum on reality and appearance is that science may study a social formation only if it is held together by mechanisms that disguise its basic anatomy. The true content of social interaction must be hidden for social science to assume a role.

When a capitalist hires a worker, each, in a flourishing capitalism, is typically unaware of the nature of the exchange they enact. The worker lacks the facilities needed in a market society to produce and sell goods. These are monopolized by the capitalist class. He is therefore constrained to submit himself to some member of that class. But he appears to dispose of his labour freely, because he can bargain, and reject what one capitalist offers in favour of a deal offered by another. In essence bound to capital, he appears to be a free agent. This appearance, generated by the opportunity to bargain, is the form his bondage takes, and under which it is concealed.[2]

One more example. According to Marxian theory, the market values of commodities are determined by the quantities of socially necessary labour time required for their production. But those values appear to be independent of human effort. The capitalist can reason that because a commodity has a high market value, it is worth hiring a large number of workers to produce it, whereas in reality it is because a large amount of labour is needed to produce it that its value is high. But again, the idea that economic values are unrelated to the expenditure of energy by human beings is nourished by ordinary experience. For in the day-to-day flux of supply and demand[3] prices do vary independently of expended labour time, and their ultimate determination by it is concealed from those who do not reach beyond daily experience to theory.

Now Marx says that relations between human beings under socialism are 'transparent' and 'intelligible'. Economic agents whose actions are integrated by a democratically formulated plan understand what they are doing. The rationale and the import of economic activity are then publicly manifest. If we conjoin Marx's conceptions of socialism and science, we obtain the conclusion that socialism renders social science superfluous. It has no function in a world

---

[1] *Capital*, i. 539-40, and see *Theories of Surplus Value*, iii. 93. The three major regimes of exploitation (slavery, feudalism, capitalism) are compared in the former passage, and also at 'Wages, Price and Profit', p. 429.

[2] See *Grundrisse*, pp. 673-4; *Capital*, i. 574, 577-8, 613-14, ii. 440; Engels, *Condition of the Working Class*, pp. 79-80, 185-6.

[3] And for deeper reasons too. See note 3, p. 347.

which has abolished the discrepancy between the surface of things and their true character.

The mysteries of capitalism, its inaccessibility to the ordinary mind, result in one way or another from the fact that capitalist production aims at the expansion of exchange value, expressed in the accumulation of money. Socialism dissolves the mysteries by abolishing the market. For it thereby eliminates money, the medium of market exchange, and without money there can be no accumulation of abstract wealth, as opposed to wealth in particular, useful, perceptible forms. Marx writes that 'if we conceive society as being not capitalistic but communistic, there will be no money-capital at all . . . nor the disguises cloaking the transactions arising on account of it'.[1] There will, for example, never be the disparity between the apparent and the real performance of an enterprise which the stock market systematically promotes.

If Marx supposed that socialism would be immune to social science, did he think all economists would be fired after the revolution? We know that he accused post-Ricardian bourgeois economists of redundancy when they spoke the language of ordinary economic agents.[2] But in their day ordinary economic language was necessarily inadequate, because it described only surface phenomena which covered the real state of affairs. Socialist economists, or many-sided socialist men who sometimes engage in economics, will have no occasion to employ a specialized conceptual apparatus. But they will still have tasks to perform. For though the rationality and thus the intelligibility of socialist production are immediately accessible, it is not the case that all the facts of the socialist economy are compresent to perception. No peak in the Urals is so high that it affords a view of every factory, field, and office in the Soviet Union. Data-gathering and data-processing are requisites of socialist planning, at any rate in the centralized socialism Marx envisaged when he emphasized the rationality of the future society in Volume II of *Capital*. But while the findings of socialist economics will exceed

---

[1] *Capital*, ii. 315. He adds that 'in capitalist society . . . social reason asserts itself only *post festum*' and therefore 'great disturbances may and must constantly occur'. Note the kinship between the idea that rationality comes in only after the event and Hegels' Owl of Minerva figure, discussed on p. 341 below.

Mandel explains '*post festum*': if something which has been produced remains unsold, there has been a waste of 'social labour time. This waste, in a consciously co-ordinated society, would have been realised in advance', and therefore prevented. 'On the market the law of value reveals it only after the event . . .' (*Marxist Economic Theory*, p. 68).

See *Grundrisse*, p. 374, for similar remarks. For more on the rationality of socialism, see *Capital*, ii. 358, 424-5, 451, iii. 184.

[2] See p. 327.

those of unaided observation, there is no reason to think they will subvert them. They will therefore not constitute science, if Marx's account of science is correct.

For Marx socialist economics is not science because it does not use specifically scientific concepts, which *are* needed to make capitalism intelligible. Above all, it dispenses with the concept of value, which is heavily impregnated with theory. It needs the concept labour time, but that is different. Labour time is not a theoretical entity, and calculations of it are performed in all economies, including Robinson Crusoe's,[1] according to principles derived not from theory but from common sense. Only under capitalism does labour time take the mystifying form of value, of which it is the secret content.[2]

By unifying social theory and social practice, socialism suppresses social science. It makes intelligible in practice spheres of human contact which had been intelligible only through theory. When social science is necessary, men do not understand themselves. A society in which men do not understand themselves is a defective society. Socialism is not a defective society, and therefore social-scientific theory is foreign to it. Capitalism is obscure. Only science can illuminate it. But in the bright light of socialism the torch of the specialized investigator is invisible.

4. Philosophy is not identical with social science. Nevertheless, in his early response to the work of Feuerbach, Marx called for a repeal of philosophy comparable to the repeal of social science entailed by his mature views of science and socialism. In each case the abolition is a consequence of the extinction of those 'illusiogenic' properties of social reality which give life to philosophy and social science alike.

In the present section I propose a somewhat novel account of Marx's Eleventh Thesis on Feuerbach. It suggests a close connection between the dictum on reality and appearance and the Marxist emphasis on the unity of theory and practice.

The concept of the unity of theory and practice has borne a number of meanings in Marxist theory and practice. In its popular use, it advances a policy for revolutionaries. In its crudest accentuation, it enjoins the revolutionary to spend half his day up in the library, and the rest down at the docks or the factory gates. But this life-style does not in itself deserve the description *unity* of theory and practice, for it is merely their juxtaposition. A further demand is that the teaching of the library be carried into the docks and the

---

[1] See *Capital*, i. 76-7.

[2] 'The mystical character of commodities does not . . . proceed from the content of the determining factors of value' (ibid. i. 71). Cf. 'Critique of the Gotha Programme', pp. 22-3.

experience of the docks be applied at the library desk. And still more sophisticated recommendations regarding correct revolutionary conduct are available.

But the unity of theory and practice may also refer not to a policy, but to a feature of an established socialist society. The integration of intellectual and manual labour is one such feature, but I have in mind something of a higher metaphysical grade, which may be expressed as a supplement to Marx's last thesis on Feuerbach. He wrote that 'the philosophers have only interpreted the world, in various ways; the point is to change it'. I suggest that we may add: 'to change it so that interpretation of it is no longer necessary'. When Engels opined that the German working-class movement was the rightful heir to German philosophy,[1] he intended that the proletariat would fulfil in practice the project of making the world intelligible which the philosophers had attempted within theory. The unity of theory and practice as a policy relates to the task of instituting a rational world. The unity of theory and practice in the present sense is a constituent of the revolutionized rational world that policy achieves. It is a world in which the theory explaining the practice of socialist man appears in his practice, and needs no separate elaboration in a theorist's head.

A certain line of reflection underlies a[2] conception of the unity of theory and practice in Marx's *Contribution to the Critique of Hegel's 'Philosophy of Right'* and *Theses on Feuerbach*. It runs as follows: Theory aims at the production of thoughts which accord with reality. Practice aims at the production of realities which accord with thought. Therefore common to theory and practice is an aspiration to establish congruity between thought and reality. Now a person might consider himself as fundamentally neither a theorist nor an activist, but as primarily dedicated to arranging a correspondence between thought and reality, by theorizing or by action or by both. He might say: 'The method of securing the correspondence is a secondary question. It is whatever, in the given circumstances, eliminates illusion.'

It was from this (unstated) point of view that Marx judged Feuerbach's programme for rescuing men from illusion to be inadequate. In certain domains thought could maintain a correspondence with reality only if reality were changed. Feuerbach demanded that people give up their illusions about their condition. He should have demanded that they give up the condition which continues to

---

[1] 'Ludwig Feuerbach', p. 402.
[2] Several semi-independent conceptions of the unity of theory and practice may be found in these documents, and I discuss only one of them.

produce illusions, even after they have been theoretically exposed.[1] When social circumstances inevitably generate discord between thought and reality, the enemy of illusion must operate on reality, not in thought alone. There are certain problems which only practice can solve.[2]

Consider the Fourth Thesis on Feuerbach: 'Feuerbach starts out from the fact of religious self-alienation, the duplication of the world into a religious, imaginary world and a real one. His work consists of the dissolution of the religious world into its secular basis. He overlooks the fact that after completing this work, the chief thing still remains to be done. . . .'[3]

It is superficial to read Marx as expressing an activist's impatience with the analytical response to illusion. He is not merely announcing his unwillingness to rest content with intellectual victories. It is false that whereas Feuerbach's concern is theory, his is practice. Their primary interest is the same. Both want to suppress illusion, and Marx's complaint is that theory alone will not do so.[4] The goal with respect to which 'the chief thing still remains to be done' is to secure intelligibility.[5] Only by bearing in mind that common aim can we understand the critique of Feuerbach as motivated by something beyond a difference of temper. There is a genuine disagreement with Feuerbach, arising out of a shared desire to destroy illusion and initiate a harmony between reality and thought.

The illusions occupying both thinkers survive theoretical exposé because theory does not cure the conditions which produce them. And that is because they are not, in the first instance, errors of thought, but distortions in the world, which theory is impotent to rectify. Marx thought social conditions must themselves be conflicted to be capable of generating a conflict between reality and appearance. And as long as society remains riven, the rift between reality and appearance will persist too.

There appears to be a straightforward clash between the Eleventh Thesis on Feuerbach and the counsel of passivity Hegel dispensed to philosophers in the Preface to his *Philosophy of Right*. Philosophy, he said, is unable to contribute actively to history. It is its office to discern the rationale of historic endeavour in the afterglow of the

[1] 'Introduction to the *Contribution to the Critique*', p. 42.
[2] See ibid., p. 50, and the portion of the Fourth Thesis on Feuerbach not quoted below.
[3] I give Engels's version of the thesis (*The German Ideology*, p. 652) because it makes explicit the Marxian thought to which I am drawing attention here.
[4] See p. 331 above.
[5] See too *The German Ideology*, p. 54.

fire of events. The owl of Minerva, emblem of wisdom, flies in the evening, when the day's work is over.[1] The Eleventh Thesis sets the tasks of a new day.

But it is not clear that Hegel thought the diurnal self-restraint of Minerva's owl permanently necessary, and if we turn to his concept of Absolute Knowledge, we may see less opposition between him and Marx than the last paragraph suggests. For Marxian socialism is, in its epistemic aspect, the fruition of Absolute Knowledge, since to have that knowledge is to know immediately, without ratiocination, the nature of the total spiritual world. Marx runs this conception to earth by projecting a community of human beings who appreciate without theory the sense of both their own actions and the actions of other men.

5. I have brought together Marx's views of reality and appearance, science and society, and theory and practice. I shall now criticize Marx's conception of science, but I shall defend his belief in the desirability of a society immune to social science.

We saw that Marx's concept of a gulf between appearance and reality depends upon an unrefined distinction between observation and theory. I shall continue to accept the distinction in its naïve form. I shall not challenge the concept of a theory-free observation report, which, moreover, counts as an observation report no matter what its context of utterance is. I shall also not question the coherence of the characterization of discrepancy between reality and appearance provided earlier. To repeat it: there is a gulf between appearance and reality when and only when the explanation of a state of affairs falsifies the description that it is natural to give of it if one lacks the explanation, this description being based purely on observation and committing the observer to no theoretical hypotheses.

These concessions do not save the thesis that *all*[2] scientific discoveries reveal a gulf between reality and appearance. Science

---

[1] *Philosophy of Right*, pp. 13–14.

[2] The texts cited in notes to pp. 326–7 suggest this strong reading, but other passages point to a possible weaker thesis, e.g., *Capital*, i. 537: 'That in their appearance things *often* represent themselves in inverted form is pretty well known in every science except political economy' (my italics). But even this is compatible with the strong interpretation, since Marx might think that science is in order only when inversion occurs.

It is no doubt impossible to establish exactly what he thought, if he thought something exact. Perhaps we should simply note, in his favour, that the thesis that a reality/appearance discrepancy is necessary for there to be a science of a domain does not entail that every assertion of the science reveals such discrepancy. Even so, the thesis seems too strong.

sometimes expands pre-scientific information without prejudicing it, and sometimes confirms it without expanding it. The claim that the work of socialist economics does not embarrass pre-theoretical belief simply does not entail that it is not science.

Some of the examples Marx uses in support of his dictum, rather than illustrating it, confirm the point just made. While it may be a 'paradox that the earth moves around the sun', it is no paradox, in the required sense, that 'water consists of two highly inflammable gases'.[1] It is true that we do not expect it to be so composed, but the discovery warrants no revision of our belief that water quenches fire, and therefore involves no gulf between appearance and reality. Even one who insists that reports of experience can be free of theoretical commitment must grant that the statement 'what extinguishes fire is not composed of inflammable substances' is not a record of experience but a piece of elementary theory. The scientific picture of the solar system arguably did subvert beliefs which were innocent responses to observation. The discovery of the constitution of water did not.[2]

Marx's dictum must be abandoned. If we accept his crude contrast between observation and theory, we may say that scientific explanation always uncovers a reality unrepresented in appearance, but that it only sometimes discredits appearance. Let us call science *subversive* when it does the latter, and *neutral* when it does not.

Now, presumably, there is a need for a science of society when and only when central social processes require theoretical explanation. I shall now maintain that it is reasonable to find the need for a science of society intrinsically regrettable. The claim will be made first for subversive, and then for neutral social science.

The thesis is easier to defend with regard to subversive social science. A gulf between social reality and its appearance is surely an unfortunate state of affairs. But we must distinguish this contention from others with which it might be confused.

One might deplore the gulf just because it means that theory is required to reveal reality. Then one is not deploring the gulf as such but the fact that reality is not pre-theoretically available. This is also true when neutral science is needed. Therefore this response to the gulf is not directed specifically against subversive science.

Suppose the gulf exists because it is necessary to conceal exploita-

---

[1] 'Wages, Price and Profit', p. 424.

[2] Marx's example of the constitution of the air is also shaky. For it is at least arguable that the air does not manifest itself as uniform, but simply fails to manifest itself as multiform; in which case the discovery that it *is* multiform is not incompatible with something it *appears* to be.

tion. Or suppose that explanation of the gulf is false, but that it does conceal exploitation. In either case one might lament the gulf because by hiding exploitation it protects it. It is more difficult to wage battle against it when it is hard to see. This again is no objection to the gulf as such.

We may also set aside objections to the gulf on the ground that it leads men into error. For we have seen[1] that it can persist after they have been enlightened.

Is the gulf still objectionable, once we ignore unhappy conditions which may be associated with it? After all, mirages, which instantiate the gulf in nature, make desert journeys more interesting. But it seems unacceptably frivolous to excuse major gulfs between appearance and social reality on similar grounds. It is surely reasonable to regret the fact that experience induces a propensity to believe falsehoods about important social matters, even when the propensity is restrained by theoretical knowledge.

But suppose Marx agreed that he was wrong to think that science is necessarily subversive. Would he continue to desire that socialism reduce the role of theoretical understanding, including neutral social science? I think he would, and reasonably so.

I believe that it is desirable for a person to understand *himself* without relying upon theory. For there is a sense, difficult to make clear, in which I am alienated from myself and from what I do to the extent that I need theory to reach myself and the reasons governing my actions.[2]

The need for a theory of the social processes in which I participate reflects a similar alienation from those processes. Hence a reduced reliance on social science is desirable. This does not, of course, make it possible. The yearning for transparent human relations can be satisfied in part, because we can specify removable social institutions, notably the market, which foster opacity. But it is futile to hope for the total transparency contemplated in the Hegelio-Marxian tradition.

---

[1] See p. 331.

[2] Theory may be used to put someone in a position where he can understand himself without drawing upon it. Consider how psycho-analytic theory is employed in the therapeutic context. The analyst does not aim to supply the analysand with the theory and show him how it applies to himself. Rather, he employs the theory so as to enable the analysand to encounter directly the images and ideas influencing his behaviour and feeling. In this respect the conclusion of the therapy resembles the attainment of Hegel's Absolute Knowledge. For though Absolute Knowledge replaces reasoning, it is possible only after prolonged engagement in it. In the psycho-analytical case too, the aim is intuition, the means is discursion. The end state of an ideal analysis counts as self-knowledge without theory in the sense here intended.

Recent developments in linguistics, in communication theory, and in realms of economics which will outlive the market are sufficient proof of this. One cannot hope to eliminate neutral theory of human phenomena, though one can understand the desire to do so. The strongest realistic hope is that subversive theory will be unnecessary and that neutral theory will be generally accessible.[1] Many would contend that if theory became generally accessible, 'observation statements' would come to be cast in the theoretical vocabulary. I shall not explore that suggestion. Its formulation violates the crude distinction between observation and theory which has framed our discussion.

[1] For excellent further discussion, see Keat and Urry, *Social Theory as Science*, p. 195.

Some Definitions

THE FOLLOWING definitions purport to codify Marx's usual conceptual practice, but they do not accommodate his every employment of the terms defined. Marx used terms clearly, yet not so carefully as to determine unique definitions of them. These aim to be simple and precise and generally faithful to his ideas.

Use-value

The term 'use-value' denotes a power, and, derivatively, things which have that power, so that what *has* (a)[1] use-value *is* a use-value. The use-value of a thing is its power to satisfy, directly or indirectly, a human desire. It satisfies a desire indirectly when it is used in the production or acquisition of another use-value. Otherwise it satisfies a desire directly.

The use-value of an automobile is, *inter alia*, its power to transport human beings, and, depending on the type of automobile, with a certain measure of speed and comfort. The desire to move with speed in comfort renders that power a use-value. The use-value of water is its power to quench thirst, to extinguish fire, and otherwise to service human desire.

It is false that all human beings desire the same things, or that, when they do, they want the same services from them. But as long as there exists at least one desire which something is able to satisfy, that thing has a use-value.[2]

As the reference to water illustrates, not all use-values are produced by human beings. The use-value of what human beings do produce is, moreover, not wholly due to the labour which produced it, partly because all production operates on a material which it transforms, transports, or extracts. The iron ore out of which the steel in the automobile is made contributes to the automobile's use-value, but it is not produced by human beings. The strength of

---

[1] We introduce a parenthesized indefinite article because wherever power is attributed, *a* power is attributed, and vice versa. Since (a) use-value is (a) power, the grammar is similar. Marx uses the term with and without the article, as here indicated.

[2] A thing has potential use-value if there could be (but is not) someone who desires a service it is able to perform. But note that a use-value which is not being used has actual, not merely potential, use-value.

the steel, which affects the car's use-value, is consequently only partly due to human effort. And the arrangement of the steel is due not only to human effort but also to the constitution of nature. Laws of nature ensure the stability of a steel structure which has been suitably assembled.[1]

Commodity

The term 'commodity' denotes use-values in virtue of a status they sometimes assume. It is thus far comparable to the term 'chairman', which denotes persons in virtue of a status persons sometimes assume. The application of 'chairman' presupposes that social relations of a certain type obtain. So does the application of 'commodity'. (The same is not true of 'use-value'.)

Because 'commodity' denotes in virtue of a status, a use-value which is at one time or in one respect a commodity may be a non-commodity at another time or in another respect. Under what conditions does a use-value assume commodity status?

It does so when it is exchanged for another use-value or is being offered in exchange for another use-value or for other use-values in general; in other words, when it is either undergoing a market transaction or is, as we say, 'on the market'.

If a farmer produces a gallon of milk for his family's consumption and does not sell or barter it, the milk is not a commodity. If someone had intercepted the milk and brought it to market, he would have turned it into a commodity.

If a man eats a bun bought at a bakery he is not, strictly speaking, eating a commodity, since the bun ceases to be one when it reaches its final purchaser. It drops out of the sphere of exchange into the sphere of consumption. It is no longer on the market.

The bun shows how commodity status may attach to a use-value at one time but not another. An example of a use-value which is a commodity in one respect but not in another is a house which is both occupied and for sale. It is at once in the sphere of consumption and the sphere of exchange.

The above severe criteria of commodity status accord with Marx's instruction that a use-value 'is a commodity in the strict sense of the word only within the framework of circulation'.[2] But he commonly relaxes the restrictions and uses the term to denote any

---

[1] 'There is not a manufacture which can be mentioned, in which nature does not give her assistance to man, and give it too, generously and gratuitously' (Ricardo, *Principles of Political Economy*, p. 76). Marx quotes this passage at *Grundrisse* (Berlin), p. 794 and *Theories of Surplus Value*, i. 61.

[2] *Theories of Surplus Value*, iii. 290, and see ibid., pp. 284–90 for a number of similar statements.

product which is on the market at some point in its history, referring to it as a commodity even when it is in the production or consumption spheres; and he sometimes uses the term more broadly still, to denote any product in a market economy, even one which is not destined to be sold.[1] We shall use 'commodity' in accordance with the first, but not the second, of the two liberalizations just mentioned.

Exchange-value

Exchange-value is a property of use-values which possess commodity status.[2] The exchange-value of a commodity is its power of exchanging against quantities of other commodities. (More vulgarly, it is a commodity's purchasing power.) It is measured by the number of commodities of any other kind for which it will exchange under equilibrium market conditions.[3] Thus the exchange-value of a coat might be eight shirts, and also three hats, and also ten pounds sterling.

Exchange-value is a relative magnitude. Underlying the exchange-value of a commodity is its value, an absolute magnitude. A commodity A has x units of a commodity B as its exchange-value just in case the ratio between the values of A and B is $x:1$. The exchange-values relative to one another of two commodities will remain the same when each changes in value if the changes are identical in direction and proportion.

According to Marx, the exchange-value of a commodity varies directly and uniformly with the quantity of labour-time required to produce it under standard conditions of productivity, and inversely and uniformly with the quantity of labour-time standardly required to produce other commodities, and with no further circumstance.

---

[1] The first liberalization characterizes most of Marx's uses of the term, but the second (see e.g. 'Results', p. 952; *Theories of Surplus Value*, ii. 64) reflects a special context. Marx is usually anxious to deny that goods which are never exchanged are commodities, even if they are produced in a capitalist society. Thus he says of the seamstress whom the capitalist retains to produce his wife's dresses that she does not produce commodities, since the dresses themselves—as opposed to her labour-power—are not sold. *Theories of Surplus Value*, i. 159, 164-5.

[2] Whether a use-value which is not on the market has exchange-value, as opposed to potential exchange-value, depends on how liberally the term 'commodity' is used.

[3] This sentence is valid on the conceptual level of volume i of *Capital* only. It needs to be qualified to cater for deviations of price from exchange-value discussed in volumes ii and iii. These deviations occur under equilibrium conditions. They are due not to short-term movements of supply and demand, but to such standing circumstances as commercial profit, divergent organic compositions of capital, and rent. The deviations raise large questions about the labour theory of value, but since the latter is not embraced in this book, the simplification introduced in the above sentence may stand.

(The first condition alone states the mode of determination of value *tout court*.) This is not a result of the definition of exchange-value, but an additional Marxist thesis, which will be neither asserted nor denied in this book. (Bourgeois economists generally hold that the use-value of a commodity influences the magnitude of its exchange-value. For Marx it is a necessary condition of exchange-value, and it affects the amounts in which different commodities are produced, but labour-time alone decides how much exchange-value a commodity has.)

Just as that which has use-value is itself a use-value, so that which has exchange-value is an exchange-value (and that which has value is a value).[1]

Money

We defined use-value as the power to satisfy, directly or indirectly, a human desire; and exchange-value as the power of exchanging against (other) commodities. But the power of exchanging against commodities serves indirectly to satisfy human desire, since it enables the acquisition of use-values. It follows that exchange-value is a species of use-value.[2] (We shall nevertheless sometimes use 'use-value' as an abbreviation for 'use-value which is independent of exchange-value', in contexts where misunderstanding is unlikely.)

We now define money as a commodity which (a) has use-value only because it has exchange-value and (b) is generally acceptable to commodity exchangers.

While money has use-value only because it has exchange-value, it is false that its only use-value *is* its exchange-value, for it also has use-value which is entirely due to *but not part of* its exchange-value. A wealthy man may obtain prestige or political power by virtue of his wealth. Yet he need not literally buy these, since he need not transfer any money to get them. They are use-values he acquires by virtue of the exchange-value he has, but, unlike the power to purchase diamond cuff-links, the power to obtain influence is not part of the exchange-value he has.

Because its use-value depends entirely on its exchange-value, money bears a unique relation to desire. A man wanting a non-

---

[1] People who read *Capital*, i. 36–8 sometimes fail to note that Marx, following Ricardo, had a concept of *value* in addition to the concepts use-value, exchange-value and socially necessary labour time. The difference between value and exchange-value has been explained, but value also differs in concept from labour time, since there can be labour time without value. Labour time is the content of value, but it assumes that form only in market economies.

[2] As Marx recognized: see, e.g., *Capital*, i. 85, and *Theories of Surplus Value*, iii. 521. On the use-value of capital, which (see p. 350) is a species of exchange-value, see *Capital*, iii. 345, 348.

monetary commodity wants it because it is an object of a certain kind, with specific distinguishing characteristics. If he wants a particular automobile, he may, indeed, want it just because it is an automobile, and not care about its more specific character. But he may want it because it is an automobile of a special sort, say a sports car or a Rolls Royce, and there is in principle no limit to the specificity of the description under which the commodity qualifies as his object of desire. By contrast, a person who desires money desires only an amount of it, and does not mind what kind he gets.[1] If he is in Scotland he will desire a Scottish pound exactly as much as he desires an English pound. If he prefers the Scottish because of its design, then it is not in its quality as money, as vessel of exchange-value, that he prefers it (whereas a man may prefer a Rolls Royce because he thinks it is very good *as* a motor car). If his interest is in money as money, then he also does not care about the currency composition of his money, where it has one. He cares only about how much he has.[2]

Regarding feature (a). All commodities have use-value by virtue of having exchange-value, in addition to the use-value they have which is realized in consumption (consumption includes productive consumption, in which one use-value is used to produce another). But money has use-value *only* by virtue of having exchange-value.

The functions commonly prescribed as definitive of money attach to it because the fact that it lacks use-value aside from its exchange-value makes it good at performing them. Money serves as medium of exchange, measure of value, store of value, etc. But it is a mistake to *define* it by reference to these services, as opposed to the properties which make it supremely eligible to fulfil them.

Regarding feature (b). This provision implies that whether a commodity is money is a matter of degree, since acceptability is a matter of degree. By demanding that acceptability be *general* we exclude such objects as stock certificates, bonds, railway tickets, etc. These and similar non-monetary documents have no use-value apart from their exchange-value, and they discharge some of the functions of money, but within restricted spheres of circulation: they cannot buy virtually anything from virtually anybody.

The definition supports a distinction between money and what is used as money. Non-money is used as money when it fulfils functions of money but lacks one or both of money's defining properties. The items mentioned two paragraphs back lack the second property.

[1] See *Grundrisse* (Berlin), pp. 872, 936.
[2] Certain counter-examples to the claims of the above paragraph will be dealt with presently, but those arising from the existence of different currency areas will not be discussed.

Certain primitive media of exchange (e.g. wheat, cattle) lack the first property. They occur in the sphere of consumption as well as in the sphere of exchange. Finally, any commodity can, at times, perform some of money's functions, even if it lacks both of the defining properties.

The definition has a certain peculiarity. Little in the world satisfies it completely, since almost nothing is capable of monetary use only. Coins can pry open tins of tobacco and notes can feather a bed. But the exchange-value of coins and notes will normally exceed that of non-monetary objects which perform similar consumption services only. It would be pointless to spend a penny or more on a tin opener which is no better than a penny at the job, does no other job better, and is not prettier. In general, money will be worth more than a cognate non-monetary material object, for otherwise it will be taken out of circulation.

Because coins and notes so predominantly owe their use-value to their exchange-value, it is wiser to pretend that they satisfy the definition than to construct a more involved one which would accommodate the extra use-value they have. It is in spite of the fact that they are money that they have these residual use-values. (The money a depositor has in the bank lacks the latter, because it has no currency composition. Here the definition is realized, for what he has is exchange-value purified of all extraneous use-value, until, of course, he withdraws it in material form.)

The residual utility—and disutility—of money also makes it necessary to modify the claim (p. 349) that currency composition is unimportant. One hundred pennies are for most purposes less convenient than a one dollar bill. But such facts impose only very minor qualifications on what was said.

Finally, a word about the use of coins as tokens. This is not a monetary use. The authority (running a subway system, or in charge of parking meters) confers non-monetary use-value on a coin by so designing a machine that the coin will make it work. Here money as money buys money as non-monetary use-value via a deftly arranged 'short circuit' in the process of exchange. Currency preferences arise, and a person might give more than ten cents for a much needed dime, but these phenomena are not serious counter-examples to important claims.

Capital

Capital is a form of exchange-value. We introduce the concept by describing some varieties of market exchange.

An exchanger can offer either money (M) or a non-monetary

commodity (C). And he can take either M or C. One kind of exchange is barter, whose schematic representation[1] is:

$$\text{I} \qquad C-C^1$$

In I a person brings a C to market and returns with a C of another kind. It might be a pair of trousers which he exchanges for a bushel of wheat. He does not want the trousers, or he wants them less than the wheat, so he surrenders them in favour of the wheat.

In another kind of exchange money appears, mediating the transaction:

$$\text{II} \qquad C-M-C^1$$

Here the man exchanges the trousers for money, with which in turn he buys the wheat.

In a third kind of exchange money functions as capital:

$$\text{III} \qquad M-C-M^1$$

In III a man acquires, say, trousers, by paying money, and sells them for a larger sum of money than he paid. He seeks M^1 not because it differs in kind from M (for it does not) but because it exceeds M in quantity. Bad luck or commercial ineptitude may lead him to accept an M^1 smaller than M, but a reduction of M is not the purpose of III. A man wanting to diminish his stock of money will give or throw some of it away rather than engage in III.[2]

In exchange-circuit III M is capital, because it is *exchange-value exchanged with a view to increasing the amount of exchange-value possessed by its owner*. A merchant capitalist proceeds as in III, by buying and selling the goods he buys. Another way money may take the form of capital is by being loaned at interest:

$$\text{IV} \qquad M(t)-M^1(t+n)$$

(The parenthesized expressions denote times when the money is transferred.)

The capitalist does not *by definition* employ money, as opposed to

---

[1] We use Marx's code, with one amendment. 'C' stands for a non-monetary commodity, and 'M' for a sum of money. The hyphen is to be read 'is exchanged for'. The amendment concerns the superscripts. We use numerical ones, and different numbers on C's and M's indicate different non-monetary commodities and sums of money, respectively. He uses a prime sign to a partly similar effect, but its use reflects his theory of value, which is not espoused in this book.

[2] M^1 may by design be less than M if, for example, C is used by a retailer as a 'loss leader', or if C is used in consumption before being resold but without being materially changed. We shall not discuss such cases.

Rationality excludes exchanges of the forms $M-M^1$ and $M-M$. Putative counter-examples depend on the residual use-values of money (e.g. paying a dime for a penny because a dime is too thin to pry open a tin) or on the use of coins as tokens or on the existence of different currency areas.

a non-monetary exchange-value. A man who lends ten cows on condition of receiving fifteen at the end of five years may be using them as interest-bearing capital. A merchant might repeatedly exchange one non-monetary commodity for another. If he does so because later commodities in the series have more exchange-value, then he acts as a capitalist, despite the fact that his transactions take the form of barter, and may be represented as I repeating itself, thus: $C^1-C^2-C^3-\ldots\ldots-C^n$. For functional reasons capitalist dealing normally involves money. But capital is by definition a species not of money but of exchange-value.[1]

A third form of capitalist exchanges his M for a C which consists of the requisites of production: labour power (LP), and raw materials, tools, premises, etc., collectively known as means of production (MP), with a view to combining them in a productive process whose result, C^1, can be marketed for more than M. This operation may be schematized as follows:

$$\text{V} \qquad M\!-\!C \begin{cases} LP \\ MP \end{cases} \!\ldots\ldots\ldots P \ldots\ldots\ldots C^1\!-\!M^1$$

'$\ldots\ldots P \ldots\ldots$' signifies the fact that in this circuit—by contrast with III—the process of exchange is interrupted by a process of production in which C is consumed and C^1 is produced through its consumption.

Marx calls capital moving in exchange circuit V *industrial* capital, though it might better be called *employing* capital, since it is distinguished by the hiring of labour power, and it appears in agriculture as well as industry. Society counts as capitalist when its production is predominantly inside circuit V, *and* there is a class of hirers of labour power distinct from the class of labourers. The first provision does not entail the second,[2] and we have occasion in Chapter XI (pp. 314–15) to describe three social forms whose production is capitalistic but which are not capitalist since they lack class division.

Two characterizations of capital common in Marxist circles do not qualify as definitions. Capital is not a relationship between purchaser and vendor of labour power.[3] Rather, it promotes that relationship and is reproduced by it. Nor may capital be identified with 'dead labour'. Dead labour is capital under certain social conditions, when it enters as MP in circuit V.[4]

---

[1] Marx implies that capital is possible without money at *Capital*, iii. 340 n.

[2] Which is not to say that there are no connections between them: see Ch. VII, section (2).

[3] Against such a definition, see *Grundrisse*, p. 259.

[4] Against the identification of capital and dead labour, see 'Wage Labour and Capital', p. 90, and Ch. IV above, p. 106.

'Capital' may be used to denote machinery, labour power (as in 'variable capital'), money, etc., but only if what is so called is an exchange-value employed with a view to expanding exchange-value. Thus Marx uses the phrase 'commodity-capital' to denote consumables which are Cs in the industrial-capitalist circuit.[1] Capital takes many forms because exchange-value can increase only through undergoing changes of form. For this reason Marx sometimes says that capital is not a thing, but a process. The motivation for that assertion may be appreciated, but it is more perspicuous to represent capital as a species of exchange-value, as exchange-value subject to a certain use.

How is capital accumulation possible? How do the various types of capitalist emerge with more exchange-value than they had initially?

The Marxist answer comes from the labour theory of value. All exchange-value is created in the productive process, none by the exchange of goods. Therefore those who acquire exchange-value by exchanging commodities always do so at the expense of producers.

This thesis does not enter the definition of capital we have given. Acceptance of that definition is compatible with rejection of the substantive claims of Marxian economics. Note too that schema V is an uncontroversial, albeit illuminating, representation of how an industrialist proceeds. The schema does not imply that it is the presence of LP in the circuit which brings it about that M^1 exceeds M. *The theses of the labour theory of value are not presupposed or entailed by any contentions advanced in this book.*

[1] See *Capital*, ii. 48.

Works Cited

By Marx and Engels:

MESW is an abbreviation for *Marx–Engels Selected Works*, a two-volume collection published in Moscow from 1958, and distinct from the more recent three-volume *Selected Works*, which began to appear in 1969. Apart from the Berlin *Grundrisse*, all references are to editions in English.

MARX, 'On the Jewish Question' (1843), in T. B. Bottomore (ed.), *Karl Marx: Early Writings*, London, 1963.

——'Economic and Philosophical Manuscripts' (1844), in Bottomore (ed.), ibid.

ENGELS, *The Condition of the Working Class in England in 1844* (1844), London, 1892.

MARX, 'Introduction to *A Contribution to the Critique of Hegel's Philosophy of Right*' (1844), in Marx and Engels, *On Religion*, Moscow, 1957.

—— and ENGELS, *The Holy Family* (1844), Moscow, 1956.

——'Theses on Feuerbach' (1845), in Marx and Engels, *The German Ideology*.

—— and ENGELS, *The German Ideology* (1846), Moscow, 1964.

——'The Communism of the Paper *Rheinischer Beobachter*' (1847), in Marx and Engels, *On Religion*, Moscow, 1957.

——*The Poverty of Philosophy* (1847), Moscow, no date.

ENGELS, 'Principles of Communism' (1847), in L. Huberman and P. Sweezy (eds.), *The Communist Manifesto*, New York, 1968.

MARX and ENGELS, 'Manifesto of the Communist Party' (1848), in MESW Vol. I.

MARX, 'Speech at the Trial of the Rhenish District Committee of Democrats' (1849), in Marx and Engels, Articles from the *Neue Rheinische Zeitung*, Moscow, 1972.

——'Wage Labour and Capital' (1849), in MESW Vol. I.

——'The Eighteenth Brumaire of Louis Bonaparte' (1852), in MESW Vol. I.

——'Speech at the Anniversary of the People's Paper' (1856), in MESW Vol. I.

——*Grundrisse der Kritik der Politischen Ökonomie* (1857–8), Berlin, 1953.

——*Grundrisse* (1857–8), Harmondsworth, 1973.

——*A Contribution to the Critique of Political Economy* (1859), London, 1971.

——*Theories of Surplus Value* (1862–3), Vol. I, Moscow, 1969; Vol. II, Moscow, 1968; Vol. III, Moscow, 1972.

——'Inaugural Address of the Working Men's International Association' (1864), in MESW Vol. I.

——'Wages, Price and Profit' (1865), in MESW Vol. I.

——*Capital* (1867, etc.), Vol. I, Moscow, 1961; Vol. II, Moscow, 1957; Vol. III, Moscow, 1962.

——'Results of the Immediate Process of Production' (186?), in Marx, *Capital*, Vol. I, Harmondsworth, 1976.

ENGELS, 'The Housing Question' (1872), in MESW Vol. I.

MARX, 'From the Resolutions of the General Congress Held in the Hague' (1872), in Marx and Engels, *Selected Works*, Moscow, 1969, Vol. 2.

ENGELS, 'On Social Relations in Russia' (1875), in Marx and Engels, *Selected Works*, Moscow, 1969, Vol. 2.

MARX, 'Critique of the Gotha Programme' (1875), in MESW Vol. II.

ENGELS, 'Karl Marx' (1877), in MESW Vol. II.

——*Anti-Dühring* (1878), Moscow, 1954.

MARX, 'Marginal Notes on Adolph Wagner's "Lehrbuch der politischen Ökonomie" ', *Theoretical Practice*, Spring 1972.

ENGELS, 'The Mark' (1882), in *The Peasant War in Germany*, Moscow, 1956.

——*The Origin of the Family, Private Property, and the State* (1884), New York, 1942.

——'Decay of Feudalism and Rise of National States' (188?), in *The Peasant War in Germany*, Moscow, 1956.

——'Ludwig Feuerbach and the End of Classical German Philosophy' (1886), in MESW Vol. II.

——'On the Erfurt Programme' (1891), in *Marxism Today*, February 1970.

——'Introduction to *The Civil War in France*' (1891), in MESW Vol. I.

——'Introduction to *Socialism, Utopian and Scientific*' (1892), in MESW Vol. II.

MARX and ENGELS, *Selected Correspondence*, Moscow, 1975.

By Others:

ABRAMSKY, C. (ed.), *Essays in Honour of E. H. Carr*, London, 1974.
ACTON, H. B., 'The Materialist Conception of History', *Proceedings of the Aristotelian Society*, 1951–2.
——*The Illusion of the Epoch*, London, 1955.
——*What Marx Really Said*, London, 1967.
——'On Some Criticisms of Historical Materialism, II', *Proceedings of the Aristotelian Society, Supp. Vol.*, 1970.
ALTHUSSER, L., *Pour Marx*, Paris, 1965.
—— *et al.*, *Lire Le Capital*, 2 vols., Paris, 1965.
——*Lenin and Philosophy*, London, 1971.
ANDERSON, P., *Passages from Antiquity to Feudalism*, London, 1974.
——*Lineages of the Absolutist State*, London, 1974.
——'The Antinomies of Antonio Gramsci', *New Left Review*, November 1976/January 1977.
ASHTON, T. S., *The Industrial Revolution*, London, 1948.

BAKER, C. E., 'The Ideology of the Economic Analysis of Law', *Philosophy and Public Affairs*, Fall 1975.
BALIBAR, E., 'Sur les concepts fondamentaux du matérialisme historique', in Althusser *et al.*, Vol. II.
BAUMRIN, B. (ed.), *Philosophy of Science: The Delaware Seminar*, Vol. I, New York, 1963.
BLOCH, M., *Feudal Society*, London, 1965.
——*French Rural History*, London, 1966.
BLUM, J., 'The Rise of Serfdom in Eastern Europe', *American Historical Review*, 1956–7.
BOBER, M. M., *Karl Marx's Interpretation of History*, Cambridge, Mass., 1950.
BOORSE, C., 'Wright on Functions', *Philosophical Review*, 1976.
BORGER, R. and CIOFFI, F. (eds.), *Explanation in the Behavioural Sciences*, London, 1970.
BOUDIN, L., *The Theoretical System of Karl Marx*, Chicago, 1907.
BRAY, J., *Labour's Wrongs and Labour's Remedy*, Leeds, 1839.
BRENNER, R., 'Agrarian Class Structure and Economic Development in Pre-Industrial Europe', *Past and Present*, February 1976.

CALVEZ, J-Y., *La Pensée de Karl Marx*, Paris, 1956.
CANFIELD, J., 'Teleological Explanation in Biology', *British Journal for the Philosophy of Science*, 1964.
CATEPHORES, G. and MORISHIMA, M., 'Is there an "Historical Transformation Problem"?' *The Economic Journal*, 1975.

COHEN, G. A., 'The Workers and the Word: Why Marx had the Right to Think He was Right', *Praxis* (Zagreb), 1968.

——'On Some Criticisms of Historical Materialism, I', *Proceedings of the Aristotelian Society, Supp. Vol.*, 1970.

——'Marx's Dialectic of Labour', *Philosophy and Public Affairs*, Spring 1974.

——'Being, Consciousness and Roles: On the Foundations of Historical Materialism', in Abramsky (ed.).

——'Robert Nozick and Wilt Chamberlain: How Patterns Preserve Liberty', *Erkenntnis*, 1977.

COHEN, P., *Modern Social Theory*, London, 1968.

DE SAINTE-CROIX, G. E. M., 'Karl Marx and the History of Classical Antiquity', *Arethusa*, 1975.

DOBB, M., *Capitalism, Development and Planning*, New York, 1967.

——*Welfare Economics and the Economics of Socialism*, Cambridge, England, 1969.

DUNCAN, G., *Marx and Mill*, Cambridge, England, 1973.

EAGLETON, T., *Marxism and Literary Criticism*, London, 1976.

FINLEY, M. I., *The Ancient Economy*, London, 1973.

FLINN, M. W. and SMOUT, T. C. (eds.), *Essays in Social History*, Oxford, 1974.

FREUD, S., 'The Future of an Illusion', in *The Complete Psychological Works of Sigmund Freud*, Vol. XXI, London, 1961.

FROMM, E. (ed.), *Socialist Humanism*, Garden City, New York, 1966.

GALBRAITH, J. K., *The Affluent Society*, London, 1958.

——*The New Industrial State*, Harmondsworth, 1969.

——*Economics and the Public Purpose*, London, 1974.

GELLNER, E., *Thought and Change*, London, 1964.

GOLDMAN, A., 'Towards a Theory of Social Power', *Philosophical Studies*, 1972.

GOLDMANN, L., 'Socialism and Humanism', in Fromm (ed.).

GOLDSTICK, D., 'On the Dialectical Unity of the Concept of Matter', *Horizons* (Toronto), Winter 1969.

GOUGH, I., 'Productive and Unproductive Labour in Marx', *New Left Review*, November/December 1972.

HANSON, N. R., *Patterns of Discovery*, Cambridge, England, 1965.

HARRIS, A. L., 'Utopian Elements in Marx's Thought', *Ethics*, 1949–50.

HARTWELL, R. M., *The Industrial Revolution and Economic Growth*, London, 1971.

HEGEL, G. W. F., 'Preface to *The Phenomenology of Mind*', trans. by W. Kaufmann in his *Hegel*, New York, 1965.

——*Logic*, trans. by W. Wallace, Oxford, 1892.

——*The Philosophy of Mind*, trans. by W. Wallace and A. V. Miller, Oxford, 1971.

——*The Philosophy of Nature*, Vol. I, trans. by M. J. Petry, London, 1969.

——*The Philosophy of Right*, trans. by T. M. Knox, Oxford, 1958.

——*The History of Philosophy*, Vol. I, trans. by E. S. Haldane, London, 1892.

——*The Philosophy of Religion*, Vol. I, trans. by E. B. Speirs and J. B. Sanderson, London, 1895.

——*The Philosophy of History*, trans. by J. Sibree, New York, 1900.

——*Lectures on the Philosophy of World History*, trans. by H. B. Nisbet, Cambridge, England, 1975.

HEMPEL, C. G., 'Explanation and Prediction by Covering Laws', in Baumrin (ed.).

——*Aspects of Scientific Explanation*, New York, 1965.

HICKS, J., *A Theory of Economic History*, Oxford, 1969.

HILL, C., *Puritanism and Revolution*, London, 1968.

——*Reformation to Industrial Revolution*, London, 1968.

——*Change and Continuity in Seventeenth-Century England*, London, 1974.

HILTON, R. H. (with P. H. Sawyer), 'Technical Determinism: The Stirrup and the Plough', *Past and Present*, April 1963.

—— SWEEZY, P., DOBB, M. *et al.*, *The Transition from Feudalism to Capitalism*, London, 1976.

——'Introduction', in Hilton, Sweezy *et al.*

——'Capitalism: What's in a Name?', in Hilton, Sweezy *et al.*

HINDESS, B. and HIRST, P. Q., *Pre-Capitalist Modes of Production*, London, 1975.

HOBSBAWM, E. J., 'Introduction', in Marx, *Pre-Capitalist Economic Formations*, London, 1964.

HOHFELD, W. N., *Fundamental Legal Conceptions*, New Haven, 1966.

HOOK, S., *Towards the Understanding of Karl Marx*, London, 1933.

HOWARD, M. C. and KING, J. E., *The Political Economy of Marx*, London, 1975.

HUME, D., *Enquiry Concerning Human Understanding*, in Selby-Bigge (ed.), *Hume's Enquiries*, Oxford, 1902.

——*A Treatise of Human Nature*, Oxford, 1964.

KANGER, H. and KANGER, S., 'Rights and Parliamentarism', *Theoria*, 1966.

KEAT, R. and URRY, J., *Social Theory as Science*, London, 1975.

KIDRON, M., *Western Capitalism Since the War*, London, 1968.

KIERKEGAARD, S., *Edifying Discourses: A Selection*, trans. by D. F. and L. M. Swenson, New York, 1958.

KOSMINSKY, L., *Studies in the Agrarian History of England in the Thirteenth Century*, Oxford, 1956.

LANGE, O., *Political Economy*, Vol. I, Oxford, 1963.

LENIN, V. I., 'The Three Sources and Component Parts of Marxism', in Marx, Engels, Lenin, *Historical Materialism*, Moscow, 1972.

——*Left-wing Communism, an Infantile Disorder*, New York, 1940.

LICHTHEIM, G., Marxism: *An Historical and Critical Study*, London, 1961.

LUXEMBURG, R., *The Accumulation of Capital*, London, 1951.

McLELLAN, D., *Marx before Marxism*, London, 1970.

——*Karl Marx*, London, 1973.

MALINOWSKI, B., *Argonauts of the Western Pacific*, London, 1922.

——*A Scientific Theory of Culture and Other Essays*, New York, 1960.

MANDEL, E., *Marxist Economic Theory*, London, 1968.

MANTOUX, P., *The Industrial Revolution of the Eighteenth Century*, London, 1964.

MERTON, R. L., 'Manifest and Latent Functions', in *Social Theory and Social Structure*.

——*Social Theory and Social Structure*, New York, 1968.

MILIBAND, R. and SAVILLE, J. (eds.), *The Socialist Register: 1965*, London, 1965.

MILL, J. S., *Principles of Political Economy*, Toronto, 1965 (comprising Vols. II and III of the definitive Collective Works, with continuous pagination).

MILLS, C. W., *The Causes of World War Three*, New York, 1958.

——*The Marxists*, New York, 1962.

MISHAN, E. J., *The Costs of Economic Growth*, Harmondsworth, 1969.

——'Ills, Bads and Disamenities: The Wages of Growth', *Daedalus*, 1973.

NOZICK, R., *Anarchy, State and Utopia*, New York, 1974.

PARKER, S., *The Sociology of Leisure*, London, 1976.

PIRENNE, H., *Economic and Social History of Medieval Europe*, London, 1936.

PLAMENATZ, J. P., *German Marxism and Russian Communism*, London, 1954.

——*Man and Society*, Vol. II, London, 1963.

PLEKHANOV, G. V., *The Development of the Monist View of History*, Moscow, 1956.

POSTAN, M. M., *The Medieval Economy and Society*, London, 1972.

PROTHERO, I., 'William Benbow and the Concept of the "General Strike" ', *Past and Present*, May 1974.

RADCLIFFE-BROWN, A. R., *Structure and Function in Primitive Society*, London, 1952.

——*A Natural Science of Society*, Glencoe, Illinois, 1957.

RENNER, K., *The Institutions of Private Law and their Social Functions*, London, 1949.

RICARDO, D., *Principles of Political Economy and Taxation*, Cambridge, England, 1951.

RITTERBUSH, P. C., *Overtures to Biology*, New Haven, 1964.

ROBERTS, M., 'On Time', *Quarterly Journal of Economics*, 1973.

RYLE, G., *The Concept of Mind*, London, 1949.

SALTER, W. E. G., *Productivity and Technical Change*, Cambridge, England, 1960.

SCHEFFLER, I., *The Anatomy of Inquiry*, New York, 1963.

SCHILLER, F., *On The Aesthetic Education of Man*, trans. by E. M. Wilkinson and L. A. Willoughby, Oxford, 1967.

SCHUMACHER, K., *Small is Beautiful*, London, 1974.

SCITOVSKY, T., *The Joyless Economy*, New York, 1976.

SHAW, W., 'Productive Forces and Relations of Production', University of London Ph.D. thesis, October 1975.

SKLAR, M. J., 'On the Proletarian Revolution and the End of Political-Economic Society', *Radical America*, May/June 1969.

SMITH, A., *The Wealth of Nations*, New York, 1937.

STRETTON, H., *Capitalism Socialism and the Environment*, Cambridge, England, 1976.

SWEEZY, P. M., *The Theory of Capitalist Development*, New York, 1956.

TAYLOR, C., *The Explanation of Behaviour*, London, 1964.

——'The Explanation of Purposive Behaviour', in Borger and Cioffi (eds.).

——*Hegel*, Cambridge, England, 1975.

THERBORN, G., *Science, Class, and Society*, London, 1976.

THOMPSON, E. P., 'The Peculiarities of the English', in Miliband and Saville (eds.).

——'Time, Work-Discipline and Industrial Capitalism', in Flinn and Smout (eds.).

——*The Making of the English Working Class*, Harmondsworth, 1968.

TÖNNIES, F., *Community and Society*, trans. by C. P. Loomis, New York, 1963.

VENABLE, V., *Human Nature: The Marxian View*, New York, 1945.

WARD, B. and DUBOS, R., *Only One Earth*, London, 1972.

WEBER, M., *The Theory of Social and Economic Organization*, New York, 1947.

——*General Economic History*, New York, 1961.

——*The City*, New York, 1966.

WHITE, JR., L., *Medieval Technology and Social Change*, Oxford, 1962.

WILLIAMS, R., 'Base and Superstructure in Marxist Cultural Theory', *New Left Review*, November/December 1973.

WRIGHT, L., 'Functions', *Philosophical Review*, 1973.

Name Index

Subject Index*

See also the names of sections in Table of Contents

* I am grateful to Robin Halpin for advice and assistance—G.A.C.